COMPETITION, EFFECTS AND PREDICTABILITY

In the US and EU, legal analysis in competition cases is conducted on a case-by-case approach. This approach assesses each particular practice for both its legality and its welfare effects. While this analytic method has the merits of 'getting the result right' by, inter alia, reducing error costs in antitrust adjudication, it comes at a cost of certainty, predictability and clarity in the legal principles which govern antitrust law. This is a rule of law concern.

This is the first book to explore this tension between Europe's 'More Economic Approach', the US's Rule of Reason, and the Rule of Law. The tension manifests itself in the assumptions in and choice of analytic method; the institutional agents driving this effects-based approach and their competency to use and assess the results of the methodology they demand; and, the nature and stability of the legal principles used in modern effects-based competition analysis. The book forcefully argues that this approach to competition law represents a threat to the rule of law.

Competition, Effects and Predictability will be of interest to European and American competition law scholars and practitioners, legal historians, policy makers and members of the judiciary.

Volume 24 in the series Hart Studies in Competition Law

Hart Studies in Competition Law

Competition, Effects and Predictability

Rule of Law and the Economic Approach to Competition

Bruce Wardhaugh

·HART·

OXFORD · LONDON · NEW YORK · NEW DELHI · SYDNEY

HART PUBLISHING

Bloomsbury Publishing Plc

Kemp House, Chawley Park, Cumnor Hill, Oxford, OX2 9PH, UK

1385 Broadway, New York, NY 10018, USA

HART PUBLISHING, the Hart/Stag logo, BLOOMSBURY and the Diana logo are
trademarks of Bloomsbury Publishing Plc

First published in Great Britain 2020

A catalogue record for this book is available from the British Library.

Library of Congress Cataloging-in-Publication data

Names: Wardhaugh, Bruce, 1960- author.

Title: Competition, effects and predictability : rule of law and the economic approach
to competition / Bruce Wardhaugh.

Description: Oxford ; New York : Hart, 2020. | Series: Hart studies in competition law |
Includes bibliographical references and index.

Identifiers: LCCN 2019052352 (print) | LCCN 2019052353 (ebook) |
ISBN 9781509926060 (hardcover) | ISBN 9781509926077 (Epub)

Subjects: LCSH: Antitrust law—United States. | Antitrust law—European
Union countries. | Competition.

Classification: LCC K3850 .W37 2020 (print) | LCC K3850 (ebook) | DDC 343.2407/21—dc23

LC record available at https://lccn.loc.gov/2019052352

LC ebook record available at https://lccn.loc.gov/2019052353

ISBN: HB: 978-1-50992-606-0
       ePDF: 978-1-50992-609-1
       ePub: 978-1-50992-607-7

Typeset by Compuscript Ltd, Shannon
Printed and bound in Great Britain by CPI Group (UK) Ltd, Croydon CR0 4YY

To find out more about our authors and books visit www.hartpublishing.co.uk.
Here you will find extracts, author information, details of forthcoming events
and the option to sign up for our newsletters.

To Jennifer, without whose support this would never have been written

PREFACE

For the sake of variety, where we are not referring to a specific jurisdiction, 'antitrust law' and 'competition law' (and their variants) are used interchangeably. We use the former when discussing the US legal regime; and the latter in discussing the European regime. We also use the term 'effects-based approach' as a generic term to describe both the American rule of reason approach and the European more economic approach (MEA), both of which are economics-focused. Further, both methodologies share a similarity determining the legality of a given arrangement through a case-by-case analysis of the welfare effects of the practice in question.

We use the present (Lisbon Treaty) numbering of the European Treaties' Articles; however, we have not renumbered Articles when they are mentioned in quotations. Where referring to an Article, without specifying a particular Treaty, the reference is to the TFEU.

Where a work (eg Cicero's *Laws*) exists in many editions, translations or has been reprinted over time, we refer to chapters and sections – this allows readers of all versions to find the text.

All websites were last visited on 1 September 2019; and, of course, no guarantees are provided for their ongoing content. The law is stated as of 1 September 2019. All mistakes and errors are – of course – mine.

ACKNOWLEDGEMENTS

This book is the result of several years of thinking and writing; earlier parts of (and ideas in) it were presented to the Competition and European Law Section at the Annual Meetings of the Society of Legal Scholars (York, 2015; Oxford, 2016; Dublin, 2017), and to the September 2017 meeting of the Competition Law Scholars Forum in Amsterdam. I thank all those who provided comments at these conferences. My institution, the University of Manchester, provided support through research leave and funding from the Law School's Research Support Fund.

But the greatest support was provided by my family, especially by my wife Jennifer who (in addition to providing assistance with copy-editing, proof-reading and reference-checking) was always there with words of encouragement when the writing got frustrating.

CONTENTS

TABLE OF CASES

Opinions of Advocates General

Judgments of the General Court of the European Union

DECISIONS OF THE COMMISSION

US CASES

ENGLISH CASES

INTERNATIONAL CASES

TABLE OF LEGISLATION

Directives

Guidelines and Notices

Recommendations

US LEGISLATION

Constitution

Legislation

Regulations

Rules

Introduction

> This Court has viewed *stare decisis* as having less-than-usual force in cases involving the Sherman Act.[1]

The above remark made by the United States Supreme Court (USSC) in a 2015 intellectual property case caused little controversy. As a statement regarding that Court's approach to precedent in antitrust matters it is certainly true. Since the 1970s US courts have taken what may appear to be a cavalier attitude towards precedent in resolving antitrust disputes. Along with this view of the 'less-than-usual' force of precedent, we also observe a view that the legal principles which govern the resolution of a particular case in antitrust take the form of malleable standards, rather than firm rules.

During this period the USSC has also reoriented the goal of antitrust. The Sherman Act is now viewed as a means to promote economic efficiency, in the sense of maximising consumer welfare. Any other goal which may have historically shaped antitrust law no longer matters. Hence antitrust analysis is now governed via economic analysis, and not the strict application of legal rules.

That Court's 2007 decision in *Leegin*[2] might be viewed as a paradigm of this new approach to antitrust. That decision overturned *Dr Miles*,[3] a 96-year-old precedent which prohibited the use of vertical agreements to implement a strategy of resale price maintenance (RPM). The Court justified its decision on the basis of recent developments in economic theory which showed that in some cases RPM can increase consumer welfare. This form of RPM is now permitted as a business strategy – with its legality ostensibly subject to case-by-case scrutiny using a rule of reason approach.

In Europe a similar approach has taken place. In 1999, the Commission introduced a new block regulation on vertical agreements.[4] This approach originally attempted to introduce a greater reliance on the use of economic methodology to assess vertical agreements, with the idea of producing greater coherence within EU competition law and policy. The Commission's thinking then expanded beyond vertical arrangements, to other sorts of agreements covered by Article 101 and practices controlled by Article 102. This is the European more economic approach (MEA) to competition law.

---

[1] *Kimble v Marvel Entertainment, LLC*, 135 S Ct 2401, 2412 (2015).

[2] *Leegin Creative Leather Products Inc v PSKS Inc*, 551 US 877 (2007).

[3] *Dr Miles Medical Co v John D Park and Sons Co*, 220 US 373 (1911).

[4] Commission Regulation (EC) No 2790/1999 of 22 December 1999 on the application of Article 81(3) of the Treaty to categories of vertical agreements and concerted practices [1999] OJ L336/21.

This book examines the effects-based, economic approach to competition law that both jurisdictions have adopted. This manner of antitrust analysis is a direct turn towards the methodology and values associated with traditional price theory and its related economic methodology. The economic approach substitutes the goal of efficiency, in the form of increased (usually consumer) welfare, for any other policy goals of the competition regime; and it uses the tools of microeconomics to evaluate legal rules and suggest the appropriate resolution of a given case. Thus this economic approach to antitrust is concerned with analysis of the effects of a given practice, and not necessarily with a more general legal rule which might govern the legality of the practice.

The argument of this book is that this economic or effects-based approach is a threat to the rule of law, in so far as it moves competition law and policy away from the rule of law ideal. This move arises for three reasons. First, the approach uses an analytic method which may not accurately describe the behaviour of agents in the marketplace, thus causing a rift between the law's goals and what the law accomplishes. Second, the approach requires a reinterpretation of the norms of the antitrust regime, which not only has been accomplished outside of the democratic norms (contrary to separation of power concerns); it also requires adjudicators to engage in activities well beyond their institutional competence, at times making rational decision-making in such cases a near-impossible task. Third, by adjudicating on a case-by-case basis, the approach eliminates much of the certainty and clarity mandated by rule of law considerations.

When speaking of 'the rule of law,' this book draws upon a thin formal theory (based on principles articulated by Fuller, Rawls and Raz) which looks at the rule of law as a set of rules (ultimately enforced by the coercive power of the state) designed to allow rational subjects the ability to make future plans. This view of the rule of law and its importance is outlined in Chapter 1. Central to this idea is the understanding that for rational individuals to make such plans, they require a degree of certainty and predictability about the future so that they can make such plans and have a reasonable reliance on the outcome. The rule of law, in this sense, is a paradigm. It is something which will almost certainly never be realised in any given legal system, or part of such a system; however, as a paradigm, this understanding of the rule of law is an aspirational ideal for any legal system.

I. The Effects-Based or 'More Economic Approach' to Antitrust

The effects-based approach to competition law is, as its name suggests, a method of antitrust analysis that focuses on a given practice's economic effects to determine (or aid in determining) its legality. In the US this is manifested in the rule of reason approach, which has, since the 1970s, become the preferred method of antitrust analysis. In the EU, this is mirrored in the MEA. This section serves as a general explanation of the effects-based approach to antitrust; and provides conceptual clarity for the remainder of the book's argument. There is a credible narrative as to how this economic turn in antitrust law and policy occurred. This narrative also raises a number of questions about how this approach is applied in practice, and what merits are presented by this approach. A further, and equally important, set of questions surrounds the similarity between the US and European approaches; and significantly for our purposes, whether or not their similarities entail that both approaches present a rule of law threat to their respective legal systems.

A. Chicago Economics and the Effects-Based Approach

One narrative of how the economic (or effects-based) approach arose begins with the Chicago School and the USSC.[5] By the mid-1970s, that Court was interventionist and was motivated out of a conception of antitrust which focused on the protection of small businesses. Kauper notes:

> At the end of World War II, the United States was the dominant economic power in the world. The industrial base of most of its rivals had been destroyed or at least severely injured. At home and abroad, US firms were doing well. Employment rates were high. Pent-up demand drove rapidly expanding production. It was easy to ignore concerns over efficiency and to adopt policies focused on protecting and rewarding small enterprises. This highly interventionist antitrust policy was a luxury we could afford.[6]

In *Brown Shoe*,[7] Chief Justice Warren expresses this interventionist view of antitrust, and thus the then view of the Sherman Act's intent:

> But we cannot fail to recognize Congress' desire to promote competition through the protection of viable, small, locally owned businesses. Congress appreciated that occasional higher costs and prices might result from the maintenance of fragmented industries and markets. It resolved these competing considerations in favor of decentralization. We must give effect to that decision.[8]

This understanding of the purpose of antitrust produced a number of antitrust rulings that were subject to immediate criticism (and in today's light appear bizarre). In *Brown Shoe*, the Court blocked a merger between Brown Shoe and Kinney Shoe. The two firms produced 4 and less than 2 per cent of the nation's

---

[5] There are of course other narratives. See also Robert Pitofsky (ed), *How the Chicago School Overshot the Mark: The Effect of Conservative Economic Analysis on US Antitrust* (Oxford, Oxford University Press, 2008), and in particular the following chapters: Richard Schmalensee, 'Thoughts on the Chicago Legacy in US Antitrust' 11; FM Scherer, 'Conservative Economics and Antitrust: A Variety of Influences' 30; and, Thomas E Kauper, 'Influence of Conservative Economic Analysis on the Development of the Law of Antitrust' 40. The narrative of these three chapters also points to Chicago, but with slightly different 'flavours' from each other (and from our narrative).

[6] Kauper, ibid 43.

[7] *Brown Shoe Co v United States*, 370 US 294 (1962).

[8] ibid 344.

shoes, respectively.[9] In *Von's Grocery*[10] four years later, using similar logic regarding the intent of the Sherman Act,[11] the USSC blocked a merger between two Los Angeles-area grocery chains whose combined market share was about 7.5 per cent.

Similar concern was expressed about the Court's treatment of vertical arrangements. Although Chapter 2 will explore these in greater detail, it is worth noting that the Court's treatment of many of these was very 'formalistic' in nature. The 1972 decision in *Topco*[12] is a paradigm of this. This case involved small and medium-sized grocery stores entering into a buyers' association. In prohibiting the arrangement, the Court failed to take into account what we would now regard as the pro-competitive efficiencies of these sorts of organisations, and treated the arrangement as a form of horizontal cartel. It reasoned, 'We think that it is clear that the restraint in this case is a horizontal one, and, therefore, a per se violation of s 1.'[13] As Kauper remarks, '[N]one of these decisions reflected what any of us today would characterize as economic analysis or anything even reasonably close to it. Antitrust of the time reflected an almost randomized mix of economic, social, and political values.'[14]

The second part of this narrative concerns the influence that the Chicago School had on the development of antitrust analysis. The 'Chicago School' is a group of economists centred at the University of Chicago who share a pro-market, limited-government approach to economic and social matters.[15] As with any grouping of thinkers, their views are not homogenous; however, there are some consistent themes running through their thought.[16] Two themes are of note. First, members of this School share a firm conviction in the superiority of market orderings, and a reservation about governmental intervention and hence role. Second, there is a strong intertwining of this belief in the superiority of a market solution with neoclassical liberal economics, and the use of price theory as the appropriate tool for economic analysis.

Chicago's influence extended beyond economic theory. Rutherford notes:

> Chicago economics, however, became much more than a combination of traditional competitive price theory and monetarism, spreading itself into a variety of new areas.

---

[9] ibid 302–03.

[10] *US v Von's Grocery Co*, 384 US 270 (1966).

[11] See ibid 274 for a statement of what the Court believed the intent of the Sherman Act to be:

> From this country's beginning there has been an abiding and widespread fear of the evils which flow from monopoly – that is the concentration of economic power in the hands of a few. On the basis of this fear, Congress in 1890, when many of the Nation's industries were already concentrated into what it deemed too few hands, passed the Sherman Act in an attempt to prevent further concentration and to preserve competition among a large number of sellers.

[12] *US v Topco Associates*, 405 US 596 (1972).

[13] ibid 608.

[14] Kauper (n 5) 43.

[15] Not all of those identified with the Chicago School were employed there. Robert Bork, although receiving his law degree from that University, taught at Yale; and Harold Demsetz also taught at Michigan and UCLA.

[16] See H Laurence Miller, Jr, 'Chicago School of Economics' (1962) 70 *Journal of Political Economy* 64 for one description of this group.

The Chicago View, with its strong pro-market, anti-regulatory, emphasis became the basis of Chicago law and economics. Simons's teaching in the Law School had begun the trend, but it was with Aaron Director and his contribution to the teaching of the antitrust course with Edward Levi, and the founding of the *Journal of Law and Economics* in 1958 that brought Chicago law and economics to the fore.[17]

It is also fair to say that Chicago's influence extended to stimulating the development of the law and economics approach to legal scholarship within the US and then abroad.[18] Scholars such as Areeda and Turner, who were unaffiliated with Chicago (and held somewhat different views from that School),[19] would use this analytic approach to reshape (at least in the US) thinking regarding predatory pricing.[20] The influence of law and economics scholarship on the courts has now become profound: one study shows that during the decade between 1967 and 1976, 30 per cent of USSC antitrust decisions cited such literature. In 1977–86, that percentage doubled to 60; and in the following decade it increased again to 78.[21]

One of the implicit tasks undertaken by Chicago was to put order into the random mixture of values which theretofore had shaped judicial understanding of US antitrust policy. The initial starting point was to advocate for a single value which antitrust could be seen to promote. From the perspective of logic, this made sense. Pursuing one goal was less likely to result in inconsistencies in reasoning than the simultaneous pursuit of multiple, and possibly incommensurable, goals. The goal of choice for Chicago was welfare.

In this regard, Chicago was mostly successful. By 1979, the USSC could state that 'Congress designed the Sherman Act as a "consumer welfare prescription",[22] and cite Bork's *The Antitrust Paradox*[23] in support. However, as used by members of the Chicago School, the term 'consumer welfare' was ambiguous as between what is commonly understood as 'consumer welfare', ie the welfare of consumers and 'total welfare', ie the sum of consumer and producer welfare.[24] While agreement on a generic goal provides the potential for greater consistency than multiple

---

[17] Malcolm Rutherford, 'Chicago Economics and Institutionalism' in Ross B Emmett (ed), *The Elgar Companion to the Chicago School of Economics* (Cheltenham, Edward Elgar, 2010) 25, 33–34.

[18] See Ejan Mackaay, 'History of Law and Economics' in Boudewijn Bouckaert and Gerrit De Geest (eds), *Encyclopedia of Law and Economics*, vol I: *The History and Methodology of Law and Economics* (Cheltenham, Edward Elgar, 2000).

[19] See Scherer (n 5) 33.

[20] Phillip Areeda and Donald F Turner, 'Predatory Pricing and Related Practices under Section 2 of the Sherman Act' (1974) 88 *Harvard Law Review* 697.

[21] Leah Bannon and Douglas H Ginsburg, 'Antitrust Decisions of the US Supreme Court' (2007) 3(2) *Competition Policy International* 14 During 1997–2006 the figure was 77 per cent, and by 'law and economics scholarship' the authors meant Areeda, Bork, Posner and Bowman, which the authors admit may be an underinclusive representation of such scholars.

[22] *Reiter v Sonotone Corporation*, 442 US 330, 343 (1979).

[23] Robert Bork, *The Antitrust Paradox: A Policy at War with Itself*, rev edn (New York, Basic Books, 1993).

[24] See eg Schmalensee (n 5) 13; Barak Orbach, 'How Antitrust Lost its Goal' (2013) 81 *Fordham Law Review* 2253.

goals, the ambiguity surrounding the exact meaning of 'consumer welfare' can import uncertainty in, for instance, merger analysis where there may be an explicit trade-off of producer gains and consumer losses.

The Chicago School's clearest success was in shaping antitrust scholarship to use classical price theory as its default method of analysis. It is now likely impossible to find an introductory text or casebook that does not contain, either as a chapter or an appendix, a discussion of 'economics for antitrust', ie traditional price theory. The use of this economic tool extends to enforcement agencies and courts; and, of course, has resulted in the development of a consulting industry specialising in providing economic expertise for antitrust litigation and commercial planning purposes.

B. The Rule of Reason and the Effects-Based Approach

In US antitrust law there are two main means of analysing potentially anticompetitive practices to determine their legality: the per se approach and rule of reason analysis. Should a practice be determined to be (or categorised as) illegal per se, analysis ends, and the practice is condemned. With rule of reason analysis, 'the factfinder weighs all of the circumstances of a case in deciding whether a restrictive practice should be prohibited as imposing an unreasonable restraint on competition'.[25]

Prior to the early 1970s, it could be said, without much exaggeration, that per se analysis was the de facto default means of analysis. As a majority of the USSC noted in the 1958 decision in *Northern Pacific Railway*, the advantage of per se analysis is that it avoids complex investigations of entire economic sectors.[26] However, since the early 1970s, the pendulum has shifted and now rule of reason is the preferred approach as a consequence of Chicago's influence.

The result of this is that, in the United States, traditional price theory has become the orthodox tool of analysis for antitrust policy; and the goal of antitrust policy is to maximise some form of welfare. Rather than relying on firm rules that are determinative of the legality of the conduct in question, this approach examines on a case-by-case basis the pro- and anti-competitive aspects of the restraint at issue to determine its 'reasonableness', and thus its legality.

Analysis under the rule of reason is therefore a very open-ended inquiry. Some classic statements of the test to be applied under the rule of reason indicate the test for legality is a matter of weighing up and balancing the pro- and anti-competitive effects that result from the arrangement in question.[27] In actual fact, the analysis

---

[25] *Continental TV Inc v GTE Sylvania Inc*, 433 US 36, 49 (1977).
[26] *US v Northern Pacific Railway*, 356 US 1, 5 (1958).
[27] See ibid; and *Ohio et al v American Express et al*, Docket No 16-1454, 25 June 2018, slip opinion 10.

is much more complex than that, requiring careful analysis presented by experts. Yet, courts have provided little guidance regarding either the manner in which the evidence is presented, or the manner which a court is required to evaluate such evidence.

There is also a threshold issue. In any consideration of the legality of a given practice, litigants and courts will need to make an initial substantive legal determination of whether the practice is to be assessed under the rule of reason or regarded as a per se violation of the Sherman Act. Getting this initial determination correct is essential. If a practice that should correctly be viewed as a per se violation of the Sherman Act is improperly characterised as being subject to rule of reason, then any savings in litigation made available by the economies of per se analysis (ie that economic evidence is, for the most, part redundant) are wasted. Similarly, pursuit of a claim under per se analysis when a rule of reason approach is appropriate may result in the dismissal of the claim.

If the boundary between the sorts of restraints which are per se illegal and those that are subject to rule of reason analysis is unclear, this poses a rule of law threat by introducing significant uncertainty into the legal regime. US courts, particularly the USSC, have never provided a clear set of criteria which could be used to demarcate that boundary. Rather the USSC has stated that when faced with a novel arrangement, courts should use care in assessing that arrangement, and rule of reason is the appropriate method of analysis. However, when courts have had sufficient experience with a particular arrangement to determine with confidence that the rule of reason would invalidate all or most instances of the practice, then – and only then – is a court justified in viewing the practice to be per se illegal.[28]

In practice, there are two problems with this formulation of the boundary. First, 'sufficient experience' and 'all or most' are inherently vague. Second, the USSC's statements about experience and the transition from rule of reason analysis to per se condemnation appears to suggest that this is a one-way street: the categorisation of a restraint shifts to per se condemnation after sufficient experience. However, in practice, traffic on this street can move in both directions, as *Leegin*[29] demonstrates. In that case, the USSC overturned longstanding precedent to hold that minimum retail price maintenance must be subject to rule of reason analysis. Given that the means of analysis determines any litigation strategy, this sort of ex ante uncertainty does little to reduce the cost of litigation, or provide certainty to those who wish to arrange their affairs to avoid litigation. These are only a few of the many rule of law issues which the rule of reason creates.

---

[28] Paraphrasing *Leegin Creative Leather Products Inc v PSKS Inc*, 551 US 877, 886–87 (2007), which in turn cites *Broadcast Music Inc v Columbia Broadcasting System Inc*, 441 US 1 (1979) and *Arizona v Maricopa County Medical Society*, 457 US 332 (1982).

[29] *Leegin* ibid.

C. Europe's 'More Economic Approach'

The present state of affairs in Europe is quite similar to that in America. Starting at roughly the turn of the present century, European has adopted a 'more economic approach' to competition analysis. This approach, driven by the Commission, does what its name suggests, and uses economic analysis shaped by traditional price theory to a greater degree than had been done in the past.

The MEA is also economics-based and effects-driven. Practices are evaluated using contemporary economic tools, to assess their pro- and anti-competitive effects and consistency with the competition rules. With very few exceptions the form that a practice takes is irrelevant to an assessment of its compatibility with the European competition rules. The exceptions are typically practices that have no purpose other than limiting (or eliminating) competition, with hard-core cartels being paradigmatic of these. Significantly, reasoning about the compatibility of a given practice based on that practice's form is eschewed, or even derided as 'formalist' by advocates of the MEA.

The European approach did not evolve in a vacuum. Although its evolution will be discussed in greater detail in Chapter 3, there was a US influence in this evolution. Among the stimulants of this process was the collapse of two globally significant mergers (*Boeing/McDonnell Douglas* and *GE/Honeywell*). The US authorities had approved them, yet the Commission blocked them, on grounds that were purported to be driven by bad economics. Additionally, US scholars[30] subjected the European approach (and particularly its treatment of vertical restraints) to forceful criticism. As we will also see, there were of course other reasons – indigenous to Europe – which also provided this evolutionary catalyst; but one cannot deny the presence of an US influence.

Like the American approach, there is a normative element to Europe's MEA. This is the view that in competition law only economics matters. The MEA explicitly adopts a normative principle that nothing other than consumer welfare (as defined by the Commission) matters. But, a significant difference with the European approach (and which poses another set of rule of law problems than does the US approach, as we will see) is that this MEA is almost entirely driven by the Commission. Although the Courts of the European Union have been brought along to accept many of the tenets of the MEA, they have not adopted it in its entirety. This leads to a divergence between the approaches of the Commission and the Courts. This divergence is divergence in both means of analysis and in an understanding of the goals of the competition regime. A result of this divergence is inconsistency and uncertainty between the two institutions' approaches[31] which in turn drives rule of law concerns.

---

[30] See especially Barry E Hawk, 'System Failure: Vertical Restraints and EC Competition Law' (1995) 32 *Common Market Law Review* 973.

[31] See eg Anne C Witt, 'The European Court of Justice and the More Economic Approach – Is the Tide Turning?', University of Leicester Law School Research Paper No 18-10 (available at SSRN abstract=3300114).

The European MEA presents similar rule of law threats. These tend to be magnified by the sometimes-divergent approaches of the Courts and Commission. The Commission has adopted a normative position with regard to the MEA. To the Commission, only consumer welfare matters; and by 'consumer welfare' the Commission means welfare of the consumers, unlike the ambiguous situation found in the US. However, to the Courts and in the Treaties, there are other values promoted by the European competition rules.

The purpose of this discussion of the EU regime is to demonstrate not just that the EU regime is similar in its method of analysis to the US regime, but also to show that the MEA used in the European regime gives rise to rule of law concerns, similar to those in the United States. The consequences of this threat this are not merely theoretical trivialities, such as divergence from the philosopher's paradigm of an ideal legal system resting on the rule of law, but are also found in the more significant result of the introduction of uncertainty into the legal regime which governs commercial relationships.

This rule of law threat in both regimes is multifaceted, and is centred around three foci: the 'tools' (or methodology) used by the economic approach, the institutions driving the change in approach to antitrust law, and the legal uncertainty and unpredictability resulting from this turn. The book's final three chapters of explain each of these foci.

II. The Organisation and Scope of this Book

Given that the main focus of this work is the tendency that the effects-based approach to antitrust has in undermining the rule of law, it is necessary to have an understanding of this concept. This is the goal of Chapter 1. That chapter has two related goals: the first is to come to an understanding of a formal sense of the rule of law, which serves as the basis of the book's argument. The second goal is to demonstrate that considerations of the rule of law extend beyond 'ivory tower theorising'; and that these considerations are relevant to a well-functioning legal system, particularly one which governs market regulation – of which antitrust law is a part.

Chapter 1 begins by considering three senses of 'the rule of law': (i) a rhetorical sense (which equates the rule of law with the speaker's approval of a certain legal practice or standard); (ii) a normative or ideal sense (which tends to be the focus of the legal philosopher); and (iii) a positive sense in which these ideal standards are incorporated as (constitutional) principles in a legal regime (which is the focus of the legal scholar). The first sense is irrelevant to our present project. The focus is on the second and third senses.

Historically, the second sense of 'the rule of law' contained both a substantive dimension (in the form of mandatory moral norms incorporated into law, best seen in a natural law tradition) and a procedural dimension (of principles that make for effective law, best seen in the writings of Fuller, Rawls and Raz).

The third sense of 'the rule of law' incorporates these two dimensions into positive standards: bills of rights are instances of the former's incorporation into positive law, while legal standards of clarity and non-retroactivity are examples of the latter. Additionally, the procedural dimension will often contain standards for division of power among the constituent elements of a government.

This analysis shows that criticism of the effects-based approach to antitrust law relies on this latter sense of 'the rule of law'. And, as will be argued in the penultimate part of Chapter 1, it is rule of law in this sense that matters to our analysis. Fullerian procedural standards provide the certainty and predictability which facilitate commercial investment and exchange; and an appropriate division of power among the policy-making, enforcement and adjudicative bodies provides democratic legitimacy to the adopted legal measures.

The final part of Chapter 1 argues that rule of law considerations are not merely a form of 'ivory tower theorising'. Rather, there are pragmatic reasons such as legal certainty and predictability (which in turn facilitate reasonable expectations and commercial relationships) which suggest the importance of rule of law considerations in a positive system.

Chapters 2 and 3 outline the economic turn taken in American and European competition law. These chapters take a historical approach, as this allows for an exposition of how the approach evolved in each jurisdiction as a result of the then existing means of analysis. The chapters do not attempt to provide a comprehensive history of the antitrust law and policy of either Europe or the United States. In-depth historical accounts have been written by others. The purpose in outlining this turn is to explain how the economic approach has affected both regimes. This explanation serves as a foundation for the book's thesis, namely that this approach poses a rule of law threat to the competition regimes in both jurisdictions. This historical exposition of the effects-based approach in each jurisdiction serves as a foundation for the remainder of the argument.

Chapter 4 considers the rule of law threat posed by the uncritical reliance on traditional, neoclassical price theory as the chosen tool of analysis for antitrust problems. The argument is that while the economic tools used by this approach may have utility, these tools are not necessarily fit for all purposes for which they are deployed. The methodology deployed in the now orthodox approach to antitrust analysis, namely neoclassical price theory (with a Chicago flavour) has a number of powerful assumptions. These assumptions, the truths of which are not immediately self-evident, are such that they drive many of the effects-based approach's policy outcomes and legal conclusions. Also of significance are the challenges posed by other economic or behavioural explanations of market players' conduct. Within the last decade the discipline of behavioural economics has produced some significant results which show that if the orthodox economist's assumption of unbounded rationality is relaxed, other behaviour is predicted. These behavioural results are based on robust, empirical studies, which – if accepted – may call into question central tenets of orthodox thinking, and as a result its conclusions for antitrust law and policy.

Chapter 5 considers the rule of law threat posed by institutional forces and actors. The incorporation of the economic approach in both the US and the EU has been done through courts and administrative agencies. This raises two institutional issues. The first is a political issue: the legitimacy of the process by which legal rules adopted through a democratic process are subsequently revised (or rewritten) by non-democratic political and social actors and institutions. The book's discussion of this issue shows a correlation between the formal conception of the rule of law which it outlines, to an understanding of legitimacy in the legislative process, which suggests that the reorientation of legislation (and Treaty goals) in this manner represents a rule of law threat.

The other rule of law threat posed by intuitional agents is the issue of institutional competence: this economic approach requires a case-by-case analysis in an antitrust dispute, using the lens of a particular economic methodology. Such analysis in turn generates a significant amount of often contradictory evidence of a technical nature. To effectively evaluate this evidence, and come to a rational decision regarding the appropriate outcome of the case, those making decisions in these sorts of cases may need to have a significant amount of expertise in economic matters, which the adjudicators simply do may not possess. This absence of expertise draws this area of law away from the rule of law paradigm.

Chapter 6 considers the final set of rule of law threats. These are those posed by the type and status of legal principle which is necessary for an effects-based approach to be viable. Given that this approach requires analysis of arrangements on a case-by-case level to determine their compatibility with competition law, such an approach works only if there are few rules which govern the assessment of cases. Hence, the effects-based approach must eschew the binding nature of precedent, taking a flexible view of *stare decisis*. It will express a preference for general standards as the legal principles to be used in antitrust cases. This chapter argues that both of these consequences draw competition regimes which incorporate this effects-based approach away from the rule of law ideal.

The final part of Chapter 6 makes a suggestion about how the rule of law can be reintroduced into competition law. The suggestion is not to abandon the use of economics in competition law, rather to reorient antitrust analysis. Currently, under the effects-based approach, microeconomic methodology is focused on an analysis of a given fact pattern to determine if the practice in question is inefficient, in the sense that it is welfare reducing. It is this case-by-case approach which produces a significant amount of the threat to the rule of law. The suggestion is to refocus this economic analysis towards the production of reasonably specific legal rules, which over time will allow for an increase in such welfare. This sort of realignment of the analytic process should result in producing a legal regime which provides better guidance so that rational agents can plan their future arrangements.

III. What this Book is Not

At the outset, it should be noted that this work is not an attack on economics, experts or the appropriate use of economic analysis in policy formulation. In particular, this book is not intended to attack experts or their expertise. The general point made in this book is that economic analysis is a useful tool, and indispensably so in competition law analysis. The concern, rather, is with the present situation in antitrust law where the focus of economic analysis is directed almost entirely to the effects of individual practices in specific markets. The argument is that the focus of economic analysis ought to be towards examining the effects (or consequences) which generalised rules may have in preventing (or enhancing) a more competitive environment (eg promoting the increase of consumer welfare). In short, it argues the use of economics is better focused at the rule-making function, rather than in deciding an individual case. Focusing the analysis in this way leads to greater predictability in the application of antitrust law. Such predictability, in turn, will enhance both commercial considerations of certainty, and – possibly more abstractly – rule of law considerations in a particular jurisdiction.

Further, this book will not propose specific rules to replace existing standards. Readers who expect to find a 'Proposed Restatement of Competition Law' will be disappointed. Rather the book's purpose is to raise the rule of law problem which presently exists with an effects-based approach to competition analysis. This is the first step. Later work can consider alternative legal principles to govern competition law.

Finally, it should also be noted that this work is concerned with the antitrust law surrounding agreements and monopolisation/dominance, ie those activities regulated by Sherman Act sections 1 and 2 and TFEU Articles 101 and 102. These are the areas of law that those focusing on the MEA and rule of reason analysis are concerned with. Merger is an entirely different topic, which is beyond the remit of this work.

1

The Rule of Law and Why it Matters

The phrase 'rule of law' features prominently in current political and legal discourse. Six months to the day after his inauguration, a major American newspaper criticised the US President for showing contempt for the rule of law.[1] The President of the UK Supreme Court has criticised the popular press for undermining the rule of law in its coverage of the Brexit case.[2] The European Union has instigated legal proceedings against the government of Poland as a result of the threats to the rule of law posed by the government's judicial reforms.[3] Western governments have spent millions of dollars, pounds and euros over the past decades in an effort to improve the rule of law in developing countries.[4] This aid is provided with the expectation that, inter alia, it will improve the lives of recipient countries' citizens by bringing both the intangible benefits of improved governance and the tangible benefits obtained through greater economic development.

In addition to these understandings of the rule of law, there is also a normative element to the concept. The rule of law in its normative sense is a measuring stick by which legal systems, legal regimes and legal acts are evaluated. Hence we can meaningfully speak of the rule of law (as an abstract concept) or how this abstract concept is manifested within a particular legal system, instrument or practice.

As this book is concerned with the rule of law and its relationship to the effects-based approach taken by the US and EU competition regimes, this normative sense is essential to the book's argument. The argument is that this effects-based approach has a tendency to undermine rule of law values which are reflected in both legal systems. With this in mind, it is appropriate to address the normative

---

[1] Editorial, 'President Trump's Contempt for the Rule of Law' *New York Times* (20 July 2017) available at: https://www.nytimes.com/2017/07/20/opinion/donald-trump-sessions-interview-law.html?mcubz=1.

[2] 'Press Undermined Rule of Law in Brexit Case Coverage, Says Supreme Court Chief' *The Independent* (16 February 2017) available at: http://www.independent.co.uk/news/uk/politics/brexit-daily-mail-accused-undermining-rule-law-supreme-court-president-lord-neuberger-a7582816.html. The 'Brexit Case' is *R (on the application of Miller and another) (Respondents) v Secretary of State for Exiting the European Union* [2017] UKSC 5 on appeals from [2016] EWHC 2768 (Admin) and [2016] NIQB 85.

[3] European Commission press release, 'European Commission Acts to Preserve the Rule of Law in Poland' (26 July 2017) available at: http://europa.eu/rapid/press-release_IP-17-2161_en.htm.

[4] On the relationship to rule of law and development, see eg MJ Trebilcock and Ronald J Daniels, *Rule of Law Reform and Development: Charting the Fragile Path of Progress* (Cheltenham, Edward Elgar, 2008).

understanding of the rule of law in some (albeit limited) detail. A comprehensive discussion of the history or a detailed philosophical justification of a particular conception of the rule of law is well beyond the scope of the mandate of this work.[5] A more limited discussion is sufficient to provide the appropriate analytic clarity for this work.

The purpose of this chapter is twofold. It first examines the nature of the rule of law. This shows that the phrase is used in three senses, each of which has a distinct connotation. Of concern are two such of these: its use to describe ideal, normative standards, which are used as part of an evaluation of a legal system; and its use to denote positive features of a legal system, which typically have constitutional status. This examination will add conceptual clarity to our subsequent discussion – as far too often imprecise use and consequent equivocation resulting from different meanings of a term can be a cause of muddled thinking.

The second goal of this chapter is to outline briefly why rule of law concerns are relevant. A philosopher or legal theorist may have some intrinsic interest in exploring such ivory tower themes. A competition or commercial lawyer, however, may be interested more in pragmatic concerns, and demand some sort of practical approach to our concern. Consequently a so-called 'pragmatic' response to (or dismissal of the relevance of) our analysis may be something on the lines of 'so what – what does the rule of law matter for the real world?'

The retort is simple: there is a significant body of evidence which suggests that the respect of rule of law considerations by domestic law, particularly in commercial law, facilitates economic activity thereby enhancing the total welfare of the relevant jurisdiction.

Otherwise put, normative rule of law considerations mirror the sorts of expectations which rational beings would regard as conducive for organising their behaviour. These considerations require that principles designed to guide behaviour show consistency through time, be clear in their formulation and application, and that what is expressed in these principles is accurately reflected in the outcomes of the legal system in question. The expectations of commerce are identical. Commercial relationships will thrive where such standards are reflected in the principles governing the trading system. And where the relevant rules are uncertain, unclear or inconsistent, commercial expectations will be thwarted. Rule of law considerations are thus more than ivory tower theories. Establishing this is the second goal of this chapter.

To achieve these two goals, this chapter proceeds as follows. The next, and briefest, section of this chapter considers the rhetorical use of the phrase, 'the rule of law'. The phrase is frequently thrown around in this rhetorical sense; but as rhetoric, its use in this sense adds little to precise legal analysis of legal systems, institutions and norms. Our analysis is not only for completeness, but also serves as a caveat regarding rhetorical hyperbolae and other misuses of language.

---

[5] See eg Brian Z Tamanaha, *On the Rule of Law: History, Politics, Theory* (Cambridge, Cambridge University Press, 2004).

The second section considers normative views of the rule of law. There is no unanimity among legal philosophers regarding its content. However, it is fair to say that these views range from 'thin' theories, in which the rule of law consists of a minimal set of formal and procedural guarantees, to 'thick' theories which import substantive moral values into the concept. The chapter's focus is on thin theories, as thicker ones are built upon them. Given that the book's argument is that the effects-based approach to competition law violates thinner normative understandings of the rule of law, there is no need to consider 'thicker' theories.

The third section discusses the rule of law as a principle found in legal systems, particularly those of the US and EU. The normative discussion will show that the rule of law is one virtue of a legal system, and legal systems can incorporate rule of law considerations to varying extents. Thus it is legitimate to ask of a legal system about the extent to which it incorporates this normative good. However, in addition to particular legal systems manifesting this norm, particular elements of that system (constitutional provisions, legislation, decisions, etc.) can also be compared against that norm. This section serves to introduce a point of comparison for the US and EU regimes, through showing their efforts to incorporate rule of law norms. This section thus will provide a point of comparison by which the competition regimes of these jurisdictions can be viewed in an effort to determine the extent to which these competition regimes live up to the internally imposed standards of their jurisdictions.

The fourth section of the chapter considers the practical importance of rule of law considerations in the legal framework of a society. This serves as a retort to those who would otherwise suggest that discussion of such concepts belongs in an ivory tower and as such is divorced from reality. Rather, the contrary is the case. Rule of law considerations, and in particular those identified in the second section as constituting an element of a thin (or formal) theory of the rule of law, are the very sorts of considerations which give rise to commercial certainty. And it is commercial certainty which is a very real concern to those engaged in the planning of those sorts of commercial strategies and transactions which may be regulated by a competition regime.

I. The Rhetorical Use and Abuse of 'The Rule of Law'

Judith Shklar is perhaps the best-known exponent of this view. She writes:

> It would not be very difficult to show that the phrase 'the Rule of Law' has become meaningless thanks to ideological abuse and general over-use. It may well have become just another one of those self-congratulatory rhetorical devices that grace the public utterances of Anglo-American politicians. No intellectual effort need therefore be wasted on this bit of ruling-class chatter.[6]

---

[6] Judith N Shklar, 'Political Theory and the Rule of Law' in Allan C Hutcheson and Patrick Monahan (eds), *The Rule of Law: Ideal or Ideology* (Toronto, Carswell, 1987) 1.

In many respects, this accurately describes much of the contemporary rhetorical context in which the phrase is used.

To the extent that the phrase is used in this manner, and that legal theorists regard the emotive content of the expression as exhausting its meaning, these legal theorists share a similar moral nihilism with the proponents of logical positivism, a philosophical movement of the mid-twentieth century. This philosophical movement sought to analyse (or solve) significant philosophical problems through logical analysis and empirical observation or verification.[7] So analysed, metaphysical and theological controversies were viewed as meaningless nonsense, since their claims are neither true nor false.[8] Aesthetic and ethical claims in turn were viewed as statements about the speaker's subjective emotional state.[9] So claims such as 'honesty is a virtue' or 'lying is bad', to the logical positivist, mean nothing more than 'I prefer honesty', 'I dislike lying' or (otherwise put) 'hurrah for honesty, and boo to lying!' Similarly, in Shklar's sense, rule of law claims merely signify a speaker's preference (or dislike) for a certain state of affairs. In this use, a rule of law claim that a given practice or legal arrangement violates the rule of law merely expresses opprobrium towards that arrangement.

We will not address this first, rhetorical, sense of 'the rule of law' further, save with a caveat. It is mentioned here for completeness, and in so doing to shed light on some of the rhetoric that often finds its way into public discourse on legal and political matters. However, by way of a caveat, we note that given the other senses of the phrase, this rhetorical use of 'the rule of law' can be dangerous. The rhetorical use of the phrase can bring with it connotations of the other two senses, which thus imports some degree of normative or legal illusion into the description of the speaker's subjective mental state. As a rhetorical device it loses much, if not all, of its meaning. Hence in this sense, the phrase is subject to disingenuous use; and as 'an empty phrase [it is] so lacking in meaning that it can be proclaimed with impunity by malevolent governments'.[10]

II. The Rule of Law as a Normative Concept

A. The Rule of Law as Formal Constraints on the Exercise of Power

A constant theme of Western political thought is to determine how one can constrain rulers. We see this theme emerging in Plato's *Republic* during its

---

[7] See eg Michael Friedman, *Reconsidering Logical Positivism* (Cambridge, Cambridge University Press, 1999).

[8] See eg Rudolf Carnap, 'Überwindung der Metaphysik durch logische Analyse der Sprache' (1932) 2 *Erkenntnis* 219.

[9] AJ Ayer, *Language Truth and Logic* (London, Pelican, 1936) 103–22.

[10] Tamanaha (n 5) 114.

discussion of the nature of the just state; it is echoed in Aristotle, and via late antiquity this theme evolves into those medieval understandings of the nature of law and morality that gave rise to theories of natural law and (to these minds) a necessary link between law and morality.

Modern, liberal understandings of the concept typically start from other foundations. Some start by being focused on the individual, and consider how particular formal legal structures (and possibly substantive rights) can permit individuals to realise values such as autonomy and freedom within a political community. Other such understandings view the need for incorporation of the rule of law into a legal regime as an attempted solution to a Hobbesian problem: how can citizens constrain the sovereign, when the sovereign possess a monopoly on political power – and hence legal rule-making – within the state?

Given the differences in starting positions which include different conceptions of values that a state should promote to allow its citizens to prosper (in senses that also include development of personal abilities, and is not restricted to an economic sense of the term), it is evident why there are many competing normative under-standings of the rule of law. Providing an extensive account of this is not our task. Others have done it.[11]

Our task is somewhat briefer. It merely requires a taxonomy of rule of law theories and an exposition of, and justification for (what we will later identify as) a 'thinner', formal theory of the rule of law. Prima facie, a distinction between thick and thin theories can be drawn on the basis of goals, and the process by which goals are realised. A thick theory of the rule of law typically recognises certain substantive values which a legal system should promote. These may be (or include) property or freedom.[12] Thinner, or formal, theories tend to be concerned with the conditions of a legal system which is necessary to achieve these goals. This is a standard and prima facie distinction, which illustrates the broad differ-ences between the thick and thin ends of rule of law theories. As Tamanaha notes, 'there is not complete agreement on what falls into which category'.[13] But this lack of agreement or imprecision in the distinction is neither fatal for its illustrative use nor for the purposes of this project.

Paul Craig makes the following observation:

> Formal conceptions of the rule of law address the manner in which the law was prom-ulgated (was it by a properly authorised person, in a properly authorised manner, etc); the clarity of the ensuing norm (was it sufficiently clear to guide an individual's conduct so as to enable a person to plan his or her life, etc); and the temporal dimension of the enacted norm (was it prospective or retrospective, etc). Formal conceptions of the rule of law do not however seek to pass judgment upon the actual content of the law itself.[14]

[11] See ibid.
[12] See eg FA Hayek, *The Constitution of Liberty*, ed Ronald Hamowy (Chicago, The University of Chicago Press, 2011) 221–24.
[13] Tamanaha (n 5) 156.
[14] Paul Craig, 'Formal and Substantive Conceptions of the Rule of Law: An Analytical Framework' [1997] *Public Law* 467, 467.

As such, these understandings of the rule of law are amoral, in the literal sense of the word. This is not an insignificant point, to which we later return.

The insight underlying formal theories of the rule of law is expressed by Rawls:

> A legal system is a coercive order of public rules addressed to rational persons for the purpose of regulating their conduct and providing the framework for social cooperation. When these rules are just they establish a basis for legitimate expectations. They constitute grounds upon which persons can rely and rightly object when their expectations are not fulfilled. If the bases of these claims are unsure, so are the boundaries of men's liberties.[15]

Hayek[16] and Raz[17] make very similar arguments. In this formal sense, to be governed by the rule of law is to be subject to a set of rules (laws) which are in turn constrained by principles (or rules) that make these laws predictable in their application.

At its most minimal version, a formal theory of the rule of law is to be contrasted with rule by a person.[18] In other words the contrast is between 'rule by law' and (arbitrary) rule by a ruler. The latter connotes arbitrary and unpredictable rule by an individual exercising his or her whim; the former entails limitations (consented to or imposed) on the ruler to ensure that the ruler exercises power in a non-arbitrary fashion.[19] This minimalist sense may be of interest to those studying the legal systems of authoritarian regimes and the transition to post-authoritarian regimes.[20] It is not, however, of interest to us. In this sense 'rule by law' is merely the position that the sovereign exercises its power in a non-arbitrary fashion.

The typical exposition of a minimal, formal theory of the rule of law consists in the presentation of a set of attributes that law should possess in order to provide the necessary guarantees to underwrite citizens' ability to form legitimate expectations of the sort described above. Such presentations are accompanied by intuitive arguments establishing why or how each element advances this ability to form expectations and/or limit the arbitrary exercise of power.

Perhaps the best known of these expositions is Fuller's story, known to every student of jurisprudence, of King Rex.[21] Hapless, but well-motivated, King Rex

---

[15] John Rawls, *A Theory of Justice*, rev edn (Cambridge, MA, Harvard University Press, 1999) 207.

[16] Hayek (n 12) 221–24.

[17] Joseph Raz, *The Authority of Law: Essays in Law and Morality*, 2nd edn (Oxford: Clarendon Press, 2009) 212–13.

[18] Following Tamanaha, we do not discuss rule by law as a rule of recognition. He notes '[a rule of recognition that] "all utterances of the sovereign, because they are utterances of the sovereign, are law." Understood in this way, the rule of law has no real meaning, for it collapses into the notion of rule by the government.' Tamanaha (n 5) 92, quoting Franz L Neumann, 'The Change in the Function of Law in Modern Society' in William E Scheuerman (ed), *The Rule of Law Under Siege* (Berkeley, University of California Press, 1996) 104.

[19] See Simon Chesterman, 'An International Rule of Law?' (2008) 56 *American Journal of Comparative Law* 331, 333–34.

[20] See eg Tom Ginsburg and Tamir Moustafa (eds), *Rule by Law: The Politics of Courts in Authoritarian Regimes* (Cambridge, Cambridge University Press, 2008).

[21] Lon Fuller, *The Morality of Law*, rev edn (New Haven, CT, Yale University Press, 1973).

engaged in a process of law reform in his realm which ultimately failed. It did so because Rex's reformulated laws failed to fulfil a number of criteria which were essential to give his subjects requisite certainty and predictability. In Fuller's enumeration, these are:

- The requirement of generality;
- Requirement of promulgation;
- Non-retroactivity;
- Requirement of clarity;
- Requirement of consistency (avoidance of contradiction);
- Not mandating the impossible;
- Permanence (consistency through time); and,
- 'Congruence between official action and rule'[22]

The story of Rex provides an illustration as to why rules within a legal system need to possess the characteristics enumerated; Fuller's accompanying explanations flesh out the intuition that the story captures.

Fuller's emphasis on these necessary features of a legal system clearly follows from his understanding of law as 'the enterprise of subjecting human conduct to the governance of rules'.[23] Neither this understanding nor his enumerated features are Fuller's definition of 'law'. Rather they point towards what must be a necessary feature of law: the ability to guide people in their actions. This, in Fuller's sense, is the inner morality of law, where 'morality' is viewed in a procedural (as opposed to substantive) sense; and is a quality that a legal system can possess to a greater or lesser degree.

Raz has developed a similar list,[24] which shares the insight that the purpose of law is to guide the behaviour of its subjects.[25] Raz notes that the rule of law is meant in two senses: first, of one being governed by and obeying law; and, second, in the sense that the law must be capable of being obeyed.[26] It is with this second sense that he (and we) are concerned.

In Raz's understanding, for the law to be capable of being obeyed, it must contain certainty formal and procedural elements. His list of these elements, in part, reads:

- All laws should be prospective, open, and clear;
- Laws should be relatively stable;
- The making of particular laws ... must be guided by open, stable, clear, and general rules;
- The independence of the judiciary must be guaranteed;
- The principles of natural justice must be observed (ie, open and fair hearing and absence of bias);

---

[22] ibid 46–91.
[23] ibid 94.
[24] Raz (n 17) 214–19.
[25] ibid 214: 'This is the basic intuition from which the doctrine of the rule of law derives: the law must be capable of guiding the behaviour of its subjects.'
[26] ibid 213.

- The courts should have review powers ... to ensure conformity to the rule of law;
- The courts should be easily accessible; and,
- The discretion of crime preventing agencies should not be allowed to pervert the law.[27]

The first three elements are formal, in Fuller's sense; the latter five adopt tenets of what is viewed as natural justice. Raz admits the list is incomplete, regarding these listed elements as 'some of the more important ones'.[28] Like Fuller, Raz accepts that as so conceived, rule of law is a feature which legal systems can possess to a degree. It is almost impossible for a legal system to be entirely compliant with the rule of law; some non-compliance is at times to be preferred – some administrative discretion may be a virtue in a legal system.[29] He remarks:

> Conformity to the rule of law is a matter of degree, and though, other things being equal, the greater the conformity the better – other things are rarely equal. A lesser degree of conformity is often to be preferred precisely because it helps realization of other goals.[30]

Accordingly, in this understanding, the rule of law is only one of a number of virtues of a legal system. This is significant for both rule of law analysis and for the scope of the content of the relationship between the rule of law and justice. The virtue which the rule of law possesses is primarily negative, in that it serves as a significant check on the arbitrary exercise of state power. Although it is not a complete check, it goes a significant way to preventing arbitrary abuses. Raz notes:

> Many forms of arbitrary rule are compatible with the rule of law. A ruler can promote general rules based on whim or self-interest, etc, without offending against the rule of law. But certainly many of the more common manifestations of arbitrary power run foul of the rule of law. A government subjected to the rule of law is prevented from changing the law retroactively or abruptly or secretly whenever this suits its purposes. The one area where the rule of law excludes all forms of arbitrary power is in the law-applying function of the judiciary where the courts are required to be subject only to the law and to conform to fairly strict procedures. No less important is the restraint imposed by the rule of law on the making of particular laws and thus on the powers of the executive. The arbitrary use of power for personal gain, out of vengeance or favouritism, is most commonly manifested in the making of particular legal orders. These possibilities are drastically restricted by close adherence to the rule of law.[31]

This point is significant for the book's argument.

There are two ways in which a legal system (or, more specifically, the judiciary within a legal system) can be arbitrary, and both are an affront to the rule of law. These two senses are obviously related, insofar as they both are affronts to the

---

[27] ibid 214–18.
[28] ibid 214.
[29] ibid 222.
[30] ibid 228.
[31] ibid 219, Raz's footnote omitted.

purpose of law, which is to be a set of rules or principles to allow an individual to make rational plans. The first sense, which is of concern to Raz in the above passage, is that a legal system is arbitrary if a certain set of individuals 'win' irrespective of the merits of their case. It is in this sense that the law is arbitrarily applied when the tyrant or her friends are favoured in court decisions, in spite of legislation or other legal standards seemingly stating otherwise.

But there is a second way in which a legal system can be arbitrary, which may be more pernicious than the former sense. A legal system is arbitrary if decisions are made irrationally, or through procedures which are not directed towards obtaining truth. If legal decisions are made irrationally or the procedures by which decisions are made are not truth-seeking in their aim, the outcomes of the legal system will contain a random element. This randomness will impede (if not prevent) rational individuals from formulating and executing long-term plans.

Rawls speaks of this latter sense of arbitrariness, noting:

> If laws are directives addressed to rational persons for their guidance, courts must be concerned to apply and to enforce these rules in an appropriate way. A conscientious effort must be made to determine whether an infraction has taken place and to impose the correct penalty. Thus a legal system must make provisions for conducting orderly trials and hearings; it must contain rules of evidence that guarantee rational procedures of inquiry. While there are variations in these procedures the rule of law requires some form of due process: that is, a process reasonably designed to ascertain the truth, in ways consistent with the other ends of the legal system, as to whether a violation has taken place and under what circumstances.[32]

This latter sense may be more damaging than the former. If a legal system is arbitrary in the first sense, for favouring individuals as a result of 'extra-legal' concerns, this may be known in advance and one can take this into account in planning. Refusing to litigate a matter, in spite of having an otherwise overwhelming case, may thus be a rational choice when one's opponent is a member of the tyrant's favoured group. However, if the adjudicative process is arbitrary because of irrational or random features, then it is impossible to make judgments of even that sort.

The sense of the rule of law identified above is quite narrow. Raz himself admits this understanding of the rule of law is narrow and formal, and says nothing about the substantive content of a legal system. It also says nothing about notions of equality, human rights or any democratic (or non-democratic) features of the legal system in question.[33] Law, so understood, is amoral in content.

The immediate implication of this essential amorality is that even the most abhorrent regimes can be governed by rule of law, so long as it conforms to those

---

[32] Rawls (n 15) 210.

[33] ibid 211; on the other hand, Tamanaha, for instance, appeals to a common principle of (Western) political thought and suggests that living 'under laws of one's own making' is a common formal element of rule of law theories (Tamanaha (n 5) 99). Thus he adds some form of democratic principles to the formal principles of rule of law theories. *Pace* Tamanaha, whether or not democracy is devoid of normative content, and is therefore a purely formal element, is not self-evident.

formal principles. Raz accepts this, noting, inter alia, that slavery is consistent with the rule of law.[34] But this is viewed not as a pivot point in a *reductio ad absurdum*, but as a positive analytic feature of a formal theory of the rule of law. From an analytic perspective, if the substantive values incorporated into a legal system are scrutinised under the rubric of 'rule of law', then the analysis becomes that of 'rule of good law'.

In this context of the moral neutrality (or amorality) of formal theories of the rule of law, Tamanah remarks:

> When rules exist and are honored by the legal system formal legality operates. The essential question is: in what areas, or with respect to what activities, should legal rules govern? Formal legality has nothing to say about this question. It offers no dictates about the proportion or types of government activities that ought to be rule bound. These are matters of social choice.[35]

This point is not lost on Raz[36] and others.[37] In this regard, Summers notes:

> There is no escape from the ultimate conclusion that the satisfaction of the institutional requirements of a formal theory of the rule of law is logically compatible with the existence of laws that are bad or wrong or even evil in content.[38]

From the perspective of analytic method, this is significant. The manner by which law governs (eg through clear, prospective and stable rules) is assessed according to rule of law considerations, and it is through that lens that such governance is analysed. The areas in which law operates and the content of these laws are assessed by other norms, which include such considerations as social justice and economic efficiency. These aspects of the legal regime possess virtues different from those possessed by the rule of law, and as such they are properly viewed through other lenses.

B. The Rule of Law as Containing Procedural Standards

Procedural elements are often included in the laundry lists of standards which exemplify the rule of law. They have a tendency to be of a more administrative nature, focusing on how the law is applied particularly in individual cases to the detriment of the subject. Rawls, for instance, argues that such procedural standards 'are to ensure that the legal order will be impartially and regularly maintained'.[39] Raz echoes this point, noting the necessity for the observation of the principles

---

[34] Rawls (n 15) 221; see also eg Tamanaha (n 5) 93 and Raz (n 17) 221–22.
[35] Tamanah (n 5) 97, footnotes omitted.
[36] Raz (n 17) 211 and 221.
[37] eg Craig (n 14) 469.
[38] Robert S Summers, 'A Formal Theory of the Rule of Law' (1993) 6 *Ratio Juris* 127, 139.
[39] Rawls (n 15) 210.

of natural justice (open and unbiased hearings), judicial review and accessibility of the courts (otherwise legal rights become chimerical).[40] Democratic principles are sometimes,[41] but not universally,[42] incorporated into these lists.

Such procedural principles, which include the core of what is so-called 'natural justice', are often invoked in rule of law discourse. A common criticism of the US practice of detaining purported terrorists in Guantanamo Bay is that by depriving the detainees of key procedural standards, this treatment violates the rule of law.[43] One catalogue of this sort of procedural standards (developed in the context of Guantanamo Bay) reads:

- Conducted by an impartial judge
- Governed by established procedures that comport with due process, including:
  - Right to counsel.
  - Right to be present at all critical stages of the proceeding.
  - Right to confront witnesses ....
  - Right to present evidence.
  - Restricting evidence to evidence admissible in a court of law, unless the presiding judge finds the evidence reliable.
- Appealable to an impartial tribunal, not subject to ... influence.
- Subject to reconsideration or rehearing only according to pre-established rules.
- Subject to judicial review in the ... courts.[44]

While the above was produced in the context of US military tribunals, we have taken the liberty to redact some points specific to those sorts of hearings, thus generalising the list.

This generalised picture of procedural elements coincides with our intuitive understanding of what a *good* legal system should contain. However, the presence of such procedural elements is neither a necessary nor sufficient condition for a *legal* system. A legal system can still guide conduct and provide reasonable certainty without encompassing these procedural elements. The legal system governing the detainees at Guantanamo Bay is obviously the example. This system is governed by a set of rules[45] which provide the certainty, clarity and predictability of the sort desired by formal theories.

But that system is wanting for other reasons. It is clearly deficient as it lacks adequate procedural protections, if considerations of natural justice are taken as

---

[40] Raz (n 17) 217.

[41] See Tamanaha (n 5) 156.

[42] See eg Summers (n 38).

[43] See eg A Wallace Tashima, 'The War on Terror and the Rule of Law' (2008) 15 *Asian American Law Journal* 245.

[44] ibid 264.

[45] See eg Authorization for Use of Military Force, Pub L No 107-40, 115 Stat 224 (2001) (codified at 50 USC § 1541 note); Military Order of November 13, 2001, 66 Fed Reg 57,833 (13 November 2001), which was implemented by 32 CFR §§ 9.1–18.6; and *Detainee Treatment Act of 2005*, Pub L No 109-148, 119 Stat 2739, 2742 (2005) (codified at 10 USC § 801 note).

the standard for such protection. Likewise, this legal system contains substantive deficiencies, particularly if principles regarding proportionality of treatment (or length of detention) and international norms against torture and mistreatment are viewed as elements of a just legal system.

The deficiencies in this system demonstrate the analytic elegance of a narrow approach to the rule of law. By focusing on the lack of procedural safeguards and the inherent immorality of conduct permitted under that regime, our criticism is precisely directed. On the other hand, were one to lump these formal, procedural and substantive concerns together under the umbrella of 'the rule of law', and subsequently criticise the regime for 'rule of law violations', any criticisms become diffuse.

This is not to say that there is a sharp distinction between formal and procedural standards. There isn't; and the two sets of standards can overlap. For instance, formal considerations of congruence between what the law says and how it is applied (or operates in practice) have implications for procedural considerations about access to effective remedies. Nevertheless, analytic clarity can be improved by keeping these two sorts of considerations at least conceptually distinct.

C. The Rule of Law as Inherent Normativity

The thickest understandings of the rule of law incorporate some form of substantive moral content by which laws and legal systems are evaluated. In its most extreme form, this evaluation is critical, as failure to live up to these substantive norms can be fatal to any claim that a set of rules has to being a legal system. This thick understanding regards conformity with this moral content as a necessary condition for a law's legal validity or a system's claim to be a legal system.

This understanding of the rule of law traces its origins to thought of the classical and medieval period. Cicero[46] is perhaps the best-known classical exponent of this position; and this classical thinking was transmitted to the Western tradition through the medieval theology of, for example, Augustine (354–430) and Thomas of Aquinas (1225–1274). Their views still have some influence in modern understandings of natural law.[47]

The insight behind this early view of law is that the normative force of law results from divinely implanted, human reason.[48] In this understanding reason acts as a source for and measure of positive law; and those positive laws which are

---

[46] Cicero, *The Laws*, I.6, II.13, III.2–4.

[47] John Finnis, *Natural Law and Natural Rights* (Oxford, Clarendon Press, 1980).

[48] Thomas Aquinas, *Summa Theologica* (I II QQ XC–CXIV), literally translated by Fathers of the English Dominican Province, 2nd rev edn (London, Burns Oates and Washbourne, 1927) vol 8; I II Q XC A 4 RO 1: 'The natural law is promulgated by the very fact that God instilled it into man's mind so as to be known by him naturally.'

in accord with reason have normative force.[49] If positive law runs counter to the normative content of natural law, that so-called law has no binding force.[50]

A more modern understanding of these sorts of theories involves appeal to a relevant normative value and linking that that value to the functioning of a legal system. The typical appeal of modern natural law theories is to rationality (or some other characteristic possessed uniquely by humans) and linking that characteristic to a necessary moral value of a social system (solve a coordination problem, facilitating development of human beings as moral agents or ends, etc).

Those advocating such a theory might argue that human reason will identify fundamental human goods, and will determine certain general principles by which these goods are pursued. In turn such pursuit often needs coordination in civil society – and it is at this stage that law enters to effect such coordination.[51] The rule of law is thus the appropriate incorporation of these general principles into a positive legal regime, so that it permits the realisation of those fundamental goods.

Advocates of other thick theories of the rule of law may posit a set of normative values which are argued to be needed for a just society. These may extend to considerations such as democratic values, rights to property and welfare rights.

In a more extreme manner normativity as a yardstick for legal validity can be found in considerations of our moral obligation to be bound by an unjust law. A frequent argument which underlies civil disobedience is that certain laws are so morally abhorrent that not only do they have no moral force, but that citizens are justified (if not obliged) to disobey such laws. This normative sense and its application to the evaluation of laws and legal systems are well within the domain of social philosophy. Such a view also relies on not only a very thick conception of the rule of law, but also on a theory of social obligation which requires that our ethical obligations take priority over our legal duties, in at least some cases. This latter point, too, requires further justification, and is better viewed as being part of a larger theory of the just state or society.

There are a number of problems with any sort of thick view of the rule of law, whether founded on the basis of natural law or an alternate position. The most apparent difficulty is in establishing the normativity of the characteristics which constitute the rule of law. With natural law theories, the difficulty is in the link between the chosen uniquely human characteristic (say, rationality) and normatively desirable characteristics in a legal system. Any link is not prima facie obvious, and any argument which purports to establish such a link is open to suggestions

---

[49] ibid I–II, Q XCV A2.

[50] ibid I–II, Q XCVI A4 R: 'The like are acts of violence rather than laws; because, as Augustine says (De Lib Arb i, 5), "a law that is not just, seems to be no law at all." Wherefore such laws do not bind in conscience, except perhaps in order to avoid scandal or disturbance.'

[51] See eg Finnis (n 47) 100–27, 260–64, 354–62.

that it is based on the naturalistic fallacy and/or runs afoul of the Humeian is/ought distinction.[52] In a similar fashion, non-natural law, but nonetheless thick theories of the rule of law, need to justify why those characteristics identified by that theory are appropriate elements of the rule of law. Providing these sorts of justifications is in the domain of the moral philosopher.

Finally, the least appealing aspect and most significant problem with thick theories is their over-comprehensive nature. These are not just theories about how a system of laws ought to work to regulate social conduct. They are visions of how society ought to operate, or as Raz remarks 'a complete social philosophy',[53] rather than articulations of good legal governance.

While we are all enthusiastic about values such as equality, democracy, human dignity and development, these are ultimately social and political ideals and goals. But these values have nothing to say about how the law should operate. It is also the case that a legal system can exist in the absence of any or all of these features, and provide the legal efficacy of a system which possesses those features. A society in which these values are found may be preferable to one in which these values are absent. What this shows is that the aforementioned values are desirable, but are not necessary aspects of rule of law analysis; and incorporating a desire to achieve these goals into rule of law analysis potentially confuses issues of legal norms with wider questions of political goals and values.

For present purposes, the approach used in this work when it speaks of the rule of law in the normative sense will be that of a very thin, formal theory. This is done for a number of reasons. First, there is no present need to propound a grand social theory of either the good life or the good state. This would be a task for another monograph directed to another audience; and its argument would be much different. Rather, the present argument is in regard to the potential threats to the rule of law which are posed by an interpretative change in competition law analysis.

The set of threats considered by this book is quite narrow, and as later chapters demonstrate, results from the new approach undermining needed legal certainty. And a corollary to legal certainty is the absence of arbitrariness in the application of the rule. Legal certainty is at the core of the very narrow formal set of rule of law principles identified by, inter alia, Raz. Additionally, as theories of the rule of law become thicker, they build upon elements of thinner theories. This is not to say, however, that there is a succession of theories ordered from thin to thick, with thicker theories incorporating all elements of preceding theories. Rather,

---

[52] The naturalistic fallacy was identified by GE Moore in *Principia Ethica* (Cambridge, Cambridge University Press, 1903) where he argues that it is an error in reasoning to infer a desirable value quality (eg goodness, beauty) from a natural object or state of affairs, merely because it is natural. (And similarly, it would also be fallacious to infer a non-desirable quality from an unnatural state of affairs.) The origin of this is in David Hume's *A Treatise of Human Nature* (1738) in which he argues that facts ('is') are distinct from norms ('ought'), and one can never reason from factual premises to a normative conclusion.
[53] Raz (n 17) 211.

a better characterisation is that thicker theories tend to incorporate some, but not all, elements of thinner ones. Elements of the very thinnest theories, however, are adopted by thicker theories, as these elements tend to focus on stability and certainty, which are central to all legal regimes.

III. The Rule of Law as a Positive Legal Principle

The rule of law is a feature of the two legal systems of concern in this book. That much is trite. Of greater significance is how the rule of law features in each of these systems, which also involves a consideration of what is meant by 'the rule of law' within the system in question. Cynically, one can suggest that much of the discussion of this concept is rhetoric employed by those who are attempting to formulate a legal justification for a policy choice.[54] One commentator, lamenting on the pervasiveness of such rhetoric in US Supreme Court jurisprudence, notes:

> The result, which is regrettable, is that appeals to the Rule of Law in public, political, and legal discourse characteristically pronounce conclusions, but reveal little of the standard of judgment that the conclusions purport to reflect. The comparative utility of the concept of the Rule of Law, as either an affirmative ideal or a critical standard, suffers accordingly. Recognized or not, confusion abounds.[55]

This concern is magnified when both the majority and minority cite rule of law considerations to justify their conclusion in a politically charged, policy-driven case;[56] or where such appeals are made on an ad hoc basis to a principle which may be a constituent element of the rule of law, without either articulating a more general theory, or suggesting why and how that particular element would fit into such a theory.

Notwithstanding these concerns about rhetorical abuse, it is clear that these legal systems view the rule of law in some form as an aspirational goal of quasi-constitutional or constitutional character. American constitutional discourse will appeal to rule of law considerations as a means of underscoring the force of a particular conclusion; and such appeals are made both positively (to demonstrate how a given position is consistent with or advances a particular conception of the rule of law) and negatively (showing why the contrary position violates such considerations). As will be seen briefly below, this incorporation of rule of law considerations is found in formal, procedural and substantial elements.

---

[54] See eg Richard H Fallon, '"The Rule of Law" as a Concept in Constitutional Discourse' (1997) 97 *Columbia Law Review* 1, 38–41.

[55] ibid 41.

[56] 'In *Planned Parenthood v Casey*, for example, the plurality (joint) opinion argued that the Rule of Law required fidelity to the central holding of *Roe v Wade*, while the dissenting opinion insisted that respect for the Rule of Law required *Roe* to be reversed' (ibid 5).

In the EU, rule of law is a 'constitutional' principle – to the extent that the Treaties are a form of a Constitution of the EU. But as a principle, the rule of law is incorporated into EU law in a formal and procedural sense. This will also be seen (again briefly) below.

A. The Rule of Law as a Positive Principle of US Law

The starting point for any discussion of the rule of law as a positive principle of US law must lie in the 1803 Supreme Court decision of *Marbury v Madison*.[57] This decision is absolutely pivotal in US constitutional history, as it established the principle of judicial review (which also extended to non-discretionary actions of the Executive) and allowed the Court to declare unconstitutional Acts of Congress, thereby establishing a means of enforcing the division of powers under the Constitution.[58] In this context, Chief Justice Marshall, rather famously states (in the gendered language of the eighteenth century):

> The government of the United States has been emphatically termed a government of laws, and not of men. It will certainly cease to deserve this high appellation, if the laws furnish no remedy for the violation of a vested legal right.[59]

Chief Justice Marshall's meaning here is clear. Those applying the law are bound by the law; and if were they not, then one would be living under the 'rule of individuals'. Characteristic of this rule of individuals, where individuals (including courts) are making law under the guise of its application,[60] is the uncertain and perhaps arbitrary nature of 'rule of individuals'.

When used in US legal (and particularly constitutional) argument, rule of law claims and considerations encompass formal, procedural and substantive elements of the content of the rule of law. While extended analysis of this content of US law merits a book of its own, a brief discussion of these elements allows us to see their significance, and to provide a background which enables us to assess the rule of law threats posed by an effects-based approach to competition law.

---

[57] *Marbury v Madison*, 5 US (1 Cranch) 137 (1803).
[58] ibid 180:

> Thus, the particular phraseology of the constitution of the United States confirms and strengthens the principle, supposed to be essential to all written constitutions, that a law repugnant to the constitution is void; and that courts, as well as other departments, are bound by that instrument.

[59] ibid 163.
[60] See Fallon (n 54) 3:

> Within perhaps the most familiar understanding of this distinction, the law – and its meaning – must be fixed and publically known in advance of its application, so that those applying the law, as much as those to whom it is applied, can be bound by it. If courts (or the officials of any other institution) could make law in the guise of applying it, we would have the very 'rule of men' with which the Rule of Law is supposed to contrast.

The formal rule of law component is essentially attached to the stability and certainty of legal rules, whether constitutional or subordinate. This feature, alluded to in the 'rule of law' passage from *Marbury*, is prominent in latter argumentation, particularly in cases where *stare decisis* is a concern. At the constitutional level, the relationship between stability and *stare decisis* concerns was part of the driving feature of the plurality opinion in *Planned Parenthood v Casey*.[61] However, concerns of institutional legitimacy go hand in hand with concerns surrounding the stability of prior decisions.

In *Casey*, the plurality argued that judicial legitimacy can only be achieved through the public acceptance that courts are the ultimate arbiter of the law. This is done by the courts making legally principled decisions which are palatable to the nation. Such principled arguments contrast with politically expedient justifications of a given position. The latter are the result of political and social compromise which may have no bearing on the legal principles in question.[62] Accordingly, overturning decisions – particularly watershed decisions – is to be undertaken when only the most convincing, and principled, reasons exist. To do otherwise would give the impression that the Court is bowing to political pressure and would thereby be undermining its own legitimacy.[63]

In *Bush v Gore*,[64] another highly politicised case (as it ultimately determined the outcome of the 2000 presidential election), dissenting judges advanced similar considerations of the relationship between institutional legitimacy and the rule of law. Attacking the motivations of the petitioners in this case, the minority reasoned that underlying these motivations was a lack of confidence in the ability of the (state) judiciary to act in an impartial manner. Such lack of confidence,

---

[61] *Planned Parenthood v Casey*, 505 US 833 (1992).

[62] ibid 865–66:

The underlying substance of this legitimacy is of course the warrant for the Court's decisions in the Constitution and the lesser sources of legal principle on which the Court draws. That substance is expressed in the Court's opinions, and our contemporary understanding is such that a decision without principled justification would be no judicial act at all. But even when justification is furnished by apposite legal principle, something more is required. Because not every conscientious claim of principled justification will be accepted as such, the justification claimed must be beyond dispute. The Court must take care to speak and act in ways that allow people to accept its decisions on the terms the Court claims for them, as grounded truly in principle, not as compromises with social and political pressures having, as such, no bearing on the principled choices that the Court is obliged to make. Thus, the Court's legitimacy depends on making legally principled decisions under circumstances in which their principled character is sufficiently plausible to be accepted by the Nation.

[63] ibid 867:

But whatever the premises of opposition may be, only the most convincing justification under accepted standards of precedent could suffice to demonstrate that a later decision overruling the first was anything but a surrender to political pressure, and an unjustified repudiation of the principle on which the Court staked its authority in the first instance.

[64] *Bush v Gore*, 531 US 98 (2000).

the dissenters argued, 'can only lend credence to the most cynical appraisal of the work of judges throughout the land'.[65] They continue:

> It is confidence in the men and women who administer the judicial system that is the true backbone of the rule of law. Time will one day heal the wound to that confidence that will be inflicted by today's decision. One thing, however, is certain. Although we may never know with complete certainty the identity of the winner of this year's Presidential election, the identity of the loser is perfectly clear. It is the Nation's confidence in the judge as an impartial guardian of the rule of law.[66]

This view of the relationship between the rule of law, the stability of legal principles and the appropriate roles of courts and legislatures extends beyond the constitutional sphere.

In matters of statutory interpretation, the Court has often – but not consistently – cited rule of law considerations as grounds for not overruling previous decisions affecting matters of statutory interpretation. In *Kimble*[67] the majority of the USSC opined:

> Overruling precedent is never a small matter. *Stare decisis* – in English, the idea that today's Court should stand by yesterday's decisions – is 'a foundation stone of the rule of law'. … Application of that doctrine, although 'not an inexorable command,' is the 'preferred course because it promotes the even handed, predictable, and consistent development of legal principles, fosters reliance on judicial decisions, and contributes to the actual and perceived integrity of the judicial process.'[68]

In addition to concerns for the integrity of the judicial process, respect for *stare decisis* in matters of statutory interpretation has a division of powers element: if the policy rationale underlying a court's interpretation of a statute is unappealing, then the legislature is within its rights to modify that statute.[69]

It is unfortunate that the USSC's actual adherence to a principle of strong(-ish) *stare decisis* in matters of statutory interpretation is inconsistent with the above-quoted claims. In fact in competition matters these sorts of claims are (and hence the rule of law foundations that underlie these claims) are abandoned. Further compounding this is another inconsistency within competition matters.

As we will see in subsequent discussion,[70] the USSC has been quite amenable to overruling its own interpretations of the Sherman Act, even when so doing increases legal uncertainty. The saga of vertical restraints, culminating with the 2007 decision in *Legeen*, is the case in point. This line of cases is considered in the

---

[65] ibid 128.

[66] ibid 128–29.

[67] *Kimble v Marvel Entertainment*, 135 S Ct 2401 (2014).

[68] ibid S Ct 2409, Court's references to *Michigan v Bay Mills Indian Community*, 572 US 782 (2014) and *Payne v Tennessee*, 501 US 808 (1991) omitted.

[69] *Kimble* ibid: 'What is more, *stare decisis* carries enhanced force when a decision … interprets a statute. Then, unlike in a constitutional case, critics of our ruling can take their objections across the street, and Congress can correct any mistake it sees.'

[70] See below, pp 50–54 and 190–96.

next chapter. Yet at the same time, the USSC can be adamant in adhering to some interpretations of the Sherman Act (and suggesting that it is Congress's, not the Court's, responsibility to correct these) even when confronted with the absurdity of that interpretation. Professional baseball's exemption from the Sherman Act is the case in point.[71] These inconsistencies in the application of the doctrine of *stare decisis* give rise rule of law concerns. Given the relationship between *stare decisis* and legal certainty, the policy-making function of courts and the need for integrity within the judicial process, and the over-arching need for the appearance of consistency within a legal system, these concerns are magnified in the case of competition law.

Procedural elements of the rule of law are also well ensconced in American thinking. While procedural and formal understandings of the rule of law are difficult to distinguish at the margins, *Marbury's* focus on the necessity that a remedy be available to protect a right is a clear statement of this value existing as an extra-constitutional norm which extends into the realm of positive law. Although the availability of a remedy may sit on the border of form and procedure, the clear constitutional protections against the deprivation of life, liberty or property by either the federal or state governments without due process of law[72] clearly imposes some – albeit ill-defined – procedural requirements on any attempted deprivation.

The Constitution (and the Bill of Rights, in which this clause appears) is silent about the content of 'due process'. It contains, at minimum, a reasonably well-understood procedural aspect, and a substantive aspect. There is less of a consensus concerning the content and boundaries of the latter.

Procedural due process requires (again blending with the formal aspect of the rule of law) that any deprivation be done according to some pre-existing law.[73] It also requires the use of appropriate or 'fair' procedures in the processes by which

---

[71] As a result of the decision in *Federal Baseball Club of Baltimore Inc v National League of Professional Baseball Clubs et al*, 259 US 200 (1922), which upheld the decision in *National League of Professional Baseball Clubs et al v Federal Baseball Club of Baltimore Inc*, 269 F 681, 684 (DCCA 1921) that: 'The business in which the appellants were engaged, as we have seen, was the giving of exhibitions of baseball.' This was not commerce; hence s 1 of the Sherman Act was inapplicable. This was upheld in *Toolson v New York Yankees, Inc*, 346 US 356 (1953). And in *Flood v Kuhn et al*, 407 US 258, 284 (1972) the Court, when confronted with the inconsistent treatment of baseball relative to other professional sports, remarked:

> Accordingly, we adhere once again to *Federal Baseball* and *Toolson* and to their application to professional baseball. We adhere also to *International Boxing* and *Radovich* and to their respective applications to professional boxing and professional football. If there is any inconsistency or illogic in all this, it is an inconsistency and illogic of long standing that is to be remedied by the Congress and not by this Court. If we were to act otherwise, we would be withdrawing from the conclusion as to congressional intent made in *Toolson* and from the concerns as to retrospectivity therein expressed. Under these circumstances, there is merit in consistency even though some might claim that beneath that consistency is a layer of inconsistency.

On the baseball exemption, see eg Stuart Banner, *The Baseball Trust: A History of Baseball's Antitrust Exemption* (Oxford, Oxford University Press, 2013).

[72] US Const amend V 2 and US Const amend XIV, s 1, respectively.

[73] See *Murray's Lessee v Hoboken Land and Improvement Co*, 59 US (18 How) 272, 276 (1856).

deprivations are conducted.[74] However, further discussion of substantive due process as a positive principle of US law is beyond the scope of this work. Our concern, as noted above, is with a minimalist conception of the rule of law, which is reflected in positive law via these formal and (procedural) due process concerns.

In addition to these formal and due process aspects, US law indisputably contains substantive rule of law considerations. The rights enumerated in first ten amendments to the Constitution (the 'Bill of Rights') were added to the US constitutional order through the efforts of the Anti-Federalists (of whom Patrick Henry, Samuel Adams and James Monroe were the best known) to ensure protection of individual liberty. This was, of course, in contrast to the position taken by the Federalists (particularly Madison) who – basing their thinking on Montesquieu[75] – argued that the tripartite division of governmental powers was sufficient to protect individuals against tyranny, ie the arbitrary exercise of power.[76] However, irrespective of the historical reasons for and the means by which these values are incorporated into the constitutional order, these need not be considered in any detail, for reasons made clear.

B. The Rule of Law as a Positive Principle of EU Law

The EU takes pride in being subject to the rule of law, and rule of law considerations permeate its legal order. We read, for instance, in Article 2 of the Treaty on the European Union (TEU):

> The Union is founded on the values of respect for human dignity, freedom, democracy, equality, the rule of law and respect for human rights, including the rights of persons belonging to minorities. These values are common to the Member States in a society in which pluralism, non-discrimination, tolerance, justice, solidarity and equality between women and men prevail.[77]

Further substantive content is added by TEU Article 6's recognition of the EU Charter of Fundamental Rights (along with it having identical legal force as the Treaties) and the (at present unrealised) goal of accession to the European

---

[74] ibid:

> The constitution contains no description of those processes which it was intended to allow or forbid. It does not even declare what principles are to be applied to ascertain whether it be due process. It is manifest that it was not left to the legislative power to enact any process which might be devised. The article is a restraint on the legislative, as well as on the executive and judicial, powers of the government, and cannot be so construed as to leave Congress free to make any process 'due process of law,' by its mere will.

[75] Charles Louis de Secondat, Baron de Montesquieu, *The Complete Works of M de Montesquieu*, 4 vols (London, T Evans, 1777) vol 1, bk XI, ch 6, 198–99, available at: http://oll.libertyfund.org/titles/837.

[76] *Federalist 47* (Madison), 1 February 1788.

[77] Consolidated version of the Treaty on European Union [2012] OJ C326/13.

Convention on Human Rights.[78] Article 7 TFEU protects the values enumerated under Article 2 (which include the rule of law) in Member States, and provides for a procedure for sanctioning a non-compliant Member State. This process has been invoked against Poland, due to interference by the government of that Member State with the independence of the judiciary.[79] The European Parliament has commenced Article 7 proceedings against Hungary.[80] Additionally, rule of law considerations play an important role in the accession process of candidate Member States, as respect for EU values is a necessary condition for accession.[81]

Rule of law considerations have been addressed in the case-law of the European Courts. Most famously, in *Les Vertes*,[82] the ECJ opined:

> It must first be emphasized in this regard that the European Economic Community is a Community based on the rule of law, inasmuch as neither its Member States nor its institutions can avoid a review of the question whether the measures adopted by them are in conformity with the basic constitutional charter, the Treaty. ... Natural and legal persons are thus protected against the application to them of general measures which they cannot contest directly before the Court by reason of the special conditions of admissibility laid down in ... the Treaty. Where the Community institutions are responsible for the administrative implementation of such measures, natural or legal persons may bring a direct action before the Court against implementing measures which are addressed to them or which are of direct and individual concern to them and, in support of such an action, plead the illegality of the general measure on which they are based. Where implementation is a matter for the national authorities, such persons may plead the invalidity of general measures before the national courts and cause the latter to request the Court of Justice for a preliminary ruling.[83]

Rule of law considerations include the availability of judicial review of acts of EU institutions. Further, in *Unión de Pequeños Agricultores*,[84] the Court held these rule of law considerations also include the right to effective judicial protection (ie the possibility of a remedy).

While the Court and Treaties note that the rule of law considerations which govern the EU are based on principles common to the legal and constitutional traditions of the Member States,[85] indications or enumerations of the extent and content of these principles are scarce. Perhaps the best enumeration one can hope

---

[78] In Opinion 2/13, ECLI:EU:C:2014:2454, the ECJ held the then agreement for accession was incompatible with EU law. The agreement is currently being redrafted.

[79] Commission Recommendation of 20 December 2017 regarding the rule of law in Poland complementary to Commission Recommendations (EU) 2016/1374, (EU) 2017/146 and (EU) 2017/1520. See also Case C-619/18 *Commission v Poland*, ECLI:EU:C:2019:531.

[80] On 12 September 2018 the European Parliament instituted such proceedings against Hungary, the matter is now with the Council: see Outcome of the Council Meeting 19 February 2018 6547/19.

[81] See TEU Art 49.

[82] Case 294/83 *Parti écologiste 'Les Verts' v European Parliament*, ECLI:EU:C:1986:166.

[83] ibid para 23.

[84] Case C-50/00 P *Unión de Pequeños Agricultores v Council of the European Union*, ECLI:EU:C:2002:462, paras 38–39.

[85] See eg TEU Art 2 and *Unión de Pequeños Agricultores* (ibid) para 39.

for is provided by the Commission in its Recommendation on the Rule of Law in Poland. This reads:

> Case law of the Court of Justice of the European Union and of the European Court of Human Rights, as well as documents drawn up by the Council of Europe, building notably on the expertise of the European Commission for Democracy through Law ('Venice Commission'), provides a non-exhaustive list of these principles and hence defines the core meaning of the rule of law as a common value of the Union in accordance with Article 2 TEU. Those principles include legality, which implies a transparent, accountable, democratic and pluralistic process for enacting laws; legal certainty; prohibition of arbitrariness of the executive powers; independent and impartial courts; effective judicial review including respect for fundamental rights; and equality before the law. In addition to upholding those principles and values, State institutions also have the duty of loyal cooperation.[86]

We may wish to add a requirement of clarity to this list.

In tax and tariff matters, where unclarity can lead to confusion about one's legal status, the ECJ has been adamant about this latter principle. In *Gondrand Frères*,[87] the Court held that: 'The principle of legal certainty requires that rules imposing charges on the taxpayer must be clear and precise so that he may know without ambiguity what are his rights and obligations and may take steps accordingly.'[88] And similarly in *Gebroeders van Es*:[89]

> However, that still leaves the question of legal certainty to be addressed. In that regard, it should be noted that the principle of legal certainty is a fundamental principle of Community law … which requires in particular that rules imposing charges on a taxpayer be clear and precise so that he may be able to ascertain unequivocally what his rights and obligations are and take steps accordingly.[90]

It would be erroneous to attempt to distinguish these cases on the basis that they are revenue matters, and not see them as expressing a more general principle requiring of clarity and certainty when an individual's rights and obligations are at issue.

The meaning of 'rule of law' in the EU is very wide, encompassing formal, procedural and substantive elements. Although casual reading of EU legislation and soft law may suggest that considerations of the latter two elements are the exclusive focus of rule of law concerns, formal principles of the rule of law are nevertheless well ensconced in the EU's legal order. This is particularly the case when questions of legal certainty and ambiguities of an individual's legal position arise.

---

[86] Commission Recommendation of 20 December 2017 regarding the rule of law in Poland (n 79) Recital 4.

[87] Case 169/80 *Administration des Douanes v Gondrand Frères*, ECLI:EU:C:1981:171.

[88] ibid para 17.

[89] Case C-143/93 *Gebroeders van Es Douane Agenten BV v Inspecteur der Invoerrechten en Accijnzen*, ECLI:EU:C:1996:45.

[90] ibid para 27.

The significance of this should not be understated. Unclarity in legal rules, whether this lack of clarity arises from the wording of the rule or the rule's interpretation, will lead to situations where a legal individual is unable to act. In a taxation situation, for instance, legal uncertainty results in the financial uncertainty of a potential liability. Similarly, in a situation where a particular commercial course of action may or may not be prohibited, the surrounding legal uncertainty may result in the undertaking forgoing a profitable (or otherwise socially beneficial) course of action.

What this section has shown is that both the legal systems of the US and EU take rule of law considerations, and in particular their formal manifestations, seriously. This is significant for two reasons. First, certainty and similar formal rule of law considerations (including elements such as congruence in how the law reads and how it is applied, and stability over time) will give rise to the social and economic circumstances which support longer-term planning and investment decisions. These considerations are reflected in the literature of law and development, law and investment, and transaction cost economics.

The second point of significance is one of contrast: both of these jurisdictions recognise the importance of these sorts of formal rule of law considerations. Yet this recognition of these considerations does not always translate well into practice, particularly in competition matters. The focus of subsequent chapters is on this latter point, and the remainder of this chapter is concerned with the former.

IV. Why the Rule of Law Matters

We began this chapter by noting that over recent decades, millions of dollars, euros, pounds and other currencies have been spent across the world to bring rule of law principles into the legal orders of other countries. Indeed, one commentator has somewhat cynically remarked: 'One cannot get through a foreign policy debate these days without someone proposing the rule of law as a solution to the world's troubles.'[91] While the rule of law may not be a universal panacea to all the problems which ail the world, or even a particular country, it is nevertheless a useful element of any legal system.

However, if the early part of this chapter has taught us anything, it is that rule of law talk is very broad; and its very breadth is liable to be the source of problems in analysis. Two people can meaningfully agree that enhancing 'the rule of law' may be a solution to a particular problem, yet they may disagree as to the precise aspect of the rule of law that will provide the needed solution.

[91] Thomas Carothers, 'The Rule of Law Revival' (1998) 77 *Foreign Affairs* 95, 95.

A. The Rule of Law and Development Status: The Evidence

The relationship between the rule of law and development is one such, albeit important, example. There is a relationship between the strength of a country's commitment to the rule of law and to its state of development.[92] Development, it should be noted, has both an instrumental and normative sense, and rule of law considerations dovetail with both of the senses. When development is spoken of in an instrumental sense, considerations of citizens' economic and physical well-being (such as increased GDP, life expectancy at birth, availability of health care) come to mind. The normative sense of development, which Sen elaborates in detail,[93] involves the recognition that human freedoms (such as democratic elections, ability to fairly participate in the labour market, the possession of certain civil liberties) are necessary to permit citizens' realisation of their capacities, and it is the purpose of (economic) development to facilitate this. The rule of law plays a profound role in both these senses of 'development.'

From an instrumentalist perspective, the work of the New Institutional Economists[94] has been influential, if not conclusive. These theorists start from the traditional neoclassical economist approach which recognises market actors as self-interested, utility-maximizing agents. They also recognise the importance of the nature of the legal and social institutions which govern the interactions among these economic agents. These institutions are – in effect – the 'rules of the game' when it comes to marketplace interaction, and the quality of these institutions is determinative of a country's development status.[95] This is also borne out by other statistical correlations of markers of the rule of law with economic development.[96]

These considerations have been adopted by institutions such as the World Bank as a means of measuring how a country is governed; and:

> This includes the process by which governments are selected, monitored and replaced; the capacity of the government to effectively formulate and implement sound policies; and the respect of citizens and the state for the institutions that govern economic and social interactions among them.[97]

---

[92] See Trebilcock and Daniels (n 4) 1–57.

[93] Amartya Sen, *Development as Freedom* (Oxford, Oxford University Press, 1999).

[94] See eg Douglass North, *Institutions, Institutional Change and Economic Performance* (Cambridge, Cambridge University Press, 1992).

[95] Dani Roderick, Arvind Subramanian and Francesco Trebbi, 'Institutions Rule: The Primacy of Institutions Over Geography and Integration in Economic Development' (2004) 9 *Journal of Economic Growth* 131, 135.

[96] eg Daron Acemoglu, Simon Johnson and James Robinson, 'The Colonial Origins of Comparative Development: An Empirical Investigation' (2001) 91 *American Economic Review* 1380, 1386 showing a correlation between protection from expropriation (a common component of a rule of law yardstick) and economic development.

[97] See World Bank, Worldwide Governance Indicators, http://info.worldbank.org/governance/wgi/#doc.

In its consideration of the indicators of governance, the World Bank considers six dimensions of governance:

- *Voice and Accountability* ('the extent to which a country's citizens are able to participate in selecting their government, as well as freedom of expression, freedom of association, and a free media');
- *Political Stability and Absence of Violence* ('the likelihood of political instability and/or politically-motivated violence, including terrorism');
- *Government Effectiveness* ('the quality of public services, the quality of the civil service and the degree of its independence from political pressures, the quality of policy formulation and implementation, and the credibility of the government's commitment to such policies');
- *Regulatory Quality* ('the ability of the government to formulate and implement sound policies and regulations that permit and promote private sector development');
- *Rule of Law* ('the extent to which agents have confidence in and abide by the rules of society, and in particular the quality of contract enforcement, property rights, the police, and the courts, as well as the likelihood of crime and violence'); and,
- *Control of Corruption* ('the extent to which public power is exercised for private gain, including both petty and grand forms of corruption, as well as 'capture' of the state by elites and private interests').[98]

The rule of law, in this context, concerns the efficacy and independence of judicial institutions, and how well these institutions provide strength and security of contractual and property rights, equal treatment of individuals (particularly non-citizens) before the law, and security of the person and property.

While these data show a strong positive correlation between governance (as measured by these indicators) and development outcomes,[99] there are two obvious difficulties with any attempt to generalise this result. First, the data on which the quantitative measures of governance indicators are based are themselves highly subjective, as they relate to individual belief and confidence in aspects of the legal system at discrete points in time which have been aggregated as survey data or the input of expert opinion.[100] Second, as the rule of law is only one governance indicator and the formal elements of the rule of law are merely a constituent of this indicator (which do not appear to be a subject of direct inquiry), the importance of this correlation between institutional efficacy and development status for our project may be unclear.

Notwithstanding these difficulties with possible overgeneralisation, this correlation provides us with a redemptive lesson. From Sen's normative perspective, this

---

[98] ibid, links to documents which explain these qualities are found on its webpage http://info.worldbank.org/governance/wgi/-doc.

[99] See Daniel Kaufmann, Aart Kraay and Pablo Zoido-Lobatón, 'Governance Matters' (October 1999) World Bank Policy Research Working Paper 2196, 15, available at SSRN abstract=188568.

[100] See Trebilcok and Daniels (n 4) 9–12.

correlation proves the inextricable link between governance institutions of this quality with markers of development. And from an instrumentalist perspective, the data show an important link between development, and the increased social welfare which accompanies it. One can only assume that certainty and clarity of laws and decision-making processes have a foundational effect on the quality of institutional processes and decisions, as when the rules which the institution is using are clear and certain, this will have a tendency to constrain the institution's decision-making processes, by limiting (or eliminating) arbitrary options.

B. The Rule of Law and Investment: Certainty, Stability and Predictability

One can find further evidence which suggests a strong relationship between the formal rule of law considerations of interest in this work (predictability, certainty and stability over time) and a legal situation which promotes commercial confidence within the subject matter of international investment law. The backbone of international investment law is a set of treaties which govern the protection of investments made by nationals of an investment-exporting country in another country.[101]

These sorts of treaties provide guarantees regarding, inter alia, the conditions under which foreign investments are protected within a host country and a mechanism for neutral resolution of any disputes regarding the investment and its circumstances (typically through an arbitration process). Such protections usually include some form of requirement of national treatment for such investments, and protection against expropriation.

Treaty-based provisions are often supplemented with contractual provisions (between the investor and host state) to mitigate against investment risk. One frequently used such clause is a so-called 'stabilisation clause', by which the host state agrees to crystallise the regulatory environment surrounding an investment at the time the investment is made.[102] This has the consequence of reducing risk for the investor, and thereby – in what might otherwise be a marginal case – encouraging investment.

---

[101] According to the United Nations Conference on Trade and Development, as of September 2019 there were 2354 such treaties in force. See https://investmentpolicyhub.unctad.org/IIA.

[102] See Rudolf Dolzer and Christoph Schreuer, *Principles of International Investment Law*, 2nd edn (Oxford, Oxford University Press, 2012) 81–82:

> It is not surprising that investors have sought to negotiate stabilization clauses in particular with those states whose political and legal regime has in the past been subject to frequent changes or volatility. Governments of such states may have reason to agree to such clauses because they wish to attract foreign investment and because stability serves to facilitate this goal. For the host country, a stabilization clause may be more attractive than a treaty, which requires lengthy international negotiations and ratification processes. [footnote omitted]

One textbook describes the potential investor's side of the market in the following terms:

> For the investor, the long term nature of the relationship means that it must spend money immediately ... with the hope of making a profit in the future. This entails a risk that something will occur between the putting in of financial resources and the getting back of financial profits. The profit-making potential of the factory or production facilities, however, is not just contingent on the normal risks of business ..., but also on the official or unofficial actions of the government that is the host of the investment. Such governmental actions often were not, or even cannot be, foreseen at the time the investor made its decision to invest.[103]

Crystallisation of the regulatory environment thus serves to reduce the set of risks that an investor may face.

Arbitration tribunals recognise the nature of the market for international investment and the nature of host state assurances to mitigate risk and thereby make their jurisdictions a more attractive location for investment, through assurances of certainty, continuity and clarity in the regulatory environment. These assurances are taken seriously, and host states are held to their terms.[104]

This lesson from international investment law should be of no surprise. It is yet another piece of evidence that clarity and certainty promote investment (and the resulting economic gain). It is a separate lesson from, but a close corollary of, the evidence which is provided by the relationship of the rule of law in a country and its development status.

An analysis of transaction costs demonstrates the underlying link between legal certainty and the social environment that is conducive to investment and development. Coase's well-known theorem shows that in the absence of transaction costs if trade is possible bargaining will lead to a Pareto-efficient outcome, notwithstanding any initial (or subsequent) legal entitlement.[105] A corollary of this is that the presence of transaction costs can thwart an otherwise efficient transaction. Experience shows that one need not appeal to Coase's theorem for proof of this: the addition of transaction costs may push the cost of a good or service above the buyer's reservation price.

---

[103] Krista Nadakavukaren Schefer, *International Investment Law: Text, Cases and Materials* (Cheltenham, Edward Elgar, 2013) 2–3.

[104] See eg *Suez, Sociedad General de Aguas de Barcelona SA and Vivendi Universal SA v The Argentine Republic*, ICSID Case No ARB/03/19, Judgment of 30 July 2010, para 231:

> In view of the central role that the Concession Contract and legal framework placed in establishing the Concession and the care and attention that Argentina devoted to the creation of that framework, the Claimants' expectations that Argentina would respect the Concession Contract throughout the thirty-year life of the Concession was legitimate, reasonable, and justified. It was in reliance on that legal framework that the Claimants invested substantial funds in Argentina.

[105] Ronald Coase, 'The Problem of Social Cost' (1960) 3 *Journal of Law and Economics* 1.

Uncertainty is (or acts like) a transaction cost. This point is little recognised in the literature.[106] One commentator who recognises the effect of the costs created by uncertainty succinctly makes the point: 'Simply stated, uncertainty means risk, and risk avoidance involves planning costs.'[107] If these planning costs become significant, they will cause parties to abandon a course of action which may be and socially beneficial.

This section has shown that the rule of law, and in particular its formal characteristics of certainty and predictability, is not merely some 'ivory tower' ideal, which belongs exclusively to the realm of the moral philosopher. Legal certainty and predictability are not merely niceties which are pleasing to the metaphorical eye and add a superficial 'shine' to a legal system's appearance. Rather these aspects of the rule of law have significant instrumental use. The reduction of uncertainty lessens transactional risk, reducing costs associated with prediction, planning and risk mitigation.

The illustration from investment law shows that such values are actively bargained for in the international market for capital. The host state, by providing guarantees which crystallise the regulatory regime either through treaty or contract, enhances the certainty and predictability of this regime. This reduces the planning costs of a potential investor, enhancing the opportunity for investment. To the extent that deploying capital aids in the economic development of a particular country, the correlation between rule of law considerations and development can be in part explained by the certainty and predictability provided by these formal considerations. The rule of law therefore matters.

V. Conclusion

The purpose of this chapter has been to explain the nature and significance of the rule of law. In particular its concern has been with two formal elements of the rule of law, predictability and certainty. These, it was suggested, are found in the very narrow permutations of rule of law theories, and as such are incorporated to one extent or another in every such theory. Certainty and predictability serve the foundation for rational action, and provide a buffer against arbitrary rule. This minimal normative element is incorporated into both US and EU positive law. Although both jurisdictions' understanding of the rule of law is richer than the formal elements which include predictability and certainty, these elements are significant in these jurisdictions' understanding of the rule of law.

This chapter has also shown that rule of law considerations matter. When legal rules are certain and allow for predictable outcomes, planning is easier – there

---

[106] One noteworthy exception is Michael Van Alstine, 'The Costs of Legal Change' (2002) 49 *UCLA Law Review* 789.
[107] ibid 829.

is less risk to be accounted for and mitigated. This in turn facilitates commercial relationships, particularly those which involve more than a simple exchange of goods for cash. In turn, commercial certainty (with resulting commercial activity) will tend to be productive of an increased total welfare within a society. As noted, efforts to establish certainty and predictability in investment law, and the correlation between development status and rule of law indicators, shows that not only are rule of law considerations a concern, they matter.

This has thus provided a backdrop against which the current effects-based approach to competition law can be evaluated. The difficulty with this approach is that it has a tendency towards legal uncertainty and predictability, and as such actively undermines these tenets of the rule of law. However, in addition to this rule of law threat, this approach may also have the very real effect of undermining commercial certainty, as that is predicated upon these rule of law considerations. The remainder of the present work explores such themes.

2

The Effects-Based Approach in the US: The Rule of Reason

The 1890 Sherman Act[1] was the result of a decade-long legislative process spurred by popular sentiment reflected in the 1880 and 1884 presidential campaigns.[2] This process resulted in a piece of legislation which was deliberately drafted broadly, ostensibly to reflect existing common law on restraints of trade.[3] Section 1 of the Act proscribes '[e]very contract, combination in the form of trust or otherwise, or conspiracy, in restraint of trade or commerce among the several States, or with foreign nations', and criminalises the behaviour of those who enter such contracts. On its face, this sweeping provision prohibits every commercial agreement – as even a simple sale of goods contract restrains trade by removing the goods in question from the market. In light of this language, it was necessary for the judiciary to intercede. Since its first intervention, the interpretation of what restraints are permitted and prohibited under that Act has been a judicially created story.

In its most basic form the history of the Sherman Act can be divided into roughly three periods: (1) initial concerns about the meaning of '[e]very contract'; (2) the rise of the use of per se categorisation; and (3) the fall of per se categorisation and the ascendency of rule of reason analysis and the economic approach. It is not the goal of this chapter to give a comprehensive history of US antitrust law; this has been done elsewhere.[4]

The purpose of this and the next chapter is to provide accounts of the development of the effects-based approach to antitrust in both the US and Europe, and while so doing illustrate the challenges that this new approach presents for the legal principles of certainty, predictability and clarity – key elements in the formal theory of the rule of law outlined above.

This chapter will serve to introduce the threats to rule of law in the United States which are presented by the extensive use of rule of reason analysis (which is driven by an economic approach to antitrust decision-making). But as there were

---

[1] 15 USC §§ 1–7.
[2] On this, see Rudolph J Peritz, *Competition Policy in America: History, Rhetoric, Law*, rev edn (Oxford, Oxford University Press, 1996) 9–28; Bruce Wardhaugh, *Cartels, Markets and Crime: A Normative Justification for the Criminalisation of Economic Collusion* (Cambridge, Cambridge University Press, 2014) 120–25.
[3] See Peritz, ibid 20.
[4] See ibid.

reasons, which are best explained historically, for this reliance on rule of reason, a brief account of how rule of reason came to be the default analytic approach is useful. The present chapter is structured as follows: the next two sections examine the initial interpretation of the Sherman Act, and consider the early development of the rule of reason and the per se approach. Sections III and IV look at the re-emergence of the rule of reason, and how it operates in practice. This is followed by a brief section on 'Quick Look' analysis, for completeness. Section VI shows that the means of analysis matter, as this is often determinative of the outcome of the litigation.

Finally, the substantive component of the chapter ends with a brief consideration of Sherman Act section 2, its provision on monopolisation. This is done for two reasons. Courts have taken a similar economic approach to analysis of conduct under section 2 as they have done with section 1 cases. This has resulted in similar rule of law concerns arising out of the sorts of legal analysis conducted under that section. Second, in Europe, the more economic approach is very much a part of analysis under Article 102, which is Europe's abuse of dominance rule. Hence a brief discussion of the US approach provides an illuminating point of comparison.

I. The Early Background to Sherman Act Interpretation

Although in its very early interpretation of the Act[5] the USSC took a literal view of Sherman Act section 1, this literalism was soon to be rejected. In the 1911 case of *Standard Oil*,[6] the Court considered the common law tradition in which the Court felt the Act originated. In light of this tradition, the majority reasoned:

> [I]t inevitably follows that the provision necessarily called for the exercise of judgment which required that some standard should be resorted to for the purpose of determining whether the prohibition contained in the statute had or had not in any given case been violated. Thus not specifying, but indubitably contemplating and requiring a standard, it follows that it was intended that the standard of reason which had been applied at the common law and in this country in dealing with subjects of the character embraced by the statute was intended to be the measure used for the purpose of determining whether, in a given case, a particular act had or had not brought about the wrong against which the statute provided.[7]

But seven years later in *Chicago Board of Trade (CBOT)*,[8] the test for legality would be described by Justice Brandeis in a well-known formulation:

> The true test of legality is whether the restraint imposed is such as merely regulates and perhaps thereby promotes competition or whether it is such as may suppress or even

[5] *US v Trans Missouri Freight Federation*, 166 US 290 (1897).
[6] *Standard Oil Company of New Jersey v US*, 221 US 1 (1911).
[7] ibid 60.
[8] *Board of Trade of the City of Chicago v US*, 246 US 231 (1917).

destroy competition. To determine that question the court must ordinarily consider the facts peculiar to the business to which the restraint is applied; its condition before and after the restraint was imposed; the nature of the restraint and its effect, actual or probable. The history of the restraint, the evil believed to exist, the reason for adopting the particular remedy, the purpose or end sought to be attained, are all relevant facts.[9]

Two points need to be made about this early formulation.

First, as Stucke has noted, the *CBOT* test represents a shift away from the common law understanding of restraints of trade which was incorporated into the *Standard Oil* test.[10] The former is based on the 1711 King's Bench decision in *Mitchel v Reynolds*,[11] a decision regarding what would now be viewed as an ancillary restraint. On the other hand, the *CBOT* test is applicable to a wider class of restraints than those used to ensure the success of another transaction. Second, and more significantly, the *CBOT* test is unsatisfactory. If its goals were to delineate the types of agreements proscribed by the Sherman Act, or to adduce a set of criteria to differentiate the two sorts of arrangements, it would fail on both accounts. As to the former goal, it is almost tautologous: restraints which promote competition are permitted; those that suppress it, prohibited. As to the latter, to determine whether a restraint is pro- or anti-competitive, this statement of the rule of reason provides a list of factors, in which anything can seemingly be relevant. This second problem could be (and, indeed, was) addressed through later decisions of both the USSC and the Courts of Appeal. However, as Stucke notes, by its decisions before and after *CBOT* the Supreme Court limited whatever discretion the judiciary might have had in clarifying that case's statement of the rule of reason.[12]

II. Per Se Rules and the Limits to the Rule of Reason

These limits arose as a result of judicial determination that certain commercial arrangements, particularly price-fixing, had no procompetitive advantages; and as a result such practices were immediately condemned. The most prominent early

---

[9] ibid 238.

[10] Maurice E Stucke, 'Does the Rule of Reason Violate the Rule of Law?' (2009) 42 *UC Davis Law Review* 1375, 1397–98.

[11] *Mitchel v Reynolds* (1711) 24 ER 347 (KB); see *National Society of Professionals Engineers v US*, 435 US 679, 688 (1978):

> The legislative history [of the Sherman Act] makes it perfectly clear that it expected the courts to give shape to the statute's broad mandate by drawing on common-law tradition. The Rule of Reason, with its origins in common-law precedents long antedating the Sherman Act, has served that purpose.

And at 689: 'The Rule of Reason suggested by Mitchel v Reynolds has been regarded as a standard for testing the enforceability of covenants in restraint of trade which are ancillary to a legitimate transaction.'

[12] Stucke (n 10) 1399.

case in this regard was *Dr Miles*.[13] In this case, decided six weeks before *Standard Oil*, the Court examined a distribution system in which the minimum retail price of certain proprietary medicines was stipulated in the (wholesale) sales agreement. Although counsel for Dr Miles made submissions on the advantages that such minimum pricing would bring, these arguments were rejected by the Court.[14] Rather the Court felt that any advantages obtained by the distribution system in question would flow to the retailers (and not to Dr Miles, the manufacturer/complainant)[15] and were identical to the advantages which would be obtained a network of horizontal agreements among the retailers themselves.[16] The Court reasoned:

> But agreements or combinations between dealers, having for their sole purpose the destruction of competition and the fixing of prices, are injurious to the public interest and void. They are not saved by the advantages which the participants expect to derive from the enhanced price to the consumer.[17]

Such practices, the Court noted, are condemned by both the common law and the Sherman Act.[18]

Three subsequent cases[19] would define the Court's approach to what it felt to be patently unreasonable restraints, before the high-water mark of per se reasoning in *Topco*[20] decided in 1972. The first two, *Trenton Potteries*[21] and *Scoony Vacuum Oil*,[22] involved price-fixing agreements; the third, *Northern Pacific Railway*,[23] concerned tying. All three cases represented incremental, but significant, advances on the Court's earlier decisions.

---

[13] *Dr Miles Medical Company v John D Park and Sons Co*, 220 US 373 (1911).

[14] ibid 407.

[15] ibid: 'But the advantage of established retail prices primarily concerns the dealers. The enlarged profits which would result from adherence to the established rates would go to them, and not to the complainant.'

[16] ibid 408: 'As to this, the complainant can fare no better with its plan of identical contracts than could the dealers themselves if they formed a combination and endeavored to establish the same restrictions, and thus to achieve the same result, by agreement with each other.'

[17] ibid.

[18] ibid 409: 'The questions involved were carefully considered and the decisions reviewed by Judge Lurton [in the court below], and, in following that case, it was concluded below that the restrictions sought to be enforced by the bill were invalid both at common law and under the act of Congress of July 2, 1890. We think that the court was right.'

[19] I have omitted consideration of *Appalachian Coals Inc v US*, 288 US 344 (1933). While this decision evokes a rule of reason approach, it is fair to regard this case as a Depression-era outlier where the Court may have incorporated its own social preferences in applying the rule of reason. In any event, the Court viewed the approach 'not on point' (and likely overruling it *sub silentio*) in a subsequent Depression-era case also involving a shrinking resource/energy industry: *US v Scoony Vacuum Oil et al*, 310 US 150, 214 (1940). See Stucke (n 10) 1400–01 and Wardhaugh *Cartels* (n 2) 136–38.

[20] *US v Topco Associates*, 405 US 596 (1972).

[21] *US v Trenton Potteries et al*, 273 US 392 (1927).

[22] *US v Scoony Vacuum Oil* (n 19).

[23] *Northern Pacific Railway v US*, 356 US 1 (1958).

In *Trenton Potteries*, the defendants (who controlled about 82 per cent of the market[24]) were convicted of establishing the trading conditions (which included fixing prices) of toilets and related fixtures. As part of their defence, the defendants wished to suggest that the prices which they fixed were 'reasonable'; and, as such, this practice was permitted under the Sherman Act's rule of reason. The trial judge refused the defence's request to charge the jury in that manner. Rather the judge's charge included a statement that, as a matter of law, such an agreement among members 'controlling a substantial part of an industry, upon the prices which the members are to charge for their commodity, is in itself an undue and unreasonable restraint of trade and commerce'.[25] On appeal, the Court of Appeal for the Second Circuit held this to be an error.[26]

The USSC reversed the Court of Appeal. Writing in the background of its earlier jurisprudence on price-fixing,[27] the Court held that merely because a fixed price was purported to be 'reasonable', this does not render the practice of price-fixing legal under the Sherman Act:

> That only those restraints upon interstate commerce which are unreasonable are prohibited by the Sherman Law was the rule laid down by the opinions of this court in the Standard Oil and Tobacco Cases. But it does not follow that agreements to fix or maintain prices are reasonable restraints and therefore permitted by the statute, merely because the prices themselves are reasonable.[28]

In concluding that price-fixing is an unreasonable practice, the Court focused on the effects of the practice, noting:

> The aim and result of every price-fixing agreement, if effective, is the elimination of one form of competition. The power to fix prices, whether reasonably exercised or not, involves power to control the market and to fix arbitrary and unreasonable prices. The reasonable price fixed today may through economic and business changes become the unreasonable price of tomorrow.[29]

The Court's view about the effects of price-fixing would be echoed in another Depression-era case, *Socony*.

The arrangement of concern in *Socony* involved a price stabilisation agreement for 'distressed gasoline'. The oil-production technology of the day did not allow for a well, once opened, to be temporarily closed: were pumping to cease, changes in the geological structure surrounding the well would result in its collapse, rendering the well unusable in the future. Due to a decline in demand for gasoline, the need to pump oil to keep wells open and producers' lack of storage capacity, there was a glut of gasoline on the Midwestern US market from about 1926

---

[24] *Trenton Potteries* (n 21) 394.
[25] ibid 396.
[26] *Trenton Potteries et al v US*, 300 F 550 (CA2 1927).
[27] See the cases cited in *Trenton Potteries* (n 21) 397–401.
[28] ibid 396.
[29] ibid 397.

until the time of the agreement (1935). The gasoline which resulted from the overproduction ('distress gasoline') was sold by minor producers on the spot market, further depressing the price.[30] As a result of the surplus, gasoline could be sold at less than the costs of its production.

To stabilise the prices, the major oil producers established a scheme where they would buy distressed gasoline from the minor producers, and incorporate it into their inventories, thus keeping the distressed gasoline out of the spot market. This arrangement had the effect of 'stabilising' the spot price, and – given the relationship between the spot and retail market – stabilising the retail price.[31]

The US government charged 27 corporations and 57 people with violating section 1 of the Sherman Act due to their participation in this arrangement. At trial, the District Court charged the jury that it was an offence under that Act for 'a group of individuals or corporations to act together to raise … prices'.[32] The Court of Appeal held that this was a reversible error, as the trial judge's charge was premised on 'the theory that such a combination was illegal per se. In [his] view respondents' activities were not unlawful unless they constituted an unreasonable restraint of trade.'[33] As the jury had not had the opportunity to consider that point, the Court of Appeal ordered a new trial.

The respondents argued that the appellate court was correct in its assessment, and:

> there was evidence that [the respondents] had affected prices only in the sense that the removal of the competitive evil of distress gasoline by the buying programs had permitted prices to rise to a normal competitive level; that their activities promoted rather than impaired fair competitive opportunities; and therefore that their activities had not unduly or unreasonably restrained trade.[34]

The Supreme Court would have none of this. After reviewing its previous price-fixing cases, the Court concluded:

> Thus for over forty years this Court has consistently and without deviation adhered to the principle that price-fixing agreements are unlawful per se under the Sherman Act and that no showing of so-called competitive abuses or evils which those agreements were designed to eliminate or alleviate may be interposed as a defense.'[35]

The Court held that any combination formed 'for the purpose and with the effect of raising, depressing, fixing, pegging, or stabilizing the price of a commodity in interstate or foreign commerce is illegal per se'.[36] The all-important footnote 59 to this decision makes it explicit that all claims (and hence evidence for) the

---

[30] ibid 169–209.
[31] ibid 198–99.
[32] ibid 210.
[33] ibid 211.
[34] ibid 211–12.
[35] ibid 218.
[36] ibid 223.

reasonableness of price-fixing agreements are irrelevant. There the Court noted: 'Whatever economic justification particular price-fixing agreements may be thought to have, the law does not permit an inquiry into their reasonableness. They are all banned because of their actual or potential threat to the central nervous system of the economy.'[37] Hence defences such as 'ruinous competition', 'price stabilization' and lack of market power are unavailable.

Eighteen years later, the USSC stressed the forensic advantages of such presumptions in *US v Northern Pacific Railway*, where the majority opined:

> However, there are certain agreements or practices which because of their pernicious effect on competition and lack of any redeeming virtue are conclusively presumed to be unreasonable and therefore illegal without elaborate inquiry as to the precise harm they have caused or the business excuse for their use. This principle of per se unreasonableness not only makes the type of restraints which are proscribed by the Sherman Act more certain to the benefit of everyone concerned, *but it also avoids the necessity for an incredibly complicated and prolonged economic investigation into the entire history of the industry involved, as well as related industries, in an effort to determine at large whether a particular restraint has been unreasonable – an inquiry so often wholly fruitless when undertaken.*[38]

This statement is followed by an enumeration of practices which theretofore were regarded as 'unlawful in and of themselves'.[39] Thus if the practice in question is among that set, courts need not undertake a costly inquiry into the purported 'reasonableness' of the practice.

The high-water mark of per se reasoning was likely reached in the 1972 decision of *Topco*. The case involved a cooperative association of small grocery chains formed for the purposes of obtaining and marketing quality food under private labels.[40] To aid in the marketing of its products, the association's bylaws provided for territorial restrictions on the distribution of products by its members. It was this latter aspect of the arrangement which concerned the authorities.

The USSC held the arrangement to be a per se violation of the Sherman Act. Three aspects of the decision are instructive. First, the majority displays a high degree of formalism in its reasoning. It expresses its legal conclusion in one brief sentence: 'We think that it is clear that the restraint in this case is a horizontal one, and, therefore, a *per se* violation of § 1.'[41]

Second, this formalism displays the need for careful categorisation: the restraints in concern were categorised as horizontal in nature; from which the Court

---

[37] ibid 224 fn 59.

[38] *Northern Pacific Railway* (n 23) 5, emphasis supplied.

[39] These were: price fixing (*Socony-Vacuum Oil Co* (n 19)); division of markets (*Addyston Pipe & Steel Co*, 85 F 271 (CA6 1898), affd and modified, *Addyston Pipe and Steel Co v United States*, 175 US 211 (1898)); group boycotts (*Fashion Originators' Guild of America v FTC*, 312 US 457 (1941)); and perhaps some tying arrangements (*International Salt Co v United States*, 332 US 392 (1947)).

[40] *Topco* (n 20) 599.

[41] ibid 608.

made an immediate inference of illegality. In so categorising the arrangement in question,[42] the Court relied on its earlier decision in *Sealy*,[43] which considered a similar distribution system viewed by the Court as horizontal in nature.[44] But this reliance is correct only to the extent that *Sealy* 'got it right', and that *Sealy* is sufficiently analogous to *Topco*. If *Sealy* involved vertical restraints,[45] then a different outcome may have be appropriate in that case. Alternatively, if the agreement in *Sealy* was horizontal, but if *Topco's* arrangements incorporated a vertical element,[46] the former case may not have been immediately controlling.

Finally, the Court stresses the advantages self-characterised 'rigid'[47] means of reasoning. According to the majority of the Court, this sort of reasoning based on per se rules entails that courts need not engage examining economic problems (or perform balancing exercises) and ensures commercial certainty. The Court makes the former point thus:

> The fact is that courts are of limited utility in examining difficult economic problems. Our inability to weigh, in any meaningful sense, destruction of competition in one sector of the economy against promotion of competition in another sector is one important reason we have formulated per se rules.[48]

And in the all-important footnote 10 to the above passage, the Court remarks:

> Without the per se rules, businessmen would be left with little to aid them in predicting in any particular case what courts will find to be legal and illegal under the Sherman Act. Should Congress ultimately determine that predictability is unimportant in this area of the law, it can, of course, make per se rules inapplicable in some or all cases, and leave courts free to ramble through the wilds of economic theory in order to maintain a flexible approach.[49]

Chief Justice Burger was to dissent vigorously. The Chief Justice's prediction that the majority's decision would result in private label groceries vanishing from the shelves of all but the largest chains would prove to be inaccurate.[50] But his comments advising caution in the use of per se rules and of the need for courts to recognise that antitrust cases will require judges to make difficult economic decisions seem to foreshadow later disagreements among antitrust scholars.

---

[42] ibid 609: 'United States v Sealy … is, in fact, on all fours with this case.'

[43] *US v Sealy, Inc*, 388 US 350 (1967). The defendants here were a group of mattress manufacturers who manufactured mattresses under licence from Sealy, which in turn was almost wholly owned by the manufacturers. The licensing agreement imposed territorial restrictions on the licensees.

[44] *Topco* (n 20) 609.

[45] This was suggested by Justice Harlan, in his dissent in *Sealy* (n 43) 358.

[46] In *Topco*, the association was held to be a 'purchasing agent for its members': *Topco* (n 20) 598.

[47] ibid 610.

[48] ibid 609–10.

[49] ibid 610 fn 10.

[50] ibid 624; Topco is one of the largest retail group purchasing organisations in the US foods sector: www.topco.com/Who-We-Are/About.

III. The Renaissance of the Rule of Reason

A change in Court composition beginning with the Nixon administration[51] and the broadening influence of the Chicago School[52] had an effect on how the Supreme Court would address antitrust concerns. The shift from the reliance on per se approach to rule of reason examination is best seen in a trilogy of cases involving vertical restraints, which played out during the 1960s and 1970s: *White Motor*,[53] *Schwinn*[54] and *Continental TV*.[55] All three cases involved vertically imposed territorial restrictions in distribution arrangements.

In the first, *White Motor*, the Court was asked to review a summary judgment in favour of the US government, which had condemned the appellant truck manu-facturer's use of customer and territorial restrictions in allocating dealerships. The District Court summarily held that this practice was a per se violation of the Sherman Act, and enjoined the practice.[56] In considering the appeal, the USSC noted that this was the first case involving vertically induced restrictions, and as a result courts know very little about the impact of these sorts of arrangements.[57] Previous judicial experience suggests that horizontal territorial limitations hinder competition; but the Court recognised that vertical restrictions (particularly when used by a small company attempting to break into or compete in a mature market – as was the case here) may not have this effect.[58] Realising that courts must need to know more 'about the actual impact of these arrangements on competition',[59] the Court held that it was inappropriate for the District Court to resolve this matter through summary judgment, and remanded it for a full hearing – where the competitive effects of customer and territorial restrictions could be established on their merits. The retrial never took place.

Fours later in *Schwinn* (decided the same day as *Sealy*) the USSC was to recon-sider its approach to verticals. Schwinn, a then important manufacturer of bicycles, was facing a decline in sales and attempted to enhance its market position through a new distribution system. The controversial element of the system involved Schwinn's imposition of resale restrictions on dealers who had purchased bicycles from Schwinn (ie title had passed to the dealers). The District Court held that

---

[51] See Andrew I Gavil, 'Moving Beyond Caricature and Characterization: The Modern Rule of Reason in Practice' (2012) 85 *Southern California Law Review* 733, 745.

[52] The influence of the Chicago School, including the writings of William Comanor, Richard Posner and Robert Bork, should not be underemphasized here. Their works are cited in eg *Continental TV Inc et al v GTE Sylvania Inc*, 433 US 36 (1977).

[53] *White Motor Co v US*, 372 US 253 (1963).

[54] *US v Arnold, Schwinn and Co*, 388 US 365 (1967).

[55] *Continental TV* (n 52).

[56] There was an element of price fixing in White Motor's distribution system. The District Court's injunction also applied to this practice; however, White Motor did not appeal against this element of the District Court's order.

[57] *White Motor* (n 53) 261.

[58] ibid 263.

[59] ibid.

this was a per se violation of the Sherman Act; and the Supreme Court – relying on 'the ancient rule against restraints on alienation'[60] – agreed.[61] This represents an obvious shift from *White Motor*. The Court's earlier reticence to draw a priori conclusions regarding the competitive effects of vertical relationships, based on judicial inexperience, seems to have vanished. Similarly, although the trial before the District Court lasted 70 days,[62] the USSC incorporated none of the evidence in establishing its conclusion. This seemed to show that per se analysis was still the pre-eminent mode of antitrust reasoning.

This pre-eminence would remain an integral part of the antitrust analysis of commercial arrangements (particularly those involving the distribution of goods) until 1977. In *Continental TV* the Court was in effect invited to reconsider whether its earlier per se condemnation of vertically induced territorial restrictions could – as the Court itself put it – 'be justified under the demanding standards of *North Pac R Co*'.[63] The standards of the latter case require the practice in question to have a pernicious effect on competition and be devoid of any redeeming competitive virtues.[64] This reconsideration, as the Court recognised, raised considerations of *stare decisis*.[65] Yet considerations of what could be termed 'getting it right' also came into play. The Court noted that the *Schwinn* decision had not only been subject to a significant amount of negative academic commentary, but lower courts had also limited *Schwinn's* holding.[66] The Court justified its willingness to revisit *Schwinn* on the basis that 'the experience of the past 10 years should be brought to bear on this subject of considerable commercial significance'.[67]

The focus of this criticism was on *Schwinn's* purported distinction between vertical restrictions in non-sale arrangements (which were governed by the rule of reason) and sale arraignments (prohibited per se). The majority in *Schwinn* offered no principled justification for this distinction, rather it appeared to be based on 'the Court's unexplained belief that a complete *per se* prohibition would be too "inflexibl[e]"'.[68] Further, the Court noted, *Schwinn's* distinction between sale and non-sale arrangements may work against those firms who could most benefit from invoking sale restrictions: small firms whose financial position precludes them from using non-sale arrangements.[69] Accordingly, the majority reasoned that the analytic focus must be on the economic effects which the agreements in question have, and not their form.[70]

---

[60] *Schwinn* (n 54) 380.
[61] ibid 382.
[62] ibid 367.
[63] ibid 50.
[64] *Northern Pacific Railway* (n 23) 5.
[65] *Continental TV* (n 52) 47–49.
[66] ibid 47–48.
[67] ibid 48–49.
[68] ibid 54, quoting *Schwinn* (n 54) 379.
[69] ibid 56.
[70] ibid 58–59: 'But we do make clear that departure from the rule-of-reason standard must be based upon demonstrable economic effect rather than as in *Schwinn* upon formalistic line drawing.'

From the perspective that the Sherman Act prohibits unreasonable restraints on trade, and that it is judicial experience with the practice and its effect on the competitive structure of the market which determines the extent of the inquiry (and thus the evidential requirements) which is needed to evaluate the reasonableness of a given restraint, the approach of the Court in *Continental TV* is almost certainly correct. The judicial decisions and academic writings produced in the decade since *Schwinn* could provide added 'experience' upon which the Court could draw to determine the extent of evidence needed either to accept or condemn the restraint in question.

But viewed exclusively through the lens of 'getting it right', this pushes *stare decisis* considerations aside. In *Continental TV*, the majority did show some concern for *stare decisis*. It noted that 'the need for clarification of the law in this area justified reconsideration',[71] particularly given that *Schwinn* itself represented a break from earlier precedent and the sharp criticism that it in turn received.[72]

Since *Continental TV*, the USSC has been contracting the role played by per se analysis in antitrust matters. The space left by this contraction has been largely filled by a correlative expansion of rule of reason analysis, and the development of a (relatively) little used 'quick look' approach. Related to, and likely shaping, this shift in analytical approach is the influence of the so-called law and economics literature in judicial thinking about antitrust problems. *Continental TV* explicitly cites the work of scholars such as Bork, Posner and Comanor. And one study shows that during the decade between 1967 and 1976, 30 per cent of USSC antitrust decisions cited such literature. In 1977–86, that percentage doubled to 60; and in the following decade it again increased to 78.[73]

The per se anchor provides a point of contrast to the rule of reason. Per se rules are used after significant judicial experience with given practice, and such experience has shown that the practice would be invalidated by rule of reason analysis.[74] Such practices, the USSC has noted, are those which are manifestly anticompetitive, lack any redeeming procompetitive virtue and are of the sort which have a tendency to reduce competition or output.[75] As the Court noted in *NCAA*,[76] 'Per se rules are invoked when surrounding circumstances make the likelihood of anticompetitive conduct so great as to render unjustified further examination of

---

[71] ibid 47.

[72] ibid.

[73] Leah Bannon and Douglas H Ginsburg 'Antitrust Decisions of the US Supreme Court' (2007) 3(2) *Competition Policy International* 14–15. During 1997–2006 the figure was 77 per cent; by 'law and economics scholarship', the authors mean Areeda, Bork, Posner and Bowman, which the authors admit may be an underinclusive representation of such scholars.

[74] See *Leegin Creative Leather Products Inc v PSKS Inc*, 551 US 877, 886–87 (2007): 'As a consequence, the per se rule is appropriate only after courts have had considerable experience with the type of restraint at issue, … and only if courts can predict with confidence that it would be invalidated in all or almost all instances under the rule of reason.' Court's references omitted.

[75] Paraphrasing *Leegin* (n 74) 886, which in turn quotes *Business Electronics Corp v Sharp Electronics Corp*, 485 US 717, 723, and *Northwest Wholesale Stationers Inc v Pacific Stationery and Printing Co*, 472 US 284, 289 (1985).

[76] *NCAA v Board of Regents of the University of Oklahoma*, 468 US 85 (1984).

the challenged conduct.'[77] As rule of reason analysis is the preferred approach to resolving antitrust problems, the circumstances where the per se approach will be applied are limited:

> As a consequence, the per se rule is appropriate only after courts have had considerable experience with the type of restraint at issue, see ..., and only if courts can predict with confidence that it would be invalidated in all or almost all instances under the rule of reason.[78]

Only those activities which have a strong tendency to restrict competition or that reduce output are subject to this rule.[79] Hence price-fixing[80] (but not vertically imposed minimum resale prices[81]), horizontal market division,[82] concerted refusals to deal ('group boycotts')[83] and possibly some forms of tying[84] are likely the last remaining members of this set.

Notwithstanding its limited use, the USSC has recognised the analytic advantages of the per se approach: as a rule, it clearly sets out a boundary between permissible and impermissible conduct; and it does not require courts to engage in extensive economic analysis to determine the legality of a particular arrangement. The Court made this point in *Northern Pacific Railway*, remarking:

> This principle of per se unreasonableness not only makes the type of restraints which are proscribed by the Sherman Act more certain to the benefit of everyone concerned, but it also avoids the necessity for an incredibly complicated and prolonged economic investigation into the entire history of the industry involved, as well as related industries, in an effort to determine at large whether a particular restraint has been unreasonable-an inquiry so often wholly fruitless when undertaken.[85]

At one time, the Court believed that the former point was of significance, as clear rules would provide a foundation for commercial certainty and business planning. Footnote 10 to *Topco* stressed this point.[86] Yet recent jurisprudence has abandoned this view.

---

[77] ibid 103–04.

[78] *Leegin* (n 74) 886–87, citing *Broadcast Music Inc v Columbia Broadcasting System Inc*, 441 US 1, 9 (1979) and *Arizona v Maricopa County Medical Society*, 457 US 332, 344 (1982).

[79] *Business Electronics* (n 75) 723.

[80] *Catalano Inc v Target Sales Inc*, 446 US 643 (1980).

[81] *Leegin* (n 74) 885.

[82] *Palmer v BRG of Georgia*, 498 US 46 (1990).

[83] *FTC v Superior Court Trial Lawyers Association*, 493 US 411 (1990).

[84] *Eastman Kodak Co v Image Technical Services Inc*, 504 US 451 (1992); *Fortner Enterprises, Inc v United States Steel Corp*, 394 US 495, 503 (1969); *Jefferson Parish Hospital District No 2 v Hyde*, 466 US 2, 13–18 (1984); and *Illinois Tool Works Inc v Independent Ink Inc*, 547 US 28 (2006). But since any analysis of tying requires analysis of the defendant's market power with the tying product, there is room for defences, and thus some courts have suggested that tying is, at best, a 'quasi-per se' matter. See eg *US Healthcare Inc v Healthsource Inc*, 986 F 2d 589, 593 fn 2 (CA1 1993) and *PSI Repair Services Inc v Honeywell Inc*, 104 F 3d 811 (CA6 1997).

[85] *Northern Pacific Railway* (n 23) 5.

[86] *Topco* (n 20) 609 fn 10, quoted above text accompanying n 49; this point is also made in *Continental TV* (n 55) 50 fn 16.

The current expansion of the role of rule of reason analysis with its explicit focus on anti-trust as a welfare-maximising regime has led to a different view regarding commercial certainty. The commercial uncertainty caused by a retreat from per se rules is now viewed merely as an increase in the administrative costs of the antitrust system. As these additional administrative costs could be offset by the arrangement's commercial efficiencies, the current law (based on judicial fiat) regards it to be imprudent to use a sweeping rule to condemn practices that may produce competitive benefits.[87] Concerns regarding type I errors therefore dominate concerns over commercial certainty.

In practice, per se analysis acts to limit the production of evidence during litigation. If a restraint is governed by such analysis, and given that previous judicial experience with that restraint has shown that no procompetitive benefits will result, courts need not be bothered considering evidence which purports to prove the juridically impossible. Accordingly evidence of the economic benefits of such practices is irrelevant and inadmissible, and will not serve to support a defence of the legality of the restraint.[88] Hence a group of cartelists cannot invoke the defence that price-fixing established 'reasonable prices',[89] or that the practice was justified to avoid 'ruinous competition'.[90]

IV. The Rule of Reason in Practice

The rule of reason is the default standard by which commercial activities are assessed to determine their legality.[91] In contrast to per se analysis, rule of reason consideration demands the production of economic evidence. Given the sort of evidence demanded, it is a bit of a misnomer to describe the rule of reason

---

[87] See *Leegin* (n 74) 895:

> Per se rules may decrease administrative costs, but that is only part of the equation. Those rules can be counterproductive. They can increase the total cost of the antitrust system by prohibiting procompetitive conduct the antitrust laws should encourage. ... They also may increase litigation costs by promoting frivolous suits against legitimate practices. The Court has thus explained that administrative 'advantages are not sufficient in themselves to justify the creation of per se rules,' ... and has relegated their use to restraints that are 'manifestly anticompetitive.' [Court's references omitted]

[88] See Thomas G Krattenmaker, 'Per Se Violations in Antitrust Law: Confusing Offences with Defences' (1988) 77 *Georgetown Law Review* 165, who argues that per se analysis serves as a limit to the sorts of defences open to defendants (and as such precludes certain arguments being raised). It does not create specific offences. Given that the Sherman Act is concerned with (un)reasonable restraints of trade, and establishing reasonableness is ultimately a matter shaped by the evidence which the parties produce, the author agrees with Krattenmaker. A party should be precluded from presenting evidence in a futile attempt to demonstrate the purported 'reasonableness' of restraints which can never be reasonable; hence this sort of attempt at a defence should be precluded.

[89] *Trenton Potteries* (n 21) 397.

[90] *Socony* (n 22) 222.

[91] See eg *Leegin* (n 74) 885.

approach as a *rule*, rather it is more of a *set of standards for guiding an inquiry* as to whether or not the given practice is restrictive or promotive of competition.

Until recently, the USSC had provided little guidance as to the content of this standard. *Continental TV* tells us: 'Under this rule, the factfinder weighs all of the circumstances of a case in deciding whether a restrictive practice should be prohibited as imposing an unreasonable restraint on competition.'[92] This statement echoes Justice Brandeis's *CBOT* formulation – in which everything is relevant to the inquiry.

More recent statements of how rule of reason analysis is to be approached include appending to the *Continental TV* formulation:

> Appropriate factors to take into account include 'specific information about the relevant business' and 'the restraint's history, nature, and effect.' ... Whether the businesses involved have market power is a further, significant consideration. ... In its design and function the rule distinguishes between restraints with anticompetitive effect that are harmful to the consumer and restraints stimulating competition that are in the consumer's best interest.[93]

Again, this adds very little to earlier formulations.

As a result, the USSC has left it to the lower courts to develop this approach to antitrust analysis, which they have done through a process of evidentiary burden-shifting. In *Actavis*, the USSC stated of this approach:

> As a leading antitrust scholar has pointed out, '[t]here is always something of a sliding scale in appraising reasonableness,' and as such 'the quality of proof required should vary with the circumstances.' ...
>
> As in other areas of law, trial courts can structure antitrust litigation so as to avoid, on the one hand, the use of antitrust theories too abbreviated to permit proper analysis, and, on the other, consideration of every possible fact or theory irrespective of the minimal light it may shed on the basic question – that of the presence of significant unjustified anticompetitive consequences. ... We therefore leave to the lower courts the structuring of the present rule-of-reason antitrust litigation.[94]

While this permits a bespoke approach to the problem, tailoring the inquiry to the needs of the questions framing the litigation it presents difficulties for litigants. In particular, the nature of evidence needed may not be clear until well into the litigation process, past the closing of pleadings and the discovery process, making success a quixotic goal.

Nevertheless, in its recent *American Express*[95] decision, the USSC approved of the three-step rule of reason process of analysis developed by lower courts. In the first step, the evidentiary burden on in the plaintiff to demonstrate 'that the

---

[92] *Continental TV* (n 55) 49.
[93] *Leegin* (n 74) 885–86.
[94] *FTC v Actavis, Inc et al*, 570 US 136, 159–60 (2013).
[95] *Ohio et al v American Express et al*, Docket No 16-1454, 25 June 2018.

challenged restraint has a substantial anticompetitive effect that harms consumers in the relevant market'.[96] If the plaintiff succeeds, then in the second step the burden shifts to the defendant 'to show a procompetitive rationale for the restraint'.[97] Third, if the defendant meets this, the burden then shifts to the plaintiff 'to demonstrate that the procompetitive efficiencies could be reasonably achieved through less anticompetitive means'.[98]

The plaintiff can meet the first step by proof of 'actual detrimental effects'[99] directly (by establishing effects such as an increase in price, reduction of output or diminution of quality);[100] or indirectly (by proof of the defendant's market power and that the restraint harms competition).[101] Thus market definition is critical in this first stage. Without a market definition and subsequent analysis, it is difficult to determine the effects an arrangement may have on competition in a given market.

Thus the first step looks for actual detrimental effects on competition; if these are not found, a potential for adverse effects is sought. This potential can be demonstrated through proof of market power and the anticompetitive potential of the restraint in question.[102] Lower courts have described the standard of proof of actual adverse effects as those that would be 'supported by "relevant evidence that a reasonable mind might accept as adequate to support [its] conclusion."'[103] Indirect proof requires market definition, establishing that the defendant has market power within the defined market, and proof of some form of harm to competition.[104] Market power is viewed as the 'the ability to raise prices significantly without going out of business'.[105] It acts as a surrogate for proof of actual effects,[106] and without it an arrangement can have no actual or potential anticompetitive effects.

The operating principle of the rule of reason, namely that the evidence required is relative to the circumstances, is applicable to proof of each of these

---

[96] ibid slip opinion 9.

[97] ibid.

[98] ibid 10.

[99] ibid, citing *Federal Trade Commission v Indiana Federation of Dentists*, 476 US 447, 460 (1986).

[100] ibid.

[101] ibid 10, citing *Tops Markets Inc v Quality Markets Inc*, 142 F 3d 90, 97 (CA2 1998). The relevant passage from *Tops* – not quoted by the Court – reads:

> Even assuming this market share data implies that [the defendant] possessed market power, [the plaintiff] still would fail to satisfy its burden under the adverse-effect requirement. Market power, while necessary to show adverse effect indirectly, alone is insufficient. ... A plaintiff seeking to use market power as a proxy for adverse effect must show market power, plus some other ground for believing that the challenged behavior could harm competition in the market, such as the inherent anticompetitive nature of the defendant's behavior or the structure of the interbrand market.

See also *Spanish Broadcasting System of Florida v Clear Channel Communications, Inc*, 376 F 3d 1065, 1073 (CA11 2004).

[102] See *Realcomp II Ltd v FTC*, 635 F 3d 815, 827 (CA6 2011).

[103] ibid 831, quoting *In Re Detroit Auto Dealers Association*, 955 F 2d 457, 469 (CA6 1992).

[104] See the passage from *Tops Markets* quoted n 101. See also *US v Brown University et al*, 5 F 3d 658, 668 (CA3 1993); *Tunis Brothers Co v Ford Motor Company*, 952 F 2d 715, 727 (CA3 1991); *NCAA* (n 76) 110.

[105] *Agnew v National Collegiate Athletic Association*, 683 F 3d 328, 335 (CA7 2012).

[106] *Indiana Federation of Dentists* (n 99) 460.

points. However, proof of the first point mandates that the plaintiff tell a convincing story regarding the detrimental effects on competition, and typically this story is told using the tools found in conventional economic techniques.[107] But this need not always be the case: for instance, demonstrating a reduction in dealer opening hours (and output restriction) does not require significant econometric analysis.[108]

Assuming the plaintiff meets the initial burden in the first step, the burden next shifts to the defendant to show a procompetitive rationale for the arrangement in question. Typically such procompetitive virtues take the forms of new products or efficiencies in the market.[109] *BMI*[110] provides a good example of this point. Here the arrangement in question was an agreement among composers and music publishing houses in regards to blanket licensing of music performance rights. The majority recognised that this may have been 'price-fixing' in the literal sense: the composers and publishing houses joined together into an organisation that sets its price for the blanket licence it sells,[111] but the agreement nevertheless provided procompetitive benefits. Those who would want access to the performance rights could purchase a single licence and have access to millions of pieces of music from the catalogues, rather than engage in prior negotiation with individual copyright holders. The efficiencies resulting from savings in transaction costs are obvious.

Not every story told by defendants in an attempt to meet the burden imposed upon them under the second step will suffice. In the words of the Sixth Circuit, the defendant's procompetitive justification must be 'legitimate, plausible, substantial and reasonable'.[112] Courts are wary of free-riding as a justification,[113] which can be used in an attempt to justify the defendant's own economic interest.[114] Courts will reject justifications that appear to rationalise the defendant's economic self-interest[115] and condemn the practice in question as per se illegal. Similarly, proffered defences which attempt to protect weaker members in a market, or trade-off higher prices in one market against benefits in another market, tend to be rejected.

---

[107] See eg *Realcomp II* (n 102) 831–34.

[108] See *In re Detroit Auto Dealers Association Inc*, 955 F 3d 457, 470–71 (CA6 1992).

[109] See *Indiana Federation of Dentists* (n 99) 459.

[110] *Broadcast Music Inc et al v Columbia Broadcasting System Inc et al*, 441 US 1 (1979).

[111] ibid 8.

[112] *Detroit Auto Dealers* (n 103) 470.

[113] See eg *Realcomp II* (n 102) 835–36 and Herbert Hovenkamp, 'The Rule of Reason' (2018) 70 *Florida Law Review* 81, 111–13.

[114] See *Toys 'R'Us v FTC*, 221 F 3d 928, 938 (CA7 2000):

> What TRU wanted or did not want is neither here nor there for purposes of the free rider argument. Its economic interest was in maximizing its own profits, not in keeping down its suppliers' cost of doing business. ... On this record, in short, TRU cannot prevail on the basis that its practices were designed to combat free riding.

[115] See *Brown University* (n 104) 677, citing *FTC v Superior Trial Lawyers Association*, 493 US 411 (1990). This is an instance where the economic self-interest apparent in the arrangement (ie a group boycott) mandated per se treatment. *Indiana Federation of Dentists* (n 99) is another example where the defendants' economic self-interest aroused judicial suspicion of the real purpose of the arrangement.

NCAA is an example of these latter two points.[116] In that case, the defendant attempted to justify an output restriction (televised US college football games) by suggesting that the restriction helped less popular teams and promoted attendance at live games. Neither of these justifications was accepted.[117] Finally, as the USSC has stated: 'In sum, the Rule of Reason does not support a defense based on the assumption that competition itself is unreasonable.'[118]

If the defendant is able to provide the procompetitive justification demanded under the second step, the burden shifts back to the plaintiff 'to demonstrate that the procompetitive efficiencies could be reasonably achieved through less anticompetitive means'.[119] This is a balancing act, and ultimately it will be for the relevant court to determine which side of the scale is heavier. The Second Circuit noted:

> Ultimately, it remains for the factfinder to weigh the harms and benefits of the challenged behavior. The classic articulation of how the rule of reason analysis should be undertaken is found in *Chicago Bd of Trade* ... [formulation omitted]. This classic test is easier to state than to apply. It at least seems clear that the factfinder must decide the overarching question of whether the challenged action purports to promote or to destroy competition. Resolving this under the rule of reason approach requires a careful and complete analysis of the competitive effects of the challenged restraint.[120]

The difficulty is obvious: the legal standards for conducting a *CBOT*-style analysis are unclear. Further, the practice of the Circuit Courts seems to go beyond the *CBOT* test.

In *CBOT*, the arrangement in question passes muster if *on balance* the arrangement is procompetitive. Circuit application of stage three of rule of reason analysis requires proof that the arrangement is the *least restrictive means of achieving the goal*. The evidentiary burden of how this is established is also uncertain: for instance, the DC Circuit requires the defendant to establish this;[121] other Circuits (eg the Second[122] and Fourth[123]) place the burden on the plaintiff.[124] The Ninth Circuit's

---

[116] It is often suggested that *NCAA* (n 76) is an instance of the court applying a 'quick look' test. This is unlikely to be the case, as the court begins its analysis of the restraint in question (output restrictions) by recognising the actual harmful effects produced. The court does not treat the restraint as (merely) suspect or having a family resemblance to other (known) anticompetitive arrangements, as it would in a 'quick look' matter.

[117] *NCCA* (n 76) 116–20.

[118] *National Society of Professional Engineers* (n 11).

[119] *American Express* (n 95) slip opinion 10.

[120] *Capital Imaging Associates PC v Mohawk Valley Medical Associates Inc*, 996 F 2d 537, 543 (CA2 1993), cited with approval in *American Express*, ibid.

[121] *Kreuzer v American Academy of Periodontology*, 735 F 2d 1479, 1495 (DCCA 1984): '[T]he [defendant] has failed to demonstrate that the limited practice requirement is the least restrictive method available to achieve the asserted goal.'

[122] See eg *Clorox Co v Sterling Winthrop Inc*, 117 F 3d 50, 56 (CA2 1997).

[123] See eg *Continental Airlines Inc v United Airlines Inc*, 277 F 3d 499, 510–11 (CA4 2002).

[124] See Gabriel A Feldman, 'The Misuse of the Less Restrictive Alternative Inquiry in Rule of Reason Analysis' (2009) 58 *American University Law Review* 561, 582–85, who notes that this incorporates the least restrictive test of *Addyston Pipe and Steel Co* (n 39) into the *CBOT* test. See also C Scott Hemphill, 'Less Restrictive Alternatives in Antitrust Law' (2016) 116 *Columbia Law Review* 927.

test is slightly less onerous, '[the] plaintiff must then show that any legitimate objectives can be achieved in a substantially less restrictive manner'.[125] The Third Circuit requires the plaintiff to demonstrate a 'viable less restrictive alternative'.[126]

If such an alternative cannot be provided, the court is called upon to balance the pro- and anticompetitive effects of the arrangement in question.[127] There has been little discussion by the USSC of these elements of the third step.[128] Indeed, its 2018 *American Express* decision failed to discuss this step. There was no need to engage in such discussion, as the matter was resolved in preceding steps.

It is precisely because few cases proceed this far that there is little discussion of, and hence guidance for, the application of the third step. In two articles,[129] published in 1999 and 2009, Michael Carrier showed that between 1977[130] and 1999 only 4 per cent of cases decided using rule of reason analysis went to the balancing stage,[131] and between 1999 and 2009, balancing occurred in 2 per cent of cases.[132] Although balancing occurs, it is rare, and the outcome of the vast majority of cases is determined through the burden-shifting framework of the earlier stages.

V. The 'Quick Look' Approach

Consistent with a sliding scale approach in assessing the reasonableness of restraints, and given that there may not be a clear divide between the categories of antitrust analysis,[133] courts have, from time to time, adopted a 'quick look' means of analysis. Quick look is used in circumstances where: (i) the practice in question has a strong resemblance to a practice that is known to have significant anticompetitive effects with no countervailing procompetitive virtues (such as

---

[125] *Tanaka v University of Southern California*, 252 F 3d 1059, 1063 (CA9 2001).

[126] *Brown University* (n 104) 679.

[127] See *County of Tuolumne v Sonora Community Hospital*, 236 F 3d 1148, 1160 (CA9 2000): 'Because plaintiffs have failed to meet their burden of advancing viable less restrictive alternatives, we reach the balancing stage. ... We must balance the harms and benefits of the [arrangement in question] to determine whether they are reasonable.'

[128] See Hemphill (n 124) 940, who (at fn 60) cites *NCAA* (n 76) 119; *Maricopa* (n 78); *Actavis* (n 94); *NFL v North American Soccer League* 459 US 1074, 1079 (1982) (Rehnquist, J, dissenting); and *National Society of Professional Engineers* (n 11) 699–700 as examples of such discussion.

[129] Michael A Carrier, 'The Real Rule of Reason: Bridging the Disconnect' [1999] *Brigham Young University Law Review* 1265; Michael A Carrier, 'The Rule of Reason: An Empirical Update for the 21st Century' (2009) 16 *George Mason Law Review* 827.

[130] This was the year of the *Continental TV* decision (n 55) which enlarged the scope for rule of reason analysis.

[131] Carrier, 'Real Rule of Reason' (n 129) 1269

[132] Carrier, 'Empirical Update' (n 129) 828

[133] See *FTC v California Dental Association*, 526 US 756, 779 (1999):

> The truth is that our categories of analysis of anticompetitive effect are less fixed than terms like 'per se,' 'quick look,' and 'rule of reason' tend to make them appear. We have recognized, for example, that 'there is often no bright line separating per se from Rule of Reason analysis,' since 'considerable inquiry into market conditions' may be required before the application of any so-called ' per se ' condemnation is justified.

price-fixing or output reduction). (ii) This known practice is condemned by per se analysis. However, (iii) the practice in question has an idiosyncratic feature which may distinguish it from the known practice.[134] As a result of this idiosyncrasy, (iv) courts may not have had sufficient experience with the practice in question to be fully confident in assessing it under the per se approach.

In these circumstances, the practice and its anticompetitive consequences are rapidly evaluated. The USSC has stated that this means of analysis is appropriate when 'an observer with even a rudimentary understanding of economics could conclude that the arrangements in question would have an anticompetitive effect on customers and markets',[135] and the practice is accordingly condemned.

Again, the USSC has left it to the lower courts to develop the structure of quick look analysis, which these courts have done in the form of a burden-shifting framework. Courts will ask a series of questions: is the restraint in question of the sort that will obviously harm consumers? If so, it is 'inherently suspect'.[136] In that case, the defendant must provide a legally cognisable[137] procompetitive justification for the practice.[138] If the harm is not obvious, the inquiry shifts to full-blown rule of reason;[139] if the procompetitive justification is not accepted, the practice is condemned.

If the defendant successfully presents the needed procompetitive justification, the burden shifts to the plaintiff. The plaintiff can discharge this by showing either without adducing empirical evidence that the 'restraint very likely harmed consumers'[140] or (by adducing empirical evidence) that 'anticompetitive effects are likely'.[141] Should the plaintiff succeed, the burden shifts back to the defendant to establish that the arrangement does not harm consumers, or that its procompetitive effects outweigh the anticompetitive consequences.[142]

It is fair to say that this form of analysis is little used, by either the USSC[143] or lower courts.[144] Further, it is credible to suggest that with the development of a highly structured, rule of reason approach where the evidence required to shift the relevant evidentiary burdens is dependent on the circumstances of the case, there is little scope for quick look.

---

[134] See Edward D Cavanagh, 'Whatever Happened to Quick Look' (2017) 26 *University of Miami Business Law Review* 39, 40.

[135] *California Dental Association* (n 133) 770.

[136] *Polygram v FTC*, 416 F 3d 29, 35–36 (DCCA 2005), and also *In re Massachusetts Board of Optometry*, 110 FTC 549, 604 (1988).

[137] That is, not contrary to policy grounds, such as protecting a weaker product or competitor from the forces of competition or a form of disguised price-fixing. See eg *North Texas Specialty Physicians v FTC*, 528 F 3d 346, 368–70 (CA5 2008).

[138] *Polygram* (n 136) 36.

[139] *Brown University* (n 103) 669.

[140] *Polygram* (n 136) 36.

[141] ibid.

[142] ibid.

[143] See *National Society of Professional Engineers* (n 11); *NCAA* (n 76); *Indiana Federation of Dentists* (n 99); *California Dental* (n 133); and the approach is also mentioned (but its use was rejected) in *Actavis* (n 94).

[144] See Cavanagh (n 134).

If antitrust analysis involved a binary approach, with per se condemnation and full-blown, *CBOT*-style rule of reason analysis as the (only) two alternatives, developing a quick look approach makes sense from the point of view of judicial economy. Simply put, analysis of some arraignments may not require full *CBOT* analysis.

On the other hand, if rule of reason analysis does not, in every case, require such a full-blown inquiry, the need for an intermediate quick look analysis is eliminated. Should a court be required to consider an arrangement which bears a resemblance to agreements which have been previously viewed through a per se lens, but has a novel feature, rule of reason analysis is appropriate, and the required evidentiary standards can be shaped to fit the circumstances of the case. A third, intermediate, mode of analysis is thus redundant. The redundancy of quick look analysis is magnified by the USSC's pronounced preference for the use of rule of reason analysis to determine the legality of the restraint in question.

This redundancy in the face of structured rule of reason analysis may explain why in recent cases the USSC appears to have returned to a binary approach to the categorisation of unreasonable restraints. In *Leegin* and *American Express*, the words 'quick look' are never mentioned. And in *American Express*, the majority of the Court interestingly notes:

> Restraints can be unreasonable in one of two ways. A small group of restraints are unreasonable per se because they 'always or almost always tend to restrict competition and decrease output.' ... Restraints that are not unreasonable per se are judged under the 'rule of reason.'[145]

The Court does not posit quick look as an alternative, third mode of analysis. In *Actavis*, decided between *Leegin* and *American Express*, the Court rejected the submission by the Federal Trade Commission (FTC) that quick look was the appropriate analytic tool to evaluate reverse payments in the pharmaceutical industry. Given the complexities (eg size and scale of payment and its relation to future anticipated litigation costs), the majority opined that a more thorough investigation of the agreement, through rule of reason analysis, is appropriate.

This brief mention in *Actavis* may indicate that the quick look approach is not yet dead, though its treatment in *Leegin* and *American Express* shows it may be on its last legs. As an element of a continuum of structured rule of reason analysis, it is redundant. At the level of the USSC, its redundancy is shown in that court's discussions of antitrust analysis in a binary fashion. In administrative proceedings, though the FTC may apply this sort of analysis,[146] that agency typically applies it in conjunction with a rule of reason alternative. If, and when challenged, the FTC can thus defend the results of both analyses.[147] Given that the practice of appellate courts when they uphold challenged FTC decisions is to ratify them on rule of reason grounds, this again may well make quick look analysis redundant.

---

[145] *American Express* (n 95) slip opinion 8.
[146] See Cavanagh (n 134) 58–63, and *Massachusetts Board of Optometry* (n 136).
[147] See *Realcomp II Ltd v FTC*, 635 F 3d 815 (CA6 2011) and *North Carolina Board of Dental Examiners v FTC*, 717 F 3d 359 (CA4 2014) and 135 S Ct 1011 (2015).

VI. The Type of Analysis Matters

Assessing the reasonableness (and thus the legality) of an arraignment involves analysis through either a rule of reason approach or per se condemnation. Although courts (including the USSC) have said that the distinctions between per se, rule of reason and quick look analysis are not hard and fast,[148] this certainly overstates matters. First, the structured rule of reason approach requires a continuum of analysis and evidentiary standards, in which these standards vary according to the circumstances of the case. At each step in rule of reason analysis it is open to the appropriate party to discharge its evidentiary burden. In per se matters, this is not the case. Once a court has determined that per se analysis is appropriate for the agreement in question, it is simply not possible for the defendant to raise evidence to rebut this. Hence, categorisation is significant.

Second, the importance of categorisation is reflected in that categorisation is also a matter of law. It is a reversible error for a court to use the wrong mode of analysis.[149] Accordingly, where the arrangement in question is novel, a plaintiff may need to plead in the alternative that the practice fits into more than one category. This has implications for discovery and trial preparation, with the resulting implications for the cost of prosecuting the litigation.

Third, and most significantly, categorisation is almost always determinative of the outcome of the litigation. One scholar notes: 'Plaintiffs almost never prevail in a full-blown rule of reason case. Most importantly, proof of a prima facie case, whether through proof of market power or actual detrimental effects, is difficult.'[150] In this regard, Carrier's studies (which have been discussed earlier[151]) show that between 1999 and 2009, the defendant won 221 of 222 rule of reason cases.[152] Both judges[153] and scholars[154] have noted this.

The litigation (non-)strategy in *In re Sulphuric Acid Antitrust Litigation*[155] is explained by an aversion to pursue litigation under the rule of reason. This case involved a class action (the plaintiff class being American sulphuric acid

---

[148] See *California Dental Association* (n 133) 779, quoted above.

[149] See *Actavis* (n 94) 158 – 59 and *Leegin* (n 74).

[150] Alan J Meese, 'In Praise of All or Nothing Dichotomous Categories: Why Antitrust Law Should Reject the Quick Look' (2016) 104 *Georgetown Law Journal* 835, 855.

[151] See above p 59.

[152] Carrier, 'Empirical Update' (n 129) 831–32.

[153] See eg *Discon Inc v Nynex Corp*, 93 F 3d 1055, 1058–59 (CA2 1996), judgment vacated 525 US 128 (1998):

> This initial categorization is often outcome-determinative. Under one category, the arrangement may be per se illegal, while under another, it may be found permissible under the rule of reason. Due to the complexity of modern business transactions, however, courts often find that commercial arrangements can be classified theoretically under a number of different categories.

[154] See eg Frank H Easterbrook, 'Allocating Antitrust Decisionmaking Tasks' (1987) 76 *Georgetown Law Journal* 305, 305; Richard A Posner, 'The Rule of Reason and the Economic Approach: Reflections on the *Sylvania* Decision' (1977) 45 *University of Chicago Law Review* 1, 14.

[155] *In re Sulphuric Acid Antitrust Litigation*, 703 F 3d 1004 (CA7 2012).

purchasers) against Canadian sulphuric producers who entered into distribution agreements with American producers. As part of the arrangement, the American producers would reduce production of 'American' acid, and in exchange would receive exclusive territorial distribution rights to 'Canadian' acid. Prior to trial, the District Court ruled that trial must proceed under the rule of reason.

On appeal, Judge Posner questioned the plaintiff's reticence to proceed under this mode of analysis. He noted:

> The abiding puzzle of the plaintiffs' appeal is why the lawyers for the class, having spent almost nine years litigating the case in the district court, refused to go to trial. Though the trial would have been governed by the rule of reason, probably all that this would have meant in a case such as this is that the defendants would have had greater latitude for offering justifications for what the plaintiffs claim is a price-fixing conspiracy than if the standard governing the trial had been the per se rule, which treats price-fixing by competitors as illegal regardless of consequences or possible justifications. ...

> From remarks by their lawyer at the oral argument we infer that they think that in a trial governed by the rule of reason they would have had to prepare a radically different case in chief, proving not only that the defendants fixed prices (all they'd have to prove, besides damages, in a per se case), but also that the defendants had market power ... and that their collusive activity was indeed anticompetitive. ... But a plaintiff who proves that the defendants got together and agreed to raise the price ... that he pays them for their products – which is what the plaintiffs in this case would have had to prove under the per se rule to establish liability and obtain damages – has made a prima facie case that the defendants' behavior was unreasonable. He need not prove market power; ....

> But this is a detail; ....[156]

However, should Judge Posner be looking for an answer his bewilderment, he need search no further than to his own words, which he wrote some 35 years prior to this opinion: '[T]he content of the Rule of Reason is largely unknown; in practice, it is little more than a euphemism for nonliability.'[157] Faced with almost certain loss under rule of reason analysis, the appropriate strategy would be to cut one's losses, and abandon the litigation.

This suggests a number of significant reasons why plaintiffs lose rule of reason cases: the costs of assembling evidence is significant,[158] defendants can engage economic experts to present procompetitive benefits of the questioned arrangements, and courts (as well as juries – in the US) may not be capable of critically assessing this evidence. The USSC noted all of these points in 1982 in *Maricopa*:

> The elaborate inquiry into the reasonableness of a challenged business practice entails significant costs. Litigation of the effect or purpose of a practice often is extensive and

---

[156] ibid 1007–08.

[157] Posner (n 154) 14.

[158] In discussing market studies in 2013, the USSC noted that the cost of 'cost of an expert analysis necessary to prove the antitrust claims would be "at least several hundred thousand dollars, and might exceed $1 million"': *American Express v Italian Colors Restaurant*, 570 US 228, 231 (2013).

complex. ... Judges often lack the expert understanding of industrial market structures and behavior to determine with any confidence a practice's effect on competition. ... And the result of the process in any given case may provide little certainty or guidance about the legality of a practice in another context.[159]

As these comments echo similar concerns expressed earlier in, for instance, *Topco*,[160] it cannot be said that these comments in *Maricopa* represented a sudden epiphany. It is unfortunate that the USSC has done nothing to alleviate these problems; and if anything the Court's decisions in recent years have exacerbated these problems.

VII. Effects, Rule of Reason and the Sherman Act Section 2

Section 2 of the Sherman Act is worded in similar general terms to section 1. It prohibits 'monopolization' as well as attempts and conspiracies to monopolise. Like its counterpart, the history of section 2 case-law is an effort to import clarity into the general wording to the Act. The evolution of this case-law also shows an evolution in thought regarding how the goals of antitrust policy are advanced by the goals of section 2 of the Sherman Act.

The history of judicial interpretation of this section shows an initial willingness to use the anti-monopoly provisions as one of the weapons in the trust-busting arsenal. The 1911 *Standard Oil* case, the resolution of which resulted in a court-ordered dissolution of the Standard Oil Trust, is possibly the best example of this use of section 2.[161] The next shift in thought, marked by *US Steel*,[162] shows the USCC retreating from this vigorous approach, and such a retreat would continue as part of the policy of Roosevelt's New Deal, where the government 'experimented with central planning and comprehensive regulation of price and entry to spur economic recovery'.[163] By the mid-1930s, the pendulum swing back towards a more assertive enforcement of the Sherman Act, with *Alcoa*[164] being the notable case of this era. However, by the 1970s, as a result of criticism, the pendulum would reverse course and swing towards limited enforcement and stricter standards for plaintiffs to meet.

---

[159] *Maricopa* (n 78) 343.
[160] See text accompanying n 49, above.
[161] See also *US v American Tobacco Co*, 221 US 106 (1911); *US v United Shoe Machine Co*, 247 US 32 (1918).
[162] *US v United States Steel Corp*, 251 US 417 (1920).
[163] Andrew I Gavil et al, *Antitrust Law in Perspective: Cases, Concepts and Problems in Competition Policy*, 3rd edn (St Paul, MN, West, 2017) 460.
[164] *US v Aluminum Co of America*, 148 F 2d 416 (CA2 1945).

The criticism which resulted in the current state of affairs was primarily the result of, or influenced by, the Chicago School. There were four significant elements to this approach/influence. First, Chicago's normative point that the purpose behind the Sherman Act, to promote consumer welfare, should also be the focus of section 2 antitrust law and policy. Second, in light of this, the emphasis of enforcers and courts should be on protection of the competitive process, and not on the protection of competitors. Third, in an effort not to chill competition, this view takes a cautious approach to evaluation of conduct, in an effort to avoid condemning practices that may be beneficial.[165] Fourth, given Chicago's faith in the self-correcting nature of the market, this approach is concerned with avoiding type I errors (false positives). The reasoning is that wrongly condemning a procompetitive practice permanently deprives consumers of any welfare gains that this practice might produce. On the other hand, any excess return which results from failing to condemn an anticompetitive practice will – in the longer term – be competed away through the entry of competitors who see this supercompetitive return as an opportunity to be shared. This last point is a corollary of the third point.

Section 2 case-law can be characterised as an attempt to import clarity into the wording of that section, by specifying the meaning of 'monopolize' (and clarifying the prohibitions on attempts and conspiracies). 'Monopolization', as the courts were to define it, involves both market power and exclusionary conduct, a significant amount of the case-law attempts to develop tests that identify such conduct. The plural 'tests' is appropriate, as there is no unitary principle.

A. 'Monopolization' under Section 2 of the Sherman Act

The prohibition in section 2 of the Sherman Act states that '[e]very person who shall monopolize, or attempt to monopolize, or combine or conspire with any other person or persons, to monopolize'[166] is regarded as committing a crime. In *Standard Oil*, the USSC interpreted section 2 in the light of the Act as a whole, and the evil which it was designed to control, and held that to 'monopolize' requires not just power on the market, but additionally some act which furthers the position, ie which unduly restrains trade.[167] The test for such a restraint of trade is the rule of reason.[168]

---

[165] See eg *Weyerhaeuser Co v Ross-Simmons Hardwood Lumber Co*, 549 US 312, 325 (2007); *Verizon Communications Inc v Law Offices of Curtis V Trinko, LLP*, 540 US 398, 408 and 414 (2004); *Brooke Group Ltd v Brown and Williamson Tobacco Corp*, 509 US 209, 226–27 (1993); *Spectrum Sports Inc v McQuillan*, 506 US 447, 458–59 (1993); *Copperweld Corp v Independence Tube Corp*, 467 US 752, 767–68 (1984).

[166] Codified as 15 USC §2.

[167] *Standard Oil* (n 6) 61–62.

[168] ibid 62.

In *Alcoa*, a 1945 decision of the Second Circuit Court of Appeal,[169] mere possession of a monopoly position was, in the absence of other conduct, not contrary to this section. The Court reasoned that a firm might 'wake up one day' to find that it has grown to such an extent that it now had a monopoly position in the market, or alternatively a market may be such that it could only be efficiently serviced by one firm.[170]

As the Act makes 'monopoliszation' not just a civil wrong, but also a crime, the Court reasoned that it was unlikely that Congress meant to condemn the possession of a monopoly position. Rather, the feature which brings the practice under the ambit of section 2 is whether or not the monopolist engaged in exclusionary conduct.[171] While *Alcoa* set the bar quite low for exclusionary conduct[172] (and courts have resiled from this threshold in the past 75 years), its two-stage approach to section 2 liability remains the framework of the law. Indeed in 1966, a majority of the USSC was to open its discussion of the law in a monopolisation case by remarking:

> The offense of monopoly under s 2 of the Sherman Act has two elements: (1) the possession of monopoly power in the relevant market and (2) the wilful acquisition or maintenance of that power as distinguished from growth or development as a consequence of a superior product, business acumen, or historic accident.[173]

Thus analysis under section 2 requires a consideration of whether or not the firm held a monopoly position (hence a market analysis is required) and whether the conduct in question is exclusionary. The second question clearly requires an analysis of the effects of the conduct. As noted, there is no unitary test for such conduct. Given the means which can be devised to exclude competitors, this should be no surprise. Nevertheless the courts have developed a number of tests which can be applied to the practices, but this very multiplicity of tests introduces uncertainty regarding the evaluation of a new practice.

---

[169] This decision has the precedential value of the USSC, as that Court – due to a number of recusals – was unable to hear the case. See Judiciary and Judicial Procedure 1944 Act (June 9, 1944) §§ 2101 and 2109.

[170] *Alcoa* (n 164) 429–30.

[171] ibid 430–31.

[172] ibid 431:

> [Alcoa] insists that it never excluded competitors; but we can think of no more effective exclusion than progressively to embrace each new opportunity as it opened, and to face every newcomer with new capacity already geared into a great organization, having the advantage of experience, trade connections and the elite of personnel. Only in case we interpret 'exclusion' as limited to maneuvres not honestly industrial, but actuated solely by a desire to prevent competition, can such a course, indefatigably pursued, be deemed not 'exclusionary.' So to limit it would in our judgment emasculate the Act; would permit just such consolidations as it was designed to prevent.

[173] *US v Grinnell Corporation*, 384 US 563, 570–71 (1966).

B. *Aspen Skiing*: A Commercial Justification Test

Aspen Skiing[174] is an outlier in section 2 jurisprudence. Although well known, its general utility in litigation is limited. It is the only case in which the USSC has determined antitrust liability in a refusal to deal case; and the Court was thus later to state: '*Aspen Skiing* is at or near the outer boundary of § 2 liability.'[175] In that case the dominant firm (which owned three of the four slopes in the Aspen area) refused to continue with a marketing arrangement which allowed customers of the other resort owner access to its slopes, even in the face of an offer by the smaller operator to pay full retail price for access (ie a lift ticket). In extending liability in these circumstances, the Court focused not only on the effects which the practices had on the dominant firm's rival, but also on consumers as well as on any business justification that might underlie the practice.[176]

The USSC noted that resort customers had strong preferences for an 'all slope' ski pass, and that refusing the smaller operator's offer of full retail price for customers' access meant an immediate sacrifice of profit (hence lacking a commercial justification, other than as part of a long-run strategy to drive the rival out of business).[177] *Aspen Skiing* could therefore be taken as some approval for the use of a profit-sacrifice test as a means of detecting exclusionary conduct, and/or the acceptance of a commercial justification defence to potentially exclusionary conduct.

C. *Kodak*: Market Realities and Tying

In tying cases, the USSC and circuit courts have at times applied a per se test for such arrangements. A tying arrangement[178] is condemned where

> first, a tying and a tied product, ...; second, evidence of actual coercion by the seller that in fact forced the buyer to accept the tied product, ...; third, sufficient economic power in the tying product market to coerce purchaser acceptance of the tied product, ...; fourth, anticompetitive effects in the tied market, ...; and fifth, involvement of a 'not insubstantial' amount of interstate commerce in the tied product market.[179]

The USSC applied this test, somewhat controversially, to locked-in markets in *Kodak*.

---

[174] *Aspen Skiing Co v Aspen Highlands Skiing Corp*, 472 US 585 (1985).
[175] *Verizon* (n 165).
[176] *Aspen Skiing* (n 174) 605.
[177] ibid 610–11.
[178] It should be noted that although various statutory provisions (Sherman Act ss 1 and 2, Clayton Act s 3, FTC Act s 5) prohibit tying, the test for legality is the same.
[179] *Yentsch v Texaco, Inc*, 630 F 2d 46, 56–57 (CA2 1980) the court's references omitted.

In that case at dispute was the market for service and replacement parts of photocopiers. However, in the primary market for photocopiers themselves, Kodak's market share was roughly 23 per cent, hardly a dominant position. However, its share in the aftermarket was over 80 per cent.[180] Kodak suggested that a tying arrangement which would require customers to pay supracompetitive prices in the aftermarket made no economic sense, given the competitive nature of the primary market. Indeed, according to Kodak, customers make their purchasing decision on life-cycle costs, taking the purchase price and post-purchase service and repair costs into account in their initial decision. Kodak suggested that charging supracompetitive prices on the secondary market did not make business sense. If they had charged supracompetitive prices in the secondary market, Kodak suggested, this would have resulted in a loss of sales in the primary market. Accordingly, Kodak sought summary dismissal of the lawsuit.

The majority of the court rejected Kodak's argument, noting that there are considerations which may prevent the market working in the manner which Kodak assumed. These include: calculation of life-cycle costs requires a degree of information and sophistication which not all consumers may possess; the possibility of price discrimination between sophisticated and non-sophisticated consumers; and switching costs.[181] For these reasons, the majority felt that a trial, in which Kodak could inter alia demonstrate valid business reasons for the arrangements in question, was appropriate.

Beyond its utility to demonstrate how the court has expanded the prohibition of tying, *Kodak* is also of interest to us to show some initial judicial concerns about the conditions under which markets operate; and, in particular, how accurately the assumptions contained in antitrust theories of harm reflect the reality of the market. *Kodak* is considered in greater detail in Chapter 4.

D. *Brooke Group*:[182] A Joint Cost and Conduct Test for Predatory Pricing

In the mind of the USSC, a complaint about predatory pricing has two elements, alleging a two-stage strategy. First it is a complaint that pricing is 'too low', ie below a certain cost threshold, during the first stage; and, second, that in the long term, the defendant will be able to recoup any losses by, after having driven out competition in the first (price-cutting) stage, raising prices to supracompetitive levels in the second stage.[183] The Court's analysis of each of these stages is worth considering.

---

[180] *Kodak* (n 84) 457.
[181] ibid 472–79.
[182] *Brooke Group v Brown and Williamson Tobacco*, 509 US 209 (1993).
[183] ibid 222–24.

From the perspective of maximising consumer welfare, the first stage is a complaint about the price being too low. Consumers benefit from low prices, and to the extent that a goal of antitrust policy is to promote lower prices and not to protect competitors from their competitors' low pricing policies, then complaints about low prices are somewhat incongruous. The issues are how low is too low, and why? The cost measure that the courts have adopted follows the Areeda–Turner test,[184] ie prices below average variable costs.[185]

The second stage is significant, and is directly a result of Chicago. The view of the Chicago school is highly sceptical of the ability of such pricing schemes to succeed.[186] The majority judgment in *Brooke Group*[187] appeals directly to an earlier opinion in *Matsushita*[188] in which a predatory pricing conspiracy was alleged. In the latter case, the Court appealed to Chicago School reasoning (citing Bork and Easterbrook) and remarked:

> [T]he success of such schemes is inherently uncertain: the short-run loss is definite, but the long-run gain depends on successfully neutralizing the competition. Moreover, it is not enough simply to achieve monopoly power, as monopoly pricing may breed quick entry by new competitors eager to share in the excess profits. The success of any predatory scheme depends on maintaining monopoly power for long enough both to recoup the predator's losses and to harvest some additional gain. Absent some assurance that the hoped-for monopoly will materialize, and that it can be sustained for a significant period of time, '[t]he predator must make a substantial investment with no assurance that it will pay off.' ... For this reason, there is a consensus among commentators that predatory pricing schemes are rarely tried, and even more rarely successful.[189]

Given these assumptions regarding the operation of the market, now embedded in US predatory pricing law, successfully prosecuting any such claim is an uphill battle. Plaintiffs almost always lose. These market assumptions governing predatory pricing are also considered in Chapter 4.

E. *Verizon* and *linkLine*:[190] Margin Squeeze as Two Claims

Pursuing a price or margin squeeze claim is even more difficult than pursuing a predatory pricing claim. In the view of the USSC, such claims are an amalgam of two claims: a refusal to deal and a predatory pricing claim. The former represents

---

[184] Phillip Areeda and Donald F Turner, 'Predatory Pricing and Related Practices Under Section 2 of the Sherman Act' (1974) 88 *Harvard Law Review* 697.

[185] ibid 733.

[186] See eg Robert Bork, *The Antitrust Paradox: A Policy at War with Itself*, rev edn (New York, Basic Books, 1993) 149–59 and 430.

[187] *Brooke Group* (n 182) 224.

[188] *Matsushita Electrical Industrial Co v Zenith Radio Corp*, 475 US 574 (1986).

[189] ibid 590, citing Frank Easterbrook, 'Predatory Strategies and Counterstrategies' (1981) 48 *University of Chicago Law Review* 263, 268.

[190] *Pacific Bell Telephone Co v linkLine Communications Inc*, 555 US 438 (2009).

the complainant's view regarding the wholesale price charged by the dominant firm; the latter claim is in regard to the position that the complainant finds itself on the retail market. In *Verizon*, the USSC reiterated the need under section 2 to find not just the possession of monopoly power, but also the requirement that there is an element of anticompetitive conduct before a given practice is condemned as '[t]he opportunity to charge monopoly prices – at least for a short period – as what attracts "business acumen" in the first place; it induces risk taking that produces innovation and economic growth'.[191]

Further, *Verizon* permitted the Court to clarify the application of the conditions which would impose liability for refusal to deal from *Aspen Skiing*. In *Aspen Skiing*, there was a pre-existing relationship which the defendant terminated, along with the defendant's refusal to accept full retail price for the service which the defendant refused to supply.[192] *Aspen Skiing* does not support the widening of a requirement to supply.

Additionally, the service in question was unbundled access to the local loop, which Verizon was obliged to provide under the Telecommunications Act of 1996.[193] This Act also provided regulatory oversight by other federal agencies, and the significance of this specialised oversight was not lost on the USSC. It remarked: 'Antitrust analysis must always be attuned to the particular structure and circumstances of the industry at issue. Part of that attention to economic context is an awareness of the significance of regulation'.[194] The Court thus reasons that given the more generic nature of antitrust enforcement, its use in highly regulated industries – particularly as a standard bearer of refusal to supply – adds little of value to the resolution of the issue. But not only does this antitrust intervention add little of value, it opens the possibility of costly type I errors, by intervening inappropriately.[195]

Five years after *Verizon*, in *linkLine*, the Court appears to slam the door on the possibility of success for any price-squeeze claim:

> Plaintiffs' price-squeeze claim, looking to the relation between retail and wholesale prices, is thus nothing more than an amalgamation of a meritless claim at the retail level and a meritless claim at the wholesale level. If there is no duty to deal at the wholesale level and no predatory pricing at the retail level, then a firm is certainly not required to price *both* of these services in a manner that preserves its rivals' profit margins.[196]

---

[191] *Verizon* (n 165) 407.

[192] ibid 408–09.

[193] Telecommunications Act of 1996, Pub Law No 104-104, 110 Stat 56 (1996).

[194] *Verizon* (n 165) 411.

[195] ibid 414:

> Against the slight benefits of antitrust intervention here, we must weigh a realistic assessment of its costs. Under the best of circumstances, applying the requirements of § 2 'can be difficult' because 'the means of illicit exclusion, like the means of legitimate competition, are myriad.' ... Mistaken inferences and the resulting false condemnations 'are especially costly, because they chill the very conduct the antitrust laws are designed to protect.' ... The cost of false positives counsels against an undue expansion of § 2 liability. [Court's references omitted]

[196] *linkLine* (n 190) 452.

The Court's position in *linkLine* makes successful prosecution of a price-squeeze claim nearly impossible. Given the assumptions regarding the implausibility of predatory pricing claims adopted as a matter of law by the USSC in *Brooke Group*, that half of a price-squeeze claim is difficult to prove. And given the very narrow circumstances in which there is an obligation to deal, as stated in *Verizon*, the other half of such a claim is also near impossible to prove – particularly in the context of regulated industries, which are open to such abuses. It may well be the case that the result of *linkLine* is price squeezes are, in practice, per se legal, as the barrier for a successful suit is very high.

F. *Microsoft*: A Fall-Back Rule of Reason Test?

In the 2001 *Microsoft*[197] judgment, the District of Columbia Court of Appeal (DCCA) was to consider Microsoft's practice of purportedly tying Internet Explorer to its Windows operating system, thereby attempting to obtain a monopoly in the web browser market.[198] At the time, courts were unfamiliar with the market in software. This was a consequence of the software market being relatively new, more dynamic than markets courts were normally used to deal with, and also possessing other characteristics, such as network effects, all of which distinguished this market from other markets with which the judiciary was more familiar.[199] Consequently, the DCCA adopted a rule of reason methodology to assess Microsoft's practices. This approach is consistent with the USSC's practice in section 1 matters, where a novel arrangement is to be initially analysed under the rule of reason.

In applying the rule of reason, the DCCA developed a five-step test. After determining the threshold monopoly question (which requires market analysis), the first step is to determine whether the monopolist's act has an anticompetitive effect in the sense that it is exclusionary (by harming the competitive processes, and not merely by harming competitors).[200] The second step imposes the burden on the plaintiff to demonstrate that the monopolist's conduct has this anticompetitive effect, and that 'its injury is "of the type that the statute was intended to forestall"'.[201] Should the plaintiff be successful at this stage (by establishing a prima facie case), the defendant can provide a procompetitive justification for its practice, as the third step. This is 'a nonpretextual claim that its conduct is indeed a form of competition on the merits because it involves, for example, greater efficiency or enhanced consumer appeal'.[202] In support of shifting the onus on the monopolist

---

[197] *US v Microsoft*, 253 F 3d 34 (DCCA 2001).
[198] ibid 45.
[199] ibid 49–50.
[200] ibid 58.
[201] ibid 59, quoting *Brunswick Corp v Pueblo Bowl-O-Mat*, 429 US 477, 487–88 (1977).
[202] ibid.

to provide a valid business reason for the practice, the Court cited *Kodak*[203] and the Second Circuit's decision in *Capital Imaging*, a section 1 case.

In the fourth step, the plaintiff can either rebut the monopolist's procompetitive justification, or demonstrate that the anticompetitive harm from the practice exceeds the procompetitive gain.[204] The Court, citing *Standard Oil* and other Circuits' decisions,[205] noted that this balancing is identical to the (final) balancing component of the section 1 rule of reason test, and that analysis under both sections of the Sherman Act is similar.[206] The fifth step – and overarching part of the analysis – is to focus on effects of the monopolist's practice. Proof of intent, though it may go to the assessment of the practice's effects, is not necessary.[207]

At the first two steps of this section 2 rule of reason/effects test (where the given practice is analysed for its exclusionary effects) the burden on the plaintiff will differ, depending on the practice in question. Some practices, such as sham litigation[208] and fraud on the Patent Office,[209] verge on being per se illegal, hence the plaintiff will have a lighter burden than practices at the other end of the spectrum – such as monopoly pricing.[210] While the Court's five-step guide to the application of the rule of reason in section 2 cases does provide some assistance, it is nevertheless a vague standard – particularly in litigation (or ex ante advice) regarding novel practices.

G. Section 2: Multiple Tests and Lack of Clarity

This discussion of the jurisprudence which has arisen from section 2 of the Sherman Act suggests a number of legal tests, which taken together paint a rather poor picture for providing certainty or guidance for business conduct. The recent case-law adds clarity by indicating that in the view of the USSC the purpose of section 2 is to increase consumer welfare. This is done through the promotion of competition, and not through the protection of small or inefficient competitors. To this point, the case-law provides some guidance.

However, section 2 of the Sherman Act does not license the use of any means of competition. And it is at this point at which the case-law is unhelpful. There is no unique standard by which courts are to evaluate conduct under section 2. Rather,

---

[203] *Kodak* (n 84) 483.

[204] *Microsoft* (n 197) 59.

[205] In particular *Mid-Texas Communications* Systems v *American Telephone and Telegraph Co*, 615 F 2d 1372 (CA5 1980); *Byars v Bluff City News*, 609 F 2d 843 (CA6 1979) (cited in *Microsoft* (n 197)); and *California Computer Products v IBM*, 613 F 2d 727 (CA9 1979).

[206] *Microsoft* (n 197) 59.

[207] ibid.

[208] *Otter Tail Power v US*, 410 US 366 (1973).

[209] *Walker Process Equipment v Food Machinery and Chemical Corporation*, 382 US 172 (1965).

[210] See also Mark S Popofsky, 'Defining Exclusionary Conduct: Section 2, the Rule of Reason, and the Unifying Principle Underlying Antitrust Rules' (2006) 73 *Antitrust Law Journal* 435, 441–48.

it appears that individual practices are seemingly evaluated by different methods, depending on how the practice is categorised by the relevant court. Consistent with the approach taken under section 1, where a court has insufficient experience with a given business practice, the use of a rule of reason method of analysis and its resulting framework of burden shifting is appropriate.

Microsoft is illustrative of this latter point. It is strong authority: it is an *en banc*, *per curiam* judgment of the DCCA. It is cited, albeit with some caution, in *Verizon*[211] and *linkLine*.[212] And its approach is consistent with recent section 1 case-law regarding not just the default approach to be taken in antitrust matters, but the approach which should be taken with unfamiliar markets and practices. The difficulty is that *Microsoft's* rule of reason analysis is inconsistent with how courts have historically (and are still mandated to) treated other practices under section 2; predatory pricing and margin squeeze are examples.

Another point that Sherman Act section 2 caselaw has demonstrated is that Chicago School assumptions dominate the judicial analysis of the legal issues. We note the USSC's reluctance, expressed in *Verizon*, to intervene out of concern that such intervention may introduce type I errors. Further, as *Brooke Group's* analysis for the need to establish recoupment in a predatory pricing case indicates, the USSC shares the view that markets are self-correcting.[213] Accordingly, if a type II error (false negative) is introduced, any opportunity for a supracompetitive return occasioned by this error creates an opportunity for entry for other firms to chase this return, so over time these extra profits will be competed away, and price levels will drop to those in a competitive market.

The lens through which this antitrust analysis is conducted contains some powerful assumptions regarding how agents in fact operate in the market. If real actors and markets do not reflect these assumptions, then the effects-based analysis may produce results that do not accurately reflect the actual conditions of the markets in question.

VIII. Conclusion

This chapter's brief outline of US antitrust law has established a number of points. These points do not present a satisfactory picture of a regime which provides ex ante certainty and predictability for those attempting to develop business plans. First, we see an increased reliance on the use of rule of reason in antitrust analysis. With the exception of 'hard core', horizontal cartel activity, rule of reason is the default means of analysis. But, second, the application of this means of analysis is anything but certain, relying on the ability of litigants to raise and rebut

---

[211] *Verizon* (n 165) 414.
[212] *linkLine* (n 190) 458.
[213] See *Brooke Group* (n 182) 226, citing *Matsushita* (n 188) 589.

evidence regarding the potential pro- and anticompetitive effects of the arrangement in question after the practice has been implemented. Courts have provided little guidance as to how agreements, particularly novel ones, should be assessed. Third, the analytic method matters: rule of reason analysis usually means that the defendant prevails in any lawsuit. Perhaps this is the only certainty introduced by the new approach. If so, it tells against any claim that antitrust law has an underlying rule of law core.

The analysis of sections 1 and 2 of the Sherman Act shows that there has been a fundamental shift in the goals of this Act to protection of consumer welfare. This is significant. Whatever the goals were in 1890 when the Act was passed, or whatever they were in the post-World War Two-era, they are now irrelevant. The Act, as the Court has said, should (at least now) be construed as a 'consumer welfare prescription'.[214]

Consumer welfare may be an appropriate goal for antitrust policy, but its near-universal acceptance shows that it is disingenuous for US courts to claim that this is its original role. That said, from a rhetorical point, it is more convincing to present a reformulation of a doctrine as a 'return to the doctrine's original roots', than as a radical transformation. This reorientation of antitrust policy has been a judicially driven process, which raises another set of rule of law and separation of powers concerns.

In advancing an antitrust policy that maximises consumer welfare, the US courts have placed significant reliance on an examination of the potential effects which the practice in question may have on the market. In section 1 cases, this has, over time, led to the rule of reason becoming the default method of analysis in all matters, save cartels.

In section 2 cases, there has been a similar shift in goals. This is unsurprising. If (at least in the USSC's view) the overarching goal of the Sherman Act is the maximisation of consumer welfare, then consistency mandates a similar approach to monopolisation matters. However, the courts' treatment of the various practices which fall under section 2 has left no unifying standard by which practices are evaluated to determine whether or not they constitute 'monopolization'. Rather, in evaluating practices under section 2, courts will develop a test that is regarded as appropriate to the practice, and apply this test to the practice (and consider its effects) ex post.

However, all of this points towards an examination of the efficacy of a rule of reason (or more generally, an effects-based) approach for competition law analysis. The main difficulty with the rule of reason approach is that the standard is, at best, vague. While the rule of reason, when applied in litigation is primarily oriented towards burden shifting between plaintiff and defendant, and only rarely culminates in an explicit balancing test. However, the burden-shifting exercise requires a set of criteria to define what 'counts' to allow a burden to shift. There are no

---

[214] *Reiter v Sonotone*, 442 US 330, 343 (1979).

clear lists or sets of such criteria. The best we have are those listed in *CBOT*, where almost anything and everything counts. This fails to give potential market participants effective guidance regarding proposed commercial strategy: this absence of certainty, clarity and predictability is a rule of law problem.

In addition to this rule of reason framework, the effects-based approach rests on a particular view of economics – namely classical price theory – with strong assumptions incorporated into it. The difficulty of this is twofold. First, the use of this framework is appropriate only if this view of economics actually reflects how markets and agents operating in the markets work. It may well be the case that the assumptions make the theory unrealistic, when applied to actual market conditions. As we will see in subsequent discussion, some of the insights of behavioural economics show point to such a divergence.

Second, the outcome of many cases is determined not by the data, but by the initial assumptions. In resale price maintenance matters, for instance, the majority in *Legeen* was convinced that the benefits to consumers through, inter alia, improved customer service would outweigh any detriment through higher prices. Likely underlying this reasoning was unwillingness to introduce type I errors through the condemnation of a practice. However, ultimately this is an empirical argument, one that cannot be resolved through the sort of reasoning in which the Court engaged.

In section 2 matters, the same criticism applies. *Aspen Skiing* is a good case in point. In considering the refusal to deal which was the concern there, the USSC accepted the market definition as comprising Aspen resorts only. If the definition had been different – to include other destination resort areas – then the outcome may well have been different.[215] Additionally, the strong assumptions regarding market entry and entry barriers (or lack thereof) which shape the Court's view on recoupment in predatory pricing claims make such claims difficult to prosecute – in effect predetermining the outcome. If the legally mandated method of analysis fails to capture the statutory goals or if inaccurate assumptions drive the result, this leads to a situation of divergence between what the law achieves and what it mandates. This pulls antitrust away from the rule of law paradigm.

Finally, and most significantly, the effects-based approach taken by the United States is retrospective. A practice must first be implemented for its effects to become visible on a (changing) market; and then, and only then, can these effects be examined in order to determine the (il)legality of the practice. This makes business planning difficult. And these difficulties in commercial planning are exacerbated when courts are willing to overturn precedent, which experience since the 1960s shows they are willing to do.

---

[215] Stucke (n 10) 1426 fn 219 makes this point.

3

The Effects-Based Approach in the EU: The More Economic Approach

Like the Sherman Act, the European Treaty provisions regulating competition are drafted in an open-ended manner. They, too, require interpretation by the judiciary and enforcement agencies. The interpretation of these provisions, since the turn of the century, has been marked by a shift in analytic approach. This shift has moved towards an examination of the effects which a given arrangement manifests, rather on the legal form that an arrangement has.

The concern of this chapter will be to outline briefly the effects-based or more economic approach (MEA) found in EU competition law. The purpose of this chapter, like the outline of the US approach contained in the previous chapter, is to lay a foundation to establish the threats to rule of law considerations which are presented by the new European approach. To do so, this chapter takes a broadly historic perspective, considering the approaches of the Commission and the European Courts (the ECJ before 1989, both Courts thereafter).

Although the MEA has brought the European approach to competition law and policy analysis closer to that found on the other side of the Atlantic, it has also drawn EU competition law further from the ideal of the rule of law. In particular, implicit in the MEA is a reorientation of the values of European competition law. This change in values involves not only rejection of the ordoliberal foundation on which the European Treaties is founded, but also ring-fencing of competition law. As a result the redefined competition values (namely the maximisation of consumer welfare) are pursued in isolation from other values explicitly linked in the European Treaties. This refocusing of the goals of competition law has been a Commission-driven project, and raises questions of institutional legitimacy in the reformulation of European law.

Further, the MEA approach has eschewed a significant amount of the rule-based (or, as it is often derisorily referred to as, 'formalistic') reasoning. But it has also introduced greater uncertainty in some key distinctions which serve as pathways to antitrust liability. This is compounded by the Commission's practice of simultaneously prosecuting the same matters using the case-law and approach developed under the pre-MEA regime, and under the analytic method of the MEA. Not only does this method of prosecution cause expense and delay in the litigation process, but the uncertainty of the legal standards used to determine liability undermine the certainty and predictability of the European competition regime. All of this acts as a rule of law threat.

This chapter is structured into three substantive sections followed by a brief conclusion. The point of the chapter is not to give an extensive discussion of the history of the MEA. This has been done elsewhere.[1] Rather, this chapter serves as a background to illuminate rule of law difficulties posed by the MEA. The next section considers the Commission's and Courts' initial (ie pre-MEA) approach to arrangements under Article 101 and practices under Article 102. As will be shown, both institutions analyse market behaviours in a very broad context, considering them not just in the context of the economic and commercial setting in which they are used, but also against the background of the social and political objectives of the Treaties. Following that, the chapter turns to the reasons behind the shift to the MEA. This section is fairly brief, and is intended merely to illustrate the main reasons behind the shift in the EU's approach to competition analysis. The final substantive section of this chapter outlines the MEA approach taken by the Commission and Courts. This will serve to identify the features of the MEA which give rise to rule of law concerns. The chapter concludes with some brief remarks about these concerns.

I. The Pre-MEA Understanding of Articles 101 and 102

A. Article 101

Article 101(1) establishes the European prohibition against collusive anticompetitive activity; and Article 101(3) provides for an exception to the prohibition if the arrangement in question satisfies four conditions. For our present purposes, there are two significant terms in Article 101(1) which require interpretation: 'competition' and 'object or effect'. The Commission's and Courts' understanding of these terms has evolved over the past few decades, and this evolution is significant in the shift to the MEA. The Commission's (and to a lesser extent, the Courts') view of what constitutes competition has changed from a very orthodox ordoliberal understanding of the competitive process, to a view shaped by an understanding of restrictions of competition as a diminution of consumer welfare.

Likewise, the shift in how 'object or effect' has been applied in the analysis of competitive restraints is also significant to the development of the MEA approach. Prior to the turn of the twenty-first century, these were two alternative pathways for liability, and these pathways required little difference in the analytic approach

---

[1] See Anne C Witt, *The Economic Approach to EU Antitrust Law* (Oxford, Hart, 2016), who has admirably undertaken this task.

to the restraint in question that either the Commission or the judiciary would employ. In the post-MEA era the distinction takes on significant importance, as it now provides two distinct pathways to liability, with each path requiring a different means of analysis from the other. In what follows we show the significance of the change in the understanding of these two terms, and how this change in understanding of the terms was instrumental in the reshaping of European competition law and policy in the post-MEA era.

B. The Commission's Pre-MEA Approach to Article 101

Before 1 May 2004 (the date that Regulation 1/2003 became effective) the Commission had a monopoly on granting exemptions under Article 101(3). While it from time to time promulgated some guidance and block exemptions,[2] it provided no interpretative guidance regarding its views on what constituted harm to competition. However, we can tease the Commission's views on this point from its decisional practice. From this practice three points are clear. The first is the Commission's understanding of 'competition': it viewed that concept as an admixture of ordoliberal thinking and market integration goals. Second, in so considering 'competition', the Commission placed a large premium on market integration goals, to the extent that pursuit of this goal often trumped other considerations. Finally, given (or as a result of) the Commission's orientation towards the first two goals, it – for the most part – did not engage in extensive economic analysis of the sort seen today.

i. Ordoliberal Freedom and Competition

Ordoliberalism is a socioeconomic doctrine that emerged during the Weimar period, as a reaction to the then turbulent times.[3] The leading German negotiators

---

[2] These Block Exemptions concerned mainly distribution agreements (primarily vertical in nature), and were only enacted starting in the late 1980s: Commission Regulation (EEC) No 1983/83 of 22 June 1983 on the application of Article 85(3) of the Treaty to categories of exclusive distribution agreements [1983] OJ L173/1; Commission Regulation (EEC) No 1984/83 of 22 June 1983 on the application of Article 85(3) of the Treaty to categories of exclusive purchasing agreements [1983] OJ L173/5. These were modified by a series of Regulations enacted in 1999, see eg Commission Regulation (EC) No 2790/1999 of 22 December 1999 on the application of Article 81(3) of the Treaty to categories of vertical agreements and concerted practices [1999] OJ L336/ 21 (itself replaced).

[3] On the history of ordoliberalism and its influence on European competition law and policy, see also below pp 158–60; and eg Bruce Wardhaugh, *Cartels, Markets and Crime: A Normative Justification for the Criminalisation of Economic Collusion* (Cambridge, Cambridge University Press, 2014) 175–82; David J Gerber, *Law and Competition in Twentieth Century Europe: Protecting Prometheus* (Oxford, Oxford University Press 1998); David J Gerber, 'Constitutionalizing the Economy: German Neo-liberalism, Competition Law and the "New" Europe' (1994) 42 *American Journal of Comparative Law* 25; and Nicola Giocoli, 'Competition versus Property Rights: American Antitrust Law, the Freiburg School, and the Early Years of European Competition Policy' (2009) 5 *Journal of Competition Law and Economics* 747.

of the European Coal and Steel Community Treaty (the predecessor to the Treaty of Rome, Articles 65 and 66 of which were incorporated as now TFEU Articles 101 and 102) were ordoliberals. Among them was Walter Hallstein, who later became the first President of the European Commission (1958–1967).[4] Chapter Five discusses ordoliberalism in somewhat greater detail, in the context of the discussion of the normative foundations that underlie both European and US competition law and how these have been altered through the effects-based approach.[5] However, it is helpful at this point to say a few words about the ordoliberal understanding of freedom in the marketplace, as this was an important driver of the early understanding of Articles 101 and 102.

A key principle of ordoliberal thought was protection of individual freedom, not just from governmental threats, but also from threats from powerful (private) economic actors. Gerber, making this point, writes:

> For [ordoliberals], it was not sufficient to protect the individual from the power of government, because governments were not the only threats to individual freedom. Powerful economic institutions could also destroy or limit freedom, especially economic freedom. Having witnessed the use of private economic power during the Weimar period to destroy political and social institutions, the ordoliberals emphasized the need to protect individuals from misuses of such power. This meant that the state had to be strong enough to resist the influence of private power groups. In order for government officials to be in a position to create the structures of the new society, the government of which they were a part would have to be able to protect them against private influences.
>
> The Weimar experience led ordoliberals to demand the dispersion of not only political power, but economic power as well. For most, this meant the elimination of monopolies.[6]

Hence protection of freedom, both political and economic, represented a social goal, which in the context of competition was manifested through the abstract goal of protecting consumer sovereignty or freedom in the marketplace.[7]

It is not difficult to make a leap from this normative position of protecting freedom in the marketplace to a theory of competitive harm that focuses on restrictions of market actors' freedom by the agreements in question. This is a vastly different focus than a focus on the diminution of market participants' welfare as a result of those agreements. In her book, Witt[8] provides numerous examples of Commission decisions which condemned a practice, not because the practice affected consumer welfare, but because it reduced choice for or freedom of a market participant. These practices included restrictions on price, advertising and licensing.[9]

---

[4] See Giocoli ibid 767; Wardhaugh ibid 175.
[5] See below pp 159–60.
[6] Gerber, 'Constitutionalizing the Economy' (n 3) 36–37.
[7] Wardhaugh (n 3) 177.
[8] Witt (n 1) 116.
[9] ibid.

Illustrative of this is the decision in the *Dutch Cement Dealers* case.[10] This was a very simple price (and other conditions of sale) fixing and market-sharing cartel. Rather than focusing on the welfare harms caused by such agreements (as would be the case under an 'economic approach'), the Commission condemned the agreement because it limited the freedom of cement manufacturers to set their own prices to attract more custom and deprived buyers of the ability to choose among competing offers.[11] The Commission never mentioned an effect on price or consumer welfare in its decision.

ii. Market Integration

The Commission's ordoliberal focus on the limitations to freedom posed by marketplace restrictions make it easy to treat vertical restraints in a manner identical to horizontal restraints, as both types of agreements eliminate market participants' freedom to act. Additionally, the Commission's treatment of vertical restraints was also influenced by internal market considerations, particularly threats by private entities to market integration. This is best seen in the Commission's position in *Consten and Grundig*.[12] It took the view that the type (vertical or horizontal) of restraint or whether or not consumers benefited was irrelevant; rather, what was of significance was whether or not the arrangement distorted competition and trade between Member States.[13] Considerations of market integration could be paramount to consumer welfare considerations.

The *Distillers Company* decision[14] is another good example of the, at best, secondary role which consumer welfare and efficiency considerations could take when squarely confronted with a market integration imperative. The case concerned the UK-based Distillers Company Limited (DCL), an amalgamation of a number of UK liquor producers. At the time of the agreement, it was the world's largest producer of Scotch whisky. Also at the time of the agreement, although the UK market for whisky was 'mature', the whisky market in other Member States was developing. In all such states (save Belgium and Luxemburg) imported liquors faced competition from local distilled spirits. Any enterprise which sought to

---

[10] Beschikking van de Commissie van 23 december 1971 inzake een procedure op grond van artikel 85 van het EEG-Verdrag (IV/595 – *Nederlandse Cement– Handelmaatschappij NV*) [1972] OJ L22/16.

[11] ibid recital 7: 'Door deze basisovereenkomst worden de deelnemende fabrikanten *beperkt in hun vrijheid*.' ['As a result of this underlying agreement, the participating manufacturers were *limited in their freedom*.'] Emphasis supplied, author's translation.

[12] Décision de la Commission, du 23 septembre 1964, relative à une procédure au titre de l'article 85 du traité (IV-A/00004-03344 – *Grundig-Consten*) [1964] OJ 160/2545.

[13] See the Commission's submissions to the Court of Justice in the appeal of its decision in this matter. See Joined Cases 56 and 58/64, *Établissements Consten SARL and Grundig-Verkaufs GMBH v Commission*, ECLI:EU:C:1966:41, 308: 'The different types of cartel enumerated by this Article are defined in accordance with their object or their economic effects, and not by the nature of the agreements on which they are based.'

[14] Commission Decision of 20 December 1977 relating to proceedings under Article 85 of the EEC Treaty (IV/28.282 – *The Distillers Company Limited, Conditions of Sale and Price Terms*) [1978] OJ L50/16.

develop the market share for whisky outside of the UK would need to invest in a strong promotional effort.

To enable this promotion of whisky outside of the UK, DCL introduced a two-tiered pricing system (by which the wholesale prices in the UK were less than those outside) and imposed conditions of sale in an effort to make it uneconomic for non-UK customers to buy from UK sources. The increased non-UK wholesale prices would be used to fund this promotional activity. In its decision, the Commission focused on the effect that the agreement had in the partitioning of the Common Market and that the export restrictions reduced the freedom of UK exporters to sell their goods to other customers in other (Common Market) countries.[15] In addition, the Commission dismissed DCL's arguments relating to the need for promotional activity to develop the non-UK's markets on the grounds that whisky was not a new product which required exceptional marketing efforts.[16]

A similar analysis can be seen in the *Hennessy-Henkell* decision[17] which involved the appointment of Henkell as Hennessy's distributor in Germany. The agreement in question included exclusive sales, partial exclusive purchase and non-compete clauses.[18] Additionally, the agreement included provisions that guaranteed Henkell an 18 per cent margin, but restricted Henkell's ability to establish prices based on market conditions.[19]

The Commission summarily condemned the agreement on three grounds. First, it created a sole direct importer of Hennessey cognac into Germany. Second, it sought to prevent parallel imports of the relevant products into Germany. Third, 'because Henkell's lack of freedom to fix its retail prices may deflect trade from the direction it would naturally take if there was total freedom to form prices'.[20] The emphasis on the freedom to establish prices and the absence of consumer welfare considerations is telling.[21]

iii. *Economic Analysis – Or Lack Thereof*

As seen from the above, the Commission typically avoided deep economic analysis or lengthy discussions of consumer welfare in its analysis of these agreements. From an ordoliberal perspective in which the normative value of market participants' freedom is a goal of competition policy, economic analysis is redundant.

---

[15] ibid 27.

[16] ibid 28.

[17] Commission Decision of 11 December 1980 relating to a proceeding under Article 85 of the EEC Treaty (IV/26.912 – *Hennessy–Henkell*) [1980] OJ L383/11.

[18] ibid recital 19.

[19] ibid recital 20.

[20] ibid recital 21.

[21] See Witt (n 1) 115: '[T]he Commission therefore saw the restriction of competition in the fact that the agreement restricted the parties' own freedom as well as the opportunities of their competitors. The effects on customers and end consumers are not even mentioned in this assessment.'

But from the perspective of market integration, such analysis may be needed. Hawk, a critic of the Commission's pre-MEA position writes:

> A second explanation for the frequently sparse economic analysis under Article 85 (both (1) and (3)) derives from the market integration goal which impels both the Commission and the Community courts, according to the critics, to emasculate the economic analysis by rejecting in principle efficiency arguments/justifications and by favouring intrabrand competition over interbrand competition. This criticism is most relevant with respect to territorial restraints. I shall limit myself here to only one comment. The economic freedom notion above and the market integration goal raise very different issues. The former effectively eliminates economics and should be discarded; the latter requires a more sophisticated economic analysis whose task is to reconcile the consumer welfare (efficiency) considerations with the market integration goal (eg an assessment of distributional (in the economic sense) variances among the different Member States).[22]

Applying 'sophisticated economic analysis' to the fact patterns found in *Distillers Company* and *Hennessey-Henkell* may well have led to different conclusions.[23]

iv. Object and Effect – Pathways to Liability

Article 101(1) captures agreements (etc) that are anticompetitive by their 'object or effect'. This disjunction was immediately recognised as setting out alternative grounds, rather than cumulative conditions, for prohibiting agreements.[24] And given that it is the curtailment of 'competition' which is at issue, the phrase cannot be understood in isolation. Thus central to its interpretation is the meaning which the two European institutions import to 'competition'. This meaning, discussed above, centres around the concepts of (ordoliberal) limits to freedom and market integration.

It is notable that this disjunction, at least in the early, pre-MEA days, served as alternative pathways to immediate liability, rather than pathways which required differing analytic methods to support a finding of liability – as is the case now.[25] In this regard, 'object or effect' could be seen as something of a pleonasm in pre-MEA days.

If the Commission could show that an agreement was directly effecting or limiting competition (as understood), the Commission would condemn that agreement under the provisions of 101(1). The *Preserved Mushrooms* decision[26]

---

[22] Barry E Hawk, 'System Failure: Vertical Restraints and EC Competition Law' (1995) 32 *Common Market Law Review* 973, 981; Hawk's footnote omitted.

[23] However, see Joanna Goyder, *EU Distribution Law*, 4th edn (Oxford, Hart, 2005) 75 fn 29, who in regard to the former case opines: 'The same result would probably be reached today even under the Commission's new economics-based policy, so strong is the market integration imperative.'

[24] See Case 56/65 *Société Technique Minière v Maschinenbau Ulm GmbH* ('*STM*'), ECLI:EU:C:1966:38, 249–50.

[25] See below pp 101–06.

[26] Commission Decision of 8 January 1975 relating to a proceeding under Article 85 of the EEC Treaty (IV/27.039 – *Preserved Mushrooms*) [1975] OJ L29/26.

illustrates this. The arrangement in question involved European and Asian mushroom processors' coordination of production and sales within Europe. This involved production quotas (including the allocation of markets), a commonly agreed pricing policy and an obligation to share information to facilitate the enforcement of the regime. In other words, it was a naked cartel. The Commission condemned it in no uncertain terms.[27]

Similarly, any proffered justification under Article 101(3) was summarily dismissed. The Commission concluded that market sharing and price-fixing 'could not produce the improvements required by Article 85(3). Nor could they make a valid contribution to promoting technical or economic progress; they can only harm the interests of consumers.'[28] It may be a mistake to read the last phrase as a reference to consumer welfare. Rather, it is a rejection that consumers could obtain their fair share of any benefits which such an agreement could generate. This is evident given the Commission's paraphrase of Article 101(3) two paragraphs earlier, which introduced its rejection of this defence.

The *Preserved Mushrooms* decision can be fruitfully compared with the decision in *Ceramic Wall and Floor Tiles*.[29] The latter case concerned agreements in the German ceramic tile sector which provided for progressive rebates and bonuses on annual purchases of (German) ceramic tiles made from members of the manufacturing syndicate in question. Depending on the monetary value of tiles purchased, the rebates and bonuses ran from 10 to 20 per cent of purchases. The arrangement was analysed under Article 101, rather than Article 102 – notwithstanding that the tile manufacturers' syndicate satisfied over 60 per cent of the then German market. The arrangement was held to be a restriction or distortion of competition by object or effect, as it limited the commercial freedom of the parties to the arrangement. It hindered syndicate members' ability to compete through offering a different (more rewarding) system of rebates; thus it limited the freedom of buyers by preventing them from obtaining better rates.[30]

The syndicate offered three reasons why the practice should be justified under Article 101(3)'s first ground, namely its 'contribut[ion] to improving the production or distribution of goods or to promoting technical or economic progress.'[31] Rather than summarily rejecting these, the Commission very briefly considered them. But its consideration – occupying fewer than two pages of the *Official Journal* – resulted in a finding that the first ground of Article 101(3) was

---

[27] ibid 28: 'The sole object of the agreement was to restrict competition within the common market.'
[28] ibid 29.
[29] Entscheidung Der Kommission vom 29 Dezember 1970 betreffend ein Verfahren nach Artikel 85 des Vertrages (IV/25107 – '*Rabattbeschluß der Interessengemeinschaft der deutschen keramischen Wand- und Bodenfliesenwerke*') (71/23/EWG) [1971] OJ L10/15.
[30] ibid 18–19.
[31] Namely, the common rebate system provided for commercial certainty with regard to the terms of a transaction, that the scheme improved the competitive position of the (German) industry from competition from other (non-German) products and allowed the tile manufacturers to provide appropriate advice to customers, and it encouraged specialisation in tile production.

inapplicable to the arrangement. One can only speculate why the Commission did not summarily dismiss these possible Article 101(3) justifications.

One thought may be that the Commission did not have a great deal of experience with such rebate practices, as they would have had with more obvious cartels, hence there was a need at least to consider the justifications. In related fashion, the need for (some) greater consideration of these possible justifications may have been due to their anticompetitive consequences not being apparent. In any event, this decision provides some evidence that the Commission subjected 'non-standard' cartels to (slightly) greater scrutiny than those of the sort that they were familiar with. This thus may be indicative of a nascent germ of a form of Article 101 analysis which requires more extensive analysis when the Commission is either unfamiliar with the type of arrangement in question or where the object of the agreement is not immediately apparent.

But to draw these conclusions may be reading future developments into earlier analysis. To the extent that *Ceramic Tiles* can guide our understanding of the Commission's analytic method, it is safer to conclude that in the pre-MEA era, if an analytic distinction between 'object-based' and 'effects-based' analysis exists (which is not certain), then such a distinction is very undeveloped.

If the phrase 'object or effect' had any special significance in the pre-MEA era, it was an exhortation for the Commission to consider an agreement within its commercial context. However, these sorts of examinations would be viewed by present standards as meagre to inadequate in their analysis of the market. While the Commission may consider market share, it was used as an immediate proxy for market power. Typically, the Commission gave very little consideration to substitutability of goods, entry barriers and other factors that would today be taken into account in assessing an undertakings power on the market.

C. The Court's Pre-MEA Approach to Article 101

There was no significant divergence in approach between the positions of the Commission and the Court regarding the constituent elements of the competitive harm that Article 101 was designed to prevent. The Court would view market integration and commercial freedom in a similar manner as the Commission, viewing restraints which fragmented the market or which limited the commercial freedom of market participants as presenting competition problems.

Consten and Grundig is an illustration of the former point. In rejecting the possible significance of a commercial distinction between horizontal and vertical agreements, the Court viewed the possibility that such agreements could be used to reinstitute commercial barriers between Member States as a sufficient ground to condemn the agreement.[32] A similar view can be seen in *Delimitis*,[33] decided

---

[32] ibid 340.
[33] Case C-234/89 *Stergios Delimitis v Henninger Bräu AG*, ECLI:EU:C:1991:91.

15 years after *Consten*. There, the cumulative effect of distribution agreements, which limited a pub operator's choice of beers to those produced by the brewer/landlords, was considered. These agreements diminished the commercial opportunities (hence freedom) of both the pub operator and other breweries who may wish to put their product on the market.[34] Further, because the supply contract limited[35] the pub operator's ability to purchase for resale beer produced in other Member States, these sorts of contracts – forming a network of distribution agreements – will fragment the internal market.

i. Limits on Commercial Freedom: Limits to Competition

Early cases reflecting Commission decisions and Court judgments recognise that the commercial context of particular restraints is important.[36] This was perhaps the most significant result of administrative and judicial consideration of the phrase 'object or effect'. Although the Court mentions the need to examine the economic circumstances of an agreement,[37] 'economic circumstances' seems to be a synonym for 'commercial context'. Nevertheless, an understanding of the commercial context of an agreement is significantly different than an examination of a particular agreement's economic effects and consequences. But by today's expectations the analysis is sparse.

Rather, both the Commission and Court viewed this commercial context against the backdrop of the ordoliberal value of market freedom and the Community goal of market integration. The difficulty is that neither of these principles could (even with the meagre economic analysis employed by the Commission) be used to distinguish good from bad restraints on 'competition', as defined. Further, as the US courts recognised early in their consideration of the Sherman Act, all contracts and commercial agreements restrain trade, and hence limit the market freedoms of those operating on the given market. This necessarily imported an expansive, and possibly overbroad, scope to Article 101(1). These institutions soon developed two escape paths from the overbreadth of this provision (so interpreted).

The first such path was to determine that some types of agreements do not eliminate the commercial freedom of the parties. Where the restriction of competition is necessary for the existence of the commercial practice in question, that restriction will not be viewed as falling within the scope of Article 101(1).[38] Hence both the Commission and the Court accepted and developed a doctrine

---

[34] ibid 27.

[35] The scope of this limitation was significant. The clause in question only permitted the pub operator 'to purchase competing beers in other Member States' (ibid 29), rather than purchase beer imported by other undertakings. Further, the contract also included a requirement for the pub operator to buy a minimum quantity of beer from the brewery. If this minimum quantity was large, the Court noted, this would nullify the effect of the ability to bring in imported beers (paras 29–30).

[36] See *STM* (n 24) 250.

[37] See eg Cases 40–46 and 114/73 *Suiker Unie et al v Commission*, ECLI:EU:C:1975:174, para 548.

[38] See *STM* (n 24) 250, first para.

of ancillary restraints,[39] and systematically (but likely – from an economist's perspective – inconsistently) assessed elements of vertical agreements for their inclusion under Article 101(1). As Hawk notes,[40] some restrictions on supply under selective distribution schemes (eg prohibitions on dealers supplying classes of customers[41] and similar restrictions on wholesalers[42]) were excluded from the ambit of this paragraph.

However, other restrictive elements of selective distribution systems such as 'minimum sales and stocking obligations'[43] are within the scope of Article 101(1) when they occur in the context of a selective distribution system. Yet, in the context of a franchise arrangement (another vertical distribution system), such provisions are acceptable – in the sense that they do not fall within the provisions of Article 101(1).[44] Similarly, a franchisee may be required not to change their business location without the consent of the franchisor,[45] yet (exclusive/absolute) territorial protection will generally infringe Article 101(1) (and in the pre-MEA era required an Article 101(3) exemption, which the Commission from time to time approved[46]).

This inconsistent treatment of vertical restraints led – quite rightly – to accusations that the European antitrust regime was built upon a set of formalistic distinctions, where the categorisation of an agreement was determinative of its legality, rather than the consequences that the agreement had for other market participants (consumers, rivals). Indeed, as is evident from the above discussion of franchise and selective distribution systems, a practice engaged in by a franchisee may be legal, but if practised by a member of a selective distribution system is illegal, notwithstanding the consequences in the market are identical. And it only compounded the problem that such inconsistent treatment of these arrangements (the result of inconsistent reasoning in Commission decisions) became carved in the stone of the Commission's Block Exemptions.[47]

The second path of escape from a broad reading of Article 101(1) was to develop a wide interpretation of Article 101(3) exemptions. This was a frequent feature of the Commission's practice in the pre-MEA era. The Commission would take into

---

[39] See Case 42/84 *Remia v Commission*, ECLI:EU:C:1985:327, paras 17–20.

[40] Hawk (n 22) 985.

[41] ibid, citing Commission Decision of 16 December 1985 relating to a proceeding pursuant to Article 85 of the EEC Treaty (IV/30.665 – *Villeroy and Boch*) [1985] OJ L376/15.

[42] ibid, citing, inter alia, Case 26–76, *Metro SB-Großmärkte GmbH & Co KG v Commission*, ECLI:EU:C:1977:167, and *Villeroy and Boch* (ibid).

[43] ibid.

[44] Commission Decision of 2 December 1988 relating to a proceeding under Article 85 of the EEC Treaty (IV/31.697 – *Charles Jourdan*) [1989] OJ L35/31, recital 20.

[45] Case 161/84 *Pronuptia de Paris GmbH v Pronuptia de Paris Irmgard Schillgallis*, ECLI:EU:C:1986:41, para 19.

[46] Décision de la Commission, du 28 octobre 1970, relative à des procédures au titre de l'article 85 du traité CEE (IV/10.498, 11.546, 12.992, 17.394, 17.395, 17.971, 18.772, 18.888 et ex 3.213 – *Omega*) [1970] OJ L242/22.

[47] Hawk (n 22) 984.

account welfare considerations, eg agreements which they viewed as improving consumer choice[48] and quality of service.[49] In addition to welfare considerations, the Commission considered social goals to justify Article 101(3) exemptions, permitting the establishment of crisis cartels,[50] promoting environment considerations,[51] and the creation of a joint venture with the explicit goal of promoting employment in less economically developed regions of a newly acceded Member State.[52] These latter social goals are less readily convertible into welfare considerations, yet in the pre-MEA era they were accepted as part of an Article 101(3) justification.

D. Article 102

In contrast to the number of decisions regarding Article 101 matters, the Commission delivered very few Article 102 decisions in the pre-MEA era.[53] This was likely a result of capacity pressures on the Commission, given that Regulation 17's[54] clearance regime consumed a significant proportion of Commission resources. This, in turn, would have limited the Commission's resources to engage in own-initiative investigations of such conduct or investigate complaints raised by other undertakings. An obvious consequence of few Commission decisions is a paucity of Court judgments.

i. The Commission's Pre-MEA Approach to Article 102

For a business practice to run afoul of Article 102, it must be committed by an undertaking which holds a dominant position on the given market, and the practice must be an abuse of this dominance. A fortiori there are three elements to an adequate analysis of the practice: an examination or definition of the relevant market, a test for dominance, and a test for abuse. Typically, the Commission (and in turn the Court) would consider these points seriatim in a decision or judgment.

---

[48] See eg *Charles Jourdan* (n 44) recital 37.

[49] Commission Decision of 13 December 1974 relating to a proceeding under Article 85 of the EEC Treaty (IV/ 14.650 – *Bayerische Motoren Werke AG*) [1975] OJ L29/1, recital 28.

[50] Commission Decision of 4 July 1984 relating to a proceeding under Article 85 of the EEC Treaty (IV/30.810 – *Synthetic fibres*) [1984] OJ L207/17 and Commission Decision of 29 April 1994 relating to a proceeding under Article 85 of the EC Treaty (IV/34.456 – *Stichting Baksteen*) [1994] OJ L131/15.

[51] Commission Decision of 24 January 1999 relating to a proceeding under Article 81 of the EC Treaty and Article 53 of the EEA Agreement (Case IV.F.1/36.718 – *CECED*) [2000] OJ L187/47.

[52] Commission Decision of 23 December 1992 relating to a proceeding pursuant to Article 85 of the EEC Treaty (IV/33.814 – *Ford Volkswagen*) [1993] OJ L20/14, recital 36.

[53] Witt (n 1) 143 notes: 'Between 1964 and 1998, the Commission decided 311 cases pursuant to Article 101. During the same period, it decided only 44 cases under Article 102.'

[54] Regulation No 17: First Regulation Implementing Articles 85 and 86 of the Treaty [1962] OJ 204.

However, notwithstanding this comparatively thin decisional corpus, it provides sufficient detail to allow one to see the Commission's methods of analysis and competition. In particular, the decision in *Chiquita*[55] (which was later considered by the Court as *United Brands*[56]) shows the Commission's approach.

Chiquita is paradigmatic of the Commissions reasoning in Article 102 matters in the pre-MEA era. The Commission had a number of concerns with United Brand's (UBC) practices governing the sales of its 'Chiquita' brand bananas. Most relevant for our purposes were: (i) UBC's practice of prohibiting its distributors from reselling 'green' (unripened) bananas in some Member States;[57] (ii) its differential pricing among different Member States (prices in some northern Member States were at times twice that paid in Ireland);[58] and (iii) the withdrawal of banana supplies to a distributor that had taken part in a campaign advertising competing bananas.[59]

To address these concerns, the Commission first engaged in market analysis, identifying the unique features of the product market, and the geographical market. In turn, it examined UBC's position within this market, finding that UBC to be highly vertically integrated (owning, inter alia, plantations, ships, ripening facilities), had significant financial resources, a large market share, and through well-developed marketing practices has fostered an immediately identifiable and distinct brand. As such, the Commission concluded that it was dominant on the markets in question.[60]

It then turned to the nature of the abuses, and in concluding that its practices constituted an abuse of dominance, the Commission made the following conclusions. First, the prohibition on the resale of green bananas has two anticompetitive consequences. It restricts the ability (hence freedom) of UBC's ripeners to enter into competition with UBC at the wholesale level; and as only ripe (and soon perishing) bananas can be resold, the resale prohibition at the wholesale level acts as an export prohibition, hence segregating the market.[61]

Second, the Commission regarded UBC's practice of charging different prices for the same product in different Member States to be an abuse of its dominance. Relying on an earlier decision of the ECJ which held that the ability to charge different prices in different Member States, in the absence of an objective justification, was an indicium of abuse,[62] the Commission noted the wide difference

---

[55] Commission Decision of 17 December 1975 relating to a proceeding under Article 86 of the EEC Treaty (IV/26699 – *Chiquita*) (76/353 /EEC) [1976] OJ L95/1.

[56] Case 27/76, *United Brands Company and United Brands Continentaal BV v Commission* ('*UBC*'), ECLI:EU:C:1978:22.

[57] *Chiquita* (n 55) 13–14.

[58] ibid 14–16.

[59] ibid 16–17.

[60] ibid 13.

[61] ibid 13–14.

[62] Case 78/70 *Deutsche Grammophon Gesellschaft mbH v Metro-SB-Großmärkte GmbH & Co KG*, ECLI:EU:C:1971:59, para 19.

in price and UBC's lack of objective justification for this spread. It concluded: 'In conclusion, the prices which are currently charged to customers in the BLEU, Denmark, Germany ... and the Netherlands are unfair and therefore constitute an abuse by UBC of its dominant position.'[63] The reasoning seems to be a direct inference from 'unfair pricing' to 'abuse'.

Finally, the core of the Commission's condemnation of UBC's withdrawal of banana supplies to a customer characterised as 'one of its most important customers among the distributor/ripeners, which had reconstructed its ripening facilities in 1967/68 in order to be able to distribute Chiquita bananas',[64] focused on the harm that this refusal did to the customer's business interests and commercial freedom.

After noting the obvious commercial harm to the distributor and rejecting UBC's justification for terminating the supply of bananas, the Commission remarked:

> A buyer must be allowed the freedom to decide what are his business interests, to choose the products he will sell, even if they are in competition with each other; in effect to determine his own sales policy. When dealing with a supplier in a dominant position, such buyer may well find it worthwhile to sell several competing products, including those of the dominant firm, and to advertise them, but to an extent which he must remain free to decide for himself.[65]

This intermediate premise used to support the conclusion that UBC abused its dominance by refusing to supply its former distributor is flavoured with an ordoliberal view of commercial freedom.[66]

It would be fair to say that that three values form the core of the Commission's pre-MEA understanding of abuse. These are market integration, a sense of 'fairness', and an ordoliberal understanding of freedom in commercial behaviour. Unfortunately, two of the concepts are vague; and the other may require greater analysis than the Commission has given to it.

'Fairness' is an inherently vague concept, and unless it is grounded on some normative principle of distribution, it is inherently subjective. The Commission does not appear to have engaged in any principled discussion of what it means by this concept. In this regard, Akman remarks:

> [T]here is not a single or coherent conception or test of 'fairness'. 'Fairness' has been understood as *absolute necessity, equality, proportionality, transparency, objectivity, certainty* and so on regarding the practices of dominant undertakings. ... As such, assessment of 'fairness' turns very much on the facts of the case and it seems as if 'fairness' has sometimes been used as an umbrella notion under which to condemn practices that the EU authorities would like to sanction under Article 102.[67]

---

[63] *Chiquita* (n 55) 16.
[64] ibid.
[65] ibid 16–17.
[66] Hence this view of freedom does not necessarily extend to the freedom to engage (or not) in commerce with parties of one's choosing.
[67] Pinar Akman, *The Concept of Abuse in EU Competition Law* (Oxford, Hart, 2012) 156–57.

Similar criticisms can be made regarding the Commission's interpretation of 'freedom'. The *Chiquita* decision makes this very evident. There is a prima facie clash between the freedom of the distributor (to be supplied and compete against the supplier) and the freedom of UBC (in its choice of customers) which is not addressed in a principled manner. And although subsequent refusal to supply cases did engage with these concerns, they were not addressed in a comprehensive or principled manner. That said, however, in its decision, the Commission's market integration concerns were likely well founded, and as an overarching goal of the European project these concerns had normative significance independent of commercial or other concerns.

Finally, it should be noted that the Commission did at least implicitly differentiate between some forms of abuse; however, at least in the pre-MEA era, the reasons for such anticompetitive practices were not cogently expressed. Exploitative and discriminatory abuses, such as the high prices which UBC charged in certain Member States, were subsumed under the rubric of 'unfairness'. Exclusionary abuses, such as UBC's refusal to supply its former distributor, thereby preventing it from engaging in market activity, were explained as a form of inappropriate restrictions on the freedom (in an ordoliberal sense) of a market participant.

ii. The Court's Pre-MEA Approach to Article 102

During the pre-MEA era, the Article 102 jurisprudence of the courts did not diverge significantly, if at all, from the Commission's thinking. The Commission's views regarding the defining characteristic of dominance and the nature of abuse were accepted by the ECJ. In *UBC*, that Court was forced to consider the behaviour of that undertaking in the markets on which it was operating, in an effort to determine whether UBC was competing fairly (as it maintained) or abusing its dominant position. The Court accepted the Commission's view of dominance:

> The dominant position referred to in this article relates to a position of economic strength enjoyed by an undertaking which enables it to prevent effective competition being maintained on the relevant market by giving it the power to behave to an appreciable extent independently of its competitors, customers and ultimately of its consumers.[68]

The Court found UBC to be dominant, and agreed with most of the Commission's reasoning. The Court did, however, annul one point of the decision on evidentiary grounds: that UBC had charged 'unfair' prices.[69]

Although, like the Commission, the Court identified a number of types of abuses, it, too, failed to provide a unifying analysis of this sort of conduct. In *UBC*, we see that exploitative abuses occur when a dominant undertaking charges an excessive price, ie a price that has 'no relation to the economic value of the

---

[68] *UBC* (n 56) para 65.
[69] ibid paras 235–68.

product supplied'.[70] This, as the Court acknowledges, requires the production of data regarding the cost structure of a particular undertaking. Although the Court (perhaps optimistically) notes that this is not an insuperable problem, the Commission did not do that in the case in question – leading to the annulment of that aspect of the decision.

Continental Can[71] provides an early indication of the Court's thinking regarding exclusionary abuses. While that case was, strictly speaking, a case where a merger was (sought to be) controlled through recourse to Article 102, the concerns extend beyond this sort of situation to one of pure unilateral conduct. The Court noted

> [I]t can, irrespective of any fault, be regarded as an abuse if an undertaking holds a position so dominant that the objectives of the Treaty are circumvented by an alteration to the supply structure which seriously endangers the consumer's freedom of action in the market, such a case necessarily exists, if practically all competition is eliminated. Such a narrow precondition as the elimination of all competition need not exist in all cases.[72]

The Court reiterated this view of exclusionary abuses in *Hoffmann-La Roche*:[73]

> The concept of abuse is an objective concept relating to the behaviour of an undertaking in a dominant position which is such as to influence the structure of a market where, as a result of the very presence of the undertaking in question, the degree of competition is weakened and which, through recourse to methods different from those which condition normal competition in products or services on the basis of the transactions of commercial operators, has the effect of hindering the maintenance of the degree of competition still existing in the market or the growth of that competition.[74]

This has become the classic, textbook[75] definition of abuse, frequently repeated by the Court in subsequent cases.[76] The significance of this definition is that as stated it focuses on market structure and the behaviour of and opportunities for commercial operators within that structure. The consequence for consumers of a market where a dominant undertaking is present is expressed in terms of 'freedom', rather than welfare.

Similarly, market integration goals can be pursued by condemning the commercial rewards of a fragmented market. This 'reward' is, of course, the ability to profitably discriminate within the market. Again such conduct is directly caught by the Treaty, and likewise judicial silence is expected.

---

[70] ibid para 250.
[71] Case 6/72 *Europemballage Corporation and Continental Can v Commission*, ECLI:EU:C:1973:22.
[72] ibid para 29.
[73] Case 85/76 *Hoffmann-La Roche & Co AG v Commission*, ECLI:EU:C:1979:36.
[74] ibid para 91.
[75] See Alison Jones, Brenda Sufrin and Niamh Dunne, *EU Competition Law: Text, Cases and Materials*, 7th edn (Oxford, Oxford University Press, 2019) 366.
[76] See eg in the pre-MEA era Case 322/81 *NV Nederlandsche Banden Industrie Michelin v Commission*, ECLI:EU:C:1983:313, para 70; and in the post-MEA era, Case C-52/09 *Konkurrensverket v TeliaSonera Sverige AB*, ECLI:EU:C:2011:83, para 27; and Case C-549/10 P *Tomra Systems ASA and Others v Commission*, ECLI:EU:C:2012:221, para 17.

It should be apparent that during the pre-MEA period, both the Commission and the Courts analysed dominance and abuse in terms of their consequences for markets and with market structure, and not in terms of their effects on consumers. In this regard, both institutions seem to be driven by adherence to the wording of the Treaty (which in itself is a merit, from a rule of law perspective), which was informed by the market integration goals of the European project and influenced by ordoliberal concerns of freedom. While it may be easy to seize on this ordoliberal approach and overstate its influence,[77] it is nevertheless present.

II. The Shift to the More Economic Approach

The shift towards the more economic approach did not appear in a vacuum. There were at least five considerations which influenced the Commission to refocus its analytical methodology in competition matters.[78]

In no particular order, the first two were occasioned by what could be called transatlantic concerns, and the latter three more indigenous to Europe. First, in light of the shift in US thinking post-*Continental TV*,[79] which considered the legality of vertical restraints through the lens of the rule of reason (and hence explicitly recognising that such restraints are not always harmful), academic commentary soon turned to question the wisdom of the existing European position on such restraints.[80]

But transatlantic concerns did not just rest with academic commentary. Antitrust authorities on both sides of the Atlantic were faced with considering three significant cases: two mergers (*Boeing/McDonnell Douglas*[81] and *GE/Honeywell*[82]) and a monopolisation/dominance investigation (*Microsoft*[83]). The outcome of the two merger cases was identical: they were approved in the United States, but were blocked by the Commission. As a result, the transactions collapsed. This led to recriminations flowing across the Atlantic that the European competition regime protected competitors, but the US regime protects competition.[84] Whether or not

---

[77] See Akman (n 67) 151–53, who similarly cautions against an overinclusive reading-in of ordoliberalism.

[78] Witt speaks of these as 'triggers and catalysts' (n 1) 7–39.

[79] *Continental TV Inc et al v GTE Sylvania Inc*, 433 US 36 (1977).

[80] See especially Hawk (n 22).

[81] Commission Decision of 30 July 1997 declaring a concentration compatible with the common market and the functioning of the EEA Agreement (Case No IV/M.877 – *Boeing/McDonnell Douglas*) [1997] OJ L336/16.

[82] Commission Decision of 03 July 2001 declaring a concentration to be incompatible with the common market and the EEA Agreement (Case No COMP/M.2220 – *General Electric/Honeywell*).

[83] Commission Decision 2007/53/EC of 24 March 2004 relating to a proceeding pursuant to Article 82 [EC] and Article 54 of the EEA Agreement against Microsoft Corp (Case COMP/C-3.37.792 – *Microsoft*); appealed to the CFI under Case T-201/04 *Microsoft Corp v Commission*, ECLI:EU:T:2007:289.

[84] See eg Eleanor M Fox, 'We Protect Competition, You Protect Competitors' (2003) 26 *World Competition* 149.

this accusation is accurate is irrelevant; the non-rhetorical concern was the divergence in analysis which led to the different outcomes (and subsequent collapse of the proposed merger).

Microsoft was slightly less problematic. No deals collapsed. Authorities on both sides of the Atlantic condemned Microsoft's behaviour. But Microsoft's legal matters were for the most part settled through consent orders in the United States; however, in Europe they were a subject of a Commission decision, fines and commitments.

In addition to the transatlantic criticism of the Commission's economic methodology, in June through October 2002 the Court of First Instance (CFI, now the General Court) would direct similar criticism towards the Commission in three merger cases: *Airtours*,[85] *Schneider Electric*[86] and *Tetra Laval*.[87] In each of these cases, a Commission decision prohibiting the merger was overturned as a result of the Court finding significant problems in the Commission's reasoning. Indeed in *Schneider Electric*, the CFI commented: 'The Court considers the errors, omissions and inconsistencies which it has found in the Commission's analysis of the impact of the merger to be of undoubted gravity.'[88] In the light of this highly embarrassing criticism of its use of economics in legal analysis, the Commission needed to 'up its game'. And with the possibility that judicial annulment of decisions as a result of inadequate economic analysis could result in a claim for non-contractual damages against the Commission,[89] the necessity to improve in this regard was underscored.

This drive to enhance the Commission's economic expertise saw the appointment of Mario Monti as Competition Commissioner and the establishment (and staffing) of the office of Chief Competition Economist in the Competition Commission. Monti was the first holder of a PhD in economics to serve as Competition Commissioner, and from the outset of his term vowed to reshape the Commission's approach to antitrust analysis. As a result of the Commission's legal defeats in 2002, the office of Chief Economist was established in 2003. Its mandate is to support and advance the MEA. It was and is well staffed. Through its analytic input into matters in which the Commission is involved, the drafting of academic and policy papers, and input into the drafting of guidance and legislation, this office attempts to ensure that the economic analysis used by the Commission is fit for purpose.

Perhaps the final item which influenced the move to the MEA was contained in some of the reasoning behind the modernisation package which resulted in

---

[85] Case T-342/99 *Airtours plc v Commission*, ECLI:EU:T:2002:146.

[86] Case T-310/01 *Schneider Electric SA v Commission*, ECLI:EU:T:2002:254.

[87] Case T-80/02 *Tetra Laval BV v Commission*, ECLI:EU:T:2002:265.

[88] *Schneider Electric* (n 86) recital 404; see also *Tetra Laval* (ibid) recitals 336–37, and *Airtours* (n 85) recital 294.

[89] See Case T-351/03 *Schneider Electric SA v Commission*, ECLI:EU:T:2007:212, upheld (but limited) on appeal: Case C-440/07 P *Commission v Schneider Electric SA*, ECLI:EU:C:2009:48.

the adoption of Regulation 1/2003.[90] One of the features of the post-2003 regime was that undertakings could no longer notify the Commission of proposed agreements to seek an exemption under Article 101(3). Rather, post-Regulation 1/2003 it would become the responsibility of undertakings to self-assess the agreement to determine if it can benefit from Article 101(3).

To guide undertakings in their self-evaluation with an eye to facilitate consistency and predictability in the process, the Commission would need to promulgate guidance to those engaging in this process.[91] Additionally, to facilitate consistent results (and to reduce the opportunities to game the system) the Commission also needed to ensure that any trade-offs or balancing required by Article 101(3) were made using commensurable and measurable criteria.

Pre-2003 Commission practice had granted exemptions for agreements which were predicated on values that included environmental considerations,[92] orderly industry-wide restrictions (with the goal of mitigating mass unemployment),[93] and promotion of regional development in recently acceded, and less wealthy, Member States.[94] The goals pursued by these agreements could not be measured exclusively through a comparison or 'balancing' of (consumer) welfare gains and losses, nor in the Commission's analyses of the agreements did there appear to be any attempt to do so. Further, consumer welfare is apparently an inappropriate measuring stick by which the myriad of values captured by each of these agreements (economic development, concerns regarding environmental/energy conservation, and mitigating the social costs of sudden mass unemployment) are compared. To come to a resolution as to whether or not such agreements are compatible with the provisions of what is now Article 101(3) requires the superimposition of non-economic considerations to mediate among the competing values.

Parenthetically, strictly speaking, as these arrangements required the evaluation of economic and non-economic concerns, it is inappropriate to use terms such as 'balancing' or 'weighing' to describe the reasoning process in determining the compatibility of these agreements with EC competition law. These two terms describe a process of comparing several items by using one common metric, but by hypothesis such agreements involve values that cannot use a common metric.

It can be fairly said that pre-2003 the Commission incorporated values beyond the maximisation of consumer welfare in its antitrust analysis. When the Commission had the monopoly in granting Article 101(3) exemptions, there was little harm in this. The Treaties appear to recognise competition as one of a number of goals in the (then) Community's objectives. As the sole arbiter of exemptions,

---

[90] Council Regulation (EC) No 1/2003 of 16 December 2002 on the implementation of the rules on competition laid down in Articles 81 and 82 of the Treaty [2003] OJ L1/1.

[91] Which they did; see eg Guidelines on the application of Article 81(3) of the Treaty [2004] OJ C101/97.

[92] See *CECED* (n 51).

[93] See *Synthetic Fibres* and *Stichting Baksteen* (n 50).

[94] See *Ford Volkswagen* (n 52) particularly para 36.

the Commission could be expected to apply these non-economic values objectively, and it had sufficient institutional memory to ensure consistency over time. The similarities in the facts and results of *Synthetic Fibres* and *Stichting Baksteen*, notwithstanding the decade between them, seem to be evidence of this position.

However, once the Commission lost its monopoly in this regard and undertakings became responsible for the self-assessment of their own commercial agreements, such guarantees of consistency became tenuous. Viewed benignly, undertakings would have little sense of how to accurately apply incommensurable standards in an analysis of an agreement which may potentially benefit from Article 101(3). More cynically, one could add that the existence of such incommensurable standards may result in cases where undertakings could 'over-emphasise' non-economic values, at the expense of economic concerns – suggesting that a price increase (and consequent transfer of wealth from consumers) could be justified by other concerns.[95] Therefore, to shift away from a multifaceted approach to an approach that relies on a single metric (consumer welfare) and demands objective and verifiable evidence of the economic effects of the proposed arrangement[96] is more likely to produce consistent results.

III. The More Economic Approach

A. Article 101

i. *The Commission's Post-MEA View of Article 101*

In 1999 the Commission promulgated its first Vertical Restraints Block Exemption Regulation.[97] This was the first significant guidance produced by the Commission which was influenced by the MEA. This Regulation specifically noted the correlation of possible anticompetitive effects of agreements and the market power of parties to the agreement. Recognising that low market shares reflect low market power, it created a safe harbour of a 30 per cent market threshold (subject to a turnover limit) for most verticals.[98] In 2001, in its De Minimis Notice,[99] the Commission publicly recognised agreements (both horizontal and vertical)

---

[95] In previous work, the author suggested that the UK dairy industry case (OFT Case CE/3094-03 (Decision 10 August 2011); *Tesco et al v OFT* [2012] CAT 31) had an element of this. See Bruce Wardhaugh, 'Crisis Cartels: Non-Economic Values, the Public Interest, and Institutional Considerations' (2014) 10 *European Competition Journal* 311.

[96] As the Commission insists, see eg Commission Notice Guidelines on the application of Article 81(3) of the Treaty [2004] OJ C101/97, points 13 and 51–58.

[97] Commission Regulation (EC) No 2790/1999 (n 2).

[98] ibid Arts 2 and 3, see recitals 8 and 9.

[99] Notice on agreements of minor importance which do not appreciably restrict competition under Article 81(1) of the Treaty establishing the European Community (de minimis) [2001] OJ C368/13; this was replaced in 2014, see below n 101.

between undertakings that possess very low market shares will not have an appreciable effect on competition, and again set safe harbours based on low market shares.[100]

The economic premise behind the Commission's thinking in the Regulation and Notice was that as agreements by parties with low market share have little consequences for the markets in which they were found, they either did not violate Article 101(1), or – if they did – they generated sufficient efficiencies to be excused by Article 101(3). Both documents would be subsequently revised and reissued, in the case of the Regulation without great change to its import; but in the case of the Notice, to rectify its treatment of object ('hard-core') restraints, in light of developments in the ECJ.[101] Over time, the Commission would produce further guidance on other sorts of agreements, which not only aided somewhat in the post-2003 self-assessment process by introducing some certainty for undertakings and their advisors, but were also predicated on the view that there was little chance of competitive harm from the coordinated activities of undertakings possessing small market shares.

The Commission's 2004 Guidelines on the Application of Articles 101(3) illustrates the MEA. This document outlines the Commission's reasoning behind earlier published guidelines and attempts to provide needed guidance to national courts and undertakings in their assessment of agreements which may infringe Article 101.[102]

The approach is explicitly focused on consumer welfare. Point 16 makes this evident:

> Agreements between undertakings are caught by the prohibition rule of Article 81(1) when they are likely to have an appreciable adverse impact on the parameters of competition on the market, such as price, output, product quality, product variety and innovation. Agreements can have this effect by appreciably reducing rivalry between the parties to the agreement or between them third parties.[103]

These Guidelines also provide a template for production of the sort of evidence and argument that the Commission should expect to see in Article 101(3) analysis. The Guidelines and expected method of analysis here could have been produced in Chicago. Freiburg's ordoliberal considerations are completely absent from this new approach.

The Commission's position on the 'object or effect' jurisdictional requirement of Article 101(1) also subtly changed, and the distinction becomes significant. If a restriction is 'by object', then further proof of anticompetitive effects is unnecessary,

---

[100] See ibid points 7–9.
[101] See Case C-226/11 *Expedia Inc v Autorité de la concurrence and Others*, ECLI:EU:C:2012:795, which required the Commission to reformulate its 2001 De Mimimis Notice: Notice on agreements of minor importance which do not appreciably restrict competition under Article 101(1) of the Treaty on the Functioning of the European Union (De Minimis Notice) [2014] OJ C291/1.
[102] ibid 3–5.
[103] Guidelines on Art 81(3) (n 96) para 16.

and subsequent analysis proceeds under Article 101(3). A finding that an agreement contains a 'by object' restriction on competition acts thus to shift the burden of proof. The Commission is no longer required to produce (presumably significant) evidence of anticompetitive effects, rather the burden then shifts to the undertakings involved to present the procompetitive efficiencies under Article 101(3).[104]

The difficulty with the Commission's reliance on this distinction (particularly given the burden-shifting consequences which the distinction has) is its imprecision. Paragraph 21 states:

> Restrictions of competition *by object* are those that by their very nature have the potential of restricting competition. These are restrictions which in light of the objectives pursued by the Community competition rules have such a high potential of negative effects on competition that it is unnecessary for the purposes of applying Article [101](1) to demonstrate any actual effects on the market. This presumption is based on the serious nature of the restriction and on experience showing that restrictions of competition by object are likely to produce negative effects on the market and to jeopardise the objectives pursued by the Community competition rules. Restrictions by object such as price fixing and market sharing reduce output and raise prices, leading to a misallocation of resources, because goods and services demanded by customers are not produced. They also lead to a reduction in consumer welfare, because consumers have to pay higher prices for the goods and services in question.[105]

Restrictions are considered 'by object' if experience shows that they have a 'high potential' to produce 'negative effects on the market' and 'jeopardise the objectives' of the competition rules. The examples given are price-fixing and market-sharing. These create reduced output with corresponding deadweight loss. The harm is explained in light of underproduction of the product with resulting that prices.

This new view redefines the goals of the competition rules in terms of consumer welfare. Market allocation is contrary to these goals due to its detrimental welfare effects, and not because of its consequences for the internal market. The Commission provides further examples of object restrictions which are identified by reference to other Commission documents.[106]

ii. Commission's Post-MEA Decision Practice Concerning Article 101

Among the consequences of the post-Regulation 1/2003 self-assessment regime was that a significant amount of the Commission's resources were freed up. The Commission would now have greater opportunities to select its own enforcement priorities. It initially chose hard-core cartels as its primary target.

---

[104] Regulation 1/2003 (n 90) Art 2.
[105] Guidelines on Art 81(3) (n 96) para 21, Commission's footnotes omitted.
[106] See ibid point 23.

From the perspective of cartel enforcement, the Commission's efforts were successful. Its investigations resulted in significant fines,[107] raised awareness of the harmful effects this behaviour has on consumers, and made some contribution to certainty in what was considered permissible coordination of commercial activity. However, this focus on cartel activity meant that the Commission's resources were concentrated less on non-cartel matters, with the result that it produced relatively few non-cartel decisions.[108]

The most significant of the post-MEA, non-cartel decisions are *MasterCard et al*[109] and *Cartes Bancaires* (*CB*).[110] Both concerned the market in bank cards and involved arrangements which diminished competitive conditions in that market. In *CB*, the concern was with an additional per-card membership fee which would be imposed on network members that had (relatively) small numbers of customers. The obvious effect of this is to increase the costs of new entrants to the network, to the benefit of the larger incumbents. In *MasterCard*, the issue was MasterCard's Multilateral Interchange Fee (MIF – a fallback interchange fee, applied in the circumstance where there was no bilateral agreement between issuing and acquiring banks). The Commission took the position that the MIF acted to set a floor, which in turn artificially inflated the merchant fee.[111] This then would be passed on to consumers, increasing prices.

These two decisions illustrate the Commission's new approach. Their most immediately noticeable feature is extensive market analysis. *CB* devotes 29 paragraphs to the issue, but in *MasterCard* market analysis runs to a full 80 paragraphs. This is more extensive than the scope of analysis found in pre-MEA matters.

The route the Commission takes to establish an infringement in both of these cases is also remarkable. The Commission first establishes that the arrangement in question is an object restriction. Legally this is sufficient to ground an infringement of Article 101(1). However, in both cases the Commission pursues an alternative effects-based path to liability. While legally unnecessary in the first instance, this supplemental analysis will make the decision 'appeal-proof' in the likely event of an appeal should the undertakings involved convince the Court that the restriction in question was not 'by object'.[112] But this completeness is at the expense of

---

[107] The Commission takes apparent pride in publishing its statistics on fines, see https://ec.europa.eu/competition/cartels/statistics/statistics.pdf.

[108] Witt (n 1) 123 fn 57 remarks: 'Between 2000 and July 2015, the Commission published 11 Art 101 infringements in non-cartel cases, as opposed to 97 cartel infringements.' However, in 2018 and 2019 the Commission issued a number of decisions fining participants of cartels in financial markets, undertakings which fixed prices in online markets, and undertakings which interfered with the cross-border flow of goods.

[109] Commission Decision of 19 December 2007 Relating to a Proceeding Under Article 81 of the EC Treaty and Article 53 of the EEA Agreement (Cases COMP/34.579 – *MasterCard*, COMP/36.518 – *EuroCommerce*, COMP/38.580 – *Commercial Cards*).

[110] Commission Decision C (2007) 5060 final of 17 October 2007 relating to a proceeding under Article [81 EC] (COMP/D1/38606 – *Groupement des cartes bancaires (CB)*).

[111] *MasterCard Decision* (n 109) recitals 733–42.

[112] As was the case in Case C-67/13P *Groupement des cartes bancaires (CB) v European Commission*, ECLI:EU:C:2014:2204, paras 96–99.

any efficiencies brought about by the evidentiary shift in burden of proof that 'by object' analysis brings.[113]

The final and perhaps most startling feature of this new mode of analysis is explicit reliance on a theory of harm anchored to consumer welfare.[114] There is no discussion of any interference with the parties' freedom to set their own prices. In this regard, it is illuminating to compare these decisions (particularly *MasterCard*) to say, the decision in *Distiller's Company*[115] where the harm resulting from pricing policies which fixed a 'floor price' is explained in ordoliberal terms as limits to commercial freedom. The Commission's analytical approach now fully incorporates a consumer welfare goal.

iii. The Courts' Post-MEA View of Article 101

Although a superficial reading may suggest otherwise, there are some points of divergence between the Courts' and Commission's post-MEA positions. Some differences are significant, as they go to the scope of the object restrictions (with corresponding implications for shifts in evidentiary burden), the means or criteria by which restrictions by object are distinguished from those which have anti-competitive effects, and the harms which the competition rules are to prevent. I consider each of these points of divergence.

The starting point for the legal analysis of any agreement under Article 101(1) is whether it has as its 'object or effect the prevention ... of competition'. This distinction is also significant to the Courts, as they have long accepted that these are alternative pathways to liability. Hence should an agreement be found to be restrictive of competition by its object, there is no need to analyse its effects on the market. This proposition is, as the Courts note, as old as *Consten and Grundig*, and words to this effect are repeated as mantra in a typical Article 101 case.[116] Once the agreement (or concerted practice) is determined to be a 'by object' restriction, it can be condemned (fairly) immediately. Although there is – in principle – a possible Article 101(3) defence open to the parties to legitimise the agreement.[117] But such a defence seems to be theoretical, rather than practical.[118]

---

[113] See above text accompanying n 104.

[114] See eg *CB Decision* (n 110) recital 245, *MasterCard Decision* (n 109) recital 408.

[115] See above pp 80–81.

[116] See eg Case C-209/07 *Beef Industry Development Society and Barry Brothers* ('*BIDS*'), ECLI:EU:C:2008:643, para 16; also Case C-32/11 *Allianz Hungária Biztosító Zrt and Others v Gazdasági Versenyhivatal*, ECLI:EU:C:2013:160, para 34; and *Expedia* (n 101) para 35.

[117] See Case T-17/93 *Matra Hachette SA v Commission*, ECLI:EU:T:1994:89, para 85; *BIDS* ibid para 21; and Joined Cases C-501/06 P, C-513/06 P, C-515/06 P and C-519/06 P *GlaxoSmithKline Services Unlimited v Commission* ('*GSK*'), ECLI:EU:C:2009:610, paras 89–96, not interfering with the CFI's remarks at Case T-168/01 *GlaxoSmithKline Services Unlimited v Commission*, ECLI:EU:T:2006:265, para 233.

[118] *BIDS* ibid para 39.

On the other hand, if the agreement (etc) is determined to be restrictive of competition by its effects, then condemnation is not a summary process. Rather, as the ECJ noted in *Maxima Latvija*, it is necessary to find that the agreement appreciably restricts or distorts competition.[119] Analysis of agreements that are restrictive of competition by effect is a more extensive process. This requires the determination of the pro- and anticompetitive effects of the practice, and a judgment about how these effects balance out each other. But this is an extensive, economics-focused fact-finding exercise.

There are adjudicative efficiencies which result from this dichotomy. These efficiencies are gained from the fact that the categorisation of a restraint as 'by object' infringement eliminates the need for an extensive fact-finding exercise. Yet such gains can be easily squandered if agreements which on balance are procompetitive are wrongly condemned as anticompetitive by object (type I errors). Second, where agreements which are not anticompetitive 'by object' are not recognised as such, the savings of immediate condemnation will be lost. If an agreement is wrongly characterised as 'by effect', then adjudicators will be obliged to engage in a full-blown, effects-based analysis of the agreement. This will in the end show that the agreement was indeed highly restrictive (ie restrictive by object) of competition. Thus any advantages of immediate assessment and condemnation will be foregone. Finally, as a related point, the advantages of 'by object' categorisation are lost if extensive analysis is required to confirm that a given restriction is indeed 'by object'.[120]

For this approach to be workable, the Court would need to provide guidance on at least three points. In particular, first the Court must create an accurate distinction between 'by object' and 'by effect' restrictions which are found in anticompetitive agreements. In so doing, the Court must draw the line in the right place, and with sufficiently clarity. This will both reduce the occurrence of type I errors and ensure that only effects-based agreements are subjected to full-blown analysis. This will address the first two issues mentioned in the preceding paragraph.

Similarly, when the line is drawn, in addition to being drawn with precision, ie in 'the right place', the Court must ensure that it draws it with sufficient clarity. It goes without saying that an unclear rule or standard is of little use to those relying on it for guidance. Hence clarity in demarcating the boundaries between these two sorts of agreements is essential for business planning. Firms may well forego entering into arraignments which are restrictive of competition by effect (but which they believe to have, on balance, a procompetitive result) if they are uncertain how

---

[119] Case C-345/14 *SIA Maxima Latvijva v Konkurences padome*, ECLI:EU:C:2015:784, para 17, citing *Allianz Hungária* (n 116); and *CB* (n 112) para 52; and Case C-286/13 P *Dole Food and Dole Fresh Fruit Europe v Commission*, EU:C:2015:184, para 116.

[120] This appears to be one of the consequences of the ECJ judgment in *Allianz Hungária* (n 116) para 48. On this see Csongor István Nagy, 'The Distinction Between Anti-competitive Object and Effect after Allianz: The End of Coherence in Competition Analysis?' (2013) 36 *World Competition* 541, 561–62. However, in *CB* ibid para 82 the Court appears to recognise its mistake in *Allianz Hungária*.

the agreement is regarded. They may choose not to risk summary condemnation (with only a theoretical possibility of an Article 101(3) defence, and significant fines), if the dividing line is insufficiently clear.

Second, for related reasons, the Court needs to provide a clear indication of the nature (and extent) of the analysis required when both types of agreements are scrutinised. To ensure that savings are realised by subjecting 'by object' restrictions to lesser scrutiny than 'by effect' restrictions, analysis of the former must *in fact* be done with a lighter touch than is the case with the latter. This is the third issue raised above.

Finally, the Court needs to articulate a view of competitive harm, ie what it is that the competition regime is to promote. Without a clear indication of the nature of competitive harm (or harms, if there in fact more than one type), there can be no measuring stick by which pro- and anticompetitive consequences of commercial arrangements can be examined.

It is fair to say that there is both some divergence between the Commission and the Courts in their responses to these three issues and some evolution (or otherwise put, correction or clarification) by the Courts in their views. The difference in Treaty interpretation between the Commission (as enforcer of the Treaty provisions) and the Courts (as authoritative interpreter of these provisions) introduces uncertainty into the regime. This can also create a rule of law problem for the regime as a whole.

iv. *The Court on 'By Object' and 'By Effect' Restrictions*

The ECJ's judgment in *CB* is an excellent case to illustrate the Court's approach to the MEA. It also demonstrates the uncertainties which result from the lack of a clear line between 'object' and 'effect'. Additionally, *CB* involved a two-sided market, which is analytically more complex than the usual sorts of markets investigated by the Commission. And, finally, in a few cases[121] prior to *CB*, the Court made some infelicitous remarks regarding the expansion of 'by object' restrictions and of the sort of analysis to which such restrictions should be subjected. Thus *CB* can be seen as an effort by the Court (with the assistance of Advocate General Wahl) to get the Court's analysis 'back on the rails' again.

The Court began its analysis with a consideration of the by object/by effect distinction, noting that earlier guidance is apposite. The starting point of the ECJ's analysis in *CB* is the line of case-law culminating in *Allianz Hungária*, where the ECJ noted that the object/effects distinction 'arises from the fact that certain forms of collusion between undertakings can be regarded, by their very nature, as being injurious to the proper functioning of normal competition'.[122]

---

[121] Case C-8/08 *T-Mobile Netherlands BV and Others v Raad van bestuur van de Nederlandse Mededingingsautoriteit*, ECLI:EU:C:2009:343, para 31; and *Allianz Hungária* (n 116) para 48.

[122] *CB* (n 119) para 50; see *Allianz Hungária* (n 116) para 35; *Expedia* (n 101) para 36 which in turn cites *BIDS* (n 116) para 17; and *T-Mobile* (n 121) para 29.

The conclusion that a form of collusion is a restriction by object is evidence driven. In *CB*, the Court (after repeating the form of words used in, for example, *Allianz Hungária*) explains:

> [I]t is established that certain collusive behaviour, such as that leading to horizontal price-fixing by cartels, may be considered so likely to have negative effects, in particular on the price, quantity or quality of the goods and services, that it may be considered redundant, for the purposes of applying Article 81(1) EC, to prove that they have actual effects on the market .... Experience shows that such behaviour leads to falls in production and price increases, resulting in poor allocation of resources to the detriment, in particular, of consumers.[123]

Explicit in the Court's reasoning is that 'experience' has shown that collusion on price or quality and output restrictions lead to a reduction of consumer welfare.

The Court cites price-fixing by horizontal cartels as an example, noting: 'Experience shows that such behaviour leads to falls in production and price increases, resulting in poor allocation of resources to the detriment, in particular, of consumers.'[124] The Court is correct on this point. There a significant body of empirical evidence that shows that prices are higher and quality is lower in markets where collusion is present. Further, it is a simple exercise in microeconomic theory to a priori demonstrate these effects. It is this sort of experience, ie empirical evidence confirmed by (or at minimum, consistent with) reasoned analysis, which will justify the classification of a restriction as 'by object'.

Advocate General Wahl's Opinion in *CB* makes this point clear. Noting the advantages in judicial economy which follow from a restraint being condemned 'by object', the Advocate General cautions against hasty categorisation of a particular restraint, and does so by making two important points. First, central to the object–effects distinction is that restrictions 'by object' have no net beneficial procompetitive consequences; and their anticompetitive nature is readily identifiable through informed experience. Second, since classification as a 'by object' restraint will truncate the legal analysis (resulting in almost inevitable condemnation of the restraint), competition authorities must exercise caution in concluding that a particular restriction is 'by object'. The implication of these two points taken together is that the default classification for restraints will be a 'by effect' classification, and for legal purposes will remain so until competition authorities have sufficient experience with the restraint.[125]

The Court agreed with this analysis. In rejecting the General Court's analysis, the ECJ remarked:

> First, ... the essential legal criterion for ascertaining whether coordination between undertakings involves such a restriction of competition 'by object' is the finding that such coordination reveals in itself a sufficient degree of harm to competition.

---

[123] *CB* (n 119) para 51.

[124] ibid.

[125] Case C-67/13 P *Groupement des cartes bancaires (CB) v Commission*, ECLI:EU:C:2014:1958, Opinion of AG Wahl, paras 55– 59.

... [Second, t]he concept of restriction of competition 'by object' can be applied only to certain types of coordination between undertakings which reveal a sufficient degree of harm to competition that it may be found that there is no need to examine their effects, otherwise the Commission would be exempted from the obligation to prove the actual effects on the market of agreements which are in no way established to be, by their very nature, harmful to the proper functioning of normal competition. The fact that the types of agreements covered by Article 81(1) EC do not constitute an exhaustive list of prohibited collusion is, in that regard, irrelevant.[126]

The ECJ's concern regarding the General Court's peremptory classification is found in paragraphs 71–90 of the judgment. While the Court did not say so in as many words, the Commission and General Court's inexperience with two-sided markets meant that their analyses failed to identify possible procompetitive aspects of the arrangement in question. This thus serves as a warning about the pitfalls of hasty 'by object' classifications.

CB (and the case-law which precedes it) stands for the position that 'by object' restraints are those which have no net benefits to the competitive process, and can be identified as such by significant and informed experience. Thus authorities must examine novel restraints with care, and accordingly not immediately cast them into 'the object box', in the slang of the competition community.[127] Although this clarification is significant, *CB* does not explicitly address another concern, left open by earlier case-law.

This concerns the level at which analysis of a restraint should occur. This analysis can occur at two levels:[128] at the level of individual restraints (eg a particular contract between a manufacturer and its distributors), or by the type of restraints (eg retail price maintenance, taken generally). The reasoning in *CB* makes it clear that where the court or competition authority does not have extensive experience with a given restriction, then 'by effect' analysis at the level of the individual agreement in question is mandated. On the other hand, if the authority has significant informed experience with a set of practices and a given agreement falls within that set, then little analysis should be required before the agreement is prima facie condemned. To require otherwise would eliminate any adjudicative economies that may arise from the object/effect distinction.

But the issue is how 'little' is sufficient? The case-law recognises that agreements cannot be analysed in the abstract, and those examining the competitive effects of an agreement must take heed of the commercial context in which it is found. For instance, in *GSK*, the ECJ notes:

According to settled case-law, in order to assess the anti-competitive nature of an agreement, regard must be had inter alia to the content of its provisions, the objectives it seeks to attain and the economic and legal context of which it forms a part .... In addition, although the parties' intention is not a necessary factor in determining

---

[126] *CB* (n 112) paras 57–58.
[127] This is a traditional view of the object–effect distinction. See eg Richard Whish and David Bailey, *Competition Law*, 9th edn (Oxford, Oxford University Press, 2018) 123.
[128] See Luc Peeperkorn, 'Defining "By Object" Restrictions' [2015] No 3 *Concurrences* 40, 43–46.

whether an agreement is restrictive, there is nothing prohibiting the Commission or the Community judicature from taking that aspect into account.[129]

The extent of such contextual analysis is crucial.

Unfortunately, the case-law prior to *CB* failed to give a clear answer to this question; and indeed the approach the ECJ took in *Allianz Hungária* could have been ruinous for any adjudicative efficiencies which the distinction may have provided. In paragraph 48 of that case, the Court remarked:

> Furthermore, those agreements would also amount to a restriction of competition by object in the event that the referring court found that it is likely that, having regard to the economic context, competition on that market would be eliminated or seriously weakened following the conclusion of those agreements. In order to determine the likelihood of such a result, that court should in particular take into consideration the structure of that market, the existence of alternative distribution channels and their respective importance and the market power of the companies concerned.[130]

This requirement would force a full-blown economic analysis of each instance of a so-called 'object' restriction, before it could be condemned.

This passage from *Allianz Hungária* has been termed 'disastrous'.[131] If this represents the case-law, then by requiring 'by object' restrictions to be subjected to full-blown economic analysis, the Court blurs the distinction between object- and effect-based restrictions. By obscuring this distinction, the Court also eliminates any adjudicative efficiencies which can be produced by a light-touch analysis of 'by object' restrictions. Such light-touch analysis can occur only if type-based categorisation is possible.[132]

In *CB*, the Court implicitly resiles from the approach which it appears to have taken in *Allianz Hungária*. Implicit in its reasoning in *CB* is an acceptance that 'by object' analysis must be focused on *types of restrictions*, and *not on individual restrictions* themselves. For instance, at paragraph 49, the Court states: 'In that regard, it is apparent from the Court's case-law that certain types of coordination between undertakings reveal a sufficient degree of harm to competition that it may be found that there is no need to examine their effects.' This statement is followed by further discussion of harms which *types* of agreements (and horizontal price-fixing is named as one such type of agreement) can inflict on the market.

The Court's clarification on this point is welcome. Yet the case-law leaves a number of other issues obscure. First, we are told that when a competition authority is faced with a restriction which, based upon informed experience, presents no net competitive effects, that restriction can be viewed as 'by object'

---

[129] *GSK* (n 117) para 58; Court's citation of case-law omitted.

[130] *Allianz Hungária* (n 116) para 48.

[131] Nagy (n 120) 561.

[132] See Nagy ibid; he also, correctly, points out the Court's suggestion in *Allianz Hungária* that all agreements be subjected to such full-blown analysis also contradicts earlier case-law in *Expedia* (n 101) paras 35–37 which holds that 'by object restrictions' are so, irrespective of the structure of the market and the power of the undertakings on that market.

and summarily condemned (subject to a – theoretical – Article 101(3) defence). However, beyond a few generalities such as the commercial context or 'real conditions of the functioning and structure of the market or markets in question'[133] in which the agreement is found, the Court fails to provide any meaningful guidance about what might suffice to ground the informed experience. The Court informs us that the list of agreements in Article 101(1) is not an exhaustive enumeration of 'by object' restrictions,[134] but does not provide a clear set of sufficient conditions for a type of agreement to be added to that list.

We are also told that in the absence of this informed experience, the default classification is 'by effect', thus subjecting the agreement to full-blown analysis. As the border between object and effect restrictions is unclear, those considering restrictions which are close to that border must apply a full-blown, effect-based analysis to determine their legality. Thus the adjudicatory advantages of 'by object' classification are lost at the margin.

Beyond the default classification, the nebulous nature of the process we have termed 'informed experience' further contributes to the unclarity of the European competition project. In addition to the paucity of description as to the sort and depth of analysis required to inform our experience, the Court is silent on whether or not the move to classification of restrictions as 'by object' from 'by effect' is a one-way street.

In other words, once a particular kind of restraint is classified as a 'by object' restraint, will it always remain so? Presumably, at least at one time, there was sufficient informed experience to justify that classification. Yet informed experience ought to change when more data become available. If such data, perhaps explained by further refinements in economic analysis, do arise, should this result in a 'reclassification' of the restraint? One can envisage a situation where instances of a type of restraint which had been condemned as 'by object' restraints are successfully defended under Article 101(3). A situation such as this would suggest that the initial classification should be reconsidered. As shown by the US experience in *Leegin*,[135] this is not merely a theoretical concern. In that case, the majority of the USSC were of the view that there had been a sufficiently significant shift in economic thinking (ie informed experience had evolved) to now justify the use of rule of reason analysis to consider resale price maintenance agreements, and abandon their per se condemnation.

Finally, and this is a significant point, the Court is unclear as to the nature of the competitive harms which the competition regime is to prevent. Paragraphs 50 and 51 of *CB* state that the negative effects in concern are those which involve 'price, quality and quantity' of the goods in question. In other words, these types of 'by object' restraints will reduce consumer surplus without producing countervailing benefits.

---

[133] *CB* (n 112) para 53.
[134] ibid 58.
[135] *Leegin Creative Leather Products Inc v PSKS Inc*, 551 US 877 (2007).

But according to the case-law of the Court, an agreement's reduction in consumer surplus (with no offsetting benefits) may be a sufficient, but not a necessary condition, for it to be treated as a 'by object' restriction. In *GSK*, the ECJ unequivocally rejected the CFI's view to the contrary. The Court noted that neither the case-law nor the Treaties support the views that consumer harm is necessary.[136] Part of the reasoning is clear. The Court alludes to *T-Mobile*, which condemned information sharing notwithstanding that the shared information was never acted upon. In this circumstance, no harm was done to the consumer.

However, the Court puzzlingly mentions 'the interests of competitors', 'the structure of the market' and 'competition as such'. These are vague terms reflective of an ordoliberal approach to the market; and their use as policy goals is inconsistent with a competition policy exclusively devoted to the maximisation of consumer welfare. If anything, the Court's use of these terms seems to indicate reluctance to completely and wholeheartedly adopt an exclusively consumer welfare focused approach to competition policy, and thereby abandon any remaining vestiges of ordoliberal thinking in its analytic approach.

The Commission's position is prima facie inconsistent (at least at the margins) with the Court's authoritative interpretation of the Treaty. Further, as we will see in the following exposition of the Court's position on Article 102, its interpretation of that Article does not validate the Commission's interpretation, thus compounding legal uncertainty and rule of law considerations.

B. Article 102

i. *The Commission's Post-MEA View of Article 102*

In 2005, the Commission released a report by its Economic Advisory Group for Competition Policy[137] and a Discussion Paper on the Application of Article 102 to Exclusionary Abuses.[138] The publication of these documents was used to guide the Commission in preparing its enforcement strategy regarding Article 102 abuses. This strategy was promulgated by the Commission in its 2009 Communication, the so-called 'Guidance Paper'.[139] The explicit argument of the Report was to argue

---

[136] *GSK* (n 117) paras 63–64.

[137] EAGCP, Economic Advisory Group for Competition Policy (Jordi Gual, Martin Hellwig, Anne Perrot, Michele Polo, Patrik Rey, Klaus Schmidt, Rune Stenbacka) 'An Economic Approach to Article 82: Report by the European Advisory Group on Competition Policy', available at: http://ec.europa.eu/dgs/competition/economist/eagcp_july_21_05.pdf.

[138] Commission, 'DG Competition Discussion Paper on the Application of Article 82 of the Treaty to Exclusionary Abuses: Public Consultation' (Brussels, 2005) available at: http://ec.europa.eu/competition/antitrust/art82/discpaper2005.pdf.

[139] Commission, Guidance on the Commission's Enforcement Priorities in Applying Article 82 of the EC Treaty to Abusive Exclusionary Conduct by Dominant Undertakings [2009] OJ C45/7.

for an economics-based approach to Article 102 analysis, similar to the post-MEA approach taken in Article 101 matters and merger control.[140]

Although the Advisory Group is independent of the Commission, its views were highly influential of the latter's thought process. The economic focus of the Report's authors is old-style Chicago School. They are open about this.[141] Further, and commendably so, the authors explicitly recognise the challenges that an effects-based policy will pose for the legal process.[142] They recognise that much will depend on the allocation of burden of proof, and how (rebuttable) evidentiary presumptions are developed. Two principles follow from this:

> First, in the absence of additional evidence to the contrary, an argument based on established economic theory and supported by facts that according to the theory, are material to the assessment of the practice in question should be deemed more credible than a counterargument that does not have such a basis. ... Second, if the story of competitive harm that is brought forth by the competition authority fulfils the criteria listed above and the validity of the counter-story brought by the firm hinges on data in the domain of the firm, then it should be incumbent upon the firm to provide these data.[143]

In summary, the authors note the consequences of this, namely:

> Both of these principles require a certain degree of flexibility in the handling of proof requirements. However, this cannot be avoided if the effects-based approach is to be practical. Whereas a form-based approach hinges on data that the competition authority should in principle be able to provide, an effects-based approach also requires interpretations of data where discrimination is more difficult.[144]

These honest remarks by the authors point to difficulties inherent in any effects-based approach.

The efforts of the Advisory Group and the Commission's consultation process were consolidated into the above-mentioned Guidance Paper. The Guidance Paper is notable for a number of reasons. First, it merely sets out enforcement *priorities* in the Commission's enforcement of Article 102 abuses. As the softest of soft law it merely announced the Commission's approaches to competition law analysis and enforcement in Article 102 cases. The Commission noted that it will focus on exclusionary abuses.[145] However as Guidance, it neither compels the Commission

---

[140] The Executive Summary to the Report (n 137) remarks:

> This report argues in favour of an economics-based approach to Article 82, in a way similar to the reform of Article 81 and merger control. In particular, we support an effects-based rather than a form-based approach to competition policy. Such an approach focuses on the presence of anti-competitive effects that harm consumers, and is based on the examination of each specific case, based on sound economics and grounded on facts.

[141] See eg p 27 of the Report, ibid.
[142] ibid 15–16.
[143] ibid.
[144] ibid 16.
[145] Guidance (n 139) points 5 and 6.

to act in a particular way, nor does it prohibit them from focusing their attention on other forms of abuse – particularly exploitative abuses – when the situation merits.[146]

The starting point of the Guidance Paper is a statement of the sort of harm that its enforcement activities are directed at preventing. Following on the case-law which has held that a dominant undertaking has a special responsibility not to allow its conduct to further impair the functioning of the market,[147] the Commission suggests that this is best done by focusing on those activities which most harm consumers, such as abuses that prevent competition on price and quality.[148] In spite of this consumer welfare focus, the Guidance Paper mentions that the 'Commission is mindful that what really matters is protecting an effective competitive process and not simply protecting competitors',[149] and of the need for intervention to protect 'the proper functioning of the internal market'.[150] It doubtful that the Commission's view of the competitive harm prohibited by Article 102 is coextensive with the Court's view.

The Commission does add some certainty to its analytical approach. In point 22, for instance, it notes that when the harm in question likely results in consumer harm and presents no offsetting efficiencies, the Commission will infer an anticompetitive effect. This is analogous to analysis under Article 101's object restrictions. Additionally, the Guidance Paper appeals to cost- and efficiency-based criteria as markers for abusive conduct. The focus is on excluding 'as efficient competitors' (AEC).[151] As an undertaking is aware of its own costs and efficiencies, the AEC benchmark provides some certainty as to the standard against which its conduct will be evaluated.[152] Further, in considering cost-based exclusionary conduct, the Commission states that it will use average avoidable costs (as failure to cover these indicates profit sacrifice) and long-run average avoidable costs (failure to cover indicates failure to recapture all fixed costs of the good's production) as benchmarks. Pricing below either is an indication that the dominant undertaking is capable of excluding AECs; and as an undertaking is well positioned to know its own cost structures, such benchmarks are capable of providing ex ante legal certainty regarding future commercial strategies.

Notwithstanding this clarification of some benchmarks, the Guidance Paper does introduce an element of uncertainty into the assessment process. Legal guidance can enhance clarity and certainty by presenting standards and presumptions which can be taken into account by those planning on engaging in the sort of activity contemplated by that guidance.

---

[146] ibid point 7.
[147] ibid point 1; however, this merely restates the ECJ in eg *Michelin* (n 76) para 57.
[148] ibid point 5, see also point 19.
[149] ibid point 6.
[150] ibid point 7.
[151] See points 23–27.
[152] However, this absolute certainty is reduced in cases where a less efficient competitor can provide a competitive constraint on the dominant undertaking. See eg ibid point 24.

For instance, in its discussion of dominance, the Guidance Paper notes that undertakings which have less than 40 per cent of market share will unlikely to be viewed as dominant.[153] However, turning its back on existing case-law which establishes presumptions of dominance when market share exceeds certain percentages,[154] the Commission announces that its assessment of dominance will take into account the competitive structure of the market and constraints imposed by suppliers, actual and potential competitors, and buyer power.[155]

The Guidance Paper also considers defences to potentially abusive practices. In an effort to ensure consistency between Articles 101 and 102, the Commission suggests that a defence similar to that in Article 101(3) is available to allegations of abuse.[156] While, of course, consistency between Articles 101 and 102 is a merit, it is meritorious only if the case-law permits it and offers solutions that are realistically available to those who might need them. It is not clear whether an Article 101(3)-like defence is consistent with the case-law. As Monti notes, that case-law does not require the undertaking involved to demonstrate 'that the conduct in question does not eliminate competition, so the Guidance Paper may be stricter than necessary'.[157] Further, demonstrating that a particular practice generates the required efficiencies will be a difficult task; and if lack of success in Article 101(3) defences is a measure of this task, the Guidance Paper's defence is likely illusory.

The Guidance Paper is best regarded as an indication of the Commission's thinking. Unfortunately, beyond putting the business community on notice that it will be focusing on exclusionary abuses, it fails to live up to its name, and give market players clear guidance. Indeed, by failing to provide such guidance, via, for instance, suggestion of safe harbours and (rebuttable) evidentiary presumptions, it could be suggested that the Commission not only lost a chance to clarify its approach, but muddied the waters even further. It may well be that the Guidance Paper represents a rule of law threat.[158] Although the Guidance Paper is the softest of soft law, and has no legal effect, it nevertheless can establish expectations among the business community. Hence any departure from the Court's interpretation of law by the Commission is a non-trivial concern.

ii. *The Commission's Post-MEA Decisional Practice Concerning Article 102*

It appears that the Guidance Paper seems to have changed little in the way the Commission conducts its analysis. The majority of the Commission's Article 102

[153] Guidance (n 139) point 14.
[154] See *Hoffman-La Roche* (n 73) para 59; Case T-30/89 *Hilti AG v Commission*, ECLI:EU:T:1991:70, para 92.
[155] Guidance (n 139) point 12.
[156] ibid points 28–31.
[157] Giorgio Monti, 'Article 82 EC: What Future for the Effects-Based Approach?' (2010) 1 *Journal of European Competition Law and Practice* 2, 9.
[158] On this point, see Pinar Akman, 'The Reform of the Application of Article 102 TFEU: Mission Accomplished?' (2016) 8 *Antitrust Law Journal* 145.

enforcement activities have resulted in commitment decisions, with only 11 prohibition decisions being issued between February 2009 and August 2019 (the time of writing).[159] Three of the nine decisions have yet to be released in a public version.

Commitment decisions are an effective means of resolving a competitive concern in a manner which avoids the time and cost of protracted administrative hearings (and the likelihood of subsequent judicial review). However, the ad hoc nature of these decisions makes it difficult to distil general principles from them. The delay in promulgating public versions of decisions, given that they may provide guidance for others active on the market, compounds the rule of law threat.

Nevertheless, the prohibition decisions can give us some indications of general principles in the Commission's reasoning. What is clear from these decisions is that the Commission now engages in a redundant two-stage process when it wishes to rest on the position it took in the Guidance Paper. This is noted by Witt in her analysis of the *Intel* and *Telekomunikacja Polska* decisions, in which the Commission engaged in two-step analysis of the practice in question.[160] In both cases, the Commission first analysed the practice under the pre-MEA case-law and analytic approach, and found the practice in question to be an abuse. The Commission then applied the criteria established in the Guidance Paper to demonstrate the practice's anticompetitive foreclosure. The latter step is redundant. It is also costly. But it mirrors recent Commission practice in Article 101 decisions.

Yet in some cases, the Commission eschews this latter step. *Google (Shopping)* is worth noting in this regard. Here the abuse consisted in the dominant undertaking's self-preference, ie positioning related sites (eg Google-affiliated shopping, finance and travel providers) more prominently than similar third-party sites. The Commission's analysis is very traditional. It relies on case-law which holds that abuse under Article 102 extends to beyond diminution of consumer welfare, to include harms to 'an effective competition structure'.[161] The analysis of the particular harm in question (a form of tying) also proceeded using the traditional approach, indicating that the gravamen of the abuse consists of the dominant undertaking seeking to strengthen its position on an adjacent market.[162]

Google (Shopping) could have been an ideal case for the Commission to develop its new approach. It did not. Rather the Commission's analysis would not have

---

[159] COMP/C-3/37.990 – *Intel*, 13 May 2009; COMP/39.525 – *Telekomunikacja Polska*, 22 June 2011; AT.39984 – *Romanian Power Exchange/OPCOM*, 5 March 2014; AT.39985 – *Motorola (Enforcement of GPRS standard essential patents)*, 29 April 2014; AT.39523 – *Slovak Telekom*, 15 October 2014; AT.39759 – *ARA Foreclosure*, 20 September 2016; Case AT.39740 – *Google Search (Shopping)*, 27 June 2017; AT.39813 – *Baltic Rail*, 2 October 2017; AT.40099 – *Google (Android)*, 18 July 2018, no public version available; AT.40411 – *Google (AdSense)*, 20 March 2019, no public version available; AT.39711 – *Qualcomm Predatory Pricing (Baseboard Chipsets)*, 18 July 2019, no public version available.

[160] Witt (n 1) 151–52.

[161] *Google (Shopping)* (n 159) recital 333.

[162] ibid recitals 332–34.

been out of place in the pre-MEA era. And it is noteworthy that the word 'foreclosure' does not appear in the non-confidential version of the decision. Similarly, in *Baltic Rail*, a clear exclusionary case which involved the dominant undertaking's removal of a stretch of rail track, forcing its competitors to take a longer journey (thus increasing their costs), the Commission's approach was very traditional.

Arguably, the MEA did little to alter the Commission's practice in Article 102 cases. Although the Guidance Paper advocates an economics-focused approach, its practice is different. Commentators have suggested that this signified risk-aversion on the part of the Commission: an unwillingness to defend in court a standard which differs from the existing case-law.[163] Alternatively, the two-stage process is a form of 'cakeism'[164] on the part of the Commission: the two-stage process ensures that in spite of its desire to use the new approach, if challenged before the courts the Commission will win, given the alternative reliance on the traditional case-law.[165] (For a department populated by results-focused litigators, such a strategy makes sense.[166]) But such a litigation strategy is not without its flaws. In addition to the expense (for the Commission and undertaking involved) which this bifurcated process involves, it also creates uncertainty regarding the status of not just the Commission's Guidance Paper, but also the economic approach to Article 102.

iii. The Court's Post-MEA View of Article 102

If one word had to be chosen to describe the approach taken by the CJEC in response to the Commission's post-2009 approach to TFEU Article 102, that word would be 'continuity'. Neither the ECJ nor the General Court adjusted their analysis of Article 102 cases as result of the Commission's new agenda. Arguably, given the Commission's two-step process (eg as exemplified in the *Intel* decision), there was no need to do so. The Court could – and did – continue to rely on the reasoning embedded in its previous case-law in its consideration of abuse of dominance cases.

---

[163] Liza Lovedahl Gormsen, 'Why the European Commission's Enforcement Priorities on Article 82 Should Be Withdrawn' (2010) 31 *European Competition Law Review* 45, 50–51.

[164] A neologism meaning 'to have one's cake and eat it too' – it has been derisorily applied to positions taken by some Brexit advocates. See the footnote below.

[165] See Frédéric Louis and Cormac O'Daly, 'Unfulfilled Promise: Is the Commission's Guidance Going the Way of the Dodo?' *Global Competition Law Review* (15 August 2017) 1, 5:

> Eight years on since the Guidance Paper's publication, the Commission needs to commit wholeheartedly to the economics-based approach lest the Guidance Paper become insignificant. The 'have your cake and eat it' approach in cases like Intel (albeit the Intel investigation admittedly was initiated pre-Guidance Paper) – where, on the one hand, the Commission demonstrates that rebates are unlawful under the courts' case law and, on the other, purports to apply an AEC test while making it clear it feels such a step is not necessary – is all too comfortable with the Commission ensuring that it will win either way.

[166] See Jorge Padilla, 'Whither Article 102 TFEU: Comments on Akman and Crane' (2016) 8 *Antitrust Law Journal* 223, 229.

As a result of the Commission's litigation strategy and its reliance on earlier case-law of the Court (at the expense of the sort of analysis proposed by the Guidance), the force of the Commission's MEA was muted before the Court. Further, the Courts' position on the nature of harm which Article 102 is to prevent did not change.

Although the Commission took a consumer welfare orientation in its approach to this harm, this approach is not wholeheartedly shared by the Courts. Rather, in clarifying these harms, the Court appeals to earlier case-law, particularly *Michelin* and *British Airways*.[167] For instance, in *Post-Danmark III*,[168] the Court remarks:

> As regards the application of Article 82 EC to a rebate scheme, it should be recalled that, in prohibiting the abuse of a dominant market position in so far as trade between Member States could be affected, that article refers to conduct which is such as to influence the structure of a market where, as a result of the very presence of the undertaking in question, the degree of competition is already weakened and which has the effect of hindering the maintenance of the degree of competition still existing in the market or the growth of that competition.[169]

In addition to this ongoing concern regarding market structure, the Court would refer to other non-welfare goals. In *Tomra* (a rebates case), for instance, echoing ordoliberal values, the ECJ relates abuse to limiting the buyer's freedom of choice of supplier;[170] and in *TeliaSonera*, the Court returns to its mantra that dominant undertakings have a special responsibility to ensure that competition in the market in which they operate is not further distorted by their practices.[171]

In addition to its consistency with its pre-2009 views regarding the harms that Article 102 is designed to prevent, the Court also appears to develop some consistency in its analysis of Article 101 and 102 matters. The object–effect distinction is key to analysis of Article 101 matters. Post-2009, it appears that the Court is developing something similar for Article 102 matters.

In Article 101 matters this distinction is often determinative of the outcome of the case. If a practice is found to be a 'by object' restriction, there is no need to engage in any detailed analysis of the practice. Through informed experience competition authorities have recognised that certain practices have no net procompetitive benefits. These are condemned; however, undertakings involved in such arrangements can (in theory) justify their conduct by appeal to the criteria of Article 101(3). Where informed experience does not point to the practice having no net procompetitive benefits, the court (or agency) will engage in a more

---

[167] *Michelin* (n 76) para 70, and C-95/04 P *British Airways v Commission*, EU:C:2007:166, para 66.
[168] Case C-23/14 *Post Danmark A/S v Konkurrencerådet* ('*Post Danmark III*'), ECLI:EU:C:2015:651.
[169] ibid para 26, references to *Michelin* and *BA* omitted.
[170] *Tomra* (n 76) para 71.
[171] Case C-52/09 *Konkurrensverket v TeliaSonera Sverige AB*, ECLI:EU:C:2011:83, para 24, see also para 27.

comprehensive analytic process, balancing the pro- and anticompetitive consequences of the arrangement, as part of its assessment.

In Article 102 matters, the Court appears to be taking a similar approach, which has not gone unnoticed in the literature.[172] Certain practices, when engaged in by dominant undertakings, are self-evidentially exclusionary. Once identified, these are condemned, subject – of course – to possible defence based on commercial reasonability. Other practices may have the potential to exclude competitors of the dominant undertaking, but may produce some benefits for consumers. This latter set will be subjected to more intensive scrutiny – in a manner similar to Article 101's 'by effect' analysis.

Rebates are also paradigmatic of practices which may have an exclusionary effect, but may have countervailing benefits. *Post-Danmark III* indicates that in considering the effects which the given practice has, the assessor is to take into account 'all the circumstances of the case, in particular, the criteria and rules governing the grant of the rebates, the extent of the dominant position of the undertaking concerned and the particular conditions of competition prevailing on the relevant market'.[173] In *Intel*, the Court added a price–cost test into the considerations which a competition authority or other assessor must take into account when evaluating a rebate. In particular, the relevant authority must assess whether or not the rebate is capable of excluding an AEC before the balancing any of pro- or anticompetitive effects.[174] The use of the AEC test will add some clarity to the process which evaluates legality of the rebate arrangement. Indeed, it may be suggested that as an undertaking is aware of its own cost structure, this stage of the evaluation can be done on an ex ante basis. However, notwithstanding the clarity that can be obtained through the AEC test, the case-law (particularly as crystallised in *Post-Danmark III*) permits an extensive range of commercial and economic factors to be taken into account in evaluating the effects of the practice. This provides little in the way of useful ex ante certainty and guidance for undertakings and their advisors.

IV. Conclusion

It can be rightly said that the MEA in European competition law is marked by the following features. First, it is almost entirely Commission driven, albeit as a response to judicial perception of inadequacies of the prior approach. But to the extent that it is Commission driven, this approach can lead to a divergence in analytic approaches between the Commission and the European Courts.

---

[172] Pablo Ibáñez Colomo, 'Beyond the "More Economics-Based Approach": A Legal Perspective on Article 102 TFEU Case Law' (2016) 53 *Common Market Law Review* 709.

[173] *Post Danmark III* (n 169) para 50.

[174] Case C-413/14 P *Intel Corp v European Commission*, ECLI:EU:C:2017:632, para 140.

From a rule of law perspective, this divergence can be problematic. As the first-line enforcer, the Commission takes decisions regarding the acceptability of a given practice or proposed merger. Although Commission decisions are reviewable by the Courts, when Commission practice diverges from the Court's previous interpretation, this divergence undermines legal certainty by the promulgation of guidance (and possible enforcement action pursuant to such guidance) that does not coincide with decided law. While an appeal to the Courts may resolve any inconsistent or incongruent interpretation, such a process is inherently risky and expensive.[175] (The alternative method of placing a reference before the ECJ is also an unsatisfactory means of ensuring alignment between the Commission's views and the Courts' statement of law. Such a litigation strategy also involves risk and expense and may not result in unequivocal realignment of Commission policy and practice with case-law.)

In addition, the Commission's unilateral reinterpretation of EU competition law in a manner which may not be congruent with precedent (and quite possibly the Treaties) raises rule of law concerns at an institutional level. The Commission's role is prescribed by TEU Article 17(1). For it to go beyond this role and to in effect rewrite aspects of the law through adopting and enforcing a different legal understanding than the Courts is a concern. There are significant rule of law issues presented by such a unilateral reorientation of the values surrounding the competition regime.

As an analytic approach the MEA focuses exclusively on the economic effects of the practices (or arrangements) in question. The form of the arrangement is (for the most part) irrelevant. Two consequences flow from this. The first is that there needs to be some guidance on how these effects are to be measured and evaluated. While the Commission has produced numerous documents providing guidance in this regard, the Commission has not been particularly consistent in its own application of its advice. This is well seen in some Article 102 matters where it uses both a MEA approach and a pre-MEA approach for assessment of some practices. The difficulties of this position are exacerbated when the Court (which is the authoritative interpreter of European law) takes a position that is not absolutely congruent with the Commission's position.

A further consequence of the MEA is that parties to a dispute are required to engage in a significant process of evidence gathering and subsequent analysis, in an effort to determine and explain these effects. This is a time-consuming and expensive process, with results being only as good as the evidence obtained and the analysis performed. It is also a problematic exercise. Given the crux of any dispute will be focused on the effects of the agreement or practice in question, and

---

[175] Anne C Witt, 'Public Policy Goals Under EU Competition Law – Now Is the Time to Set the House in Order' (2012) 8 *European Competition Journal* 443; Bruce Wardhaugh, 'Crisis Cartels: Non-Economic Values, the Public Interest, and Institutional Considerations' (2014) 10 *European Competition Journal* 311.

there will necessarily be an adversarial element to the presentation of cases (with at minimum parties being able to challenge the economic evidence presented by others).[176] The culmination of this process will be that adjudicators may be faced with situations where they are required to decide between the conflicting results of varying data sets and models. In legal systems where inexpert judges are called on to resolve these conflicts,[177] rule of law considerations regarding certainty and predictability become legitimate concerns. This is explored in Chapter 5.

Third, the MEA contains a normative attitude that in competition law only economics matters. But more specifically, and more worryingly, it explicitly adopts a normative principle that nothing other than consumer welfare (as defined by the Commission) matters and it implicitly adopts classical price theory as the sole yardstick by which it conducts economic analysis. From the point of view of economic analysis the advantage of relying exclusively on this approach keeps matters simple: there is only one approach to antitrust analysis; there are no additional complicating factors such as choice of methodology and comparing the results of two different approaches. However, if markets do not mirror the assumptions contained in classical price theory, then this approach starts on the wrong foot.[178] This is further discussed in the next chapter.

Further, and perhaps most significantly, the exclusive focus on consumer welfare, while ignoring other normative considerations, is problematic from a rule of law point of view. The Treaty fabric which underlies the European competition regime reflects not just an ordoliberal approach, but also a recognition that values other than consumer welfare matter. The process of effectively rewriting Treaty-based rules to ignore these values draws this regime away from the rule of law ideal.

---

[176] See Case T-194/13 *United Parcel Service v Commission*, ECLI:EU:T:2017:144, paras 214–22. There the GC annulled the Commission's merger prohibition decision on the basis that UPS was not provided with the Commission's final econometric model, and this deprived UPS of its rights of defence (ie its ability to challenge the Commission's model and its results).

[177] Particularly where such a finding may be considered a finding of fact, against which there may be little room for appeal.

[178] See pp 127–49, below and eg Herbert Hovenkamp, 'Post-Chicago Antitrust: A Review and Critique' [2001] *Columbia Business Law Review* 257.

4

Economics and the Effects-Based Approach

This work has focused on the rule of law considerations relating to certainty, predictability and clarity. These allow rational agents to plan and order their lives. Other rule of law considerations suggest that rational planning also requires consistency between what the law says it does and what it in fact does. Although this goal was not expressed in these terms in the discussion in Chapter 1, it is nevertheless latent in the rule of law characteristics found in the theories discussed there. For instance, when Fuller speaks of congruence between official activity and rule,[1] implicit in his words is that the goal which the law seeks to implement can be achieved through the practices of those who are responsible for implementation.

The effects-based approach in antitrust involves a normative goal, and a methodological tool to aid in the realisation of that goal. The normative goal is that enhancing consumer welfare is the sole objective of the competition regime (and a corollary of which is that nothing else should matter). The methodology of choice is traditional price theory.

Both the normative goal and the assumptions underlying the choice of economic methodology are essential to the effects-based approach. The exclusive use of economic methodology makes sense if and only if consumer welfare is the sole objective of competition policy. If competition policy incorporates non-welfare goals, policy makers and enforcers need methodological tools other than price theory to measure and reconcile welfare and non-welfare goals to determine an appropriate legal response to a particular practice.

The 'flavour' of the economic methodology used in modern antitrust has a Chicago taste to it. A significant part of this taste is some strong assumptions about how markets in fact work, and how people actually operate within the market. If these assumptions are correct (or at least not wildly inaccurate), and if increasing consumer welfare is the sole goal of antitrust policy, then the MEA is well designed to advance this goal. But if antitrust is not a 'consumer welfare prescription' or if the adopted methodology contains incorrect assumptions, then the approach may well be dictating solutions that are inconsistent with the actual operation of markets.

---

[1] Lon Fuller, *The Morality of Law*, rev edn (New Haven, CT, Yale University Press, 1973) 81–91.

The consequences of this are obvious. First, if the goal, as stated by the courts or enforcement agencies, differs from the goal as determined by a legislature or a Treaty (in case of the US and EU, respectively), then a strong case can be made that such a reinterpretation of antitrust's goals raises a rule of law issue. This concerns the appropriate exercise of quasi-legislative authority within a political community. This is an issue in any democratic society which considers itself governed by the rule of law, and which views such rule as containing limits to institutional exercise of power. This problem is addressed in the next chapter.

Second, if the methodology adopted by the MEA fails to realise the ostensible goal of antitrust policy, this raises the rule of law considerations of divergence from the stated goal that were outlined earlier. This is the focus of the present chapter.

The first part of this chapter examines the economic tools adopted by the proponents of the effects-based approach. It initially considers these from within their own assumptions, and secondly from an external viewpoint – that of behavioural economics. This first aim is to show that the strong presumptions contained in the sort of economics which has been used in traditional antitrust analysis fail to accurately capture market behaviour, and generate results that may be incompatible with the stated goals of competition policy.

The second and third parts of the chapter examine the challenge posed by behavioural economics to antitrust policy. The second part outlines some principles of behavioural economics which challenge the traditional view of the rational economic actor. Behavioural economics is now a mainstream subdiscipline: it is increasingly taught as a post-secondary subject, with textbooks being produced to fill market demand. It serves as a part of the basis for 'nudge' theory, which is being increasingly used to formulate public policy and governmental action. But most significantly, the insights presented by behavioural economics pose a significant challenge for the assumptions that underlie the orthodox, effects-based approach to antitrust analysis. If actors in the market place do not possess unbounded rationality and consequently fail to maximise their own welfare, then the effects-based approach may be built on foundations of sand.

The third part of this chapter considers the examples of tying, predatory pricing and market entry. The results obtained by orthodox analysis of each of these activities differ from those generated by behavioural analysis. These different outcomes suggest that the insights of behavioural economics pose a significant challenge for this traditional approach, and indicate that the traditional approach's analysis of business practices may not be accurate in distinguishing practices which are anticompetitive from those which enhance competition.

These three sections set the basis for this chapter's conclusion. It stresses that as a result of the strong assumptions inherent in the traditional view, and the challenges posed by the behavioural approach, there is a significant risk that this traditional approach yields incorrect results. Given that these results are not in concordance with the stated purpose of the legal regime, this presents a rule of law issue.

I. The Economics of the Effects-Based Approach

It is not too controversial to state that the economic approach to antitrust law arose from the Chicago School's approach to law and economics.[2] Chicago's approach and methodology added some critical rigour into not just antitrust law, but also legal scholarship generally, by showing the inconsistencies and difficulties with established legal doctrine. Underlying this methodology is a view that efficiency is the sole normative goal, which is followed by some other strong assumptions. The efficiency which antitrust should pursue is interpreted as consumer welfare. And of Chicago's other assumptions, perhaps the most fundamental is that market solutions are to be preferred over governmental solutions.[3] There are, of course, other assumptions. These include that governmental intervention (which includes judicial rulings) is usually suboptimal as such intervention in the market can perpetuate costly errors;[4] and a related assumption that markets are self-correcting.

To those adhering to these assumptions, it follows from the self-correcting nature of the market that type II errors ('false negatives') are less of a concern than type I errors ('false positives'). Entry will 'compete out' monopoly profits, but will not undo the harm imported by incorrectly denying consumers the benefit of an (efficiency-enhancing) arrangement. In addition to these assumptions regarding the operation of the market, this school makes other strong assumptions about the exercise of monopoly power, in particular that monopolies will innovate to compete (this is a corollary of the proposition that markets are self-correcting), and that there is only one single monopoly profit.

These assumptions pervade US antitrust law and policy, and are also present in EU antitrust thinking. We see Chicago's influence on the Commission's thinking.[5] But Chicago's assumptions are not universal truths. They do not hold in a significant number of cases, which casts doubt on the validity of any general proposition that can be drawn from them. And as these assumptions are shared in EU antitrust thinking, a similar concern extends to EU competition policy.

In what follows, three of the strong assumptions that have shaped antitrust thinking since the 1960s are examined. While they remain 'anchors' of the American approach to analysis, they have to some degree or another influenced European thought. These assumptions are: (i) the self-correcting nature of markets; (ii) in antitrust analysis type II errors are to be preferred over type I errors, as market entry will cancel the former out (this is a corollary of (i)); and, (iii) that

---

[2] See eg Richard Posner, *Economic Analysis of Law* 9th edn (New York, Wouters Kluwer, 2014) 29–31.

[3] See George L Priest, '"The Limits of Antitrust" and the Chicago School Tradition' (2009) 6 *Journal of Competition Law and Economics* 1, 7.

[4] See eg Frank H Easterbrook, 'Limits of Antitrust' (1984) 63 *Texas Law Review* 1; Priest, ibid; and Jonathan B Baker, 'Taking the Error out of "Error Cost" Analysis: What's Wrong with Antitrust's Right' (2015) 80 *Antitrust Law Journal* 1.

[5] See Dzmitry Bartalevich, 'The Influence of the Chicago School on the Commission's Guidelines, Notices and Block Exemption Regulations in EU Competition Policy' (2016) 54 *Journal of Common Market Studies* 267; and Chapter 3, above.

monopolies must continue to innovate in order to compete. But more significantly, this discussion calls into question the extent that these assumptions can be used to uncontroversially guide antitrust law and policy.

A. The Self-Correcting Nature of the Market

This assumption is based on a simple and elegant theoretical model. If a market offering supracompetitive returns exists, then firms will enter to capture this return. This entry will enhance competition on that market, driving the price closer to the price that would exist in a perfectly competitive market. Given sufficient entry, over time, any supracompetitive return will be 'competed away', and prices will return to the marginal cost of production of the good or service in question.

This assumption is evident in the US case-law on predatory pricing. *Matsushita*[6] is an elegant case in point. There, the USSC dismissed allegations of a two-decade-long predatory pricing conspiracy. The Court analysed predatory pricing as a two-stage strategy, the first stage involving price cutting to drive competitors from the market; and the second stage involving supracompetitive pricing to recoup all the losses incurred in the first stage. The USSC, explicitly relying on Chicago School views,[7] remarked that in the second stage 'it is not enough simply to achieve monopoly power, as monopoly pricing may breed quick entry by new competitors eager to share in the excess profits'.[8]

A similar view is reflected in the Commission's thinking on monopolistic practices. In its review of Article 102 policy which it began in 2005, the Commission had an opportunity to rethink its treatment of abuse. In the EAGCP Working Paper of July 2005[9] (which served as the starting point of this reflection) the authors consider two possible responses to monopoly pricing (and the potential for exploitation which arises). This is worth quoting in detail:

> As an illustration of these considerations, consider the problem of monopoly pricing. One response to the problem might be for the competition authority to intervene, citing excessive pricing by a monopolist as an infraction of the abuse-of-dominance prohibition in Article 82 of the Treaty. Another response might be to leave the matter alone, hoping that the profits that the monopolist earns will spur innovation or imitation and entry into the market, so that, eventually, the problem will be solved by competition.
>
> The choice between these two alternative responses to the problem of monopoly pricing involves a choice among competition policy regimes, as well as an intertemporal trade-off. If it was just a question of short-run versus long-run effects, one might be tempted

---

[6] *Matsushita Electric Industrial Co v Zenith Radio Corp*, 475 US 574 (1986).
[7] See the references cited ibid 589–90.
[8] ibid 589.
[9] EAGCP, Economic Advisory Group for Competition Policy (Jordi Gual, Martin Hellwig, Anne Perrot, Michele Polo, Patrik Rey, Klaus Schmidt, Rune Stenbacka), 'An Economic Approach to Article 82: Report by the European Advisory Group on Competition Policy', available at http://ec.europa.eu/dgs/competition/economist/eagcp_july_21_05.pdf.

to put the immediate gain of today's consumers above everything else. However, a policy intervention on such grounds requires the competition authority to actually determine what price it considers appropriate, as well as how it should evolve over time; for this it is not really qualified. Moreover, such a policy intervention drastically reduces, and may even forego the chance to protect consumers in the future by competition rather than policy intervention. A regime in which consumer protection from monopoly abuses is based on competition is greatly to be preferred to one in which consumer protection is due to political or administrative control of prices. In most circumstances therefore, the competition authority ought to refrain from intervening against monopolistic pricing and instead see to it that there is room for competition to open up.[10]

As noted, the framework chosen by this report's authors is explicitly based on a Chicago-influenced approach.[11]

Such thinking was continued in the DG Competition's 2005 Discussion Paper on Article 102 abuses, which served as the basis for a subsequent public consultation. In this Discussion Paper, the Commission recognised:

> If the barriers to expansion faced by rivals and to entry faced by potential rivals are low, the fact that one undertaking has a high market share may not be indicative of dominance. Any attempt by an undertaking to increase prices above the competitive level would attract expansion or new entry by rivals thereby undermining the price increase.[12]

Although this European approach is slightly more tempered than its US counterpart in as much as it recognises a gradient in entry barriers, it still very much drives EU enforcement priorities.

Subsequent to the public consultation, the Commission published its Guidance on Enforcement Priorities in Applying Article 102.[13] This document announces that the Commission will focus its Article 102 enforcement efforts towards exclusionary abuses. Such focus is justified on the grounds that so doing 'ensur[es] that markets function properly and that consumers benefit from the efficiency and productivity which result from effective competition between undertakings'.[14] The assumption here is that the 'proper functioning' of markets entails that competitors are able to enter the market unhindered by artificial entry barriers created by dominant incumbents.

The Commission's approach is more moderate than that taken by its US counterpart; it focuses on exclusionary conduct, in particular whether or not a dominant undertaking impairs effective competition by erecting artificial entry barriers, thereby foreclosing the market to its competitors.[15] The Commission's

---

[10] ibid 10–11.

[11] See above pp 106–07.

[12] DG Competition Discussion Paper on the application of Article 82 of the Treaty to Exclusionary Abuses (Brussels, December 2005) para 34.

[13] Guidance on the Commission's Enforcement Priorities in Applying Article 82 of the EC Treaty to Abusive Exclusionary Conduct by Dominant Undertakings [2009] OJ C45/7.

[14] ibid point 5.

[15] ibid point 19.

approach recognises that there may be barriers to entry (which may be endoge-
nous to the industry or artificially imposed by an incumbent) that may prevent the
competitive process from competing away any supracompetitive returns in these
sorts of markets.[16] While both approaches see market entry as a main means of
ensuring competitive prices within a market, the European view is that entry is not
necessarily as fast or easy as is assumed by US policymakers. Yet both assume that
at some point entry will occur.

But market entry is not as timely or fast as policymakers in either the US or EU
assume.[17] By definition, those active in a cartelised market are receiving a supracompetitive return. If the assumptions underlying the self-correcting nature of
markets were true, we would expect to see rapid entry into cartelised markets as
a response. Instead, we see cartels persisting over numerous years, some lasting
decades. One study which analysed the 110 cartels sanctioned by the EC Commission between 1990 and 2008 found: 'The longest lasting cartel in the dataset is the
Belgium Architect Association which lived 36 years. The average mean duration of
the cartels is 8.08 years where the median life is 6 and standard deviation is 6.32.'[18]

This data set has three limitations – all of which strengthen our criticism. First,
the duration of the cartel is only the duration which the Commission was able
to prove. In many cases the cartel was suspected of operating for a longer period
(some as much as two and a half times the proven duration).[19] Second, this data
set only captures cartels which the Commission sanctioned. There is a second
set of cartels which would not have been sanctioned by the Commission, either
because they failed the jurisdictional requirements for a European investigation
(and hence were left to Member States) or were not an enforcement priority for the
Commission. Third, these are only discovered cartels. Once can safely assume that
other cartels remained unnoticed.

These figures are confirmed by other studies. Levenstein and Suslow's work is
illuminating.[20] They show that numerous cartels have lasted for several decades,
that although industrial concentration enhances cartel stability, cartelisation will
occur even in unconcentrated industries, and the mean duration of cartels was five
to six years.[21] Again, these are detected cartels.

This evidence from cartels is significant. It shows that notwithstanding this
belief in an invisible, correcting 'hand' in the marketplace, entry does not occur
as predicted or expected. Rather these anticompetitive practices persist, allowing
their perpetuators an opportunity to reap supracompetitive returns over a lengthy

[16] ibid point 16.
[17] See Baker's findings (n 4) 11–12.
[18] Oindrila De, 'Analysis of Cartel Duration: Evidence from EC Prosecuted Cartels' (2010) 17 *International Journal of the Economics of Business* 33, 44.
[19] ibid 45.
[20] Margaret C Levenstein and Valerie Y Suslow, 'What Determines Cartel Success?' (2006) 44 *Journal of Economic Literature* 43.
[21] ibid 44.

period. If anything, this body of evidence casts doubt on one of the fundamental assumptions of the economic approach to antitrust policy, at least in its more extreme versions.

B. Preference for Type II Errors Over Type I Errors

A corollary of the self-correcting market hypothesis is that in drawing conclusions about antitrust matters, type II errors (false negatives) are to be preferred over type I errors (false positives). There are three reasons for this. First, if the assumption that markets are self-correcting is correct, the harm resulting from anticompetitive practices mistakenly rendered legal as a result of type II errors will be 'competed out' through the invisible correcting hand of the market, described above. The second reason is that if a type I error renders a beneficial practice illegal, consumers (ie society) will be deprived of the gains which that practice could have delivered. Third, the possibility of enforcement authorities (particularly courts) making type I errors leaves the door open for meritless litigation, designed to attack a competitor rather than promote consumer welfare.

While the antitrust regimes of both the US and EU are reticent about admitting type I errors through their policies and rules, there is a difference of degree in this reticence. The European position is slightly more tolerant of this sort of errors than the American regime. The likely reason for this relates to the relationship between attitudes towards accepting market intervention (via government or its agencies) and acceptance of type I errors. This in turn relates to the strength of belief in the self-correcting nature of the market: if one is sceptical about the efficacy of intervention (and at least implicitly has faith in a self-correcting market), then one is less tolerant of type I errors.

In the United States, a preference for type I errors is apparent in the USSC's consideration of section 2 of the Sherman Act in *Verizon*,[22] which – in turn – relied on its earlier thinking. *Verizon* concerned an incumbent telecoms operator's antitrust obligation to supply a competitor access to the local loop. Although this case was discussed earlier, the Court makes several significant points that merit repetition.

First, the Court sees that reaping the rewards of a monopoly, and in particular the supracompetitive prices a monopolist can charge, is to be considered a reward for the 'business acumen' which created the monopoly.[23] To compel a firm to involuntarily deal and hence share its product would not only reduce the incentives which monopoly profits provide, but would also require the courts to make

---

[22] *Verizon Communications Inc v Law Offices of Curtis V Trinko LLP*, 540 US 398 (2004).

[23] ibid 407: 'The opportunity to charge monopoly prices – at least for a short period – is what attracts "business acumen" in the first place; it induces risk taking that produces innovation and economic growth. To safeguard the incentive to innovate, the possession of monopoly power will not be found unlawful unless it is accompanied by an element of anticompetitive *conduct*.'

decisions as with whom to deal and at what price the good (or service) is to be sold. Somewhat hyperbolically the Court views this as a central planning exercise and a gateway to collusion, and suggests that in general terms the law expressed in *Colgate*[24] that there is no antitrust obligation which compels a trader to deal with another party is generally correct. The USSC recognises that *Colgate* was somewhat limited by *Aspen Skiing*,[25] and that in some very limited cases, there may be a very limited duty to deal. However, the Court notes: 'We have been very cautious in recognizing such exceptions, because of the uncertain virtue of forced sharing and the difficulty of identifying and remedying anticompetitive conduct by a single firm.'[26]

But *Verizon* was not a simple antitrust claim; it also concerned that firm's regulatory obligations under the Telecommunications Act 1996: this additional layer of statutory complexity further deterred the USSC from intervening. Here the desire to avoid type I errors is explicit. In this context, the Court opines:

> Against the slight benefits of antitrust intervention here, we must weigh a realistic assessment of its costs. Under the best of circumstances, applying the requirements of § 2 'can be difficult' because 'the means of illicit exclusion, like the means of legitimate competition, are myriad.' ... Mistaken inferences and the resulting false condemnations 'are especially costly, because they chill the very conduct the antitrust laws are designed to protect.' ... The cost of false positives counsels against an undue expansion of § 2 liability. One false-positive risk is that an incumbent LEC's [local exchange carrier, ie owner of the local loop] failure to provide a service with sufficient alacrity might have nothing to do with exclusion.[27]

Verizon is almost a Platonic paradigm of a desire to avoid type I errors.

This desire takes two forms. First, more broadly, the *Colgate* doctrine (that a firm is under no obligation to deal) is itself a concretisation of the reluctance to make type I errors. It draws a bright line in favour of freedom not to trade. This bright line eliminates the possibility of type I errors (which would require the firm to deal with a competitor when such dealing would not advance the welfare goal), but recognises that type II errors (here, not requiring dealing when dealing would enhance the goal) may occur.[28] Second, there the Court expresses unwillingness to make mistakes which might chill 'the very conduct the antitrust laws are designed to protect' (in the words of *Matsushita*). The assumption is simply: if the Court is to make a mistake, it is to make a mistake in favour of avoiding type I errors.

In the EU, there is a similar, albeit more tempered, desire to avoid such errors. For instance, in the Commission's Guidance Paper on Enforcement Priorities, it

---

[24] *United States v Colgate and Co*, 250 US 300, 307 (1919), see below p 194, n 48.

[25] *Aspen Skiing Co v Aspen Highlands Skiing Corp*, 472 US 585 (1985), discussed above p 67.

[26] *Verizon* (n 22) 408.

[27] ibid 414; references to *United States v Microsoft Corp*, 253 F 3d 34, 58 (CADC 2001); and *Matsushita* (n 6) 594, respectively, omitted.

[28] See Alan Devlin and Michael Jacobs, 'Antitrust Error' (2010) 52 *William and Mary Law Review* 75, 116.

notes that it will take care in the imposition of a duty to supply, as a broad obligation to supply will undercut the incentives to invest.[29] This point echoes the remarks which Advocate General Jacobs makes in his Opinion in *Bronner*:

> Secondly, the justification in terms of competition policy for interfering with a dominant undertaking's freedom to contract often requires a careful balancing of conflicting considerations. In the long term it is generally pro-competitive and in the interest of consumers to allow a company to retain for its own use facilities which it has developed for the purpose of its business. For example, if access to a production, purchasing or distribution facility were allowed too easily there would be no incentive for a competitor to develop competing facilities. Thus while competition was increased in the short term it would be reduced in the long term. Moreover, the incentive for a dominant undertaking to invest in efficient facilities would be reduced if its competitors were, upon request, able to share the benefits. Thus the mere fact that by retaining a facility for its own use a dominant undertaking retains an advantage over a competitor cannot justify requiring access to it.[30]

Yet notwithstanding the expressed reluctance in imposing such a duty, EU authorities and Courts will do so when appropriate conditions (which are beyond the scope of this section to describe) are met. Nevertheless, there is an aversion to type I errors by European authorities.

The primary concern driving avoidance of type I errors is to ensure that consumers are not harmed through incorrectly prohibiting practices that in fact promote consumer welfare. This view has been described by the USSC as 'chill[ing] the very conduct the antitrust laws are designed to protect'.[31] Easterbrook makes this point:

> If the court errs by condemning a beneficial practice, the benefits may be lost for good. Any other firm that uses the condemned practice faces sanctions in the name of stare decisis, no matter the benefits. If the court errs by permitting a deleterious practice, though, the welfare loss decreases over time. Monopoly is self-destructive. Monopoly prices eventually attract entry. True, this long run may be a long time coming, with loss to society in the interim. The central purpose of antitrust is to speed up the arrival of the long run.[32]

While this may be a real concern, it is likely overblown.

The suggestion that it is a permanent loss of the entire benefit is wrong. Employment of a practice is binary: either the practice is used or it is not. But the alternative to not using a given practice (because its use has been erroneously prohibited) is to use a second-best practice. Thus the loss from type I errors is

---

[29] Guidance (n 13) point 75:

The existence of such an obligation – even for a fair remuneration – may undermine undertakings' incentives to invest and innovate and, thereby, possibly harm consumers. The knowledge that they may have a duty to supply against their will may lead dominant undertakings – or undertakings who anticipate that they may become dominant – not to invest, or to invest less, in the activity in question.

[30] Case C-7/97 *Oscar Bronner GmbH and Co KG v Mediaprint Zeitungs- und Zeitschriftenverlag GmbH and Co KG and Others*, ECLI:EU:C:1998:264, Opinion of AG Jacobs, para 57.

[31] *Matsushita* (n 6) 594.

[32] Easterbrook (n 4) 2.

not the entire loss to consumer welfare which would have been prevented by the employment to the wrongly condemned practice; rather it is loss of the difference in welfare between the condemned practice and the second-best practice.[33]

There are usually second-best practices. In the United States, prior to *Legeen*, although resale price maintenance was condemned by *Dr Miles*, the *Colgate* doctrine could be used to promote this practice. In Europe, though the practice is a hard-core restraint, a manufacturer can turn to other means of distribution (eg agency) to circumvent this rule to some degree.

The loss is also in no meaningful sense 'permanent'. While there may be some welfare loss occasioned by the use of second-best practices which may never be recaptured, it is somewhat hyperbolic to assume that this stream of losses continues infinitely. When type I errors are made, there are frequent legal responses to distinguish (or overrule) the erroneous precedent or principle. US antitrust law is replete with such cases.[34] In resale price maintenance cases, *Colgate* limited *Dr Miles* (which was overruled by *Leegin*), *Socony Oil* limited *Appalachian Coal*, and the *White Motor–Schwinn–Continental TV* saga did the same with vertical restraints. But this is not a feature exclusive to antitrust law; the history of the common law shows rules and precedents being distinguished to the point of irrelevance. And of course, objective discussion of consumer welfare losses resulting from type I errors must also consider consumer welfare losses from the type II errors that this approach is more willing to embrace.

Similarly the claim that type I errors are more productive of meritless lawsuits is odd. Easterbrook makes this claim.[35] It appears to be an US response. It is implicit in Chief Justice Robert's conclusion in *linkLine*,[36] in which a price squeezing claim was dismissed. The Chief Justice remarked: 'Plaintiffs' price-squeeze claim, looking to the relation between retail and wholesale prices, is thus nothing more than an amalgamation of a meritless claim at the retail level and a meritless claim at the wholesale level.'[37] It is significant to note that the plaintiff's theory of harm (that the margin between a dominant firm's wholesale and retail prices does not allow for a competitor to make a return) has been accepted in Europe.[38]

This claim is bizarre. All legal rules and processes are capable of being misused by parties who, for whatever reason – vexatious or otherwise – decide to invoke them for a purpose for which they were not designed. Casual empiricism shows

---

[33] See Devlin and Jacobs (n 28) 98.
[34] See also Baker (n 4) 23–25.
[35] Easterbrook (n 4) 33–39.
[36] *Pacific Bell Telephone Co v linkLine Communications Inc*, 555 US 438 (2009).
[37] ibid 452 (2009).
[38] Case T-271/03 *Deutsche Telekom v Commission*, ECLI:EU:T:2008:101, para 237:

> If the applicant's retail prices are lower than its wholesale charges, or if the spread between the applicant's wholesale and retail charges is insufficient to enable an equally efficient operator to cover its product-specific costs of supplying retail access services, a potential competitor who is just as efficient as the applicant would not be able to enter the retail access services market without suffering losses.

The CFI was affirmed by ECJ on this point: Case C-280/08 P *Deutsche Telekom AG v Commission*, ECLI:EU:C:2010:603, para 255.

this occurring in many areas of the law. Intellectual property (IP) and personal injury litigation come rapidly to mind. However, judges are able to distinguish meritorious from meritless lawsuits in these cases. Antitrust is not an exception.

C. Monopolies Must Innovate and Compete

This is a US position, found most prominently in the USSC's opinion in *Verizon*. In it, Justice Scalia remarks:

> The mere possession of monopoly power, and the concomitant charging of monopoly prices, is not only not unlawful; it is an important element of the free-market system. The opportunity to charge monopoly price – at least for a short period – is what attracts 'business acumen' in the first place; it induces risk taking that produces innovation and economic growth. To safeguard the incentive to innovate, the possession of monopoly power will not be found unlawful unless it is accompanied by an element of anticompetitive conduct.[39]

This point is noteworthy for several reasons. It accurately restates the position that a monopoly position is not in itself a contravention of the antitrust laws. Rather it is the monopoly position plus some anticompetitive conduct which serves as the basis of an antitrust violation. Also, the Court regards acquiring a monopoly position as a reward for risk and innovation. This reward will take the form of *short-term* monopoly profits.

Implicit in this quote is the idea of self-correcting markets. Oligopolies and monopolies reflect innovation and efficiencies. Market entry will occur by other efficient firms or firms which can bring other, innovative products to the market.[40] To prevent such entry, the monopolist must further innovate in the more efficient production of better (more innovative) products.

This argument contains a number of assumptions. The first surrounds the temporal horizon of 'short'. If the innovation is protected by a patent or some other IP right, 'short' is as long as either the right lasts or until a substitute can be put onto the market. This period allows for supracompetitive pricing, the acquisition of producer surplus and an increase in deadweight loss. Further, there is evidence that rather than investing the return on innovation, monopolists chose to spend the return to enhance the efficiencies of their production processes. While this may lower the price of the monopolised good, there is a net increase in deadweight loss, due to the increase in output.[41] On its own terms (classical price theory) this result undercuts the assumption contained in *Verizon*.

---

[39] *Verizon* (n 22) 407.

[40] See Robert Bork, *The Antitrust Paradox: A Policy at War with Itself*, rev edn (New York, Free Press, 1993) 196.

[41] See Michael Reksulaka, William F Shughart II and Robert D Tollison, 'Innovation and the Opportunity Cost of Monopoly' (2008) 29 *Managerial and Decision Economics* 619, 621: 'As a monopolist becomes more efficient, deadweight social welfare losses loom larger because the output that would have been produced under competitive market conditions increases proportionately more than the monopolist's output does.'

Finally, the idea that an equally as efficient competitor can (and is willing) to enter the market is itself suspect in many cases. A monopolist possesses an advantage of economies of scale that are unavailable to potential competitors. In addition to these cost advantages, if the monopolist is a legacy of a previous regulated industry (as was the case in *Verizon*), it will have had years to develop distribution networks and other barriers which establish challenges for entrants to overcome. This point is recognised by Europeans, who – given the ordoliberal thinking[42] which shaped their antitrust policy – have a different attitude towards monopolies.

D. Chicago School Economics and Antitrust Analysis

The previous section has briefly shown a few of the strong assumptions which underlie the Chicago approach to antitrust analysis. Based upon classical price theory, this methodology is the foundation on which the effects-based approach is built. There is no doubt that this methodology is a powerful and elegant tool with which to analyse competition problems. But the utility of any tool depends on some assumptions, in particular the purpose for which it was designed, and the purpose for which it is used. Although it might be an extreme analogy, a bone saw is useful in orthopaedic surgery, but should not be used to remove cataracts.

However the power and elegance of traditional antitrust economics may be misplaced if it does not describe the reality of the markets 'out there'. The above discussion shows that there is good reason to believe that the assumptions contained in this methodology are simply not reflective of the realities of the market. The tool might be powerful, but it may well be the wrong tool for such analysis.

Further doubts as to whether or not this classical price theoretical model is an appropriate tool can be raised by comparing it to the methodology developed by behavioural economists. This, perhaps more empirical, approach suggests that agents in the marketplace do not always act in the manner predicted by the a priori approach of this classical model. The next section of this chapter investigates this behavioural challenge.

II. The Challenge of Behavioural Economics

Behavioural economics is an empirically driven methodological approach which uses data from the social sciences (primarily psychology and sociology) to examine how people in fact act and interact in a market environment. In recent decades,

---

[42] See Guidance (n 13) points 16–17, and Case C-23/14 *Post Danmark A/S v Konkurrencerådet*, ECLI:EU:C:2015:651, paras 60–62 in which the ECJ notes that with high entry barriers in a market with a (former statutory) monopolist it may be inappropriate to use the 'as efficient competitor' as the comparator for the assessment of antitrust harm.

the insights of behavioural economics have become sufficiently published, known and accepted to become mainstream. Its insights have been applied to marketing, finance, governmental policy design and implementation, health care, and antitrust[43] – to name merely a few areas of application.

The main insight of behavioural economics runs counter to a fundamental tenet of neoclassical economics. Neoclassical economics relies on the axiom that economic agents are unbounded rational maximisers, ie economic agents select the best of those options available to the agent at a given time. In addition, the agent has the abilities to so do. In 1955, Simon described this agent in the following terms:

> Traditional economic theory postulates an 'economic man,' who, in the course of being 'economic' is also 'rational.' This man is assumed to have knowledge of the relevant aspects of his environment which, if not absolutely complete, is at least impressively clear and voluminous. He is assumed also to have a well-organized and stable system of preferences, and a skill in computation that enables him to calculate, for the alternative courses of action that are available to him, which of these will permit him to reach the highest attainable point on his preference scale.[44]

This rationality assumption permeates contemporary antitrust analysis.

For instance, the decisions in *Matsushita* and *Brook Group*[45] indicate that most lawsuits alleging predatory pricing should be rejected, on the grounds that recoupment (a necessary element to the practice) is economically irrational, as it requires the predator to forgo an immediate, undiscounted, loss of profit in the anticipation of recovering a greater (but time-discounted) return in the future, when entry to the market may be fairly easy. Similarly, in *Leegin*[46] the majority of the USSC determined that although resale price maintenance has a tendency to raise prices, the fact that rational manufacturers adopted the practice demonstrates that the practice otherwise stimulates demand (via, for example, enhanced presale service) to make up for revenue which would otherwise be lost.[47] Given this use by profit-maximising market agents, the majority of the Court used this as part of their justification that there must be procompetitive justifications for this practice, and consequently overturned a 96-year-old precedent which deemed the practice to be per se illegal.

---

[43] See Amanda P Reeves and Maurice E Stucke, 'Behavioral Antitrust' (2011) 86 *Indiana Law Journal* 1527, 1528–31; on the use of behavioural economics to implement policy, see Richard H Thaler and Cass R Sunstein, *Nudge: Improving Decisions about Health, Wealth, and Happiness* (New Haven, CT, Yale University Press, 2008); on the use of behavioural economics in antitrust, see eg Aviahalom Tor, 'Understanding Behavioral Antitrust' (2014) 92 *Texas Law Review* 573. Texts on behavioural economics include Nick Wilkinson and Matthias Klaes, *An Introduction to Behavioral Economics*, 3rd edn (London, Palgrave, 2018) and Eyal Zamir and Doron Teichman, *Behavioral Law and Economics* (Oxford, Oxford University Press, 2018).

[44] Herbert A Simon, 'A Behavioral Model of Rational Choice' (1955) 66 *Quarterly Journal of Economics* 99, 99.

[45] *Brooke Group Ltd v Brown and Williamson Tobacco Corp*, 509 US 209 (1993).

[46] *Leegin Creative Leather Products Inc v PSKS Inc*, 551 US 877 (2007).

[47] ibid 895–96; see also Tor (n 43) 585–87.

This very strong assumption of unbounded rationality is undermined by some of the empirical results produced by behavioural research. This research shows that economic agents (ie humans) do not possess the ability to identify and assess all options open to them, and the further ability to rationally calculate or assess the utilities of these options before deciding on a course of action. Rather, people use shortcuts (heuristics) to make these decisions, which are likely to be influenced by biases and predispositions which we hold. These heuristics and biases affect not just the demand side of the market (though their effects may be most vivid on that side, as we can readily see them), but also the supply side. A firm acts through its employees/agents, who are also susceptible to these limitations of rationality.

The next part of the chapter discusses the challenge that behavioural economics poses to the traditional approach to economic analysis in antitrust matters. This approach stems from the empirical evidence that suggests economic agents act with bounded rationality. As a result of the constrained rationality some of the conclusions of the traditional approach regarding antitrust problems may not hold true. This of course poses significant problems: if the chosen methodological approach underlying a particular legal justification for a choice of rule does not accurately describe or represent the conditions in which that rule is to operate, this raises rule of law questions. In particular, by being designed with inaccurate (or even false) assumptions of its subjects, the legal rule may be demanding the impossible.

In exploring this challenge of behavioural economics, this part considers some of the biases and heuristics which this branch of scholarship has identified, showing how these constraints undermine claims that economic agents operate with unbounded rationality. It further discusses the implications posed by this bounded rationality for three significant areas of concern to the antitrust lawyer and policymaker: predatory pricing, tying and market entry. This part demonstrates that the empirical results presented by behavioural economics weaken (or perhaps even falsify) some of the traditional conclusions in these areas. The chapter concludes with a few remarks about the implications of behavioural economics for antitrust generally. In particular, and somewhat paradoxically, its existence and results do not make the antitrust community's life easier.

A. Biases, Heuristics and Bounded Rationality

Human beings are not the rational economic agents described by Simon above. In recognising this, later he described human faculties and approach to reasoning as 'bounded rationality'.[48] People simply do not have the abilities to assess the expected utilities of a large set of outcomes (particularly in the relatively short

---

[48] Herbert A Simon, 'Behavioral Economics' in John Eatwell, Murray Milgate and Peter Newman (eds), *The New Palgrave Dictionary of Economics* (New York, Stockton Press, 1987) 222.

amount of time in which they are called upon to make some decisions). Rather humans use heuristics, ie 'short cuts' or 'rules of thumb', to guide analysis. The use of heuristics is often quite reasonable: it can often be rational to use rules of thumb that result in people making a good (eg 'utility-maximising') decision without engaging in an elaborate process of reasoning. However, rules of thumb are just that – rough and ready guides to facilitate decision-making. They provide neither the certainty of a deductive inference nor the inductive confidence of strong statistical reasoning. The use of these heuristics can, and often will, lead people astray.

Further, unlike the idealised unboundedly rational economic agent, humans do not begin our deliberative process with a blank slate. People typically start their reasoning from a given perspective, which has an effect on the outcome of the process, ie the conclusions drawn (and the actions consequent on these conclusions). These starting points, or biases, can result in choices which – from the perspective of utility maximization – are irrational. There is an extensive literature on biases and heuristics in decision-making,[49] and the area is the foundation on which much of behavioural economics is built.

This part of the chapter considers several of these short cuts. The emphasis is on those which undermine the assumptions that underlie the conventional economic analysis of rational behaviour in the marketplace, in particular the practices of predatory pricing and tying; and the implications these short-cuts to reasoning have for understanding traditional assumptions regarding entry barriers. The latter point is significant, as it underpins much of the analysis of theories of harm in dominance cases and drives a significant amount of antitrust enforcement, particularly in the EU.

B. Five Sets of Biases Affecting Market Behaviour

Biases are cognitive processes (often starting points for reasoning) which, when viewed from the perspective of the rational agent, induce systematic error into the reasoning process of deliberative agents. The earliest studies identified three such biases: representiveness, availability, and adjustment and anchoring.[50] However, recent work has shown the existence of many more.

i. Overconfidence

A key set of biases which undermines the neoclassical axiom of rationality is those surrounding *overconfidence*. People's overestimation of their abilities is a well-known and all-too-frequent phenomenon. The literature is replete with studies

---

[49] The seminal paper in this area is Amos Tversky and Daniel Kahneman, 'Judgment under Uncertainty: Heuristics and Biases' (1974) 185 (NS) *Science* 1124.
[50] ibid.

demonstrating the existence of bias.[51] Overconfidence manifests itself in the form of overestimation, overplacement and overprecision.[52]

Overestimation, as a bias, is the overestimation of 'one's actual ability, performance, level of control or chance of success'.[53] We see instances of this very frequently.[54] When asked, far more than 50 percent of the driving population view themselves as above-average drivers,[55] athletes overestimate their abilities,[56] and people frequently underestimate the time that it will take them to complete given tasks.[57]

ii. Optimism

Related to overconfidence and the set of related biases is *optimism*. This is the well-known trait which causes humans to underestimate, inter alia, costs, adverse effects, risk and time to completion of projects, while overestimating the benefits of projects. This bias is sufficiently endemic in planning processes that the *Green Book*, published by the UK Treasury in order to provide guidance 'to help officials develop transparent, objective, evidence-based appraisal and evaluation of proposals to inform decision making'[58] specifically cautions decision-makers about this bias. It also contains an Appendix[59] to provide direction to planners

---

[51] For a short list of such studies, see eg Wilkinson and Klaes (n 43) 128–31.

[52] ibid 118–19.

[53] ibid 118.

[54] Notably David Cameron, when asked why he wanted to be Prime Minister, is reputed to have said: 'Because I think I'd be rather good at it.' Dominic Sandbrook 'How Will History Treat David Cameron?' *New Statesman* (29 August 2016) available at: https://www.newstatesman.com/politics/uk/2016/08/how-will-history-treat-david-cameron. And, of course, Donald Trump's boasts about his intellectual abilities are well known: see eg Avi Selk, 'Trump Says He's a Genius. A Study Found these Other Presidents Actually Were' *Washington Post* (7 January 2018) available at: https://www.washingtonpost.com/news/retropolis/wp/2018/01/07/trump-says-hes-a-genius-a-study-found-these-other-presidents-actually-were/?noredirect=on&utm_term=.49cd94918971.

[55] Ola Svenson, 'Are We All Less Risky and More Skilful than Our Fellow Drivers?' (1981) 47 *Acta Psychologica* 143.

[56] A Peter McGraw, Barbra A Mellers and Ilana Ritov, 'The Affective Costs of Overconfidence' (2004) 17 *Journal of Behavioral Decision Making* 281.

[57] Roger Buehler, Dale Griffin and Michael Ross, 'Exploring the "Planning Fallacy": Why People Underestimate their Task Completion Times' (1994) 67 *Journal of Personality and Social Psychology* 366; and Roger Buehler, Dale Griffin and Michael Ross, 'Inside the Planning Fallacy: The Causes and Consequences of Optimistic Time Predictions' in Thomas Gilovich, Dale Griffin and Daniel Kahneman (eds), *Heuristics and Biases: The Psychology of Intuitive Judgment* (Cambridge, Cambridge University Press, 2002) 250.

[58] HM Treasury, *Green Book* (London, HM Treasury, 2018) available at: https://assets.publishing.service.gov.uk/government/uploads/system/uploads/attachment_data/file/685903/The_Green_Book.pdf. See para 5.43: 'Optimism bias is the demonstrated systematic tendency for appraisers to be over-optimistic about key project parameters, including capital costs, operating costs, project duration and benefits delivery. Over-optimistic estimates can lock in undeliverable targets.'

[59] HM Treasury, *Supplementary Green Book Guidance: Optimism Bias*, available at https://assets.publishing.service.gov.uk/government/uploads/system/uploads/attachment_data/file/191507/Optimism_bias.pdf.

and decision-makers in order to mitigate this phenomenon. The *Green Book's* authors note:

> There is a demonstrated, systematic, tendency for project appraisers to be overly opti-mistic. To redress this tendency appraisers should make explicit, empirically based adjustments to the estimates of a project's costs, benefits, and duration.[60]

This bias affects not just estimations in project planning, but affects decision-making in matters such as health (particularly in regard to adverse consequences of risk[61]), views towards the pleasure we will obtain from an upcoming holiday, and expectations regarding a career and salary.[62] In short: 'The optimism bias is defined as the difference between a person's expectation and the outcome that follows. If expectations are better than reality, the bias is optimistic; if reality is better than expected, the bias is pessimistic.'[63] This bias is pervasive, by some esti-mates occurring in 80 per cent of the population, and appears across race, gender and national bounds.[64]

In a commercial context, optimism bias is seen in behaviour that would otherwise be described in strictly rational terms as risk-seeking. Such a bias can manifest itself in the form of acting on a risky strategy such as pursuing a practice which objectively has a negative net present value, on the (optimistic) grounds that the negative conse-quences are unlikely (or less likely than the objective data suggest). As seen below, there is a behavioural explanation of predatory pricing explaining the second (ie recoup-ment) stage as a form of risk-seeking behaviour, resulting from decisions shaped by this bias. In effect, those engaging in the practice are overoptimistic about their chances of recouping the losses incurred in the first (ie predation) stage.

iii. Desirability

This is a bias related to overconfidence and optimism. The *desirability bias* is 'the overestimation of the probability of desirable future events'.[65] This phenomenon has been well studied in the psychological community, and robust results show that it is a cross-cultural phenomenon.[66] More tellingly, these results show that professionals working in their area of expertise are susceptible to this bias.[67] And quite early results show that both the degree of ambiguity in which the agent finds him- or herself and the importance of the situation's outcome to the agent correlates positively with a

---

[60] ibid para 1.1.
[61] Nathan Radcliffe and William Klein, 'Dispositional, Unrealistic, and Comparative Optimism: Differential Relations with the Knowledge and Processing of Risk Information and Beliefs about Personal Risk' (2002) 28 *Personality and Social Psychology Bulletin* 836.
[62] Tali Sharot, 'The Optimism Bias' (2011) 21 *Current Biology* R941.
[63] ibid.
[64] ibid R942.
[65] Robert Olsen, 'Desirability Bias among Professional Investment Managers: Some Evidence from Experts' (1997) 10 *Journal of Behavioral Decision Making* 65, 66.
[66] See eg ibid and the results cited therein.
[67] ibid.

subjective (positive) weighting of desired outcomes.[68] The desirability bias should not be confused with the social desirability bias. The latter manifests itself in skewed responses that survey participants provide so that the respondents may appear to be 'better' than they believe themselves to be, through their self-reporting of behaviour (exercise and smoking levels, etc) and overreporting perceived 'virtuous' behaviour and similarly under-reporting 'vices'.[69]

iv. Default

To avoid making complex decisions which require additional tasks of enumerating and evaluating all options, humans tend to select that option which is immediately at hand. This tendency is known as the *default* or *status quo bias*. It is a well-known phenomenon.[70] Understanding this phenomenon is significant, as it has important real-world implications. For instance, organ donation rates are significantly higher in jurisdictions with opt-out policies (ie the default is to grant permission for donation) than in opt-in jurisdictions. One study on the default position and organ donation concludes:

> When donation is the default, there is a 16.3% (P < 0.02) increase in donation, increasing the donor rate from 14.1 to 16.4 .... Using similar techniques, but looking only at 1999 for a broader set of European countries, including many more from Eastern Europe, [others] report an increase in the rate from 10.8 to 16.9, a 56.5% increase.[71]

Policy-makers can shift default options to encourage retirement savings,[72] healthy eating[73] and other sorts of choices. However, default choices can be used perniciously to guide the behaviour of those making choices. A default option of opting-in to automatic renewal of contracts or granting access to personal data will have a different result than the alternative opt-out default. This can be seen in consumer contracts ('automatic renewal') and in the EU's General Data Protection Regulation[74] which requires active consent to the collection of most data. This

---

[68] Douglas McGregor, 'The Major Determinants of the Prediction of Social Events' (1938) 33 *Journal of Abnormal and Social Psychology* 179, 192–93.

[69] Pamela Grimm, 'Social Desirability Bias' in Jagdish N Sheth and Naresh K Malhotra (eds), *Wiley International Encyclopedia of Marketing* (Hoboken, NJ, John Wiley, 2011).

[70] William Samuelson and Richard Zeckhauser, 'Status Quo Bias in Decision Making', (1988) 1 *Journal of Risk and Uncertainty* 7; Brigitte Madrian and Dennis Shea, 'The Power of Suggestion: Inertia in 401(K) Participation and Savings Behavior' (2001) 116 *Quarterly Journal of Economics* 1149; Eric J Johnson and Daniel Goldstein, 'Do Defaults Save Lives?' (2003) 302 *Science* 1338.

[71] Johnson and Goldstein, ibid 1339, citing Ronald W Gimbel, Martin A Strosberg, Susan E. Lehrman, Eugenijus Gefenas and Frank Taft, 'Presumed Consent and Other Predictors of Cadaveric Organ Donation in Europe' (2003) 13 *Progress in Transplantation* 17.

[72] See Madrian and Shea (n 70).

[73] Muireann Quigley, 'Nudging for Health: On Public Policy and Designing Choice Architecture' (2013) 21 *Medical Law Review* 588.

[74] Regulation (EU) 2016/679 of the European Parliament and of the Council of 27 April 2016 on the protection of natural persons with regard to the processing of personal data and on the free movement of such data, and repealing Directive 95/46/EC (General Data Protection Regulation) [2016] OJ L119/1.

mandates a collection strategy which precludes the use of passive, opt-out default options.[75] These results show that the default position matters insofar as this starting point has significant consequences for any action which follows.

v. Sunk Cost Fallacy

From a normative perspective, a rational decision-maker should not take into account past expenditures which cannot be recovered ('sunk costs') in determining a future course of action. The *sunk cost fallacy* (or *effect*) is the tendency of an agent to continue on a course of action once some expenditure has been made, in effect 'throwing good money after bad'.[76] This is a pervasive (and again well-studied) phenomenon, which is pervasive in individual and group (eg governmental and firm) behaviour. A plausible explanation for this behaviour is provided by Arkes and Blumer, who remark:

> One reason why people may wish to throw good money after bad is that to stop investing would constitute an admission that the prior money was wasted. The admission that one has wasted money would seem to be an aversive event. The admission can be avoided by continuing to act as if the prior spending was sensible, and a good way to foster that belief would be to invest more.[77]

This behaviour is common.[78] Further it seems that some governmental decisions (or more properly, decisions not to cancel projects after significant expenditure) may be driven by this fallacy.

In their important early article on the sunk cost fallacy, Arkes and Blumer quote the comments of two US Senators regarding the possible cancellation of a significant infrastructure project (the Tennessee–Tombigbee Waterway Project). They defended further expenditure in terms which focused on the amount of past expenditures: 'To terminate a project in which $1.1 billion has been invested represents an unconscionable mishandling of taxpayers' dollars.'[79] And: 'Completing Tennessee–Tombigbee is not a waste of taxpayer dollars. Terminating the project at this late stage of development would, however, represent a serious waste of funds already invested.'[80] So rather than treating past expenditures as what they were, unrecoverable sunk costs, they were viewed as an investment, and further expenditure was justified on that basis. Similar behaviour is found in the selling activities of investment fund managers, who express a reluctance to sell securities for a loss.[81]

---

[75] ibid Recital 32.

[76] Hal R Arkes and Catherine Blumer, 'The Psychology of Sunk Cost' (1985) 35 *Organizational Behavior and Human Decision Processes* 124, 124; Corina Haita-Falah, 'Sunk-Cost Fallacy and Cognitive Ability in Individual Decision-Making' (2017) 58 *Journal of Economic Psychology* 44, 44.

[77] Arkes and Blumer ibid 132.

[78] See Wilkinson and Klaes (n 43) 239–40 for a discussion of some of the studies.

[79] Senator Jeremiah Denton quoted in Arkes and Blumer (n 76) 124.

[80] Senator Jim Sasser quoted ibid.

[81] Daniel Kahneman, *Thinking Fast and Slow* (New York, Farrar, Strauss and Giroux, 2011) 344.

As an aside, another term for the sunk cost fallacy is the 'Concorde fallacy', named after the decisions of the UK and French governments to expend ever-increasing sums of money on that project, in spite of its increasingly apparent commercial unviability. The latter term, however, now appears to be used in a restricted way to describe the behaviour of non-human animals[82] with 'sunk cost fallacy' referring to the bias exhibited by humans.

The above is far from an exhaustive enumeration of cognitive biases. Rather, the above have been selected for discussion for illustrative purposes. In addition to biases, people often use heuristics, or 'rules of thumb', in coming to a conclusion over the set of options which may be available to them at a given time. The use of heuristics can be understood in the context of bounded rationality. Humans simply do not have the cognitive captivity to – among other things – enumerate all options, adequately assess all probabilities, or calculate the expected outcomes of possible options or events from which they must choose. As a result people use short cuts to enumerate and assess in rapid fashion. Doing so is efficient: this avoids being in a state of (in)decision paralysis, ie a state of being overwhelmed by the choices, options, probabilities, etc, that the agent might otherwise face. And, on the whole, such rules of thumb work fairly well, most of the time – otherwise people would not use them. But as rules of thumb, they do not have deductive certainty. Working 'fairly well' and 'most of the time' can leave room for error. Accordingly, this chapter next discusses two further heuristics, which can cause the decisional behaviour of economic agents to deviate from the so-called rational behaviour on which neoclassical economics is predicated.

C. Two Heuristics Affecting Market Behaviour

i. Availability

The *availability heuristic* is a rule of thumb that people use to calculate from probabilities or frequency of occurrence how readily particular instances or occurrences come to mind.[83] Tversky and Kahneman illustrate:

> For example, one may assess the risk of heart attack among middle-aged people by recalling such occurrences among one's acquaintances. Similarly, one may evaluate the probability that a given business venture will fail by imagining various difficulties it could encounter. This judgmental heuristic is called availability.[84]

And, they remark, 'It is a common experience that the subjective probability of traffic accidents rises temporarily when one sees a car overturned by the side of the road.'[85]

---

[82] See eg Patrick J Weatherhead, 'Do Savannah Sparrows Commit the Concorde Fallacy?' (1979) 5 *Behavioral Ecology and Sociobiology* 373.
[83] Tversky and Kahneman (n 49) 1127.
[84] ibid.
[85] ibid.

There are a number of considerations, or biases, which enter into the formulation of the search set from which the inferences are made. These include retrievability or ease of recall (the traffic accident example of the last paragraph as an instance), effectiveness of the search set, the imaginability of the search set, and illusory correlation.[86]

The *effectiveness* of the search set concerns how easily a particular set can be enumerated, with a resulting bias to overestimate the occurrence of its members. The classical example is to ask an English speaker if more words begin with 'r' than have 'r' as their third letter. As it is easier to enumerate words which begin with 'r' than words with 'r' as the third letter, the usual answer is to answer that there are more words that begin with 'r'. In fact, the opposite is true: there are about three times more words whose third letter is 'r' than the number of words which begin with 'r'.[87]

Imaginability is the bias of generating a search set not from memory, but using a particular rule, and judging the probability of an event occurring on the basis of the ease of generating that particular instance.[88] The real-world implications are significant. On this Tversky and Kahneman note:

> Imaginability plays an important role in the evaluation of probabilities in real-life situations. The risk involved in an adventurous expedition, for example, is evaluated by imagining contingencies with which the expedition is not equipped to cope. If many such difficulties are vividly portrayed, the expedition can be made to appear exceedingly dangerous, although the ease with which disasters are imagined need not reflect their actual likelihood. Conversely, the risk involved in an undertaking may be grossly underestimated if some possible dangers are either difficult to conceive of, or simply do not come to mind.[89]

While the days of the Victorian explorer are long over, people often engage in risky (whether commercially or physically) behaviour, and thus this observation remains salient.

Illusory correlations occur as a result of human tendency to find a relationship between items or impose order on a set. There is a tendency for this to occur when two events, which are on their own infrequent, coincide.[90] An explanation for this rests in the strength of the association between the two events: experiencing the coincidence of two rarely occurring events would tend to produce a strong association between them, leading to a belief of correlation or even causality.[91]

---

[86] ibid 1127–28.
[87] ibid 1127.
[88] ibid.
[89] ibid 1128.
[90] Scott Plous, *The Psychology of Judgment and Decision Making* (New York, McGraw-Hill, 1993) 164–67.
[91] See Tversky and Kahneman (n 49) 1128.

ii. Representativeness

The *representativeness heuristic* is a rule of thumb that people use to calculate the probability that an object or event belongs to a given class of objects or events based on the extent to which the object resembles members of the class.[92] In general, such rules of thumb 'work' because resemblance often correlates with class membership of the sort in question. However, correlation of this sort is never perfect, and when used in reasoning governed by other biases and heuristics, representativeness will frequently lead people into error.

In particular, biases or misunderstandings regarding base rates, sample sizes and independence of events can lead to erroneous conclusions. Wilkinson and Kleas provide a good illustration of erroneous reasoning regarding the base rate. They suggest the example of Jane, who 'likes aromatherapy, new age music, reads her horoscope regularly and belongs to a spiritualist group'.[93] People would be more likely to state that she is a holistic healer than a school teacher, in spite of the population at large containing more teachers than healers.[94]

Similarly, insensitivity to sample size imposes another form of limitation on the accuracy of the results obtained through the use of this heuristic. People will often believe that the results generated from large and small samples will be equally as robust.[95] Similarly, a lack of understanding of the independence of events can lead to erroneous probabilistic inferences. For instance, people will naïvely believe that a coin toss outcome of H-H-T-T-H is much more likely than an outcome of H-H-H-H-H, when they are equally as likely. Similarly this feeds into the 'hot hand fallacy' and 'gambler's fallacy'. The latter involves the view that a sequence of similar chance events (say, a slot machine not paying out over time) will necessarily mean that the next outcome will be of a different sort (eg the slot machine will soon pay out). The 'hot hand fallacy' is seen, for example, among sports participants and fans, who believe that based on immediate past results, a given player may be 'hot' (eg in being successful with a shot) so it may merit passing the ball to that player (or, focusing one's defence on that player).

The 'hot hand' phenomenon has been studied in basketball, and shown to be a cognitive illusion.[96] While the nature of the 'hot hand phenomenon' in sport may be merely a matter for amusing discussion, 'hot hand' beliefs are pervasive elsewhere, and include beliefs in and about financial markets. The authors of one study remark:

> The hot hand fallacy and the gambler's fallacy are two important behavioral biases in financial markets. People who are affected by these biases misinterpret random

[92] ibid 1127.
[93] Wilkinson and Kleas (n 43) 121.
[94] See also Tversky and Kahneman (n 49) 1124–25.
[95] ibid 1125.
[96] Thomas Gilovich, Robert Vallone and Amos Tversky, 'The Hot Hand in Basketball: On the Misperception of Random Sequences' (1985) 17 *Cognitive Psychology* 295.

sequences. Specifically, when prone to the hot hand fallacy, people misidentify a non-autocorrelated sequence as positively autocorrelated, generating beliefs that a run of a certain realization will continue in the future. In financial markets, for instance, this bias is observable when investors delegate decisions to experts like professional fund managers. Specifically, people mostly buy funds which were successful in the past, believing in the managers' ability to prolong the performance record.[97]

The biases which lead to this latter set of conclusions can be more costly to the average person than a belief in a hot hand or foot of an athlete.

Since human cognitive capacity is limited, people use heuristics as a short cut or quick rule of thumb to allow them to make a decision. Given that heuristics work reasonably well, most of the time, their limited use is justified. For instance, the similarity heuristic is useful since resemblance is a mark of membership in the same set. The difficulty with any truncated process of reasoning is that people can be led astray through a cursory process. While using the resemblance heuristic can allow us to make quick judgements, this short cut is – in many significant ways – reliant on the use of stereotypes to allow its user to draw rapid conclusions. Reasoning using stereotypes can lead people astray, particularly in cases where underlying rules of probabilistic reasoning are poorly understood by those using these short cuts.

Similarly, biases in our cognitive processes will shape our decisions. For instance, people can be overoptimistic and discount (or ignore) adverse future events. Similarly overconfidence in one's ability or chances of success is a well-observed phenomenon. Indeed, as remarked, the latter of these two biases is so pervasive that the UK's Treasury warns project planners and assessors to take them into account when appraising the costs, benefits and duration of a project.

The presence of biases and use of heuristics in the human cognitive process entails that many decisions made by people differ from the decision that an agent who possesses unbounded rationality would make. But classical price theory assumes the existence of agents with unbounded rationality acting in a market, with their resulting decisions being necessarily optimal. Thus people's actual choices, as explained by the behavioural approach will be other than the choices that classical economics would predict. Or, to put it another way, these behavioural studies cast doubt that classical economics' assumption (or axiom) of rationality is universally true.

This has significant implications for a classical economics approach to law, and in particular competition law. The purported advantage of the economic approach to competition law is that it is based on what it perceived to be market

[97] Thomas Stöckl, Jürgen Huber, Michael Kirchler and Florian Lindner, 'Hot Hand and Gambler's Fallacy in Teams: Evidence From Investment Experiments' (2015) 117 *Journal of Economic Behavior and Organization* 327, 327, citing ER Sirri and P Tufano, 'Costly Search and Mutual Fund Flows' (1998) 53 *Journal of Finance* 1589 and BM Barber, T Odean and L Zheng, 'Out of Sight, Out of Mind: The Effects of Expenses on Mutual Fund Flows' (2005) 78 *Journal of Business* 2095.

realities, and not on 'formalistic' principles or distinctions. However, should its 'market realities' turn out to be based on incorrect assumptions of actual behaviour, this advantage is lost. But more problematically, if the approach does not accurately reflect reality, then the legal prescriptions produced using this approach are themselves a concern, for they may be based on faulty presuppositions. This clearly raises rule of law considerations driven by the necessity of legal rules to accord with reality.

In the next section, this point is developed further by considering three problems in competition law where insights from the behavioural approach cast doubt on the accuracy of some of the solutions provided by the neoclassical (or 'more economic') approach. These are tying, predatory pricing and market entry. The latter problem is significant, as a powerful assumption made by the adherents to the more economic approach is that markets will self-correct through market entry. If this assumption is incorrect, then much thinking about type II errors and the (benign) presence of monopolies is misguided. There is an assumption of rationality which underlies the classical analysis of tying and predatory pricing. If this assumption is incorrect (or, at minimum, too strong) then the orthodox approach to these two problems may also be misguided.

III. The Behavioural Challenge to Antitrust

One of the key drivers of divergence between behaviourist analysis and traditional analysis in competition law focuses on the assumption (or axiom) of rationality which governs the actions of market players. This section considers two practices and one antitrust assumption where the differing analyses of the two approaches yield divergent results. These are tying, predatory pricing and market entry. In all three cases, the results of the behavioural approach undermine the predictions of the traditional approach. As the traditional approach has served to shape legal and policy responses to the problems, the behavioural approach also serves to undermine these solutions.

A. Tying

The differences between the two approaches to tying are perhaps most vividly displayed by examining the majority and dissenting opinions of the USSC in *Kodak*.[98] This case concerned allegations by Image Technical and other independent service organisations that Kodak was tying the sale of service for its copying and micrographic machines to the sale of parts for these machines. Its procedural

---

[98] *Eastman Kodak v Image Technical Services*, 504 US 451 (1992).

origins are significant. The complaint was filed with the District Court of Northern California,[99] where on summary judgment the District Judge ruled, inter alia, that Image had failed to provide sufficient evidence that Kodak had sufficient market power in the service and parts markets to establish a tying claim, given their lack of power in the equipment market. The Ninth Circuit Court of Appeal reversed the District Court's judgment.[100]

The factual situation in *Kodak* was somewhat different from the typical tying case. First, the tie – if it existed – was between a manufacturer's original equipment (the tying primary market) and the parts and service for that equipment produced by that manufacturer (the tied aftermarket). Second, there is robust interbrand competition in the primary market (for micrographic and copying machines): the primary market was competitive, and Kodak lacked market power in it.[101] This was different from the usual tying situation, where the monopolist has a dominant position in the primary market and uses that position to leverage its position in the secondary market.

The majority and dissenting opinions of the USSC illustrate two approaches to this problem. We start with the dissenting opinion of the Court, authored by Scalia J. This opinion illustrates the orthodox approach to analysis of a tying problem. It recognises (and appears to accept) the rationale of the Sherman Act's sections 1 and 2 prohibitions against tying. In both cases (ie whether by agreement or by monopolistic imposition), the arrangement allows the perpetuator to extend its position in one market into a second market, through exclusionary behaviour.[102] Yet, in Scalia's mind, this was not the case in *Kodak*.

Adopting Kodak's theory of the case, Scalia first examined the type of alleged tie in question. That tie concerned a manufacturer's power over its distinctive aftermarket parts. This according to him makes no economic sense, as it 'is possessed by every manufacturer of durable goods with distinctive parts'.[103] The subsequent argument in his opinion is an attempt to show this lack of economic sense. His starting point is Kodak's lack of power in the market for machines, ie the primary market. Given the lack of power on this market, Scalia reasons as follows:

> In the absence of interbrand power, a seller's predominant or monopoly share of its single-brand derivative markets does not connote the power to raise derivative market prices *generally* by reducing quantity. As Kodak and its principal amicus, the United States, point out, a rational consumer considering the purchase of Kodak equipment will inevitably factor into his purchasing decision the expected cost of aftermarket support. ... If Kodak set generally supracompetitive prices for either spare parts or repair services without making an offsetting reduction in the price of its machines, rational consumers would simply turn to Kodak's competitors for photocopying and

---

[99] *Image Technical Services Inc et al v Eastman Kodak Co*, 1988 WL 156332 (ND Calif 1988).
[100] *Image Technical Service Inc et al v Eastman Kodak Co*, 903 F 2d 612 (CA9 1990).
[101] *Kodak* (n 98) 466 fn 10.
[102] ibid 487–88.
[103] ibid 489.

micrographic systems. … True, there are – as the Court notes … – the occasional irrational consumers that consider only the hardware cost at the time of purchase (a category that regrettably includes the Federal Government, whose 'purchasing system,' we are told, assigns foremarket purchases and aftermarket purchases to different entities). But we have never before premised the application of antitrust doctrine on the lowest common denominator of consumer.[104]

Justice Scalia's argument is quite simple.

He argues that in arriving at the decision to buy a product such as those in question, a rational consumer will look at their use of the product over the lifecycle of that product, and factor all expected costs into the purchasing decisions. Such costs include not just the initial outlay for the equipment in question, but also service, replacement costs and (presumably, though not mentioned by Scalia) consumables. Should Kodak (or a similarly placed firm) price the goods and services in the aftermarket supracompetitively, customers will notice this in their assessment. As a result, customers would not purchase from a firm which engaged in such supracompetitive aftermarket pricing. The key is robust, interbrand competition in the primary market for machines. The existence of such competition will 'punish'[105] firms who exploit their aftermarket position, as (rational) consumers will avoid dealing with them. Interbrand competition will act as a check on exploitation in tying matters, much as it acts a check in the use of vertical restraints.[106]

While there may be some 'irrational consumers' who fail to take into account aftermarket costs, antitrust law and policy can safely ignore this 'lowest common denominator of consumers'.[107] Apparently this set of individuals can be ignored, without regard to their number or their level of participation in the market (ie consumption). This is of course significant. If there is a non-trivial amount (either in number or by spend) of irrational, 'lowest common denominator' consumers, the opportunities for Kodak (and other firms) to use this practice are significant. Given that US federal government procurement decisions used one office (or set of accounts) to obtain equipment (as a capital expenditure[108]), and another for aftermarket transactions (operating expenses), it is likely the case that the former office will have attempted to minimise its costs, without regard to the budgetary implications for the latter office. And as the government is a large customer of such products, supracompetitive pricing in the aftermarket leaves opportunities for exploiting it (and other customers with similar procurement processes).

Blackum J's majority decision, on the other hand, identifies what might be a flaw in the theory which served as the core of Scalia's reasoning. The flaw involves

---

[104] ibid 495–96, quotations from the amicus brief of the US and references omitted.
[105] ibid 503.
[106] ibid 501.
[107] ibid 495–96.
[108] ibid 475.

the acquisition of the data relevant to lifecycle pricing. Such acquisition is a significant task:

> For the service-market price to affect equipment demand, consumers must inform themselves of the total cost of the 'package' – equipment, service, and parts – at the time of purchase; that is, consumers must engage in accurate lifecycle pricing. Lifecycle pricing of complex, durable equipment is difficult and costly. In order to arrive at an accurate price, a consumer must acquire a substantial amount of raw data and undertake sophisticated analysis. The necessary information would include data on price, quality, and availability of products needed to operate, upgrade, or enhance the initial equipment, as well as service and repair costs, including estimates of breakdown frequency, nature of repairs, price of service and parts, length of 'downtime', and losses incurred from downtime.[109]

Additionally, to determine the best deal in a market characterised by robust inter-brand competition, a customer must obtain the same information about every brand on that market.

The majority discussed this evaluation exercise in terms of a cost (likely reflecting the analytic framework economic framework in which the Court was operating). This is not an inaccurate description of the evaluation: one can envisage the procurement department of a large organisation undertaking such an exercise. Another way of describing this, though, is that the need to acquire and process this information to make an appropriate purchasing decision shows the limits of our cognitive capacity; and thereby undermines the truth of the assumption of unbounded rationality which is posited by traditional analysis.

Yet 'costs' in this sense are only one element to be taken into account in assessing the practice. The behaviourist perspective would suggest that the assessment of lifecycle costs is even more complicated than the majority describes. Biases, such as optimism and overconfidence, will affect this assessment. Those engaged in lifecycle pricing may be susceptible to underestimating their future consumption (and costs), and perhaps be overconfident about their ability to predict this. Further, once a customer makes the decision to purchase a particular brand of machine, other biases may prevent a so-called 'rational' response to aftermarket exploitation. Inertia, a form of the default bias, may simply prevent a customer from attempting to recalculate the costs of continuing to use the existing machines in comparison with other alternatives.

Further, even if the customer recalculates, the sunk cost fallacy may prevent the customer from appropriately 'recosting' a switch. Rather than viewing the difference between the purchase price and the present salvage value of the machine's initial purchase price (if bought; or, if leased, the 'buy-out' costs of the lease) as a sunk cost, there may be a tendency to view it as a form of investment to be maximised by further consumption and 'investment' (in the form of purchase of parts, service and tied consumables).

---

[109] ibid 473 footnotes omitted.

Viewed through the additional lens of behavioural economics, the majority's argument becomes stronger. The acquisition and processing of lifecycle costs provide a challenge to people's cognitive abilities, whether in terms of a 'cost', or as a counterexample to the axiom (or truth of the assumption) of unbounded rationality. Furthermore, even if a potential customer attempts a lifecycle costs assessment, biases may shape the calculation, and hinder the willingness of customers to shift out of what might be an exploitative commercial arrangement.

B. Predatory Pricing

The US law regarding predatory pricing, as developed in *Matsushita* and *Brooke Group*, requires both pricing below a cost threshold and an element of recoupment, namely that the predatory firm will recover any losses occasioned by the price cutting in the first stage of the strategy through supracompetitive pricing in the second (recoupment) stage. The orthodox approach, seen for instance in Bork[110] and reflected in the case-law, holds that given the risks inherent in the second stage, the strategy is unlikely to be attempted, never mind be successful.[111] This is because an agent which possesses unbounded rationality would assess the losses incurred in the first stage and compare them with the discounted value of the gains obtained in the second stage, and determine that given the discount and risks involved, the strategy had a negative net present value. Accordingly, that actor would not pursue the strategy. And given that this strategy is unlikely to be successful or pursued, attempts to identify and control apparent instances of this practice run the risk of miscategorising beneficial (cost-cutting and welfare-promoting) practices as pernicious ones.[112]

The European prohibition regarding predatory pricing does not require proof of recoupment.[113] It merely requires proof that a dominant undertaking sold goods either below average variable costs, or between average variable costs and average total costs as part of a plan to eliminate competition.[114] Although recoupment is not part of the legal prohibition, if the practice is analysed from an orthodox perspective, the possibility of recoupment must be part of any strategy involving low cost pricing, for only the possibility of making a future gain which exceed the present loss could justify that loss.

The behavioural analysis of this phenomenon leads to a different result. The Achilles' heel of the orthodox approach is its reliance on the assumption of an

---

[110] Bork (n 40) 144–59.

[111] See eg *Matsushita* (n 6) 589, cited in *Brooke Group* (n 45) 226.

[112] See *Brooke Group* ibid 226–27.

[113] Case C-202/07 P *France Télécom SA v Commission*, ECLI:EU:C:2009:214, paras 109–11.

[114] Case C-62/86 *AKZO Chemie BV v Commission*, ECLI:EU:C:1991:286, paras 70–72; Case C-333/94 *Tetra Pak v Commission* ('*Tetra Pack II*'), ECLI:EU:C:1996:436; Case C-202/07 P *France Télécom v Commission*, ECLI:EU:C:2009:214.

unboundedly rational agent, which would not pursue a strategy that has a negative net present value. If one were to relax this assumption, a different result ensues. Indeed, Tor has studied predatory pricing from this behaviourist perspective, and notes that 'the behavioral approach to antitrust law and economics does reveal that predatory pricing may be more likely than rational actor models predict, at least in specific settings.'[115] Given the biases and heuristics that influence peoples' thinking, it is not unrealistic to relax this assumption in order to obtain a description of how market agents actually operate.

Tor suggests that predatory pricing may occur in some circumstances, particularly when a dominant firm sees its market share being eroded by a new entrant.[116] A manager in such a situation may start with her reference point of the firm's previous success as framing her subsequent decisions, and operating under an overconfidence bias, may take excessive risks. On this, Tor remarks:

> The evidence on boundedly rational choice behavior reveals that decision makers perceive expected outcomes above the reference point as positive and those below it as negative. A negative change relative to the reference point – that is, a loss – looms large, so managers will try harder to avoid the threatening loss from an eroding market share, Therefore, a manager whose current competitive strategy is unable to stanch a market share slide may be inclined to engage in negative expected value predatory pricing (ie, without a rationally sufficient likelihood of recoupment). Such managers may be willing to take higher risks than rational profit maximizing justifies, hoping they will succeed in reestablishing the firm's lost long-term market position.[117]

Once a manager begins such a strategy, it may be too late to terminate it.

If the strategy makes initial losses, optimism bias (the present strategy will 'beat the odds' and succeed[118]) on the part of the manager pursuing this strategy may 'kick in'. And this, in turn, may be combined with fallacious reasoning about sunk costs, viewing previous losses as some form of investment. Tor notes:

> Unlike the hypothetical rational actor, who always ignores sunk costs and lets bygones be bygones, real world managers are far more inclined to hold to a course they have committed to despite dim prospects for success – as long as there are any prospects at all – and often exhibit a tendency to escalate commitments in the face of losses.[119]

Further, predation can work as a discipline strategy, given the availability bias. Under that bias, people view occurrences which are more easily recalled as being more probable. Hence, as Tor argues 'the availability bias will tend to make highly publicized, colorful instances of predation stand out in the imagination and memory of market participants. This effect may sometimes be reinforced through

---

[115] See especially Avishalom Tor, 'Illustrating a Behaviorally Informed Approach to Antitrust Law: The Case of Predatory Pricing' (2003) 18 *Antitrust* 52, 57.
[116] ibid 55–56.
[117] ibid 55, Tor's footnotes omitted.
[118] ibid.
[119] ibid.

the law of small numbers'.[120] As such, threats of price reduction in this form may be used by larger firms in a market to discourage price competition by smaller firms, and as a disciplinary threat among cartel participants.

The behavioural analysis of predatory pricing is significantly divergent from the orthodox analysis of the same problem. This analysis shows that should people's cognitive ability diverge from the unbounded rationality assumed by the orthodox perspective, predatory pricing is a strategy which may in fact be pursued. Indeed, there is some fairly convincing evidence that firms do pursue predatory pricing strategies.[121] One recent study shows that there seems to be strong evidence for this practice in the US passenger air transport market,[122] and according to that study:

> [N]o particular technological, organizational, or regulatory characteristic obviously limits this phenomenon to the airlines. So long as a large, multi-market incumbent has some market power and ability to discriminate, it could be profitable to terrorize entrants and capital with predatory signals.[123]

And in contemporary industries marked by firms characterised by large negative cash-flows (eg Amazon and Netflix) a predatory pricing strategy may not only be rational, but also undetectable.[124]

C. Market Entry

Assumptions around market entry are central to much of the orthodox analysis of antitrust law and policy. If market entry is felt to be is easy, ie there are few barriers to prevent firms from entering the market and challenging incumbent players, then this will shape analysis of a significant number of competition problems associated with monopoly. In particular, in the presence of low barriers, any supracompetitive profit made by a monopolist will attract entry, which in turn will compete away such returns. In the EU, the Commission's position that it will focus its enforcement efforts towards exclusionary practices, as opposed to exploitative practices, is a direct result of this line of thought.[125] In the US, this approach to market entry has informed the preference to avoid type I errors over those of type II.

---

[120] ibid 56.

[121] See Bruce H Kobayashi, 'The Law and Economics of Predatory Pricing' in Keith N Hylton (ed), *Antitrust Law and Economics* (Cheltenham, Edward Elgar, 2010) 116, 124–29; see also Zamir and Teichman (n 43) 384.

[122] Chris Sagers, 'Rarely Tried, and ... Rarely Successful: Theoretically Impossible Price Predation among the Airlines' (2009) 74 *Journal of Air Law and Commerce* 919; see also Christopher R Leslie, 'Rationality Analysis in Antitrust' (2010) 158 *University of Pennsylvania Law Review* 261, 318–24.

[123] Sagers ibid 957.

[124] See Shaoul Sussman, 'Prime Predator: Amazon and the Rationale of Below Average Variable Cost Pricing Strategies Among Negative-Cash Flow Firms' (2019) 7 *Journal of Antitrust Enforcement* 203.

[125] Guidance (n 13).

The behavioural analysis of market entry[126] yields a possibly prima facie coun-terintuitive result. This approach shows that market *entry* may be more frequent than predicted under the orthodox approach, but this 'excess entry' does not imply survival. In a world where agents are unboundedly rational, one would expect agents to enter the market only when the net present value of entry (after a discount for risk) is positive.[127] Yet this is not the case.

Tor reviews studies that examine US, UK and German data, and concludes:

> The empirical evidence strongly suggests that negative net present value entry is commonplace. First, while entry is pervasive, amounting on average to about 50% of all existing firms every five years across all domestic manufacturing industries, entrants also exhibit strikingly high mortality rates. Within ten years, only about 20% of any entrant cohort still operates. Attrition, moreover, begins right from the start, with more than 25% of new entrants exiting within two years, over 60% disappearing within five years. In fact, high-volume exit accompanies the high volume of entry in most industries, such that the two phenomena are strongly correlated, and result in little net entry.[128]

The reasons for this can be explained in the heuristics and biases with which boundedly rational agents assess market opportunities and subsequently react.

A boundedly rational, prospective market entrant cannot enumerate and assess all pitfalls, risks and rewards associated with entering into a particular market. The agent's cognitive capabilities are insufficient to do this. Rather, that agent will use shortcuts and be influenced by biases in their assessment of these risks and rewards.

Both the boundedly and unboundedly rational agent calculate the risk, rewards and expected outcomes of market entry based on some indication of the expected value of market entry. This, of course, requires that agent to consider a vast array of variables, from the form that the entry can take, to the details of financing, the likely response(s) of competitors, future demand for the products in question, etc. The main difference between the two agents is that the unboundedly rational agent has the cognitive capacity to know all relevant variables in this array, and as a result can calculate the optimal entry and subsequent survival strategy.

On the other hand, the boundedly rational agent's assessment of entry is shaped through biases and heuristics in assessing the probability and value of the alterna-tives open to the agent.[129] The availability heuristic is a short cut which people use to enumerate and evaluate instances, events or occurrences. That heuristic holds that which is most visible is most frequent or likely. In this way, someone may

---

[126] See Avishalom Tor, 'The Fable of Entry: Bounded Rationality, Market Discipline, and Legal Policy' (2002) 101 *Michigan Law Review* 482, 504. This paper has shaped my thinking about this issue, and I have drawn upon it for this discussion. See also Amanda P Reeves and Maurice E Stucke, 'Behavioral Antitrust' (2011) 86 *Indiana Law Journal* 1527, 1557–58.

[127] Tor ibid 488–89.

[128] ibid 490–91.

[129] ibid 504.

think that heart attacks are more frequent if they have had acquaintances who have suffered from this in the near past, since these events very readily come to mind. Similarly, in assessing the potential for market entry, those using the availability heuristic will recall successful market entrants, rather than all entrants – as those that have failed will have fallen from memory. When looking at, say entry into the local restaurant market, it is easier to recall existing successful restaurants than the myriad of failed start-ups which have long since disappeared from the scene (and memory).

Further, assessment of success is limited by sample size. A sample of market entrants enumerated using the availability heuristic will necessarily be smaller than the set of all entrants, and these will show characteristics of being successful. This may lead to the inference that successful market entry is more likely than it in fact is.

In combination with the optimism, desirability and overconfidence biases, one can see how the probabilities and resulting value of alternatives regarding market entry will differ from those calculated by the unboundedly rational agent. Both the optimism and overconfidence biases will point the boundedly rational agent towards entry. The former will cause that agent to underestimate risks and other adverse circumstances, while overestimating the benefits and returns. The latter bias will influence the market entrant's perceptions of its ability to succeed encouraging entry.[130] The related desirability bias will magnify this perception of success, given that people often overestimate the likelihood of a desired outcome. The result of this is that people will overestimate their chance of success in a given endeavour, including market entry. This result has been robustly demonstrated, and it is quite pronounced when people think that success is down to their own skill, when competing against similarly skilled individuals.[131] People are more likely to be overconfident in situations where success appears to be based on their own skill, rather than a random event.[132]

The behaviourist approach will predict excess entry into markets, and also provides a powerful explanation of why such excess entry will occur. However, the behavioural approach on its own does not dictate an immediate response for antitrust law or policy. Rather, this result should inform subsequent consideration (if not development) of such law and policy.

The conclusion that entry will occur more frequently than what the orthodox approach predicts may be prima facie (but only prima facie) paradoxical. Indeed, if entry occurs more frequently than expected, this might suggest that the orthodox approach is roughly correct, namely that entry does occur, and thus concerns about type II errors are misplaced. And given that – if the behavioural approach is correct – market entry occurs even more often than predicted, antitrust enforcers

---

[130] On overconfidence bias and entry, see Colin Camerer and Dan Lovallo, 'Overconfidence and Excess Entry: An Experimental Approach' (1999) 89 *American Economic Review* 306.
[131] ibid.
[132] ibid 311 and 314–15.

and policy-makers should be even more relaxed about this monopoly phenomenon than the orthodox approach alone would suggest.

Alternatively, the behaviourist approach could suggest that orthodox analysis
considers the wrong phenomenon. It is not market *entry* which is key to control of
monopolies, rather it is market *survival* and post-survival market presence. Tor's
data, cited above, shows that even with (or possibly, because of) pervasive entry, a
quarter of entrants will exit within two years, and only 20 per cent will remain after
ten years. However, ephemeral entry, even frequently and by numerous competitors, may be insufficient to provide a solution to an incumbent monopolist (or
otherwise large undertaking) which has obtained or entrenched its position as a
result of a type II error.

The behavorialist approach to market entry challenges the orthodox view of
the way firms that can attract a supracompetitive profit can be controlled. The
orthodox approach suggests that market entry is sufficient to address this monopoly problem. The behaviourist approach suggests that this is not the case: indeed,
market entry may be attempted more often than the orthodox approach suggests.
It may therefore be something else, eg survivability, which is the solution to that
problem. Accordingly, prioritisation of enforcement in dominance cases based on
an assumption of the self-correcting nature of the market, which in turn is predicated on market entry as a disciplining force, is likely misguided in its approach.[133]

By exclusively focusing on market entry and the barriers to entry, the orthodox
approach to competition policy has incorrectly identified the place in the competitive process where control of dominant entities takes place. Competitive constraint
to dominant entities takes place not at the initial point of entry by a challenger, but
later in the competitive process where the non-incumbent firm can exert competitive pressure. Accordingly, exclusive focus on dominant firms excluding equally as
efficient competitors may be too strong a test, for nascent entrants may be somewhat behind more established and more dominant firms in the industrial 'learning
curve' characterised by the development of productive and distributive efficiencies
and networks.[134]

This argument thus provides a hypothesis for further investigation. If such
investigation establishes that a key competitive moment is not merely entry, but
survival, this would tend to show that the orthodox approach's exclusive focus
on entry is misguided, and leads to failing to solve the problem. It is further

---

[133] Guidance (n 12) paras 1 –17.
[134] This may be recognised by the ECJ; see, for example, its statement in *Post Danmark* (n 42) para 59:

> On the other hand, in a situation such as that in the main proceedings, characterised by the holding
> by the dominant undertaking of a very large market share and by structural advantages conferred,
> inter alia, by that undertaking's statutory monopoly, which applied to 70% of mail on the relevant
> market, applying the as-efficient-competitor test is of no relevance inasmuch as the structure of the
> market makes the emergence of an as-efficient competitor practically impossible.

While the Court's reasoning immediately applies to former statutory monopolies with existing
networks and large market shares, there is no a priori reason that this reasoning cannot apply to other
markets characterised by well-entrenched incumbents.

suggested that if further investigation establishes that it is survival (and not entry) which provides this constraint, remedies which facilitate entrants' chances of survival are not directed at protecting the competitor. Rather they are to protect the competitive process, as a means of perhaps mitigating the unintended consequences of enforcement authorities' unwillingness to intervene out of concern of committing type II errors. And it is not just in assessing monopolistic practices (eg in possible Sherman Act section 2 and Article 102 violations) that concerns about the corrective force of market entry are in play: these concerns are equally applicable to merger control.

D. Some Concluding Remarks on the Behavioural Approach

The orthodox approach assumes that market agents possess a significant degree of cognitive capacity – so-called 'unbounded rationality'. With this capacity, such agents are able to identify all options or opportunities open to them at a given time, compute the probabilities of each option, and thus assess the expected value of all options open to them at a given time. The unboundedly rational agent will rank these options, and select that which provides the greatest expected value. With this axiom of unbounded rationality in hand, traditional price theory – as favoured by the Chicago School and popular elsewhere – works well as a theoretical description of markets. And if this is the case, then this orthodox approach may well be an adequate analytical tool.

But it is folly to assume that people possess the unbounded rationality which is assumed by the orthodox approach. Human cognitive capacities are limited; people use short cuts, or heuristics as a means of coping with these limitations. For instance, rather than enumerating a long list of what may potentially occur, people are likely to turn to what first comes to mind. While such heuristics can be useful – after all they work reasonably well most of the time – they nevertheless lead people astray. Further, in addition to being led astray by reliance on these sorts of short cuts, people frequently exhibit biases in their cognitive processes. The behavioural approach to market interactions (and hence economics) shows that this use of heuristics and influence of bias causes people to behave in a way different to that which would be predicted by the orthodox approach.

This divergence in behaviour is significant. To the extent that observed behaviour differs from the behaviour predicted by a theory, then that theory is in need of revision, if not outright rejection and replacement. And it may well be dangerous to use such a theory as the exclusive analytic tool, or 'organizing principle',[135] on which to base legal principles or socioeconomic policy.

---

[135] Gregory J Werden, Luke M Froeb and Mikhael Shor, 'Behavioral Antitrust and Merger Control' (2011) 167 *Journal of Institutional and Theoretical Economics* 126, 138 rejecting the behavioural approach, particularly in merger control.

IV. Conclusion

The effects-based approach to competition law is built on two related principles. The first principle is that the sole goal of competition law and policy is the maximisation of welfare. There is some dispute among proponents of this view whether total welfare or consumer welfare is the appropriate quality which a competition regime should seek to maximise. But among proponents of this view there is no dispute about other, non-economic goals. These goals are simply not a concern for this area of law and policy. The second principle is that economic theory, in the form of classical price theory, is the appropriate methodology to guide the construction and interpretation of legal rules in order to promote the maximisation of consumer or total welfare.

This is the orthodox approach to competition analysis. But this chapter has shown that there are concerns with this orthodox approach. These concerns are evident from what we can call an internal and an external analysis. An internal analysis considers the orthodox approach 'on its own terms', ie questioning whether it provides an adequate explanation or prediction of the phenomena it sets out to explain or predict, as the case may be.

This was briefly done in the first part of the chapter, showing than many of the assumptions inherent in the orthodox approach were likely too strong, and failed to accurately describe markets or predict market behaviour in some fundamental principles of concern to the competition policy analyst. These include the self-correcting nature of the market, that in antitrust analysis type II errors are to be preferred over type I errors (as the former are, over time, benign), and the need for monopolies to innovate and compete. Upon even brief examination, the self-evident nature of each of these claims became suspect. And given the central place which these principles have in orthodox competition analysis, particularly market self-correction and the preference of type II errors, our argument generates some doubt that this analytic tool is entirely appropriate for the task entrusted to it.

These concerns were magnified when the chapter took an 'external' approach to considering the orthodox toolkit. This external approach was provided by the results of behavioural economics, and the results of this analysis are powerful. In short, the behavioural approach suggests that market actors do not act as the orthodox approach predicts. The significant variation between predicted and actual behaviour can be explained in terms of the orthodox approach's assumption of agents possessing unbounded rationality. Simply put, this assumption is false. Rather, boundedly rational agents compensate for their cognitive limitations by using mental short cuts (heuristics) and also approach their reasoning through mental 'lenses' which impose biases on the outcome of their cognitive processes. These short cuts and biases lead agents to act differently to how the orthodox theory predicts (or assumes). Not only do the results of the behavioural approach robustly demonstrate this, but the behaviouralist can also provide a rigorous explanation of why this is the case.

From a rule of law perspective these results are problematic for the ortho-dox approach. For the sake of argument, suppose that welfare maximisation is (or should be) the goal of competition law and policy. If that is the case, policy-makers and legislators must design competition legislation and policy instruments in a manner that gives guidance to market participants on how to achieve that goal, and in this design (and in the resolution of cases or controversies) adopt an analytic approach which realises this goal of welfare maximisation.

If the analytic approach chosen does not achieve the goal, then this choice of methodology has introduced a 'rule of law gap'. In other words, if the methodo-logical approach incorporated into the legislation (and its underlying policy basis) prevents the ostensive legislative goal from being achieved, the legal regime will in actual practice be directing behaviour away from the desired goal. As a conse-quence, this divergence poses significant rule of law issues. Such divergence, in Fullarian terms,[136] leads to breaches of rule of law due to inconsistency,[137] not mandating the impossible,[138] and incongruence between rule (or policy underly-ing the rule) and official action.[139] Each of these, on its own, is a serious problem for the normative acceptability of a legal arrangement. Taken together, these concerns suggest that the methodology incorporated into the orthodox approach to competition law poses a genuine rule of law threat.

The aspirational principles of the rule of law enumerated by Fuller (and Raz) set out certain desiderata of a legal system. As the purpose of law is to guide human conduct, a legal system must contain rules which can be known and followed by its human subjects. Thus, at minimum, the demands and expectations which law imposes must be capable of being addressed by (boundedly rational) human beings. To require otherwise would mandate the impossible.

---

[136] See the discussion in Chapter 1, particularly pp 18–19.
[137] Fuller (n 1) 65–70.
[138] ibid 70–79.
[139] ibid 81–91.

5

Institutional Legitimacy and Competence

The effects-based approach to competition law, whether in the form of the EU's 'more economic approach' or the American 'Chicagoist' approach, contains two principles: one normative, the other methodological. The former is that only economic values (particularly consumer welfare) matter for competition law and policy. The latter is that traditional welfare economics is the appropriate means for assessing the welfare-enhancing effects of a given policy or legal rule. The previous chapter examined the latter principle. This examination showed that the orthodox methodological approach used in competition analysis will give rise to rule of law problems due to inaccurate (and over-strong) assumptions about how markets work and how boundedly rational humans actually behave in markets.

This chapter considers the rule of law issues arising from the activities of institutional actors in the antitrust enforcement process. In both the United States and the European Union, as part of these regimes' normative reorientation towards this economics-focused approach, the main institutional actors (in the US, the courts; in the EU, the Commission) have reinterpreted the legislative basis underlying the competition regime from a multivalued system to a single-valued system. These systems now regard the maximisation of consumer welfare as their sole principle. As a result of this reorientation of antitrust values, these institutions now compel the use of the methodology of orthodox economic analysis in antitrust matters.

This raises two immediate rule of law concerns. The first rests in the institutional legitimacy in reorienting the legislative (or treaty) norm for competition law and policy. In many relevant ways, to narrow competition policy so that it focuses exclusively on one goal (and thereby excluding other goals) is to significantly rewrite competition policy. However, in a democratic society it is not self-evident that it is legitimate for either courts (in the case of the US) or an executive body (in the case of the EU) to serve as appropriate entities to undertake this sort of revision.

The second rule of law concern rests in institutional competence to evaluate the sort of evidence required by this approach. The effects-based approach requires parties to muster and present a significant amount of economic evidence, which, in most instances, will determine the outcome of the controversy. If courts lack the expertise to assess such evidence, then the economic approach may be directing courts to do the impossible. Thus a 'correct' outcome may be the result of chance, rather than judicial expertise.

This chapter examines these two institutional concerns which are consequent on the effects-based approach. The first part of the chapter examines the reorientation of both US and EU competition law from a multivalued system to one which focuses exclusively on consumer welfare. This book has already considered how the economic approach manifested itself in the competition regimes of these two jurisdictions. The focus of this part of the chapter is to examine the starting and end points of this transition to an effects-based approach, to illustrate the normative shift which this transition has caused. The argument is that this rewriting of the normative underpinnings of competition law by the judiciary (or executive of the sort that the Commission is) is an inappropriate exercise of power in a democracy, which has significant implications for the rule of law.

The second part of the chapter concerns the institution of the judiciary itself. The demands that the effects-based approach place on the judiciary to assess complicated evidence are significant. The approach also places similar demands on litigants. The assessment of such evidence, even with the 'aid' of experts, is a Herculean task that may well be beyond the capability of all but the most specialised courts. The argument is that these institutional concerns raise fundamental rule of law concerns.

I. The Reorientation of Antitrust

In spite of what some have recently said about the US antitrust regime, both it and its European counterpart were, in their original instantiations, multifaceted regimes. In these early regimes considerations other than consumer welfare counted. In the preceding analysis of the European regime, it was shown that considerations such as the social costs of unemployment, which could be mitigated through 'orderly downsizing' of an industry, were taken into account by authorities in their consideration of agreements in the Dutch brick and European synthetic fibre industries. Further, the European approach was also built upon ordoliberalism, which is normatively different from an economic approach with exclusive focus on welfare maximisation. Prior to the ascendency of the effects-based approach, US courts took into account the need to protect small businesses.[1] Neither of these results necessarily maximise consumer welfare; but they were the decisions of the Commission and USSC.

This section considers the shifts that have taken place in both the US and EU in regard to the goals of competition law and policy. That shift is, in the US, entirely a result of the judiciary, driven by the influence of the Chicago School; and in Europe, driven by the Commission. The result of these shifts is that the original purpose of the competition regimes has been changed by judicial or administrative fiat, respectively.

---

[1] See eg *US v Von's Grocery Co*, 384 US 270 (1966).

A. Antitrust: As Originally Viewed by the US Regime

The USSC has famously stated 'they [the Congressional floor debates which preceded the passage of the *Sherman Act*] suggest that Congress designed the Sherman Act as a "consumer welfare prescription."'[2] As a statement of law, this is of course correct. It is an interpretation of the Sherman Act, by that jurisdiction's highest court (from which there is no appeal), and any adequate rule of recognition would identify it as law. However, as a statement of a historical proposition it is false.

It is often difficult to determine with certainty the legislative intent behind a piece of legislation. Legislators do not have a common intention when they speak to or vote on a piece of legislation. Even with the clearest of statutes this may be a difficult task; with statutes that are worded in an open-ended manner like the Sherman Act, this task is monumental. In his study of the Sherman Act's origins, Lande remarks:

> It is not possible to ascertain with certainty the original goals of the antitrust laws. Not only are there conflicting statements of legislative purpose, but it is often difficult to decide whether certain statements represent isolated, unimportant views or infrequently mentioned but nevertheless significant motivating factors.[3]

Further, as a result of political rhetoric what is said in debate may not be what is meant. Lande again notes: 'For example, legislators might have stated that they condemn monopolization out of a concern for consumers when they actually were more concerned with providing small businesses fair opportunity to compete.'[4] Nevertheless, a consideration of legislative history – and hence intent – can aid us in possibly ruling out purported original goals, and enumerating some of the values which the legislators believed to be advanced by a particular piece of legislation.

One purported goal that can be ruled out by even a cursory examination of the legislative background to the Sherman Act is that Congress's exclusive goal in passing this Act was to promote consumer welfare.[5] Given the activities of the trusts, high prices would have been a concern to Senator Sherman. Indeed section 1 of the Bill he originally introduced would have explicitly prohibited 'all arrangements, contracts, agreements, trusts, or combinations between persons or corporations

---

[2] *Reiter v Sonotone Corporation*, 442 US 330, 343 (1979), quoting Robert Bork, *The Antitrust Paradox: A Policy at War with Itself*, rev edn (New York, Basic Books, 1993) 66.

[3] Robert H Lande, 'Wealth Transfers as the Original and Primary Concern of Antitrust: The Efficiency Interpretation Challenged' (1982) 34 *Hastings Law Journal* 65, 81.

[4] ibid 81 fn 65.

[5] *Pace* Bork (n 20) 20–21: '[T]he delegation was confined by the policy of advancing consumer welfare. ... [And, t]he variety of other policy goals that have since been attributed to the framers of the Sherman Act is not to be found in the legislative history'); and 65–66 as well as statements of the USSC, see eg *Sonotone* (n 2).

designed, or which tend, *to advance the cost to the consumer of any such articles*.[6] In debate Senator Sherman stated that the purpose of his legislation was *not*

> to cripple combinations of capital and labor, the formation of partnerships or of corporations, but only to prevent and control combinations made with a view to prevent competition, or for the restraint of trade, or to increase the profits of the producer at the cost of the consumer.[7]

This latter statement (and particularly its final clause) in the eyes of a twenty-first century competition scholar may be viewed as a statement which suggests an early understanding of consumer welfare.

But Senator Sherman's statement on its own does not give support for a view that allocative efficiency was in the minds of the legislator when considering the Sherman Act.[8] The economic analysis which could support such a position was yet to be widely known. Marshall's *Principles of Economics* was not published until 1890, and the first edition of that work did not contain any significant account of the inefficiencies that resulted from monopolistic reduction of output.[9] This was a twentieth-century development.

Yet this is not too say that Congress (and Senator Sherman) was unware of productive efficiencies obtained by economies of scale. The gains from such efficiencies were somewhat begrudgingly accepted by the Senator. He remarked: 'It is sometimes said of these combinations that they reduce prices to the consumer by better methods of production, but all experience shows *that this saving of cost goes to the pockets of the producer*.'[10] This focus on consumer welfare (as it is now termed) is consistent with the view that protection of consumers against wealth extraction by producers was among Senator Sherman's original goals in his eponymous Act.[11]

Senator Sherman was only one of many senators, all with different views as to the purpose of the Act. These other views included the protection of small businesses, a view shared by several senators.[12] While this view did not extend to a general position that the concerns of small business could trump other goals,[13]

---

[6] 21 *Congressional Record* S 1, 51st Cong 1st Sess 2455 (18 March 1890), emphasis supplied.

[7] 21 *Congressional Record* S 1, 51st Cong 1st Sess (20 March 1890).

[8] *Pace* Bork (n 2) 26–31.

[9] See Lande (n 3) 88 fn 97; see also Bruce Wardhaugh, *Cartels, Markets and Crime: A Normative Justification for the Criminalisation of Economic Collusion* (Cambridge, Cambridge University Press, 2014) 220.

[10] Senator Sherman, quoted with emphasis added in Lande ibid 91.

[11] See also Lande ibid 93–96.

[12] See ibid 101–05.

[13] See ibid 103. As Lande notes, only one Congressman (Representative Mason) explicitly took this view; however, Lande continues (at 103 fn 149):

> In addition, some of the proconsumer statements may have disguised the desires of a few members of Congress who really favored aid to small businesses. But a few isolated statements do not represent the intent of Congress. Nor can they establish the policy or spirit of the Sherman Act. This is especially true because Representative Mason's views run counter to the strong consumer orientation of the Sherman Act.

it was a position that the courts would later come to accept to some degree,[14] prior to the ascendency of the now orthodox position.

A further goal inherent in the congressional understanding of the Sherman Act was to control the political and economic power of the trusts. This was one of the leading political questions of the 1880s, receiving significant press coverage in the major newspapers of the day.[15] Trusts were a target of editorial cartoons, and a focus of much discussion on the floors of Congress. In remarks introducing his Bill, Senator Sherman famously stated:

> [W]e will not endure a king as a political power we should not endure a king over the production, transportation, and sale of any of the necessaries of life. If we would not submit to an emperor we should not submit to an autocrat of trade, with power to prevent competition and to fix the price of any commodity.[16]

Sherman was not alone in his condemnation of the trusts on this basis.[17] Some 21 years after the Act's passage, in *Standard Oil v US*, White J opined:

> They conclusively show, however, that the main cause which led to the legislation was the thought that it was required by the economic condition of the times; that is, the vast accumulation of wealth in the hands of corporations and individuals, the enormous development of corporate organization, the facility for combination which such organizations afforded, the fact that the facility was being used, and that combinations known as trusts were being multiplied, and the widespread impression that their power had been and would be exerted to oppress individuals and injure the public generally.[18]

In the late 1880s people were not necessarily concerned about prices, as prices for most consumer goods were stable or declining.[19] The popular (and political) concern seemed to be about the process by which the prices were set.[20] The public

---

[14] See, most especially, *US v Aluminum Co of America*, 148 F 2d 416, 429 (CA2 1945); see also *US v Trans-Missouri Freight Association*, 166 US 290, 323–24 (1897); *Fashion Originators' Guild v FTC*, 312 US 457, 467 (1941); and *Brown Shoe Co v US*, 370 US 294, 344 (1962) (the latter albeit in the context of a merger – Clayton Act s 7 – situation).

[15] William L Letwin, 'Congress and The Sherman Antitrust Law: 1887–1890' (1956) 23 *University of Chicago Law Review* 221, 224–25.

[16] 21 Cong Rec S 1, 51st Cong 1st Sess 2457 (20 March 1890).

[17] See Lande (n 3) 99–101, fnn 136–40.

[18] ibid 50.

[19] See Lande (n 3) 97 fn 128, citing US Census Bureau statistics. These show a significant drop in the CPI, cost of living indices and wholesale price indices in the period between 1880 and 1890. Ironically, this may have been due to economies of scale achieved by some of the larger trusts. Notwithstanding the decrease in prices, during this decade there was a popular view that the gap between the 'haves' and 'have nots' was increasing, due to trust activity. Further, and related to this, was the decline in farmers' income, again in part due to the activities of the trusts. On these latter points, Letwin (n 15) 225, remarks:

> The low income of farmers, for which remedies were constantly being considered, was often said to be aggravated by various trusts, such as those that sold farmers bags and bought their linseed and cotton-seed. The general problem of poverty, a great concern of the time, was regularly said to be accentuated by the trusts, which were accused of dividing the country into two classes, the very rich and the very poor.

[20] ibid 101.

felt that prices were set by fiat by the trusts, rather than through a fair, market-based process.

With this background in mind, it would be incorrect to suggest that Congress's intent behind enacting the Sherman Act was to promote a unique goal, particularly one driven by later, twentieth-century economic thinking. If there had been a dominant goal, it is likely that this was to ensure that consumers paid a price which was fair for the product, ie not imposed artificially by a trust. In paying such a price, they would therefore not see their wealth being inappropriately transferred to (or appropriated by) these trusts. Implicit in criminalising anticompetitive activities is the assumption that there is a property right to consumer surplus, and to deprive a consumer of this through improper means is tantamount to theft. Congress's concern extended beyond low prices (or more appropriately 'fair') prices.[21] It was also concerned about protection of small businesses, and preventing trusts from both gaining further economic power and exercising those powers that they had already acquired.

It may also be a similar mistake to view an exclusive focus on consumer welfare as the sole goal of a contemporary antitrust policy. To look at this policy through an exclusively consumer welfare lens ignores both concentrations of market power and consideration of the competitive process. Khan, in her influential article, writes:

> Focusing antitrust exclusively on consumer welfare is a mistake. For one, it betrays legislative intent, which makes clear that Congress passed antitrust laws to safeguard against excessive concentrations of economic power. This vision promotes a variety of aims, including the preservation of open markets, the protection of producers and consumers from monopoly abuse, and the dispersion of political and economic control. Secondly, focusing on consumer welfare disregards the host of other ways that excessive concentration can harm us – enabling firms to squeeze suppliers and producers, endangering system stability (for instance, by allowing companies to become too big to fail), or undermining media diversity, to name a few. Protecting this range of interests requires an approach to antitrust that focuses on the neutrality of the competitive process and the openness of market structures.[22]

Khan is not alone in promoting view that antitrust has lost its original focus. The idea that US antitrust law should incorporate goals other than the promotion of consumer welfare has recently re-emerged within the legal and policy formulation

---

[21] The distinction may be significant. Lande gives the example of unsuccessful predation, where consumers benefit by obtaining (for a short term) goods at below the marginal cost of their production. When the predator attempted to raise prices to a monopoly level, they were prevented by market entry. However, during the (short) predatory phase, other (likely smaller) businesses left the market, thus resulting in harm. To the extent that Congress enacted the Sherman Act to protect small businesses and control the economic power of larger ones, such conduct would likely fall within the Act's ambit. See Lande (n 3) 105 fn 152.

[22] Lina M Khan, 'Amazon's Antitrust Paradox' (2017) 126 *Yale Law Journal* 710, 743–44, footnotes omitted.

community in the late part of the 2010s. This view, derided as 'Hipster Antitrust'[23] (or, less pejoratively, 'The New Brandeis Movement'[24]) takes the position that in antitrust, more than consumer welfare counts. Concerns such as those identified by Khan above should be a concern to policy-makers. Although proponents of the orthodox approach have been quick to condemn this multivalued approach to antitrust,[25] the approach must be taken seriously.

B. Competition: As Originally Viewed by the European Regime

Before the advent of the MEA, European competition authorities (including the Commission) took into account values other than consumer welfare in assessing their assessment of business arrangements under Articles 101 and 102. This is apparent from the discussion in Chapter 3.

This wider view of the goals of competition law better accords with the views which shaped the design of the Treaty of Rome (which brought about the European Economic Community) and its predecessor, the European Coal and Steel Community (ECSC) Treaty. Numerous studies of the historical origins of the ECSC, the EEC and its successors have been written.[26] This history need not be rewritten, particularly since most of the history that is of concern to us is uncontroversial.

In reviewing this history, we see a number of themes that influenced the early development of European competition policy. First, these two early Treaties must be viewed against the backdrop of post-World War II reconstruction.[27] In addition to rebuilding Europe, those involved in the reconstruction project (particularly the Americans) wished to ensure that the events of 1939–1945 would never be repeated. To prevent a repetition, the architects of reconstruction

---

[23] Konstantin Medvedovsky, 'Hipster Antitrust – A Brief Fling or Something More?' *CPI Antitrust Chronicle*, April 2018.

[24] Lina M Khan, 'The New Brandeis Movement: America's Antimonopoly Debate' (2018) 9 *European Journal of Competition Law and Practice* 131.

[25] Joshua D Wright et al, 'Requiem for a Paradox: The Dubious Rise and Inevitable Fall of Hipster Antitrust' (2019) 51 *Arizona State Law Journal*, forthcoming; available at SSRN abstract=3249524.

[26] Among them are David J Gerber, 'Constitutionalizing the Economy: German Neo-liberalism, Competition Law and the "New" Europe' (1994) 42 *American Journal of Comparative Law* 25; David J Gerber, *Law and Competition in Twentieth Century Europe: Protecting Prometheus* (Oxford, Oxford University Press, 1998); Marie-Laurie Djelic, 'Does Europe Mean Americanization? The Case of Competition' (2002) 6 *Competition and Change* 233; Marie-Laurie Djelic, 'From Local Legislation to Global Structuring Frame: The Story of Antitrust' (2005) 5 *Global Social Policy* 55; Nicola Giocoli, 'Competition versus Property Rights: American Antitrust Law, the Freiburg School, and the Early Years of European Competition Policy' (2009) 5 *Journal of Competition Law and Economics* 747; Christopher Harding and Julian Joshua, *Regulating Cartels in Europe*, 2nd edn (Oxford, Oxford University Press, 2010); and Wardhaugh (n 9) 170–80.

[27] See Hans Thorelli, 'Antitrust Policy in Europe: National Policies after 1945' (1958) 26 *University of Chicago Law Review* 222; and AW Lovett, 'The United States and the Schuman Plan: A Study in French Diplomacy 1950–1952' (1996) 39 *Historical Journal* 425.

(clearly influenced by their US negotiating partners[28]) attempted to reorder the post-war economies of France and particularly Germany to reduce the chances of social and economic conditions leading to a renewal of hostilities.

This economic restructuring consisted of two elements: the elimination of restrictive business practices, particularly cartels as a means of industrial organisation, and the interlinking of the French and German economies. The cartelisation of German industry in the decades leading up to 1939 is well known.[29] This cartelisation facilitated a planned economy during the National Socialist regime, aiding the German war effort. Preventing the re-emergence of cartels in a post-1945 reconstructed economy would therefore minimise some of the economic forces which enabled World War II. Second, linking the French and German economies would not only advance the reconstruction process, but also reduce chances of future hostilities given this interdependence.

The linking of these economies was staged process. The first stage occurred with the Treaty of Paris, which in addition to establishing the ECSC (and thus connecting the French coal and German steel industries) also contained competition provisions that proscribed cartels, similar arrangements and monopolistic practices. These provisions, Articles 65 and 66 of the ECSC Treaty, would serve as the model for the competition provisions (now Articles 101 and 102) of later European Treaties. The second stage occurred with the Treaty of Rome, which set in place a process of deeper economic integration among European economies. This is an outline of a well-accepted story of post-World War II European economic integration.

But the above outline is incomplete, insofar as it omits a consideration of the influence which ordoliberal economic thinking played in the development of the European approach to the economy in the post-1945 world. While Chapter 3 briefly touched on this doctrine, and an extensive discussion of it is beyond the scope of this work,[30] it is necessary to reiterate some of its main tenets to demonstrate the significance of the normative shift which accompanied the MEA. First, it is fair to characterise ordoliberalism as an economic philosophy which focused on determining the appropriate economic conditions 'for a prosperous, free, and equitable society'.[31] These conditions required structural means to prevent the

---

[28] One account of this reads:

> On April 9, 1951 when the [ECSC] treaty was finally about to be signed, the German Minister of Economic Affairs, Ludwig Erhard, reminded the Chancellor Konrad Adenauer that the final German decision had been 'influenced by the American negotiating partners in a fashion which amounted almost to an ultimatum'.

Djelic (n 26) 245, quoting Volker Berghahn, *The Americanization of West German Industry 1945–1973* (Cambridge, Cambridge University Press, 1986) 153.

[29] See eg Djelic, ibid 236–37 (and table 1), and see also the numbers cited in Harding and Joshua (n 26) 68. Cartelisation was not a uniquely German phenomenon; this activity was authorised (or tolerated) in Italy, Belgium and the Netherlands as well.

[30] This is discussed in Wardhaugh (n 9) 175–80.

[31] Giocoli (n 26) 769.

concentration of economic power either in the government or in the hands of private economic actors. Both were threats to individual freedom, as pre-1945 experience had shown.[32]

A critical keystone of the ordoliberal approach was the protection of consumer interests in the market place, through an effective competition regime. One commentator describes the goals of ordoliberal competition policy as 'policy that aims at securing a competitive process with desirable working properties, one that works to the benefit of consumer interests'.[33] To protect consumer interests, and hence freedom in the marketplace, such a competition regime would contain provisions for the control of cartels and monopolistic behaviour. The administration of the regime would be overseen by an independent, administrative body, insulated from political interference.[34]

Ordoliberalism was not merely some nebulous academic theory that was floating around German universities in the Weimar and post-World War II periods. Rather, among the members of the Germany delegation that negotiated the ECST was Walter Hallstein (who later became the first President of the European Commission, serving from 1958 to 1967), who was an adherent to ordoliberal principles. Germany's first Minister of Economic affairs was Ludwig Erhard. He served in that role between 1949 and 1963, later serving as Chancellor until 1967. Erhard was sympathetic to ordoliberal views, particularly regarding competition policy.[35] As Giocoli, remarks: 'It seems therefore legitimate to argue that Germany's official position on the Treaty of Paris was, at least with respect to competition issues, significantly influenced by Ordoliberalism.'[36]

This is significant, for it suggests that consumer welfare – as now understood – was not among the primary concerns of those negotiating and drafting the original European Treaties. Cartels would be prohibited, not because they transferred consumer welfare to producers or created allocative inefficiencies, but because such economic concentration would limit individual freedom in the marketplace. Monopolies were similarly condemned, out of concern for freedom in the market.

C. The Original View of Antitrust

The previous two sections have shown that in their original implementation, neither the American nor the European antitrust regimes viewed consumer welfare as their sole goal. The US regime viewed protection of consumers from having

---

[32] See eg Gerber, 'Constitutionalizing the Economy' (n 26) 36–37.
[33] Viktor J Vanberg, 'The Freiburg School: Walter Euken and Ordoliberalism' (2011) Freiburger Diskussionspapiere zur Ordnungsökonomik/Freiburg Discussion Papers on Constitutional Economics No 04/11, 6.
[34] Wardhaugh (n 9) 178–79.
[35] Giocoli (n 26) 767.
[36] ibid.

their wealth transferred to (or expropriated by) producers as one of its original goals. This may be a form of protection of 'consumer welfare' in an extended sense. But this early view did not extend to the protection of such welfare to promote allocative efficiency. Rather, this is a view that a producer using its power to set prices to charge consumers more than a 'fair' or 'market' price for a good is some form of theft. Yet this was only one goal which Congress had in mind in 1890 when it passed Senator Sherman's Act.

In the original approach of the European regime, as we have seen, consumer welfare did not count among the primary goals of the competition regime. Although cartel control was a feature of this regime, cartels were not controlled in order to directly protect the consumer from increased prices; rather cartels were controlled to prevent economic concentration – which would enhance consumer freedom. It was this goal of freedom for participants in the marketplace which served as the underlying theoretical backbone of the European competition regime of the 1950s. Consumer welfare in the contemporary sense with its link to allocative efficiency played no role in the minds of the Treaties' authors.

Notwithstanding these original views, it is evident that by the second decade of the twenty-first century the main focus of both regimes is on the protection consumer welfare by ensuring that markets operate in an allocatively efficient manner. However, Chapters 3 and 4 have told two stories with a similar theme. These stories are how this consumer welfare, economic effects-based approach has developed. In the US this was driven by the Courts, primarily the USSC. In Europe, the Commission served as the driver, bringing the European Courts with it.

These shifts in the focus and goals of competition policy raise a significant question regarding the roles of courts and administrative bodies in an otherwise democratic constitutional order. The goals of the competition regime in both jurisdictions have been significantly altered (or rewritten) by bodies apparently exercising an extraconstitutional mandate. The propriety of such a mandate is further drawn into question when competition law and policy is viewed from a social perspective. There can be no doubt that market regulation, which necessarily includes competition policy, has a political content.[37]

In all but command economies, markets are the primary means by which the vast majority of goods and services are distributed. They are thus an important – if not the most important – feature of these societies. These societies are called 'market economies' for this reason; and all but the most extreme dirigiste economies contain a market element. But there is no homogenous flavour of 'market economy', as the extent of social (or governmental) intervention with market forces will vary as social conditions require, and social requirements mandate. Given the fundamental nature of the market as a means of social organisation,

---

[37] This view is obviously not unique to the author, see eg Robert Pitofsky, 'The Political Content of Antitrust' (1979) 127 *University of Pennsylvania Law Review* 1051, 1075.

a strong normative case can be made suggesting that decisions about the nature structure of market regulation should be a result of a more general process than by administrative or judicial fiat, particularly in a constitutional democracy. In other words, the reorientation of the competition rules of the sort that the US and Europe have seen gives rise to a rule of law concern.

D. Separation of Powers and the Rule of Law

A common normative justification for a separation of powers within a government rests on a desire to prevent the rise of tyranny by those that govern. From a historical perspective, this view can be found in Locke,[38] and most notably Montesquieu,[39] who in turn served to influence Madison's argument in *Federalist 47*:

> No political truth is certainly of greater intrinsic value, or is stamped with the authority of more enlightened patrons of liberty, than that on which the objection is founded. The accumulation of all powers, legislative, executive, and judiciary, in the same hands, whether of one, a few, or many, and whether hereditary, self-appointed, or elective, may justly be pronounced the very definition of tyranny.[40]

While the rise of autocrats in the second decade of the twenty-first century may give greater salience to the views of Montesquieu and Madison, however, as expressed, these are pragmatic positions. They express the need to avoid concentrations of power for the purely practical reason of avoiding tyranny. They do not provide a normative link between rule of law and separation of powers.

But such a link can be developed. This link is premised on a link between governmental action and legal authorisation for that action. Waldron[41] provides a convincing account which establishes this link, and does so in a way that explicitly follows from the rule of law principles which we discussed earlier.[42] Waldron's critical insight is to recognise that rule of law 'is the requirement that government action must, by and large, be conducted under the auspices of law, which means that, unless there is very good reason to the contrary, law should be created to authorize the actions that government is going to have to perform'.[43]

Waldron argues that such an authorisation process is a many-staged (by his count, ten) undertaking, with a number of the steps explicitly shaped by rule of law

---

[38] John Locke, *Second Treatise on Government* (1689) 2.143, 149–59.

[39] Charles Louis de Secondat, Baron de Montesquieu, *The Complete Works of M de Montesquieu* (London: T Evans, 1777) vol 1, bk XI, ch 6, 198–99, available at: http://oll.libertyfund.org/titles/837.

[40] *Federalist 47* (Madison), para 3 in George W Carey and James McClellan (eds), *The Federalist* (Indianapolis, Liberty Fund, 2001) available at https://oll.libertyfund.org/titles/788#Hamilton_0084_865.

[41] Jeremy Waldron, 'Separation of Powers in Thought and Practice?' (2013) 54 *Boston College Law Review* 433.

[42] See above pp 16–22.

[43] Waldron (n 41) 457.

considerations (of the Fulliarian/Razian flavour). In brief, and somewhat (but not entirely) paraphrased, these steps are:

1. Members of society identify the type of action they wish to perform.
2. Once identified, the 'contours of that action' are proposed and become the source of deliberation.
3. 'The representatives of the people' determine a 'clear set of formulations' for the legal norm.
4. These formulations are promulgated to the people and those responsible for the administration of the policy or rule.
5. As a result of this promulgation, those who may be affected by the rule or are responsible for administering the rule, 'order their expectations'.
6. When a dispute arises, those responsible for resolving such a dispute will initiate some sort of action.
7. Should the dispute not be resolved, the parties will have recourse to some form of judicial proceeding.
8. In such a proceeding, 'the issue of compliance will be argued out, not just factually, but in terms of how the norms that were communicated to the people are to be understood and how it is to be related to the rest of the law'.
9. After the proceeding, the court will make some kind of judicial determination.
10. If need be, this determination will be enforced.[44]

The flow between these steps, democracy and the rule of law is evident.

The first three steps identify the democratic origin of such norms within a representative legislature. Clarity, the need for promulgation and incorporation into expectations are inherent in steps 3–5. Implicit in steps 6–10 are an understanding of the rule of law shaped by considerations of natural justice. Further, the process Waldron describes is different from that which would be followed in the absence of strict division of powers. In the latter case, the body responsible for resolving (step 6) and/or the court(s) responsible for adjudicating disputes (steps 7–9) may well be defining (or redefining) the contours of the policy in the absence of democratic input (step 6, bypassing steps 1–4, which is the all-important legitimising point of the political content of any legislatively directed policy). That body potentially reformulates the legal norms, without the norms being promulgated (omitting step 4) and therefore allowing those who may be affected to reorder their expectations (step 5). Seen from this perspective, a consolidation of power into one body will violate the rule of law.

Waldron's articulation of the relationship of separation of powers to the rule of law provides support for this book's claim that the change in focus found in both American and European competition law towards a more economic effects-based means of analysis, with its related normative assumption that

---

[44] ibid 457–58.

only consumer welfare matters, represents a rule of law threat to both competition regimes. This rule of law threat is explored in the next subsection of this chapter.

E. Rule of Law, Separation of Powers and US Antitrust

The contrast between the early understanding of US antitrust law and how it is presently understood is significant. This was demonstrated in our consideration of the original views which shaped Congress's and the courts' early understandings of the purpose of the Sherman Act. These early views show that members of Congress may have had some crude understanding of what is now referred to as 'consumer welfare'. But the understanding of its protection was similar to the understanding of protection of property. In particular, it could be suggested that Congress's point here was the idea that by making consumers pay more than a fair (or the market) price for a particular good, producers (in particular, the trusts) were stealing from consumers. Expressed in later terms, Congress's understanding could be described as follows: consumers had a property right to their consumer surplus, and to deprive them of this through anticompetitive practices was tantamount to theft. However, protection of what we now understand as consumer surplus was not Congress's only goal. These other goals included protection of smaller enterprises.

This was the political consensus which gave rise to the Sherman Act. This consensus was pretty well respected by the courts until the mid-1970s. However, as shown in Chapter 3, since then the courts, directed by the USSC, have established a new understanding of the goal of the antitrust laws. This understanding, strongly influenced by the Chicago School, now puts consumer welfare as the sole goal of antitrust law and policy.[45]

This shift in focus is exclusively court driven. Being court driven, it was arrived at, and imposed, through a process that did not involve democratic institutions. Recalling Waldron's process by which governmental action is authorised,[46] we see that the shift in antitrust values that has happened in the US has occurred in the absence of democratic reflection and clear formulations which have been promulgated to the people, to allow them to order their expectations.[47]

The important role of such expectations, and the significance of legal change induced by this judicial reordering of values which underlie the legal order, has not gone unnoticed. In the dissent in *Leegin*, Justice Breyer identifies the importance of reliance interests which arise from the long-standing prohibition on resale

---

[45] *Sonotone* (n 2) 343 (1979) citing Bork (n 2) 66.

[46] Outlined above, see pp 162–63.

[47] Or, with explicit reference to the points above, this court-driven process omits steps one through five in Waldron's account.

price maintenance. To judicially do away with this prohibition undermines the expectations that various and diverse groups of people develop. Justice Breyer writes:

> [Relying on a prohibition of resale price maintenance, n]ew distributors, including internet distributors, have similarly invested time, money, and labor in an effort to bring yet lower cost goods to Americans.

> This Court's overruling of the per se rule jeopardizes this reliance, and more. What about malls built on the assumption that a discount distributor will remain an anchor tenant? What about home buyers who have taken a home's distance from such a mall into account? What about Americans, producers, distributors, and consumers, who have understandably assumed, at least for the last 30 years, that price competition is a legally guaranteed way of life? The majority denies none of this. It simply says that these 'reliance interests …, cannot justify an inefficient rule.'[48]

As noted earlier, in its 'thinnest' normative sense the rule of law is a set of requirements regarding the nature of legal rules. As the purpose of law is to enable those living under it to rationally order their lives, these rule of law considerations mirror our expectations of the necessary conditions to promote our ability to organise our behaviour. Certainty and stability of legal rules is among these.

We must distinguish judicially induced instability of this sort from the instability caused by the legislative process, when these latter institutions repeal or alter exiting law. Change through a legislative process has, by definition, a democratic element to it. This process ensures that, according to Waldron's schema, once the action which society wishes to see performed is identified,[49] then the legislature develops (and enacts) a clear formulation of the legal norm. This formulation, in turn, is promulgated, thereby allowing those affected to plan and order their lives. Such legislative change contrasts with judicial change. In the former case, the need for change is socially identified, and society's deliberative processes (eg the legislature) are invoked to provide democratic legitimacy for such an alteration of the legal framework. In the latter case, there may be no such broad social concern about problems associated with the existing rule and certainly no subsequent legislative (hence) democratic ratification of the proposed change. Where private litigation is the dominant driver of a particular area of law, the matter in dispute may not extend beyond the parties before a court (and others may not have standing to participate). Yet, the result of this litigation may well have broad implications for society as a whole. This is evidently the case with US antitrust law, which – save for the prosecution of hard-core cartels – is almost exclusively driven through private litigation, the outcome of which has strong implications for how one of society's most fundamental institutions, the market, is regulated.

---

[48] *Leegin Creative Leather Products v PSKS Inc*, 551 US 877, 925–26 (2007), the Court refers to *State Oil Co v Khan*, 522 US 3 (1997).

[49] Presumably some problem with the existing legal framework has been identified and a solution is proposed.

This normative argument linking separation of powers to the rule of law is independent from any positive argument regarding a constitutional division of powers within a particular jurisdiction, such as in the US. In that system (and those systems which share its features), the judiciary is not representative of the people. In the US federal judges are appointed and serve for life, subject to 'good behavior'.[50] This was to ensure that the judiciary was not subject to popular whims and would consequently be responsible for the impartial administration of justice.[51] The judiciary serves as an antidemocratic check on popular excesses. So, by its very design, the judiciary is necessarily non-responsive to the democratic process and democratic considerations. Hence, in a system where judicial impartiality is assured through isolation from democratic forces (and considerations) such 'judicial law-making' necessarily lacks democratic legitimacy.

F. Rule of Law, Separation of Powers and the EU Regime

The change in European competition policy towards a more economic approach which has occurred in the past 20 or so years has been almost exclusively Commission-driven. This was the focus of Chapter 3. The manner in which this alteration has been conducted leads to rule of law concerns.

These rule of law concerns are both of the normative sort and of the positive sort, and originate from the Commission's unilateral willingness to reinterpret Treaty goals. The concern here is quite straightforward. The European Treaties set out a number of goals surrounding European integration. These include economic and social goals, and the Treaties establish institutions to ensure that these goals can be achieved. In addition to conferring power on these institutions, the Treaties also limit the institutional ability to exercise power. As international treaties, these European Treaties have been ratified by each Member State in accordance with their domestic law. The democratic legitimacy of these goals and Treaty arrangements is thus ensured through the negotiation and ratification of these agreements.

According to the TEU, the Commission's role is to oversee EU law, under the Court of Justice.[52] In effect it serves as the EU's executive branch, albeit with the right of initiative. But in exercising this initiative it cannot unilaterally create secondary legislation, but must do so with the concurrence of the Parliament and/or Council. And of course, it cannot unilaterally rewrite the Treaties.

The Commission, by its reinterpretation of the provisions of Articles 101 and 102, is performing a task similar to rewriting a Treaty. The competition provisions of the TFEU do not exist in isolation from the other provisions of the Treaties.

---

[50] US Constitution, Art III, s 1.
[51] See eg *Federalist 78* (Hamilton) in Carey (n 40).
[52] TEU Art 17(1).

To read particular Articles of the Treaties in isolation is not merely an interpretative mistake,[53] but ignores the prescription of Article 7: 'The Union shall ensure consistency between its policies and activities, taking all of its objectives into account and in accordance with the principle of conferral of powers.' As the Union acts through its institutions, these institutions must therefore take into account the need to take into account multiple goals.

Immediately after Article 7, the Treaty identifies a number of social and economic goals in so-called 'integration' or 'policy linking' clauses. These clauses include Article 9's recognition of the need to 'take into account requirements linked to the promotion of a high level of employment, the guarantee of adequate social protection, the fight against social exclusion, and a high level of education, training and protection of human health'. Additionally, Article 11 provides a linkage to environmental protection and sustainable development.

The existence of such clauses imposes a legal duty on those acting under the European Treaties, which include European institutions such as the Commission to take into account these values in determining a course of action. This is a fairly uncontroversial claim regarding EU law as a whole. Townley, for instance, notes that '[g]eneral Community lawyers readily embrace this conclusion'.[54] In the case of competition concerns, such policy-linking clauses would require the Commission to take into account values such as environmental concerns and employment objectives when they faced with them in a competition matter.[55] And, in a competition matter, Article 101(3) would appear to be the appropriate place (or step in the analysis) for the Commission (or similar body) to undertake this sort of evaluation.

This appears to have been the Commission's practice in the pre-MEA era. Evidence for this can be found in the Commission's decisions in *Synthetic Fibres*,[56] *Stichting Baksteen*[57] and *CECED*.[58] The former two decisions concern industry-wide agreements for the 'orderly' shut-down of production, where due to a collapse

---

[53] Arguably a European Court would be unlikely to read a particular provision of a Treaty in isolation from other Articles. See generally Koen Lenaerts and José A Gutiérrez-Fons, 'To Say What the Law of the EU Is: Methods of Interpretation and the European Court of Justice' (2013) 20 *Columbia Journal of European Law* 3.

[54] Christopher Townley, *Article 81 EC and Public Policy* (Oxford, Hart, 2009) 51 fn 41, and the sources he cites.

[55] This view is reasonably common among academics. See eg Francis Kieran, 'A Separation of Powers Approach to Non-efficiency Goals in EU Competition Law' (2103) 119 *European Public Law* 189, 196; Townley ibid, 50–51 and 54; Johan W van de Gronden, 'The Internal Market, The State and Private Initiative' (2006) 33 *Legal Issues of Economic Integration* 105, 134; Rein Wessling *The Modernisation of EC Antitrust Law* (Oxford, Hart, 2000) 105–13.

[56] Commission Decision of 4 July 1984 relating to a proceeding under Article 85 of the EEC Treaty (IV/30.810 – *Synthetic fibres*) [1984] OJ L207/17.

[57] Commission Decision of 29 April 1994 relating to a proceeding under Article 85 of the EC Treaty (IV/34.456 – *Stichting Baksteen*) [1994] OJ L131/15.

[58] Commission Decision of 24 January 1999 relating to a proceeding under Article 81 of the EC Treaty and Article 53 of the EEA Agreement (Case IV.F.1/36.718 – *CECED*) (notified under document number C(1999) 5064) [2000] OJ L187/47.

in demand for products there was an overcapacity of production.[59] Members of the industry agreed on an orderly process of plant closures and restructuring to facilitate an orderly reduction of production.[60] If the plans were successful, not only would (after time) both industries return to profitability and normal competitiveness,[61] but the agreement would alleviate much of the social cost (such as the burden of unemployment) of industrial restructuring.[62] In both cases, the Commission exempted the agreements under Article 101(3).

These exemptions do not appear to be isolated events. They are instances of the Commission following a policy which it articulated in its *XIIth Report on Competition Policy* (1982). There, the Commission remarked:

> [T]he Commission may be able to condone agreements in restraint of competition which relate to a sector as a whole, provided they are aimed solely at achieving a coordinated reduction of overcapacity and do not otherwise restrict free decision-making by the firms involved. The necessary structural reorganization must not be achieved by unsuitable means such as price-fixing or quota agreements, nor should it be hampered by State aids which lead to artificial preservation of surplus capacity.[63]

Under this manner of applying Article 101(3) the Commission would exempt agreements to restrict output as part of a strategy to ameliorate the effects of a downturn in a particular industrial sector.

Similarly, the Commission also took a more encompassing view of Article 101(3) when it considered industry-wide arrangements designed to promote environmental concerns. *CECED*[64] is the case in point. At issue was an agreement among manufactures of household washing machines to phase out the production (and importation to the Community) of the least energy-efficient models.[65] As the least-efficient machines were typically the least expensive, phasing out such machines would require purchasers of new machines to buy a more costly (but more efficient) washing machine.[66] This industry-wide arrangement, though having a restrictive object,[67] was exempted by the Commission under Article 101(3).

In exempting the agreement, the Commission relied on the individual economic and collective environmental benefits which this arrangement would promote. Individuals would – over time – save money by using more efficient washers: the additional expense of the cost of the machine would be more than recouped through the savings in electrical consumption.[68] The collective environmental

[59] *Synthetic Fibres* (n 56) paras 28–31; *Stichting Baksteen* (n 57) paras 18–19.
[60] *Synthetic Fibres* ibid paras 35–36; *Stichting Baksteen* ibid paras 16 and 26.
[61] *Synthetic Fibres* ibid paras 35–36; *Stichting Baksteen* ibid para 26.
[62] *Synthetic Fibres* ibid para 37, *Stichting Baksteen* ibid para 27.
[63] European Commission, *XIIth Report on Competition Policy* (Brussels, Office for Official Publications of the European Communities, 1982) para 41.
[64] *CECED* (n 58).
[65] ibid paras 18–24.
[66] ibid paras 11–17.
[67] ibid paras 30–37.
[68] ibid para 52.

benefit arose from the reduction in the production of pollutants resulting from a decreased demand for electricity. The Commission noted:

> The Commission reasonably estimates the saving in marginal damage from (avoided) carbon dioxide emissions (the so-called 'external costs') at EUR 41 to 61 per ton of carbon dioxide. On a European scale, avoided damage from sulphur dioxide amounts to EUR 4000 to 7000 per ton and EUR 3000 to 5000 per ton of nitrous oxide. On the basis of reasonable assumptions, the benefits to society brought about by the CECED agreement appear to be more than seven times greater than the increased purchase costs of more energy-efficient washing machines. Such environmental results for society would adequately allow consumers a fair share of the benefits even if no benefits accrued to individual purchasers of machines.[69]

The Commission's pre-MEA approach took a broad perspective on the application of the Article 101(3) exception.

However, with the MEA and the publication of the Guidelines on Article 101(3)[70] the Commission's focus narrowed. The focus is now on the efficiencies, objectively measured, which an agreement produces.[71] Where a balancing of pro- and anti-competitive effects must take place, that balancing must occur within a relevant market.[72] Although the Commission recognises that some agreements create efficiencies which will only materialise in the future (hence requiring the application of a discount rate in their assessment), the requirement that these two types of effects must be compared with each other in the same (or at least substantially the same[73]) market prevents cross-market comparison (or balancing) of the agreement's effects. This has significant implications for the assessment of industry-wide agreements of the sort discussed above.

In an 'orderly downsizing' agreement, a significant amount of the adverse social and economic effects are regional, ie the areas supported by the factory subject to closure. Orderly restructuring of the industry allows this region (and similar regions) to 'gain', by mitigating the effects of a sudden plant closure. Yet the costs of a downsizing of this type may be imposed on others outside of the region that may be paying an increased price as a result. Similarly, environmental concerns involve not just a wide range of present beneficiaries (the 'gainers' from reduced carbon emissions are greater than those who pay more for particular goods) but also an intergenerational comparison of costs and burdens is impossible, given the need for comparison on the same market.[74]

---

[69] ibid para 56; Commission's footnote (regarding the costing of the damage from emissions) omitted.
[70] Guidelines on the application of Article 81(3) of the Treaty [2004] OJ C101/97.
[71] ibid paras 13, 33 and 48–72.
[72] ibid paras 43 and 87.
[73] ibid para 43.
[74] Further, contrary to TFEU's exhortation about animal welfare concerns, in Art 101(3) balancing, these concerns need to be monetised in a 'willingness to pay' calculation (ie how much extra are consumers in a given market for animal products willing to pay to ensure that the animals of concern are treated humanely). See Authority for Consumers and Markets (the Netherland's Competition Authority), 'ACM's Analysis of the Sustainability Arrangements Concerning the "Chicken of Tomorrow"' (26 January 2015) ACM/DM/2014/206028, available at https://www.acm.nl/sites/default/files/old_publication/publicaties/13789_analysis-chicken-of-tomorrow-acm-2015-01-26.pdf.

The result of the Commission's refocusing to the MEA is illustrated by its amicus curiae observations in *BIDS*.[75] This case, resulting from a reference to the ECJ from the High Court of Ireland,[76] concerned an industry-wide arrangement of Irish slaughterhouses, in an effort to reduce overcapacity. The arrangement in question was to all intents and purposes identical to those in *Synthetic Fibres* and *Stichting Baksteen*. The BIDS arrangement provided that some processors would exit the industry ('the goers'). The 'goers' would be compensated by 'the stayers', via a levy on the number of cattle they slaughtered.[77] The reference to the ECJ determined that this was a restriction of competition by object, and the matter was remanded back to the High Court for consideration of the Article 101(3) issue.

These amicus curae observations were highly reliant on the Guidelines on Article 101(3), and in its observations the Commission recants its previous views on the acceptability of crisis cartels. It remarks:

> The Commission wishes to emphasise that so-called '*crisis cartels*' which aim to reduce industry capacity cannot be justified by economic downturns and recession-induced falls in demand. As a general rule in a free market economy, market forces should remove unnecessary capacity from a market. … In such circumstances, it is for each undertaking to decide for itself whether, and at which point, overcapacity becomes economically unsustainable and to take necessary steps to reduce it.[78]

This statement from the Commission is a full U-turn from its position in the 1982 *Report on Competition Policy*.

This new treatment of industry-wide restructuring raises at least two of rule of law concerns. The new, Commission-driven, understanding of the role of Article 101 appears to ring-fence the Treaty's competition provisions from the remainder of the Treaty's Articles. The policy linking (or 'integration') clauses of the Treaty require those operating under and/or applying European law to take 'big-picture' perspective of the Treaties' aims. But in its reinterpretation of the competition provisions, the Commission takes a narrower perspective, thereby isolating competition concerns from the remainder of the Union's social and political objectives. This narrower perspective, focusing exclusively on the welfare effects of a given practice, replaces the ordoliberal foundation on which the European competition provisions rest.[79]

Further, with the decentralisation of the application of EU competition law[80] Member State authorities and courts can take divergent approaches to the

---

[75] *The Competition Authority v The Beef Industry Development Council and Barry Brothers (Carrigmore) Meats Ltd* [2006] IEHC 294; the Commission's observations are available at: http://ec.europa.eu/competition/court/amicus_curiae_2010_bids_en.pdf.

[76] Case C-209/07 *Competition Authority v Beef Industry Development Society Ltd and Barry Brothers (Carrigmore) Meats Ltd*, ECLI:EU:C:2008:643.

[77] ibid para 13.

[78] Commission's Observations (n 75) para 33.

[79] Note, for instance, that the reference in Art 3(3) TEU to 'a highly competitive social market economy' can be interpreted as a reference to an ordoloberal approach to the economy.

[80] Although Member State courts and authorities apply national competition law, in so doing they are also obliged to apply EU law: see Council Regulation (EC) No 1/2003 of 16 December 2002 on the implementation of the rules on competition laid down in Articles 81 and 82 of the Treaty [1993] OJ L1/1 Art 3.

substantive provisions of Article 101(3). While these Member State institutions are obliged to apply EU law, there is compelling evidence that they differ in their assessment of the (non-economic) benefits when they apply Article 101(3).[81] This divergence in the substantive understanding of this provision tells against a consistent interpretation and application of the competition provisions across the EU. While the MEA may not be the sole cause of this divergence in interpretation, it is likely to have exacerbated the inconsistency. Other courts and authorities have taken other sorts of goals into account. But by focusing exclusively on the economic benefits in its understanding of Article 101(3), the Commission has necessarily shied away from considering possible non-economic benefits, thereby depriving other authorities of possible guidance to ensure some semblance of consistency in the understanding of the competition rules.

G. Rule of Law and Institutional Legitimacy: Concluding Thoughts

In both the United States and the European Union, competition policy is an inherently political project. The political element of the US project was visible from the popular concerns which prodded legislators in the 1880s to enact the Sherman Act. The political concerns still exist today – newspapers frequently run articles and editorial pieces about the antitrust threats posed by larger companies.[82] Similarly, in Europe, competition policy is inherently political. The past and present European Treaties are parts of an evolving political process. These Treaties direct the activities of Member States and Union institutions. Competition policy is only one such activity. All of this should be fairly trite.

But two things follow immediately from this political nature of competition policy. First, the legitimacy of a given regulatory policy rests on the nature of the political (or other sorts of) process which produced and imposed that policy. Second, as with all political processes, goals and ideology matter. This is particularly the case when the policy involves market regulation, as is the case with competition law.[83] The first part of this chapter demonstrated a connection between the legitimacy of the political processes which brought about a given legislative result and the rule of law. This connection pointed to a process of ongoing democratic consent in the legislative stages when a proposed course of action is transformed into legislation. It is at this point that the ideology and goals obtain their democratic legitimacy.

---

[81] See Or Brook, 'Struggling with Article 101(3) TFEU: Diverging Approaches of the Commission, EU Courts, and Five Competition Authorities' (2019) 56 *Common Market Law Review* 121.

[82] These seem to be directed towards the 'tech giants', eg Google (Alphabet), Amazon and Facebook.

[83] See eg Marina Lao, 'Ideology Matters in the Antitrust Debate' (2014) 79 *Antitrust Law Journal* 649, 680–84.

As also argued, if the goals or ideology are changed (or 'reinterpreted') after this process – by a court or other body – the reinterpreted may lose the force of this democratic legitimacy. This has occurred in both the US and the EU.

As ideology and politics matter, it cannot be said that the MEA or the line of thinking which brought about the US effects-based approach is value free. If anything, it stresses the preference of individuals to act in the market, is suspicious of governmental intervention (lest such intervention result in type I errors), and is unwilling to consider values beyond efficiency in competition assessments. As such it possesses many of the hallmarks of a conservative political agenda.[84] While some of the methodology of this approach may be the correct approach to the analysis of competition matters, it is another matter for courts and competition authorities, by stealth, to substitute other values without democratic oversight or legislative scrutiny. Indeed, as Karel van Miert, the European Competition Commissioner from 1993 to 1999, once remarked: 'I would be worried about seeing an independent authority exercising its power without any Parliamentary control. Competition policy is not something neutral, it is "politics".[85] Although van Miert's words were in regard to a proposed European Cartel Office, they are very applicable to the Commission's new approach.

II. The Rule of Law and Institutional Competency

The previous section has identified a problem of democratic legitimacy in the economics-focused reorientation of antitrust. This was shown to be a rule of law problem. The suggestion was that this reorientation of competition law in both the US and EU by bodies which are not subject to the control of (or input from) democratic processes is a concern. This concern is exacerbated by the role which competition policy plays in regulating one of the more fundamental institutions of a liberal society: the market.

However, the sole focus on consumer welfare in the effects-based approach is only one part of the rule of law issue. There is little point in mandating an analytical approach to a competition law controversy if the results of that analysis are overly technical to the point where they may not be confidently used in a proceeding aimed at resolving that controversy. Economic analysis, whether in the form of theoretical perspectives (eg orthodox price theory versus a behaviourist approach), theories of harm, and the analysis of data used in conjunction with the former, is the vehicle which now resolves most competition disputes. But the vast majority of triers of fact, whether judicial or lay (as in the US) are not conversant

---

[84] ibid 684–85.
[85] Karel van Miert, *Agence Europe*, 6 January 1995, quoted in Stephen Wilks and Lee McGowan, 'Disarming the Commission: The Debate Over a European Cartel Office' (1995) 32 *Journal of Common Market Studies* 259, 268.

with economics, particularly the sophisticated version used in resolving antitrust disputes. This gives rise to an additional rule of law problem.

A. Gaps in Knowledge, Expert Evidence and Evaluative Competency

The economic evidence relevant to the resolution of an antitrust dispute is characteristically produced and presented by experts who have been engaged by parties to the dispute. This evidence is typically beyond the expertise of the triers of fact. Triers of fact therefore need to somehow analyse the information presented to them, come to an understanding of its significance, and then make a decision based on all of this. But there is a competency or epistemic gap in these circumstances. The triers of fact have a lacuna in their knowledge, which the parties attempt to fill through expert evidence. Yet, these epistemically challenged triers of fact must, in turn, evaluate this evidence. Therein lays an issue of competency: if there is a lack of expertise, which ex hypothesi, there is (otherwise there would be no point to introduce and/or rely on expert evidence), then triers of fact need to be somehow competent to evaluate this (often conflicting) evidence.

These concerns regarding expertise and competency can be found at the levels of assessing the broad theories which point to a source of harm. The dispute arising from the differences in analytical perspectives between the majority and minority of the USSC in *Kodak* is a case in point. In the above discussion of this case, we saw that the difference in the two views can be explained by the majority taking an early behaviourist approach while the minority's view is informed by a more orthodox approach which uses traditional price theory. The best forum for the resolution of which of these two social scientific models is appropriate is likely to be a philosophy of (social) science journal or conference, not a courtroom.

Furthermore, even if a given model is accepted as the most appropriate, it may be the case that the model can be equivocal in generating a theory of harm. The theory may or may not be applied correctly. For instance the leveraging theories of harm raised by the Commission in *Google (Shopping)*[86] may or may not accurately reflect economic reality. Again, it is not clear if a courtroom is the appropriate venue to determine this. Finally, the chosen theory may generate factually different results. Economic evidence is used in the determination of relevant market and calculation of damages, and given their significance in any given case, it is no surprise that expert assessment often varies.

---

[86] Commission Decision of 27 June 2017 relating to a proceeding under Article 102 of the Treaty on the Functioning of the European Union and Article 54 of the EEA Agreement (Case AT.39740 – *Google Search (Shopping)*) (notified under document number C(2017) 4444).

This section examines the rule of law considerations which arise from the use of economic theory and evidence in competition proceedings, and the competence of triers of fact to evaluate competing (and highly technical) evidentiary claims and explanatory theories.

B. Admissibility and Assessment of Economic Evidence

A consequence of the economic or effects-based approach in antitrust is that bright-line tests of legality are vanishing from the competition landscape on both sides of the Atlantic. Adjudication in a matter controlled by bright-line rules is conceptually simple. The inquiry need only determine if the defendant's conduct crossed a clearly defined line or legal rule, and resolve the case accordingly. However, under the effects-based approach, resolution of competition disputes requires explicit 'reliance on economic concepts, such as market power, efficiency, and conditions of entry – all of which are best introduced into evidence through an economist'.[87]

But once this evidence has been introduced, judges may not be best placed to evaluate it. Judges (or more generally, triers of fact) are unlikely to be trained economists. And gaps in judicial knowledge are not just limited to matters of economics. As a result, in legal proceedings technical evidence tends to be presented and explained by experts in a relevant field, which is then relied upon by adjudicators. One commentator has called this procedure 'epistemic deference'.[88] This is to say judges (or other fact finders) accept that experts, due to their superior understanding of a particular subject, are better placed to 'find' a particular fact which would fall within an area (or be elicited through the methodology) of that subject area.

The difficulty with this sort of deference is that not all expertise is reliable; and even in fields which produce generally reliable results, experts may disagree over the interpretation and significance of these results. In exercising such 'epistemic deference', triers of fact therefore need to be guided by standards which aid in selecting reliable expertise and assessing its results in the fact-finding process. In evidence law terms, these expert opinions must be subject to rules regarding admissibility, relevance and weight. But along with these evidence law considerations, there are some significant issues of theory acceptance which may properly be within the domain of the philosopher of science.

Legal systems have rules regarding the admissibility of expert evidence. In the US federal system, this is driven by the Federal Rules of Evidence[89] (particularly

---

[87] Andrew I Gavil, 'Defining Reliable Forensic Economics in the Post-*Daubert/Kumho Tire* Era: Case Studies from Antitrust' (2000) 57 *Washington and Lee Law Review* 831, 835.

[88] Scott Brewer, 'Scientific Expert Testimony and Intellectual Due Process' (1998) 107 *Yale Law Journal* 1535, 1553.

[89] Federal Rules of Evidence, Appendix to Title 28 USCA and USCS Rules.

Rule 702) as interpreted by the Courts (namely by the USSC's ruling in *Daubert*[90]). The Rule states:

> A witness who is qualified as an expert by knowledge, skill, experience, training, or education may testify in the form of an opinion or otherwise if:
>
> (a) the expert's scientific, technical, or other specialized knowledge will help the trier of fact to understand the evidence or to determine a fact in issue;
> (b) the testimony is based on sufficient facts or data;
> (c) the testimony is the product of reliable principles and methods; and
> (d) the expert has reliably applied the principles and methods to the facts of the case.[91]

As the USSC noted in *Daubert*, the Rule refers to *scientific* knowledge, which the Court then says 'implies a grounding in the methods and procedures of science'.[92] That Court provides a non-exhaustive listing of some of the indicia of what counts as 'science'. These include the possibility of testing and falsification, peer review and publication, error rate of a given technique, and 'general acceptance' within a particular community (presumably of experts).[93] It is noteworthy that the academic sources cited by the Court discuss 'science' in the context of the physical, natural or biomedical sciences – social science is not discussed.

There is a gatekeeping function to this rule of admissibility, ie to keep junk science out of the courtroom. But it does so at a cost – it requires judges to have sufficient competence to determine whether a particular methodological approach is 'science'. Brewer, in a significant piece, writes:

> The question, then, is this: How could a scientifically untrained judge be sufficiently epistemically *competent* to perform the gatekeeping task imposed upon it by *Daubert*'s reading of the Federal Rules of Evidence? Moreover, assuming the judge admits the evidence, how could a scientifically untrained trier of fact, whether judge or jury, be sufficiently epistemically competent to assess competing putatively scientific claims by *competing* expert witnesses when, *ex hypothesi*, that factfinder does not have the requisite expertise to judge the evidence itself?[94]

And, in the context of antitrust experts, Posner writes:

> A perfectly respectable economist might be an antitrust 'hawk,' another equally respectable economist a 'dove.' Each might have a long list of reputable academic publications fully consistent with systematically pro-plaintiff or pro-defendant testimony, and so a judge or jury would have little basis for choosing between them.[95]

While a judge may have an intuitive 'feel' about the merits of a particular theory or conclusion, a 'feel' is an insufficient basis for a principled legal justification.

---

[90] *Daubert v Merrell Dow Pharmaceuticals*, 509 US 579 (1993).
[91] Federal Rules of Evidence (n 89) R 702.
[92] *Daubert* (n 90) 590.
[93] ibid 593–94.
[94] Brewer (n 88) pp 1551–52.
[95] Richard A Posner, 'The Law and Economics of the Economic Expert Witness' (1999) 13 *Journal of Economic Perspectives* 91, 96.

But more significantly, the US standard of admissibility is shaped by appeal to the natural sciences, ie physical and life sciences. Considerations peculiar to the social science are outside of this paradigm. While an excursus into the philosophy of (social) science is well beyond the topic of this present work, it would be fair to state that the phenomena that are of concern to the social scientist (typically involving human behaviour) are of a different sort than those of concern to the physical or life scientist.[96] Thus the two use different explanatory models, with differing methodologies and experiment design (if experiments are in fact used – economics traditionally avoids experimentation).

One could cogently suggest that as the *Daubert* (or similar approach) to admissibility of evidence is skewed too far to the paradigm of science as (only) natural science, *Daubert* tests are inappropriately used to exclude evidence from the social sciences. There is significant evidence which suggests that *Daubert* has made the introduction of evidence into antitrust cases more difficult.[97] Alternatively, and more radically, it could be suggested that the failure of social science (or at least some social sciences) to fit within this paradigm of science demonstrates its unreliability for forensic purposes. If economics were thus viewed, it would of course undermine the methodological and normative foundations for the economic approach to competition law. But this may be a step (or an argument) too far.

In the European Courts, the standard for admissibility is that of relevance, and judges are thus less constrained about the sorts of economic evidence allowed into legal proceedings. Some commentators suggest that this is appropriate, as in the European Courts judges are the triers of fact, unlike in US courts where fact-finding is the purview of lay jurors.[98] But this assumes that *only* lay people are unable to separate 'good' from 'bad' science without guidance. Scientifically untrained judges suffer from the same epistemic deficiencies as scientifically untrained lay people.[99] It may therefore be appropriate for the European Courts (or legislature) to develop and articulate rules for admissibility and presentation of such evidence, and require courts to instruct themselves on these rules prior to reception of such evidence. This may prevent 'junk science' from entering the courtroom via a well-meaning judge.

In both the US and EU economic evidence in competition cases is presented by partisan experts. While practice in both the US[100] and EU permits court-appointed experts, this procedure is little used in EU Courts. In EU Courts, this

---

[96] See eg Julian Reiss, *Philosophy of Economics: A Contemporary Introduction* (London, Routledge, 2013) 1–26 and 174–94.

[97] See eg Christine P Bartholomew, 'Death By *Daubert*: The Continued Attack on Private Antitrust' (2014) 35 *Cardozo Law Review* 2147.

[98] See eg Andriani Kalintiri, *Evidence Standards EU Competition Enforcement: The EU Approach* (Oxford, Hart, 2019) 119.

[99] Indeed, in the US the likelihood that scientifically trained individuals sit on a jury is greater than that of a scientifically trained individual sitting on the bench, as juries are generally reflective of the communities from which they are selected.

[100] Federal Rules of Evidence (n 89) R 706.

has only been done twice.[101] The use of court-appointed experts is not a panacea to compensate for this judicial epistemic deficiency; judges will need the appropriate knowledge to select the appropriate or 'neutral' expert, as the above quote from Posner implicitly suggests.

Finally, and contrary to some suggestions, the use of institutions, societies and leaned academies to aid and advise in the choice of experts is no guarantee of improvement or neutrality.[102] Posner's hawk and dove situation can still arise; society membership tends towards mainstream rather than cutting-edge opinion;[103] and given that not all such institutions and societies are of equal repute, there is a regress problem in certifying the certifiers.

C. Evaluative Competency, Reasoned Adjudication and the Rule of Law

Chapter 1's discussion of the rule of law noted that there is a rule of law challenge which is posed by arbitrariness within a legal system. The purpose of law is to permit those subject to it to rationally plan their lives, and arbitrary laws and/or adjudication are an impediment to such effective planning. That discussion also indicated two ways in which laws or decisions could be arbitrary: law can serve to benefit a certain set of people, irrespective of legal merit; or law can produce unreasoned outcomes. In the former sense, 'arbitrariness' is used to describe legal systems which benefit a tyrant or those in favour with her; in the latter sense the word connotes randomness replacing legal merit in the determination of a legal outcome or state of affairs.

It is this second sense that is of present concern. A legal system which respects the rule of law, in the weak sense of concern to us, has at least two components. First, it incorporates a number of standards that allow for individuals to plan their lives. Second, in such a legal system, those applying the law (eg through making administrative or judicial decisions) do so in a rational, non-arbitrary manner. It is uncontroversial to suggest that rational decisions are made by a decision-maker under circumstances where the decision-maker either has knowledge or justified belief of the subject matter of the decision.

---

[101] Kalintiri (n 98) 117 fn 94 notes that this was only done in Case 48/69 *Imperial Chemical Industries Ltd v Commission*, ECLI:EU:C:1972:70 and Joined Cases C-89/85, C-104/85, C-114/85, C-116/85, C-117/85, C-125/85, C-126/85, C-127/85, C-128/85 and C-129/85 *Ahlström Osakeyhtiö and others v Commission*, ECLI:EU:C:1988:447.

[102] See Maarten Pieter Schinkel, 'Forensic Economics in Competition Law Enforcement' (2007) 4 *Journal of Competition Law and Economics* 1, 24–25; Posner (n 95) 97 suggests something like this.

[103] While this may screen out junk science, it may also retard the use of new techniques and methodology, as the use of DNA in forensic science shows. DNA 'fingerprinting' was quite cutting edge until the late 1980s; it is now mainstream forensic science: see eg Royal Society, *Forensic DNA Analysis: A Primer for the Courts* (London, Royal Society, 2017) available at: https://royalsociety.org/-/media/about-us/programmes/science-and-law/royal-society-forensic-dna-analysis-primer-for-courts.pdf.

The now orthodox approach to competition requires analysis and understanding of phenomena (eg market power, market definition, entry barriers, just to name a few of the 'simpler' ones) which are typically beyond the epistemic competence of most legal decision-makers. Hence data describing these phenomena are introduced by experts who proffer an explanation and interpretation of how these phenomena should cause the decision-maker to make a particular legal determination in the controversy that the decision-maker is charged with resolving. In an adversarial model, there will be two – almost certainly opposing – sets of explanations, as each side will engage their own experts to influence the decision. If there are amici curae or third parties involved in the controversy, the number of expert opinions may multiply.

The problem is how a decision-maker (eg judge) can come to a rational decision in the face of this likely complex and likely conflicting information which is outside of her expertise.[104] This is very much a rule of law problem, given the need to avoid arbitrariness. A fortiori the judge cannot make the decision based on her own knowledge, since she lacks this. Otherwise there would be no need to use experts' evidence to explain the material in question.[105] Thus to make a rational determination, the decision-maker must have a justified belief which points to an appropriate factual foundation that is sufficient to resolve the dispute. The issue therefore is how, ie under what circumstances, can the fact-finder come to acquire such a *justified* belief.

In his discussion of the problem, Brewer notes that deference to expert testimony can be justified on a number of grounds: (i) second-guessing (or making an independent judgement) about the accuracy of the evidence; (ii) subjecting the expert's testimony to the same standards of evidentiary scrutiny which apply to non-expert testimony; (iii) evaluating the expert's demeanour during testimony; and (iv) evaluating the expert's credentials.[106]

Second-guessing, or the trier of fact's making an independent judgement about the content of the expert's testimony, is what the USSC in *Daubert* suggests a judge – in exercising a gatekeeper role – must do.[107] The USSC directs the gatekeeper to focus more towards the expert's methodological approach than the conclusions which the expert draws. But this likely draws an artificial distinction between methodology and results, which may be of significance in disciplines where extensive mathematical modelling is the methodological norm, as the methodology chosen may determine the result.

---

[104] This concern extends beyond competition matters, to all areas where resolving the dispute requires engaging with a factual matrix outside of the judge's area of epistemic competence.

[105] Cases where a judge in addition to being legally trained is also an expert in the area will be dealt with below. These situations are likely to be extremely rare. But in competition matters, there have been suggestions to create specialised competition courts staffed by judges with high-level economic expertise.

[106] Brewer (n 88) 1616–30.

[107] *Daubert* (n 90) 593–94.

Subjecting the expert's evidence to identical standards of evidentiary assessment to that of non-experts is appropriate. But as Brewer notes, this may not get us far.[108] The standard criteria are principles such as consistency, coherence and explanatory value. The facts about which witnesses testify can be placed on a continuum, from the obvious to the obscure, as ordered by the trier's prior epistemic competence. The closer the testimony is to the obvious end of the spectrum, the less likely the trier of fact needs to rely on the expert's interpretation. At the other end of the spectrum, the trier of fact requires greater epistemic competence to evaluate the coherence of the expert's testimony. As Brewer remarks: 'But the more obscure the expert's failure of rational coherence, the more comprehension of the expert discipline one must have in order to see that it is a failure.'[109]

Relying on the expert's demeanour reduces to reliance on the expert's presentational skills – in other words, how the expert presents the evidence. This is hardly an effective way of evaluating what the expert says. Similarly, a battle of credentials has not only regress problems (ie who evaluates the merits of the credentials) and a non-expert evaluator of credentials may make inaccurate judgements about the credentials. But, most significantly, possession of relevant credentials is no guarantee that what the credentialled individual states is true.

Thus the usual standards of assessment are of little help to an epistemically challenged trier of fact to assess and come to a rational belief about the accuracy of a given expert's testimony. When the trier of fact is required to make a choice between the (contradictory) evidence of two experts, the difficulties with assessment and arriving at a rational belief are compounded. In these circumstances, a trier of fact is asked to determine which of two, polished presentations by similarly credentialled individuals that interpreted the same (or very similar) obscure (and perhaps complicated) data in two different ways, is best. Given that the trier is epistemically challenged, there may be little on which to found a rational belief one way or another.

If the trier has little on which to rationally justify a belief one way or the other, the trier's decision is to some greater or lesser extent arbitrary. This is significant from a rule of law perspective. As noted above, arbitrary rule is antithetical to rule of law considerations.[110] To the extent that rule of law considerations mandate a legal system the goal of which is to allow its subjects to rationally plan their lives, arbitrariness in a legal decision-making process (or dispute resolution process) impedes, if not undermines, this goal. If this argument is correct it shows that the exceptional reliance on expert evidence which an effects-based approach to competition law – whether in its American or European form – creates, and the epistemic limitations of triers of fact in an competition case, suggest that there is a significant arbitrariness to the triers' judgments. This is a real rule of law threat.

---

[108] Brewer (n 88) 1618–21.
[109] ibid 1621.
[110] See pp 18–21 above.

Of course, an immediate response is to suggest that – at least in competition matters – the epistemic gap is not as great as I have suggested. The response goes something like: judges do have experience in receiving and assessing economic evidence, and as a result they resolve the issue correctly, or at least not arbitrarily.

The issue therefore is: does judicial experience in competition cases (perhaps also supplemented by judicial training in competition economics) close this epistemic gap and allow judges to make non-arbitrary decisions in such matters? But it should be noted that resolving an issue correctly (ie the legally appropriate outcome is reached) is not identical to resolving an issue in a non-arbitrary fashion (ie the issue is resolved using the arbiter's knowledge or justified belief). In binary cases involving an 'all or nothing' outcome (eg a plaintiff obtains or is denied injunctive relief), a coin toss will decide the matter 'correctly' about half the time (assuming an equal distribution of meritorious and unworthy cases).

One plausible hypothesis regarding judicial ability to appropriately resolve (ie come to a decision based on knowledge or justified belief) would be that such ability is correlated with judicial experience in deciding competition matters and/or antecedent training in the economics of competition law. However, empirical testing of such a hypothesis does not paint an optimistic picture. Baye and Wright's study, which considered every US District Court ruling on the substantive merits of an antitrust claim between 1996 and 2006, is the leading study in this regard.[111] This study takes appeals of decisions as an indicator for judicial error, as an appeal signals that one party's economic experts believe that the original decision was incorrect, and consequently the party is willing to undertake the expense of convincing an appellate court of this error.[112] Lower appeal rates are taken to mean that a trial judge properly decided the matter in the first instance. The study also took into account the economic complexity of each case.

The results of this study are interesting. First, it shows that 'decisions involving some evaluation of economic or econometric evidence are appealed approximately 10 percent more frequently than cases demanding less economic skill'.[113] Training has some, but not a lot of bearing on the appeal rate. Baye and Wright note:

> Our second finding is that the decisions of judges who attended programs to learn basic economic skills are appealed at the same rate as those of their untrained counterparts in complex cases but about 10 percent less often in cases that do not involve the evaluation of sophisticated economic or econometric evidence.[114]

They note a plausible interpretation of this is that training helps for simple matters, but it is insufficient to resolve complex cases.[115] A further study by

---

[111] Michael R Baye and Joshua D Wright, 'Is Antitrust Too Complicated for Generalist Judges? The Impact of Economic Complexity and Judicial Training on Appeals' (2011) 54 *Journal of Law and Economics* 1.
[112] ibid 11.
[113] ibid 20.
[114] ibid.
[115] ibid.

Wright and Diveley extends this analysis to the apparently expert Federal Trade Commission.[116] They, using similar metrics, find that 'the evidence suggests the Commission does not perform as well as generalist judges in its adjudicatory antitrust decision-making role'.[117] This may be a reflection of the quality of the Commissioners,[118] who may have been appointed for reasons other than being expert economists. The empirical results show that some economics helps triers of fact to reach reasoned decisions, but it is by no means a complete solution.

A further, plausible response to this may well be: if some economics is good, more should be better; hence, what is needed are specialised courts staffed by judges who have undergone extensive training in competition economics. This training will provide such judges with sufficient knowledge to close (or at least narrow) any epistemic gaps they encounter when they are tasked with assessing expert evidence. This is a seductive, but dangerous, retort.

First of all, there is a danger in hyper-economising competition courts. The adage 'to a hammer, everything looks like a nail' is appropriate. A judge of a specialised competition court (or a competition division of a more general court) who is well versed in economics may have a tendency – encouraged by an effects-based approach to competition law – to view competition matters primarily (or perhaps exclusively) through the lens of economics, and discount (or ignore) any other issues which arise. If we are correct in our earlier suggestions that competition issues cannot be treated in isolation from other issues (in the EU) or that the US competition regime properly understood has goals other than the maximisation of consumer welfare, then treating competition problems as exclusively economic problems is likely legally erroneous.[119]

Second, even if this point is incorrect or overstates the non-economic content of competition law issues, there is a remaining concern about the sort of economics training that such a judge should undergo. Should it be narrow price theory? Should it take into account behavioural economics? And (in the EU) what of the ordoliberal approach?[120] The training that most US federal judges receive has been conducted by the George Mason University Law and Economics Center; however, critics of this training have argued that 'the programs amount to junkets designed to influence judicial decision making and are a thinly disguised attempt at indoctrinating judges with a particularly conservative, free-market-oriented style of economics'.[121] If economics is not value neutral, such training (or indoctrination)

---

[116] Joshua D Wright and Angela M Diveley, 'Do Expert Agencies Outperform Generalist Judges? Some Preliminary Evidence from the Federal Trade Commission' (2013) 1 *Journal of Antitrust Enforcement* 82.

[117] ibid 103.

[118] See ibid 84 and William Kovacic, 'The Quality of Appointments and the Capability of the Federal Trade Commission' (1997) 49 *Administrative Law Review* 915 (which is cited by Wright and Diveley).

[119] I have argued this point before: see Bruce Wardhaugh, 'Crisis Cartels: Non-Economic Values, the Public Interest, and Institutional Considerations' (2014) 10 *European Competition Journal* 311.

[120] On this approach, see eg Doris Hildebrand, *The Role of Economic Analysis in EU Competition Law: The European School*, 4th edn (Alphen aan den Rijn, Woulters Kluwer, 2016).

[121] Baye and Wright (n 111) 4.

of judges may have the consequence of importing a value-laden foundation for the judicial reinterpretation of competition law. We identified the rule of law issues raised by this sort of judicial behaviour earlier, in the first part of this chapter.

III. Conclusion

The discussion in this chapter has considered the rule of law threats posed by the judiciary (and in the case of the EU, the Commission) through their development of the effects-based approach. These threats are threats posed by both institutional legitimacy and institutional competence. This chapter has argued that law-making, in a democratic political system, involves some form of consultation with the citizenry. This process can occur in various ways (direct democracy, representative democracy or referendums are the most obvious means). This consultative process ensures democratic input into legislation and accordingly vests it with legitimacy. When such legislation is reinterpreted outside of this democratic process, such as has been done by the Commission and the US courts in their development of an economics-focused approach to competition law, this democratic input is lost. Rather the coercive force of the law has been deployed without needed democratic consent.

Further, questions of institutional competency in the application of economic analysis to legal problems also present rule of law challenges, which are exacerbated by the more economic approach. The more that economic evidence becomes conclusive of the appropriate determination of a case, the greater the need for triers of fact to be able to comprehend and evaluate such evidence. Judges need to be able to independently and critically assess the often conflicting economic evidence which parties put forward through their experts. To do this properly, and to produce a judgment that is in accord with the reasoned standards demanded by the rule of law, requires that judges have a background that the vast majority do not possess. This issue of judicial competence presents a challenge for the rule of law.

6

Commercial and Legal Certainty

[A]ntitrust rules are court-administered rules. They must be clear enough for lawyers to explain them to clients. They must be administratively workable and therefore cannot always take account of every complex economic circumstance or qualification. ... They must be designed with the knowledge that firms ultimately act, not in precise conformity with the literal language of complex rules, but in reaction to what they see as the likely outcome of court proceedings.[1]

The certainty and predictability of the principles and procedures used to resolve legal disputes are clear indicia of how well a legal system reflects the rule of law. The discussion of the rule of law in Chapter 1 demonstrated this. But Chapter 1's account was not exclusively normative. Predictability and certainty within a legal system also have instrumental value: they allow commercial relationships to be established; and when disputes arise, to be economically resolved. To the extent that the application of legal principles which govern a dispute are clear and the outcome of such application is certain, disputes are readily resolved. Indeed, if the outcome is clear and certain, then the parties may settle the dispute between themselves, with a resulting savings to the public in terms of court costs.

On the other hand, the certainty of a given legal outcome must be considered in relation to the 'correctness' of the outcome. It may be a small solace to suggest that although a legal system sometimes generates a wrong result, it is nevertheless certain and predictable in providing this result. It would be fair to characterise the effects-based approach to competition law as an attempt to align competition law towards the pole of 'getting an outcome right'. Using the tools of the economist, this approach to competition law seeks to analyse the particular behaviour in question to determine if and how it is anticompetitive. In turn, the results of this analysis are translated into a legal conclusion. From the perspective of a competition economist, this form of analysis is likely to achieve the correct result in a post facto determination of the legality of the practice in question. But from the perspective of a lawyer who is called upon to give ex ante advice regarding the legality of a proposed practice (as described in the epigraph to this chapter), this approach is far from satisfactory. This dissatisfaction should also be shared by those who take rule of law concerns – whether for normative, instrumental or other reasons – seriously.

---

[1] *Town of Concord Massachusetts et al v Boston Edison Company*, 915 F 2d 17, 22 (CA5 1990) per Judge Breyer (as he then was).

In this vein, it can be suggested that the implementation of the effects-based approach in the United States and the European Union has required both a shift in judges' and other policy-makers' understandings of the nature of legal certainty within the antitrust regime, along with a comparable view of the nature of the legal principles used to decide antitrust matters. As it has been implemented, the effects-based approach requires: (i) that the relevant legal system take a view that precedent and past practice merely weakly binds future decisions; and (ii) that the legal principles which guide decisions are of the form of standards rather than rules. But from a normative perspective, this implementation of the effects-based approach presents a significant rule of law challenge.

This chapter considers the rule of law challenges posed by a weak version of *stare decisis* and the use of standards, rather than rules, to guide legal decision-making. In this discussion the 'weakness' or 'strength' of a precedent (or a system of *stare decisis*) is relative to the willingness (and ability) of a court to overrule previous decisions. A weak version of legal precedent entails that the system is unstable, that is to say past decisions are not reliable guides to how future cases will be determined. Legal certainty, an important rule of law consideration, is undermined. Further, a system based on vaguer, less clear standards, makes predicting how courts will rule more difficult. Vagueness undermines both clarity and certainty, which are rule of law concerns.

The remainder of the chapter is organised into two substantive parts. The first discusses the role of precedent in a legal system, with focus on the use of precedential reasoning in the US and the EU. Both systems recognise the need for modification, or indeed, outright overruling of precedent, and have developed principles which assist courts in suggesting the circumstances when precedent should be overruled. However, the US system of *stare decisis* in antitrust matters promotes an unstable and uncertain legal environment. The USSC's words in its decision in *Kimble*[2] are an admission of this. The rule of law concern here is that weak – in the sense of easily overruled – precedents undermine the ability of advisors to predict how in the future courts will view a particular controversy. The EU's system, on the other hand, gives greater certainty. The threat there, however, is with the Commission and its reinterpretation of antitrust policy.

The second part of this chapter considers the nature of the legal principles (standards or rules) used to implement competition policy. Both US and EU competition regimes have eschewed strict rule-based reasoning. This has been done under the guise, in Europe, of rejecting a formalistic approach; and in the US of preferring the supposed accuracy of rule of reason analysis over per se categories. The argument is that this preference for standards, and how they are applied to antitrust matters, generates a significant amount of ex ante uncertainty for those seeking to plan their commercial affairs. Again, this is a rule of law problem. The cause of this problem

---

[2] *Kimble v Marvel Entertainment*, 135 S Ct 2401, 2412 (2015), quoted as the epigraph to the Introduction of this book.

is the manner in which standards are developed and applied. In resolving cases, the effects-based approach mandates that antitrust standards be typically applied through the mediation of the tools found in the economist's toolkit. The suggestion in this chapter is that rule of law considerations would be better respected if those tools were deployed elsewhere: in particular, to the shaping and refining of rules which are used to determine the outcome of competition disputes.

I. Precedents, Stability and the Need for Change

All legal systems rely upon previous experience (including the outcome of past litigation) to guide their decisions in future cases. By some characterisations of the rule of law, this may be a necessary condition for a set of rules enforced by state coercion to be called 'law'; and casual empiricism shows that it is an empirical fact as well as a normative desiderata. This is as it should be. Considerations of both the rule of law and judicial economy (or efficiency in adjudication) suggest that courts should rely upon their own previous decisions and decisions of superior tribunals. Those organising their legal affairs have a reasonable expectation that future disputes will be resolved in a similar, if not identical, manner to past disputes. Additionally, if future disputes are consistently decided in identical fashion to past disputes, future litigants will have no incentive to relitigate the same point, thereby needlessly expending judicial resources.

In English law, this point was made by the Earl of Halsbury LC in his speech in *London Street Tramways*:

> My Lords, 'interest rei publicæ' that there should be 'finis litium' at some time, and there could be no 'finis litium' if it were possible to suggest in each case that it might be reargued, because it is 'not an ordinary case,' whatever that may mean. Under these circumstances I am of opinion that we ought not to allow this question to be reargued.[3]

However, while rule of law considerations such as certainty are important, these considerations are only part of the goals of a legal system. Achieving justice, ensuring an equitable outcome, and ensuring that statutory goals are advanced, or otherwise put 'getting the correct outcome', are also values important to any legal system. These latter values may occasionally act in a manner opposed to the value of stability provided by *stare decisis*.

The Supreme Court of Canada has recently described this dilemma in the following terms:

> [I]n making this decision the Supreme Court engages in a balancing exercise between the two important values of correctness and certainty. The Court must ask whether it is preferable to adhere to an incorrect precedent to maintain certainty, or to correct the error.[4]

---

[3] *London Street Tramways Co Ltd v The London County Council* [1898] AC 375, 380.
[4] *Her Majesty The Queen v Craig* [2012] 2 SCR 489 [27] per Rothstein J.

The effects-based approach to antitrust law, and particularly in its US manifestation, resolves this dilemma by leaning towards getting the decision right.

A. Precedent in the USSC

In the discussion of the rule of law, we noted that the USSC has continually stressed that the US legal order is one governed by the rule of law. Although the Court recognised the constitutional significance of the division of powers in the 1790s, the Court emphatically phrased separation of powers as a rule of law consideration in its 1803 decision in *Marbury*.[5] The rule of law as stated in *Marbury* stressed the division of powers under the Constitution and the ability of the courts to subject the actions of other branches of government to review. This principle of judicial review established that everyone acting under the authority of the Constitution were subject to it, ie that the government was a government of and by law, not a government of and by individuals.

In addition to a constitutionally driven conception of the rule of law, the USSC has also adopted a formal view of the rule of law that recognised the need for stability and predictability in legal rules, whether produced as a result of constitutional interpretation or subordinate legislation and its interpretation. There is a general presumption of restraint in overturning previous decisions. This relates to the need for the Court to safeguard its own legitimacy, by ensuring that any such reconsideration is done and seen to be done only on the basis of the most convincing and principled reasons, and not as a matter of political compromise or social pressure.[6]

In reconsidering its own decisions, the USSC draws a distinction between *stare decisis* in matters of constitutional interpretation and matters of statutory interpretation. Its stated position is that in constitutional matters, it feels less bound by its previous decisions, and is willing to overrule them. But in matters of statutory interpretation, if its decision is incorrect, it is the responsibility of Congress to correct the Court's error. Given the difficulties involved in amending the US Constitution, there is a principled reason for this difference in treatment. Yet, notwithstanding the Court's view of its role in matters of statutory interpretation, it has carved out an exception for the antitrust statutes, and an exception to this exception. This antitrust exception, given how it undermines the predictability and certainty of legal principles in that area of law, is a non-trivial rule of law threat. We will see this below.

---

[5] Although *Marbury v Madison*, 5 US (1 Cranch) 137 (1805) is usually taken as the 'case on point,' the Court recognised this consequence of the constitutional allocation of power earlier. *Hylton v US*, 3 US (3 Dall) 171 (1796) and *Calder v Bull*, 3 US (3 Dall) 386 (1798) are two early cases, and see also *Federalist 78* (Hamilton). The USSC heard its first case in 1791: *West v Barnes*, 2 US (2 Dall) 401 (1791).

[6] See above pp 29–30.

i. *Constitutional Interpretation*

The USSC is a constitutional court in every sense of that term. In its first three Articles, the US Constitution allocates power to three coequal branches of government: Congress, the Executive and the Judicial branches. As a coequal branch, the Judiciary is empowered to review the activities of the other two branches, and hold that ultra vires conduct or legislation is void. The USSC has not hesitated to use this power from its early days.

Similarly, since relatively early in its history, the USSC has also not hesitated to re-examine its own decisions. This is explicit in Taney CJ's judgment in the 1849 case of *Smith v Turner*:

> After such opinions, judicially delivered, I had supposed that question to be settled, so far as any question upon the construction of the Constitution ought to be regarded as closed by the decision of this court. I do not, however, object to the revision of it, and am quite willing that it be regarded hereafter as the law of this court, that its opinion upon the construction of the Constitution is always open to discussion when it is supposed to have been founded in error, and that its judicial authority should hereafter depend altogether on the force of the reasoning by which it is supported.[7]

This is likely the correct approach in constitutional matters, as the alternative to revisiting constitutional precedent is to amend the Constitution.

Although three USSC decisions interpreting the Constitution have subsequently been nullified by constitutional amendment,[8] these are the exceptions. The US Constitution is difficult to amend. Constitutional amendment requires a resolution supported by a two-thirds vote in each of the Senate and House of Representatives (or by a Constitutional Convention called by two-thirds of the states). A proposed Amendment must then be ratified by three-quarters (ie 38) of the states. In practice:

> If only one house of thirteen state legislatures rejects a constitutional amendment, the amendment is dead. The thirteen least populous states have a combined total of less than 5 percent of the US population, which means that, in theory, constitutional amendments in the United States could be supported by more than 95 percent of the American people, and they could still fail to be ratified.[9]

The Constitution has been amended only 27 times. The first ten amendments were the original Bill of Rights (the XXVIIth Amendment was submitted to the states for ratification at the same time as the first ten – thus taking over 202 years to be ratified), three (XIIIth–XVth) were the post-Civil War reconstruction Amendments, and two (XVIIIth and XXIth) concerned prohibition. If the USSC were

---

[7] *Smith v Turner*, 48 US (7 How) 283, 470 (1849).

[8] *Chisholm v Georgia*, 2 US 419 (1793); *Dred Scott v Sandford*, 60 US (19 How) 393 (1856) and *Pollock v Farmer's Loan and Trust*, 157 US 429 (1895) were overturned by the XIth, XIVth and XVIth Amendments, respectively.

[9] Steven G Calabresi, 'Text v Precedent in Constitutional Law' (2008) 31 *Harvard Journal of Law and Public Policy* 947, 955–56.

unable to reconsider its own decisions there would be little possibility to reverse an inappropriate interpretation of the Constitution, given the inherent difficulties posed by constitutional amendment. As Roberts CJ and Alito J observed in *Citizens United*:[10]

> [S]*tare decisis* is neither an 'inexorable command,' ..., nor 'a mechanical formula of adherence to the latest decision,' ... especially in constitutional cases, ... If it were, segregation would be legal, minimum wage laws would be unconstitutional and the Government could wiretap ordinary criminal suspects without first obtaining warrants.[11]

From the perspective of public policy which recognises constitutional realities, this 'soft' view of *stare decisis* in the US constitutional order is appropriate.

ii. Statutory Interpretation

The USSC's view of *stare decisis* in matters of statutory interpretation is somewhat more complex. Ostensively, the USSC will respect previous decisions, but reserves itself the right to overrule its earlier interpretations of statutes. This has been its position from its earliest days. In *The Genesee Chief*,[12] decided eight years after *Smith v Turner*, the Court was to elaborate on this.

Chief Justice Taney, delivering the Court's judgment, held that the ability to freely reconsider previous decisions should not apply to cases which involved property or contract, given the reliance on the contractual or property rights acquired and, '[i]n such a case, *stare decisis* is the safe and established rule of judicial policy, and should always be adhered to'.[13] However, when the Court is 'convinced that the former decision was founded in error, and that the error, if not corrected, must produce serious public as well as private inconvenience and loss, it becomes [the Court's] duty not to perpetuate it'.[14] The Court then went on to overrule a previous decision which limited the jurisdiction of admiralty courts to tidal waters.

Rule of law considerations of stability and predictability underlie *stare decisis* and suggest that the Court act with strong deference towards past decisions.[15] The Court's suggested preference is that Congress rectifies previous incorrect decisions. The Court reasons that Congress can correct any errors in statutory interpretation as 'unlike in a constitutional case, critics of our ruling can take their objections across the street, and Congress can correct any mistake it sees'.[16]

---

[10] *Citizens United v Federal Election Commission*, 558 US 310 (2010).
[11] ibid 377.
[12] *The Genesee Chief*, 53 US (12 How) 443 (1857).
[13] ibid 458.
[14] ibid 459.
[15] *Kimble* (n 2) 2409.
[16] ibid.

This is particularly the case in matters of property and contract, where parties may have relied on the Court's previous interpretations to arrange their affairs.[17] The significance these reliance interests has been well recognised by the Court. In emphasising this point, the majority invokes the oft-cited words of Brandeis J in his dissent in *Burnet v Coronado Oil and Gas*,[18] namely it is 'more important that the applicable rule of law be settled than that it be settled right'.[19] Notwithstanding this deference, the Court will reverse its own decisions on statutory matters if there is a 'compelling reason' to do so. This compelling reason is something beyond a mere belief that the original decision was incorrect.[20]

In *Patterson*,[21] the Court provides three sets of 'compelling reasons' that would favour overruling a previous decision. The first set involves a change in the legal structure which underlays the earlier decision:

> In cases where statutory precedents have been overruled, the primary reason for the Court's shift in position has been the intervening development of the law, through either the growth of judicial doctrine or further action taken by Congress. Where such changes have removed or weakened the conceptual underpinnings from the prior decision, ... or where the later law has rendered the decision irreconcilable with competing legal doctrines or policies, ... the Court has not hesitated to overrule an earlier decision.[22]

According to *Patterson*,[23] this is the primary reason for the reversal of statutory precedents.

The second set of reasons enumerated in *Patterson* is related and involves the earlier precedent becoming an obstacle for legal consistency. The Court remarks:

> Another traditional justification for overruling a prior case is that a precedent may be a positive detriment to coherence and consistency in the law, either because of inherent confusion created by an unworkable decision, ... or because the decision poses a direct obstacle to the realization of important objectives embodied in other laws.[24]

The third set of reasons is where previous decisions are inconsistent with society's 'sense of justice or with the social welfare'.[25] This has its origins in Justice Cardozo's suggestion that courts are duty bound to overrule such precedents:

> [W]hen a rule, after it has been duly tested by experience, has been found to be inconsistent with the sense of justice or with the social welfare, there should be less hesitation in frank avowal and full abandonment. ... If judges have woefully misinterpreted the

---

[17] ibid 2410.
[18] *Burnet v Coronado Oil and Gas*, 285 US 393 (1932).
[19] ibid 406; this phrase appears to be the Court's 'default' citation when judges wish to maintain a previous precedent.
[20] *Kimble* (n 2) 2409, citing *Halliburton Co v Erica P John Fund Inc*, 573 US 258, 266 (2014).
[21] *Patterson v McLean Credit Union*, 491 US 164 (1989); Court's references omitted.
[22] ibid US 173.
[23] ibid.
[24] ibid.
[25] *Runyon v McCrary*, 427 US 160, 191 (1976).

> Mores of their day, or if the Mores of their day are no longer those of ours, they ought not to tie, in helpless submission, the hands of their successors.[26]

The difficulty with this latter suggestion is to differentiate between the 'Mores of their day' and a judge's values, or 'social welfare' and judicial preference of a particular state of affairs over another.

While this is the ostensive position of the USSC, its practice tells a somewhat different story. The Court will frequently overrule itself: at Chief Justice Robert's 1995 confirmation hearings it was noted that the Court had overruled itself 174 times (although mainly in a constitutional context).[27] Eskridge has examined the USSC's treatment of statutory precedent. His results show that between 1961 and 1987, the Court explicitly overruled 12 non-common law statutory precedents, implicitly overruled 24 statutory precedents, and disavowed the reasoning in 35 other statutory precedents.[28] When faced with such numbers, it is difficult not to be sceptical of the 'compelling' nature of the reasons for overruling earlier precedent.

Such scepticism is compounded when the decision to overrule is not unanimous, as the justification mounted by each position can have the appearance of an expression of personal preference rather than a reasoned evaluation of the merits of overruling the decision. *Kimble* provides an excellent case on point. Both the majority and minority consider the reasons advanced for upsetting a previous decision and do so in a rather perfunctory manner. This leaves the reader with the perception that judges are deciding these cases based on personal views towards public policy. This perception is magnified by the highly politicised nature of a large amount of the Court's business, the judicial appointment process, and the ability to appoint the 'right' judges as part of a presidential election campaign (and the subsequent spoils of victory).

iii. *'Common Law' Statutes and* Stare Decisis

'Common law statutes' are pieces of legislation which are intentionally drafted in a manner that allows for open-ended interpretation. Such statutes are written by the legislature to give the judiciary greater latitude in their interpretation and development.[29] They require the judiciary to work towards a principled approach to resolving cases, rather than applying a legislatively mandated solution.[30]

---

[26] Benjamin Cardozo, *The Nature of the Judicial Process* (New Haven, CT, Yale University Press, 1921) 149 cited ibid.

[27] Calabresi (n 9) 951.

[28] William N Eskridge Jr, 'Overruling Statutory Precedents' (1988) 76 *Georgetown Law Journal* 1361, 1427–39.

[29] PS Atiyah, 'Common Law and Statute Law' (1985) 48 *Modern Law Review* 1, 3:

> [Common law] statutes ... have deliberately adopted a very open-textured type of language, and thereby delegated to the courts the responsibility for creative development of case law. ... The case law which developed around these words was, in a sense, a mixed legislative and judicial creation.

[30] See Atiyah, ibid. Although Atiyah may have an English perspective, this is irrelevant to our argument, as the task delegated to the courts by these sorts of statutes is identical and independent of the jurisdiction.

The Sherman Act has long been recognised as a 'common law statute'. This was noted by Pound as early as 1908.[31] In *National Society of Professional Engineers*,[32] the USSC explained the common law core of the Sherman Act:

> Congress, however, did not intend the text of the Sherman Act to delineate the full meaning of the statute or its application in concrete situations. The legislative history makes it perfectly clear that it expected the courts to give shape to the statute's broad mandate by drawing on common-law tradition. The Rule of Reason, with its origins in common-law precedents long antedating the Sherman Act, has served that purpose. It has been used to give the Act both flexibility and definition, and its central principle of antitrust analysis has remained constant.[33]

As a result of this quasi-common law approach to regulation, as the Court notes, 'there is a competing interest, well represented in this Court's decisions, in recognizing and adapting to changed circumstances and the lessons of accumulated experience'.[34] As a result, considerations of *stare decisis* play less of a role in antitrust matters[35] (and other matters governed by common law statutes).

As the USSC noted in *Kimble*, in antitrust matters it will:

> [feel] relatively free to revise [its] legal analysis as economic understanding evolves and … to reverse antitrust precedents that misperceived a practice's competitive consequences. … Moreover, because the question in those cases was whether the challenged activity restrained trade, the Court's rulings necessarily turned on its understanding of economics.[36]

In other statutory matters, the drivers of change are considerations such as intervening legal developments, inconsistencies with other facets of the law, or inconsistences with the mores of the day. But in antitrust cases, the Court's 'understanding of economics' now becomes the driver of change. This is by far a lower threshold.

This low threshold to overturn previous precedents appears inconsistent with the notion of a *common law* statute. The common law process of judicial development of an area of the law or the fine-tuning of previous decisions can be accurately described as a gradual process of refinement, reasoning by analogy and distinction drawing. The process which developed the law of negligence reflects this gradual process.[37] Similarly, the development of acceptance rules for

---

[31] See eg Roscoe Pound, 'Common Law and Legislation' (1908) 21 *Harvard Law Review* 383, 383; see also Herbert Hovenkamp, *Federal Antitrust Policy: The Law of Competition and its Practice*, 5th edn (St Paul, MN, West, 2015) 74–78.

[32] *National Society of Professional Engineers v US*, 435 US 679 (1978).

[33] ibid 688.

[34] *State Oil Co v Khan*, 522 US 3, 20 (1997).

[35] See *Kimble* (n 2) 2412.

[36] ibid 2412–13; Court's references to *Leegin* omitted.

[37] See eg Lord Toulson's remarks in *Michael v Chief Constable of South Wales Police* [2015] UKSC 2, para 102:

> The development of the law of negligence has been by an incremental process rather than giant steps. The established method of the court involves examining the decided cases to see how far the law has gone and where it has refrained from going. From that analysis it looks to see whether there is an argument by analogy for extending liability to a new situation, or whether an earlier limitation is no longer logically or socially justifiable. In doing so it pays regard to the need for overall coherence. Often there will be a mixture of policy considerations to take into account.

electronic communication is an instance of the common law process of analogous reasoning.[38] This incremental process of legal change and adaptation is of a different order than that view of *stare decisis* described in *Kimble*.

iv. *Rule of Law and the 'Common Law' Approach to* Stare Decisis *in Antitrust*

This work began by developing a view of the rule of law that was informed by Fuller and his account of eight standards associated with the 'internal morality of law'.[39] These, we saw, provided us with some guidelines for the contents of a formal theory of the rule of law. Among these standards are:

• the need for prospective application of new law;

• a requirement for clarity of standards of action or inaction; and,

• respect for past decisions (*stare decisis*).

This chapter argues that the USSC's approach to *stare decisis* in antitrust matters undermines these criteria. The USSC's ruling in *Leegin*,[40] decided in 2007, can be used as a case study. The majority's decision in that case overruled the 96-year-old precedent set in *Dr Miles*[41] prohibiting resale price maintenance (RPM). The majority anchored its opinion on a purported change in thinking regarding vertical restraints.

Leegin involved a very specific dispute, between a retailer ('Kay's Kloset') and Leegin, a manufacturer, designer and distributor of leather bags and accessories (in particular its 'Brighton' line).[42] As part of its promotion strategy, Leegin required its retailers to implement a strategy of RPM by not selling the Brighton line below suggested prices. Leegin justified this strategy on the basis that sales at these prices would provide the retailers with a sufficient margin to provide customers with a quality shopping and customer service experience. The free-riding customer (who avails themselves of the pre- and post-sale services associated with the 'quality shopping experience', but buys elsewhere) was viewed (by both Leegin and the majority of the USSC) as the bogeyman that must be deterred through the use of RPM.

If a retailer breached this suggested pricing policy, Leegin would (ultimately) refuse to provide the retailer with more stock. In response to discounting of the Brighton line by competing retailers, Kay's Kloset discounted this line. Leegin

---

[38] Compare this development in England in *Thomas & anr v BPE Solicitors* [2010] EWHC 306 (Ch); *Mondial Shipping and Chartering BV v Astarte Shipping Ltd* [1995] 2 Lloyd's Rep 249, [1995] 5 WLUK 376, [1995] CLC 1011; *Brinkibon Ltd v Stahag Stahl und Stahlwarenhandel GmbH* [1983] 2 AC 34; *Entores v Miles Far East Co* [1955] 2 QB 327; *Adams v Lindsell* (1818) 1 B & Ald 681.

[39] See above pp 18–19.

[40] *Leegin Creative Leather Products Inc v PSKS Inc*, 551 US 877 (2007).

[41] *Dr Miles Medical Co v John D Park and Sons Co*, 220 US 373 (1911).

[42] *Leegin* (n 40) 882–85.

demanded that Kay's Kloset cease discounting that line. When the demand was refused, Leegin terminated its relationship with the retailer. At trial, Kay's Kloset prevailed, and was awarded damages in the amount of $3,975,000.80. Both the District and Circuit courts were bound by *Dr Miles*, and held that that case precluded Leegin from introducing economic evidence to show the efficiencies that could result from RPM strategies. The USSC, however, could examine this evidence in the course of their consideration of the matter.

In examining both the majority and the minority opinions in *Leegin*, and the economic studies cited in them, it is clear that there is no consensus among economists regarding (i) the relative benefits and harms of RPM; (ii) to whom these benefits and harms accrue; and (iii) the incidence and cost of 'free riding'. Nevertheless, the majority opined:

> Though each side of the debate can find sources to support its position, it suffices to say here that economics literature is replete with procompetitive justifications for a manufacturer's use of resale price maintenance.[43]

The minority, on the other hand, reasoned:

> Economic discussion, such as the studies the Court relies upon, can *help* provide answers to these questions, and in doing so, economics can, and should, inform antitrust law. But antitrust law cannot, and should not, precisely replicate economists' (sometimes conflicting) views.[44]

The differing approaches are significant. Noting an absence of consensus in the literature, the majority quite cavalierly accepts – without a detailed, critical examination – one side of the story. It is suggested that were a trial judge to proceed in this manner in assessing which of two sometimes-conflicting accounts to accept, that judge would commit a reversible error.

The gulf between the majority judgment and the dissent shows that there is a significant difference not only in the judges' understanding of the relevant economic theory and its consequences, but also in regard to what – in Fullarian terms – might be termed the 'criteria for action or inaction'. What is missing from the majority's opinion is a discussion of the criteria by which new developments in antitrust economics are to be evaluated as a prequel to reversing a statutory precedent. The insouciant manner in which the majority treated the conflicting positions of the economics profession is very much a rule of law threat.

A similar rule of law threat is posed by the retrospective nature of the decision, and the extinguishing of the reliance interests that *Dr Miles* may have provided. In contrast to the caution that the USSC has historically paid to property-based reliance interests (eg as found in *The Genesee Chief*), in *Leegin* these interests are dismissed by the majority, which states that such interests are secondary to an

---

[43] ibid 889.
[44] ibid 914–15.

inefficient rule.[45] The minority felt otherwise, noting the significant investments which may have been made based on the reasonable assumption that *Dr Miles'* per se prohibition on RPM would continue.[46] Again, such retroactivity in the face of actual reliance has thwarted advance planning based on rational assumptions. This is indeed a rule of law threat.

Dr Miles was not a recent decision. It was some 96 years old when it was over-ruled. Since the Court decided *Dr Miles*, Congress had not only considered that rule, and rejected repealing it by statute, but had also enacted legislation predicated on the existence of the per se prohibition of RPM.[47] If anything, the majority's decision, in Fullerian terms, failed 'to respect past decisions'. It may be true that the Sherman Act and other antitrust statutes are 'common law' statutes, inviting the judiciary to work in partnership with the legislature to develop a body of anti-trust law. However, the manner in which the USSC has treated its earlier decisions stands in contrast to the common law norm.

Under this approach, the USSC will abandon precedents, if – on their read-ing of the relevant economics – a new understanding shows the precedent to be based on an 'inefficient rule'. This is done without regard to either the usual process of legal evolution found in the common law, or any reliance interests that the business community may have. It is therefore suggested that *Leegin* shows what is wrong with the effects-based approach as adopted in the United States. The certainty (which in turn served as a reasonable foundation for reliance interests of a property or commercial nature) granted by a venerable precedent was eroded. This is a significant threat to the rule of law.

However, others may suggest that, in spite of the above, *Leegin* had very little legal significance. Manufactures could impose a RPM policy on distributors and retailers via the *Colgate* doctrine,[48] and the Court's decision merely made the practice of agreeing to a RPM policy subject to a rule of reason test for legality. This retort, however, fails to consider the commercial reality of the practice. As we noted earlier, the practical effect of analysing a commercial arrangement by the rule of reason is to consider it under a de facto rule of per se legality.[49] Second, and just as significant, the Court's overruling of *Dr Miles* was likely to have sent a signal to manufacturers that such pricing strategies were no longer unacceptable, and therefore could be implemented.[50] This appears to have been the case.

---

[45] ibid 906: 'The reliance interests here, however, … cannot justify an inefficient rule, especially because the narrowness of the rule has allowed manufacturers to set minimum resale prices in other ways.'

[46] ibid 925–26.

[47] ibid 919–20.

[48] The Colgate doctrine stems from *US v Colgate and Co*, 250 US 300 (1919), which held that it was not a violation of the Sherman Act for a manufacturer to announce in advance the price for which retailers must sell the manufacturer's product and to refuse to deal with (ie supply) retailers that did not adhere to this required price.

[49] See above pp 62–64.

[50] Subject, of course, to relevant state law.

One way of preventing *Leegin's* free-riding shopper and keeping brick and mortar retailers happy is to prevent discounting by establishing a minimum price. But in a 2017 study, as part of a symposium of the tenth anniversary of *Leegin*, Howard Marvel considered the reduction in such discounting.[51] This study showed that not only was there less variation in pricing post-*Leegin*,[52] but the market value (based on market capitalisation) of leading US price comparison websites dropped significantly as a result of a significant fall in traffic to these sites.[53] The drop is due to consumers recognising that discounts are simply no more. Marvel notes:

> The clear inference from these examples is that discounting is much less prevalent in the post-*Leegin* rule-of-reason era than previously. When discounts threaten valued retail outlets, manufacturers are now both willing and able to step in to protect those dealers' sales efforts.[54]

The reduction in discounts entails a loss of consumer welfare.

Similar results are also found in other markets where one manufacturer's standardised pricing can soften intrabrand competition. This leads to price increases of competing products with no loss of sales,[55] which is consistent with the consensus that RPM almost always causes an increase in prices.[56] The issue is whether the procompetitive gains from eliminating free-riding offset the consumer welfare losses caused by higher prices. Given that in the pre-*Leegin* era, there was no shortage of retailers of luxury goods, the free-riding problem may well have been exaggerated at the expense of consumers.[57] *Leegin* may have delivered a blow to the goal of promoting consumer welfare.

Consequently not only is *Leegin* an illustration of the rule of law threat posed by the effects-based approach (as it undermines the certainty and predictability of

---

[51] Howard P Marvel, '*Leegin* and the Economics of Resale Price Maintenance' (2017) 50 *Review of Industrial Organization* 221.

[52] See ibid 224 fn 10: 'For example [in 2010], New Balance cross-training sneakers had a range of $47.48–$69.74. In early 2017, the New Balance Men's Minimus 40 cross trainers sold for a range of $109.95–$109.99 (apart from New Balance direct, which charged $10 more). Swarovski 10×42 binoculars, which ranged from $1539.99 to $1929 in 2010, were $1799 at all sellers.'

[53] ibid 225–26.

[54] ibid 227.

[55] See eg Xiaohua Zeng, Srabana Dasgupta and Charles B Weinberg, 'The Competitive Implications of a "No-Haggle" Pricing Strategy when Others Negotiate: Findings from A Natural Experiment' (2016) 33 *International Journal of Research in Marketing* 907, which considered the 'no haggle' pricing strategy that Toyota implemented in Canada. They found:

> that for family level models, the prices of Toyota and its closest competitor Honda increased without any loss in sales. In the small car segment, which is the entry level category for both Toyota and Honda, sales expanded without any changes in their prices. Our empirical results suggest that Toyota's unilateral move to a fixed price strategy led to a market equilibrium that was more profitable for both Toyota and its main competitor Honda. (922)

[56] See the sources cited in Marina Lao, 'Free Riding: An Overstated, and Unconvincing, Explanation for Resale Price Maintenance' in Robert Pitofsky (ed), *How the Chicago School Overshot the Mark: The Effect of Conservative Economic Analysis on US Antitrust* (Oxford, Oxford University Press, 2008) 196, 223 fn 104.

[57] See ibid 216.

a long-standing rule), but it also causes legal activity in a manner contrary to the law's ostensive goal. Rather than advancing consumer welfare, *Leegin* appears to diminish it: this incongruence between the policy and the application of the rule is a yet a further rule of law concern.

The US version of the effect-based approach has increased reliance on rule of reason analysis and a willingness to pursue a perceived (but not necessarily accurate) strategy of promoting consumer welfare. This is done at the expense of precedent and the values of stability, certainty and predictability.[58] The very soft view of *stare decisis* that this approach necessarily takes in order to get decisions right erodes any confidence that previous judicial decisions can be relied upon as a guide to formulating a future commercial strategy. Further, and more alarming, the approach may not even get the result right, as the fallout from *Leegin* might suggest. If this is the case, rule of law considerations are undermined further, as this approach widens the gulf between the goals of the law and what the law actually achieves. These are all significant threats to a principled and stable legal system, predicated on the rule of law and its values.

B. Precedent and *Stare Decisis* in the CJEU

The CJEU engages in what a common lawyer would view as precedent-based reasoning. Nevertheless the Court has never felt obligated to strictly follow its previous decisions, and will overturn past decisions when it regards it necessary to so do. However, when overturning a previous decision the Court follows reasonably strict and clear criteria, so that the serious rule of law concerns of the sort found in the US are not present.

The CJEU's jurisdiction is set out in Articles 263–75 and Protocol 3 (the Statute of the Court of Justice of the European Union) of the TFEU. These provisions provide, inter alia, that the CJEU may review 'legality of legislative acts, of acts of the Council, of the Commission and of the European Central Bank',[59] and 'shall also review the legality of acts of bodies, offices or agencies of the Union intended to produce legal effects vis-à-vis third parties'.[60] Should the Court find an act to be ultra vires, having infringed essential procedural requirements, infringing the 'Treaties or of any rule of law relating to their application, or misuse of powers',[61] the Court 'shall declare the act concerned to be void'.[62] Similarly, the CJEU is empowered to give preliminary rulings regarding the interpretation of the Treaties

---

[58] This threat is further magnified when the ad hoc baseball exception to 'soft' *stare decisis* is considered. See above, p 31, n 71.
[59] TFEU Art 263, first paragraph.
[60] ibid.
[61] ibid second paragraph.
[62] ibid Art 264, first paragraph.

and the acts of Union institutions.[63] The Court has had this jurisdiction since its origins.[64] As such, to the extent that the European Treaties serve as a Constitution for a legal order, the CJEU is and always has been a Constitutional Court in the traditional sense of the term. Nevertheless, as we see below, the Court will make no distinction in precedential 'strength' when considering a Treaty provision or a piece of secondary legislation.

i. Precedential Reasoning in the CJEU

The Court has recognised its use of precedential reasoning since at least 1958. In its 20th judgment,[65] *Hauts Fourneaux de Chasse*, the Court remarks, 'consideration must be given to the substance of the case; in these circumstances, *according to the case-law of the Court*, the objection on which the defendant relies cannot stand in the way of the admissibility of the application'.[66] Any reading of recent judgments confirms the use of precedent, and its pre-1973 usage indicates that precedential reasoning is no concession to British and Irish accession.

A unique feature of much of the Court's precedential reasoning is exemplified in what Jacob[67] refers to as 'Lego reasoning' or constructing legal positions from 'preformed building blocks'. For instance, in competition matters, *Höfner and Eisner's*[68] well-known definition of an undertaking as any 'entity engaged in economic activity, regardless of the legal status of the entity and the way in which it is financed'[69] has been repeated verbatim numerous times in subsequent case-law. An interesting corollary of the Court's construction of legal positions using Lego reasoning is when the Court constructs a position using *near*-verbatim passages from previous decisions.[70] Any subtle shift in wording is likely of significance.

---

[63] ibid Art 267, first paragraph.

[64] See Treaty of Rome (1957) Arts 173–77 and the Treaty Establishing the European Coal and Steel Community (1951) Arts 33–35.

[65] See the Court's list at http://curia.europa.eu/en/content/juris/c1_juris.htm.

[66] Case 2-57 *Compagnie des Hauts Fourneaux de Chasse v High Authority of the European Coal and Steel Community*, ECLI:EU:C:1958:5, 206, emphasis supplied.

[67] Marc Jacob, *Precedents and Case-Based Reasoning in the European Court of Justice* (Cambridge, Cambridge University Press, 2014) 94.

[68] Case C-41/90 *Höfner and Elser v Macrotron*, ECLI:EU:C:1991:161.

[69] ibid para 21.

[70] See eg the Court's description of abuse in Case 85/76 *Hoffmann-LaRoche AG v Commission*, ECLI:EU:C:1979:36, para 91:

> [T]hrough recourse to methods different from those which condition normal competition in products or services on the basis of the transactions of commercial operators, has the effect of hindering the maintenance of the degree of competition still existing in the market or the growth of that competition.

This formulation is repeated in Case 32/81 *NV Nederlandsche Banden Industrie Michelin v Commission*, ECLI:EU:C:1983:313, para 70. But in Case C-209/10 *Post Danmark A/S v Konkurrencerådet* ('*Post Danmark I*'), ECLI:EU:C:2012:172, para 24 the Court adds 'to the detriment of consumers', immediately before 'of hindering'. The reference to consumers is omitted in the judgments in Case C-5549/10 P *Tomra Systems ASA and Others v Commission*, ECLI:EU:C:2012:221, para 17; and Case C-457/10 P *AstraZeneca*, ECLI:EU:C:2012:770, para 74, which were released three weeks and nine months (respectively) after *Post Danmark I*.

ii. Stare Decisis *in the ECJ*

The focus on this section will be the ECJ (rather than the CJEU as a whole), given the ECJ's role in authoritatively interpreting EU law. The ECJ will revisit its own previous decisions; and, in appropriate cases, overrule earlier decisions. This has been the Court's practice since its earliest days. For instance, in *Da Costa en Schaake*[71] the Court accepted that under the provisions of Article 177 of the EEC Treaty and Article 20 of the Statute of the Court of Justice (now Article 276 TFEU and Article 23 of the present Statute) a National Court could re-refer the same legal question to the Court.[72] Implicit in re-referral and subsequent reconsideration of the same legal question is the ability to overrule or, at minimum, not follow previous decisions on point. An early example of this was *Molkerei-Zentrale Westfalen*,[73] in which the ECJ reconsidered a previous decision, but found no grounds to give a 'fresh interpretation' of a Treaty Article.[74]

In *HAG II*,[75] the Court overruled its earlier judgment in *HAG I*,[76] a trademark issue involving the interpretation of Articles 30 and 36 of the EEC Treaty (now Articles 36 and 42). Noting that subsequent legal developments have undermined the foundation of its earlier judgment,[77] the Court explicitly reconsidered and overruled its previous decision. In the 16 years between the two cases, there had been a significant change in the legal matrix which underpinned the first decision. Accordingly revisiting and overruling it was justified 'in the light of the case-law which has developed with regard to the relationship between industrial and commercial property and the general rules of the Treaty, particularly in the sphere of the free movement of goods'.[78]

Similarly, in *Akzo Nobel*,[79] the Court viewed that 'significant recent developments "in the legal landscape"'[80] could justify the Court overruling its previous decisions. However, after considering the changes to the relevant 'legal landscape', the Court determined that 'that the legal situation in the Member States of the European Union has not evolved ... to an extent which would justify a change in the case-law'.[81]

The ECJ appears to make no distinction between Treaty interpretation (which is of constitutional significance) and the interpretation of secondary legislation when it re-evaluates its previous decisions. One only needs to point out two sets of cases to make this point.

---

[71] Cases 28–30/62 *Da Costa en Schaake v Neederlanse Belastingadminsitratie*, ECLI:EU:C:1963:6.
[72] ibid 38–39, see also Case 283/81 *Srl CILFIT and Lanificio di Gavardo SpA v Ministry of Health*, ECLI:EU:C:1982:335, paras 1 –15.
[73] Case 28/67 *Molkerei-Zentrale Westfalen v Hauptzollamt Paderborn*, ECLI:EU:C:1968:171.
[74] ibid 152–55.
[75] Case C-10/89 *SA CNL-SUCAL NV v HAG GF AG* ('*HAG II*'), ECLI:EU:C:1990:359.
[76] Case 192/73 *Van Zuylen v HAG*, ECLI:EU:C:1974:72.
[77] ibid para 10.
[78] *HAG II* (n 75) para 10.
[79] Case C-550/07 P *Akzo Nobel v Commission*, ECLI:EU:C:2010:512.
[80] ibid para 65.
[81] ibid para 76.

The first concerns the Court's reconsideration of the residence rights of third-country spouses of EU citizens.[82] In *Metok*,[83] the Court explicitly, and quite tersely, reconsiders its previous decisions on the point:

> It is true that the Court held in paragraphs 50 and 51 of *Akrich* that, in order to benefit from the rights provided for in Article 10 of Regulation No 1612/68, the national of a non-member country who is the spouse of a Union citizen must be lawfully resident in a Member State when he moves to another Member State to which the citizen of the Union is migrating or has migrated. *However, that conclusion must be reconsidered.* The benefit of such rights cannot depend on the prior lawful residence of such a spouse in another Member State.[84]

While the Court referred to previous case-law and subsequent secondary legislation, both of which undermined *Akrich*, its justification for overruling itself is perfunctory, at best, notwithstanding it overruled two previous judgments.[85]

A similar story is told – in equally as terse a fashion – by the Court's consideration of the 1976 Equal Treatment Directive.[86] In *Larsson*,[87] the Court held that the Directive did not protect women against dismissal from employment due to an absence from work which was the result of an illness which arose during pregnancy.[88] Yet, one year and a day later in *Brown*[89] the Court was to overrule *Larsson* in terse fashion:

> It is also clear from all the foregoing considerations that, *contrary to the Court's ruling in Case C-400/95 Larsson* ..., where a woman is absent owing to illness resulting from pregnancy or childbirth, and that illness arose during pregnancy and persisted during and after maternity leave, her absence not only during maternity leave but also during the period extending from the start of her pregnancy to the start of her maternity leave cannot be taken into account for computation of the period justifying her dismissal under national law.[90]

In looking at the Court's judgment, the only relevant 'foregoing consideration' to merit reconsidering *Larsson* was a realisation that pregnancy-related illnesses are a consequence of pregnancy and therefore only affect women. To dismiss a woman

---

[82] This was then governed by Regulation (EEC) No 1612/68 of the Council of 15 October 1968 on freedom of movement for workers within the Community [1968] OJ L257/2; subsequent amendments were irrelevant to the Court's reconsideration of its previous holding.

[83] Case C-127/08 *Blaise Baheten Metock and Others v Minister for Justice, Equality and Law Reform*, ECLI:EU:C:2008:449.

[84] ibid para 58, emphasis supplied.

[85] Case C-459/99 *Mouvement contre le racisme, l'antisémitisme et la xénophobie ASBL (MRAX) v Belgium*, ECLI:EU:C:2002:461; Case C-157/03 *Commission v Spain*, ECLI:EU:C:2005:225.

[86] Council Directive 76/207/EEC of 9 February 1976 on the implementation of the principle of equal treatment for men and women as regards access to employment, vocational training and promotion, and working conditions [1976] OJ L39/40.

[87] Case C-400/95 *Larsson v Føtex Supermarked*, ECLI:EU:C:1997:259.

[88] ibid para 23.

[89] Case C-394/96 *Brown v Rentokil*, ECLI:EU:C:1998:331.

[90] ibid para 27 emphasis supplied.

as a result of suffering such an illness is thus direct discrimination based on sex, which is contrary to Articles 2(1) and 5(1) of the Directive.[91]

Yet if one considers the Advocate General's Opinion, other considerations may have been lurking in the minds of the Court's members. In his Opinion, Advocate General Ruiz-Jarabo remarked:

> I confess that I find it rather difficult to reconcile those statements with the line taken in the case-law developed by the Court of Justice up to the time of that judgment, as set out in the foregoing paragraphs. The Court appears not only to maintain in *Larsson* a position contrary to what is to be inferred from a brief examination of its earlier judgments, but also directly to contradict the reading of those judgments which has been propounded over time both by its Advocates General and by the numerous authors who have commented on the judgments.[92]

In short, the Advocate General suggested that the earlier case was wrongly decided, and clearly so given its ill-fit with the Court's previous jurisprudence and subsequent commentary. The Court implicitly agreed, and summarily overruled its previous decision.

While the Court itself has never provided a comprehensive statement of when it will overrule its previous decisions, the above is indicative of those circumstances. Additionally, in his Opinion in *Merek*,[93] Advocate General Fennelly suggests that although overruling previous decisions, is rare:

> it appears that the Court will reexamine and, if need be, decline to follow earlier judgments which may have been based on an erroneous application of a fundamental principle of Community law, which interpret a Treaty provision as applicable to situations which are properly outside its scope, or which result in an imbalance in the relationship between differing principles, such as the free movement of goods and the protection of intellectual and commercial property.[94]

The rarity of the Court overruling its previous decisions is a testament that establishing a 'significant development in the legal landscape' is a difficult task.

A pair of concluding remarks about the place of precedent in the ECJ's jurisprudence is in order. First, notwithstanding the difficulty of persuading the Court that a previous decision may be incorrect, the Court's refusal to be strictly bound by its previous decision makes sense for the Court sitting as a Constitutional Court. The European Treaties are difficult to change; doing so involves the expenditure of significant political capital; and given the requirements of some Member States, the uncertainty of subjecting Treaty changes to referendums.

---

[91] ibid paras 22–25.

[92] Case C-394/96 *Brown v Rentokil*, Opinion of Advocate General Ruiz-Jarabo, ECLI:EU:C:1998:44, para 49.

[93] Joined Cases C-267 and 268/95 *Merck and Co Inc, Merck Sharp and Dohme Ltd and Merck Sharp and Dohme International Services BV v Primecrown Ltd*, Opinion of Advocate General Fennelly, ECLI:EU:1996:228.

[94] ibid para 146.

Second, the Court's apparent vision that the precedential strength of previous case-law interpreting the Treaties is identical to that of case-law interpreting secondary legislation is similarly prudent. Secondary legislation can also be difficult to alter. But secondary legislation often works in tandem with the Treaties to regulate particular areas of Union competence. In competition law, Treaty provisions regulate cartel and dominance; but merger control is governed through Regulation.[95] It would be odd, to say the least, if the case-law which governed two aspects of the competition regime had different precedential strength from that governing the remainder.

The nature of precedential reasoning and the ECJ's use of *stare decisis* do not give rise to significant rule of law problems, certainly not as exercised to date. A 'significant development in the legal landscape' is a necessary condition to the Court's overruling of its own precedent. It is unlikely that a revision to academic thinking about antitrust economics would count as such a development.

C. Commission Guidance and the Rule of Law

A short word needs to be said regarding the Commission and the guidance it provides. As discussed earlier, in order to assist undertakings with their self-assessment obligations post-Regulation 1/2003, the Commission has produced numerous guidance publications setting out its interpretation of the law, its priorities and enforcement (eg fining) practices. These publications are prospective in their content. They are binding on the Commission – indeed the Commission is subject to judicial review if it does not adhere to them.[96] As such they contribute to the rule of law framework of European competition law by providing guidance on which undertakings and their advisors can build reasonable expectations that inform their future commercial strategies.

The problem with such guidance, as noted above, is the Commission's own focus on an effects-driven analytical approach to competition policy with the sole goal of maximising consumer welfare. This is inconsistent with the multiple goals promoted by the European Treaties and the linking clauses which require Union actors to take all such goals into consideration. This was spoken of earlier. This is the true threat to the rule of law posed by the Commission's approach.

---

[95] See Council Regulation (EC) No 139/2004 of 20 January 2004 on the control of concentrations between undertakings [2004] OJ L24/1, and the implementing Regulation: Commission Regulation (EC) No 802/2004 of 21 April 2004 implementing Council Regulation (EC) No 139/2004 on the control of concentrations between undertakings [2004] OJ L133/1, amended by Commission Regulation (EC) No 1033/2008 [2008] OJ L279/3 and Commission Implementing Regulation (EU) No 1269/2013 of 5 December 2013 [2013] OJ L336/1.

[96] Joined Cases C-189/02 P, 202/02 P and 213/02 P *Danske Rørindustri A/S and Others v Commission*, ECLI:EU:C:2005:408; Case C-397/03 P *Archer Daniels Midland Co v Commission*, ECLI:EU:C:2006:328; Case C-226/11 *Expedia v Authoritié de la Concurrence*, ECLI:EU:C:2012:795; Case T-446/05 *Amann und Söhne GmbH and Co KG v Commission* ECLI:EU:T:2010:165.

D. Concluding Remarks on the Nature of Precedent and the Rule of Law

As seen in the above discussion, there is a tension between legal certainty and revisiting possibly erroneous decisions. The Canadian Supreme Court's remark in *Craig* illustrating the dilemma of maintaining certainty or correcting an error is apposite. As not following previous precedent upsets legal certainty and the expectations of those who relied on the previous precedent to order their affairs, a departure from strict *stare decisis* is simultaneously a departure from strict rule of law considerations.

But rule of law considerations are ideals, as such they will not be completely realised in any legal system. And, as this discussion of the role of *stare decisis* shows, these rule of law considerations may clash with other wanted features in a legal system, in particular the need to ensure that justice is done in particular cases. In attempting to achieve the right trade-off between certainty and individual justice, courts typically have required a significant threshold for change in the circumstances to justify not following previous precedent.

In antitrust cases, the USSC will overrule its previous decisions if *the Court's* understanding of economics changes.[97] The difficulty with the use of economic theory to justify a reconsideration of a previous decision is that it lowers the threshold for legal change, to the detriment of considerations such as certainty and predictability. A change in academic thinking is not a change in the legal matrix which underlies the dispute in question. While lawyers will be monitoring legal developments in order to provide advice to their clients and thus advise the clients to arrange their affairs accordingly, it is another matter altogether to expect legal advisors to be *au courant* with the latest academic developments in microeconomics, even if Easterbrook's claim that antitrust law is a branch of microeconomics is true.[98]

It is also clear that businesses have a significant reliance interest on the state of competition rules in planning their business development, which will include decisions concerning investment and financing, and marketing strategy. The ability to legally conduct oneself on the market in a given manner and/or to be sure that competitors or suppliers will not conduct themselves in certain ways will be a consideration in formulating and implementing these sorts of commercial decisions. If courts subsequently alter the rules due to changes in academic thinking in economics (and not as a result in the changing legal landscape), this shatters not only the reliance interests of those whose business arrangements are directly affected, but also undermines others' confidence in their own reliance interests. The nature of these interests was raised in amici curiae briefs before the USSC

---

[97] *Kimble* (n 2) 2412.
[98] Frank H Easterbrook, 'Allocating Antitrust Decisionmaking Tasks' (1987) 76 *Georgetown Law Journal* 305, 305.

in *Leegin*. The minority was concerned by these interests; however, the majority brushed these concerns aside.[99]

To the extent that US antitrust law and policy relied on the ability and willingness to overrule its earlier decisions based on a new understanding of economic theory, it creates a significant problem for antitrust advisors to give their clients clear advice of how the authorities will view their proposed (or even currently existing) business practices. This is ultimately a rule of law problem. In Europe, the rule of law problem is somewhat different. The ECJ will respect its own previous decisions, overruling them only when a development in the legal landscape has occurred. To this point, changing academic understandings of competition economics have yet to count as such a change. Rather, the European rule of law threat is from the Commission as a result of its approach of isolating competition policy from other Treaty goals.

II. Rules, Standards and Legal Certainty

The precision with which a given legal principle is stated can be a significant determinant of the certainty and predictability of decisions that are made based on the principle. Should the principle be quite precise and leave little to no room for interpretation, then parties and their advisors can better predict an outcome than in cases where the principle is phrased in vague terms. This is a point which is recognised in the rules/standards controversy which has informed a significant amount of the current discussion of the optimal form of competition legislation and rules. The literature on this topic, both in general and focused towards antitrust, is vast.[100]

Legal systems can regulate conduct with either rules or standards. To take a well-worn example,[101] should a legislature wish to prevent people from driving at too high a speed, they can chose to do so by promulgating this restriction as a rule ('no person shall drive a motor vehicle at a speed in excess of 100 kilometres per hour') or as a standard ('no person shall drive at an excessive rate of speed, given the prevailing road conditions'). There is a rule of law dimension to this rules/standards controversy, and to how conduct is regulated (ie by the choice of a rule or a standard).[102]

---

[99] See above pp 164–65 and 193–94.

[100] The two most influential articles are Isaac Ehrlich and Richard Posner, 'An Economic Analysis of Legal Rule Making' (1974) 3 *Journal of Legal Studies* 257; and Louis Kaplow, 'Rules versus Standards: An Economic Analysis' (1992) 42 *Duke Law Journal* 557. On rules and standards in antitrust, see eg Daniel A Crane, 'Rules versus Standards in Antitrust Adjudication' (2007) 64 *Washington and Lee Law Review* 49, particularly at 52–54 fn 11, which cites many other sources on this topic. On the behavioural approach and the rules–standards distinction, see Russell B Korobkin, 'Behavioral Analysis and Legal Form: Rules vs Standards Revised' (2000) 79 *Oregon Law Review* 23.

[101] See eg Kaplow, 'Rules versus Standards' ibid 560 and Korobkin ibid 23.

[102] See eg Maurice E Stucke, 'Does the Rule of Reason Violate the Rule of Law?' (2009) 42 *University of California Davis Law Review* 1375.

Typically, rules allow for better ex ante consideration of the permissibility of a proposed action. In the speeding example, it is easier to judge whether driving at 85 km/hour is (legally) acceptable if one's conduct is governed by the above hypothetical rule. However, the rule is also both over- and underinclusive. It would prohibit an ambulance from rushing to a hospital on a clear and dry day; and would condone fast driving in conditions of rain, icy roads or poor visibility. Yet a standard is useful for ex post evaluation of the given conduct. Those investigating a motor vehicle accident may wish to reconstruct what occurred, and determine whether a vehicle was being driven at an excessive rate in order to determine or apportion liability.

It is inaccurate to view rules and standards as populating two distinct sets. Rather, there is a continuum of legal prescriptions with more general standards at one end, and very specific rules at the other. In competition policy this continuum may be expressed as running from assessment by 'full scale' rule of reason approach (where economic analysis is conducted on a case-by-case basis, in order to consider and balance the relevant efficiencies and anticompetitive aspects of an individual instance of a practice) to – at the other end – the use of per se rules of legality (or illegality) to assess a given practice.[103]

As written, both the Sherman Act (and other US antitrust statutes) and Articles 101 and 102 are phrased as standards. For instance, section 1 of the Sherman Act speaks of '[e]very contract … in restraint of trade'; likewise the prohibition of Article 101 applies to 'the prevention, restriction or distortion of competition', and Article 102 refers to 'abuse … of a dominant position'. These intentionally vaguely drafted legal standards require judicial or administrative interpretation in their application to a dispute. It was, after all, judicial interpretation of '[e]very contract' which led to the development of rule of reason analysis in *Standard Oil*.[104]

Chapter 2 has shown that the development of US antitrust since the 1970s has been a progression from a regime defined by extensive use of per se rules to one in which the use of rule of reason standard is the default mode of analysis.[105] A similar movement to a more standards-driven mode of analysis has taken place in Europe, as has been illustrated in Chapter 3. In both jurisdictions, this approach has moved competition policy and law away from the rule of law ideal.

The remaining part of this chapter discusses the issue of rule versus standards, particularly as applied to antitrust matters. This will not, nor is it intended to, be a comprehensive discussion. This issue has been extensively discussed elsewhere.[106] Rather, the purpose of the present discussion is to suggest the preferability of a

---

[103] See Arndt Christiansen and Wolfgang Kerber, 'Competition Policy with Optimally Differentiated Rules Instead of "Per Se Rule vs Rule of Reason"' (2006) 2 *Journal of Competition Law and Economics* 215, 221.

[104] *Standard Oil Company of New Jersey v US* 221 US 1 (1911); see also pp 43–44 above.

[105] See Crane (n 100) 55–71, who also makes this point using judgments of Circuit Courts to show the pervasiveness of the shift to the rule of reason.

[106] See sources cited above, n 100.

rule-based system over a standards-based system. This argument flows from the normative rule of law perspective, which promotes certainty and predictability as legal virtues.

However, rules can be both over- and underinclusive. As such they can fail to generate 'the right answer' – where 'correctness' is relative to some value which informs the legal regime. So, in a competition regime focused on the protection or maximisation of consumer welfare, a rule may be clear and allow parties to plan future arrangements, but it may not well serve this welfare maximisation goal. The latter half of this section makes a suggestion for the modification of rules, through a common law-like process, to permit the capture of relevant value (eg consumer welfare; or multiple values) should the rule's scope be under- or overinclusive.

A. Rules, Standards and Governance by the Rule of Law

Normative discussions of the preferability of using rules or standards to regulate particular forms of behaviour will often[107] do so by considering the costs and benefits (or advantages and disadvantages) of particular forms of the legal principle and the activity to be related.[108] One point made in other forms of analysis of the rules versus standards distinction (shaped by critical legal studies) is to challenge the distinction.[109] We accept this challenge, noting that the rules–standards distinction is more of a continuum than a dichotomy. We also follow the cost–benefit practice, applying it to analysis of the mode of competition law regulation, keeping in mind considerations specific to competition policy.

In particular, we note that some of the harms that a competition regime may wish to control are different from the sorts of harm typically in focus in a general rules versus standards discussion. The usual harms of those discussions are incremental: the harm arising from driving too fast is one which increases with speed, the harm arising from a nuisance (eg a neighbour playing music too loud[110]) increases with the intensity of the nuisance. On the other hand, in antitrust matters, a significant amount of the activities have social value, but are harmful only after a point. Crane refers to this as the '"tipsy" [nature of the conduct] – at a certain point, the conduct tips suddenly from beneficial to harmful'.[111] For instance, in so far as the practice increases consumer welfare, price-cutting has social value. But this value ceases at the point where the low price serves to exclude competitors from the market.[112]

---

[107] Some discussions, however, address the coherency of a distinction between rules and standards; see eg Pierre Schlag, 'Rules and Standards' (1985) 33 *UCLA Law Review* 379.

[108] Korobkin (n 100) 23.

[109] See eg Schlag (n 107).

[110] Korobkin (n 100) 41 and 55–56.

[111] Crane (n 100) 85.

[112] ibid; Crane provides other examples beyond price cutting, namely product innovation (shutting out competitors in aftermarkets), cross-licensing and information exchanges.

The primary advantages of standards are that they are inexpensive to establish and when established appear to lack the over- or underinclusiveness that rules can have. It is much easier for a legislative body to mandate that an activity be conducted with 'reasonable care' than to write a catalogue which exhaustively enumerates in a precise fashion how that activity is and is not to be conducted. The latter process will be laborious, and its result will almost certainly be incomplete.

Rules are heralded as being able to provide clear guidance. This is true, to a point. Paradigmatic rules are clear. A rule stating that 'it is an offence to drive a motorised vehicle in excess of 100 km/hour' is a clear prohibition of such conduct. As it stands, that rule may need to be to be supplemented by another rule that sets out the consequences of violating the former rule; but the former rule itself is clear. However, as rules move from the paradigm (or 'rule end' of the rules–standards continuum), they have a tendency to become less clear.

The explanation for this lies in the structure and drafting of rules. Rules can be parsed as conditionals, with an antecedent and a consequent (or in Schlag's terms, a 'trigger' and a 'response'[113]). The consequent identifies the circumstances which necessitate the legal response authorised by the antecedent. Lack of clarity in rules arises with the manner in which either or both of either the antecedent or consequent is/are specified. This may arise for a number of reasons (imprecise or incomplete drafting, social/technological progress, etc) the details of which are irrelevant to this discussion. What is relevant to our discussion is that rules in themselves are no guarantee of clear guidance; rather, it is the precision with which the relevant rules are drafted that serves as the source of clarity.[114]

---

[113] Schlag (n 107) 381.

[114] One blogger, in an influential EU competition law blog, seems to make this point. Ibáñez Colomo notes:

> When people claim that rules are clear and administrable, they typically focus on the outcome of the rule. The rule determines ex ante whether a given practice is authorised or prohibited. There is no need to show, ex post or on a case-by-case basis, whether the practice has an effect on competition.
>
> As far as the above is concerned, those in favour of rules are right. The problem is that the discussion misses the other component of the rule. When we ask the question of whether a rule provides clarity and administrability, we need to pay attention not only to the outcome but also to the scope of the rule (or trigger, to use Schlag's expression).
>
> In other words: even if the outcome of the rule is clear by design, we need to ask whether the scope of the rule is clear too, or whether there is uncertainty about how broad it is and about the range of conduct that is subject to it.
>
> Legal uncertainty is inevitable when we do not know for sure the behaviour that is subject to the rule (in other words, when the trigger is 'soft', as Schlag would put it). In such circumstances, the much-touted advantages of rules are wholly absent.

Pablo Ibáñez Colomo, 'Why Rules Do Not Always Give Legal Certainty – And Why They Are Not Necessarily Administrable' *Chillin'Competition* (2 May 2018, 11:44 am) available at: https://chillingcompetition.com/2018/05/02/why-rules-do-not-always-give-legal-certainty-and-why-they-are-not-necessarily-administrable/. Ibáñez Colomo is correct, the clarity and administrability of a rule is not because a legal precept is set forth as a 'rule', but rather because the precept is drafted clearly – with sufficient precision in describing the 'triggers' and 'responses'.

A corollary of the certainty and predictability which (paradigmatic) rules provide is their ability to give greater ex ante guidance than standards. 'Certainty' here is of course relative, being a function of the precision of the clarity in drafting the rule. Nevertheless, a rule which states a firm speed limit provides greater guidance than that which requires only 'reasonable speed'. In antitrust matters there are further benefits to such certainty. First, certainty reduces litigation. Litigating over whether or not goods were priced below the marginal cost of their production (a not insignificant task, given efficiencies of scope and transparency of accounting data) is nevertheless significantly simpler than determining whether or not the goods were priced in a manner which excluded or was intended to exclude a competitor. Further, given a more certain result, a rule-based antitrust regime is less likely to be manipulated by competitors using litigation to reduce competition.[115] Similarly rules also reduce administrative and governmental discretion. This can reduce rent-seeking activities, a consequence noted not only by ordoliberals but also by constitutional economists.[116]

Second, a rule that clearly demarcates acceptable from unacceptable conduct can promote activity at the border. This has added significance in antitrust regulation, where the regulated activity manifests its harms differently from other regulated behaviour. The general approach taken with regulated behaviour is that standards and rules both demarcate the permissible from the prohibited with varying degrees of certainty. With both, near the margin, there is a 'grey zone' of activity that may or may not be subject to the prohibition. Given the nature of standards, their grey zones are larger. If the orthodox view of the economically rational person is correct, actors will direct their behaviour to approach the boundary so long as the gain from moving closer exceeds their perception of the costs. Costs are occurred when the boundary is transgressed. These costs can be significant; they include administrative penalties (which in the EU can be substantial), private damages (trebled in the US), criminal sanctions (in some jurisdictions), and the reputational consequences of committing such acts. However, a risk-adverse agent may cease the activity well before the boundary, in order to ensure that this line is not crossed and sanctions are not incurred. It will therefore be the agent's subjective perception of the location of the threshold which will determine the agent's conduct.

In a case of regulation (which does not involve antitrust) deterrence of near-boundary cases may be better met through a standard. Going back to the speeding example, a rule prohibiting driving in excess of 100 km/hour may encourage drivers to cruise at 98, irrespective of their skills or road conditions. The grey zone occasioned by a standard of reasonableness may encourage more prudent driving.

---

[115] 'The books are full of suits by rivals for the purpose, or with the effect, of reducing competition and increasing price.' Frank H Easterbrook, 'The Limits of Antitrust' (1984) 63 *Texas Law Review* 1, 34; see Jonathan B Baker, 'Taking the Error out of "Error Cost" Analysis: What's Wrong with Antitrust's Right' (2015) 80 *Antitrust Law Journal* 1, 25–29.

[116] This is noted by Christiansen and Kerber (n 103) 219–20.

Similar considerations may apply to nuisance-type behaviour. The distinguishing feature here is that these are activities where the marginal activity has little social value. Thus in these cases little of social value is lost by the grey zone caused by a standard.

In antitrust matters, given the 'tipsy' nature of much conduct, near-marginal activity is socially beneficial. In the case of low prices, for example, the lower the price, the better off the consumer is, until the low pricing strategy tips into a situation of market exclusion. A grey zone, where the relevant standard may sanction conduct, may also deter a risk-adverse (or even risk-neutral) agent from engaging in pricing practices which enter (or are near the entry point to) that zone, to the detriment of consumers. A clear, rule-based line may not have this effect, and is likely to encourage behaviour up to the border.

Should the orthodox economic approach's rationality axiom be relaxed, and the effect of standards on marginal behaviour is examined under the behavioural approach, we note that standards are more likely to encourage behaviour which crosses the border. The overconfidence bias is well known (and discussed above[117]); it shoehorns well with our earlier speeding example. Svensen found that over 50 per cent of drivers view themselves as above-average drivers.[118] Armed with this overconfidence, a 'reasonable speed' may be faster than prudence would otherwise suggest; hence attracting behaviour which crosses the margin. Similarly in an antitrust matter, such a bias may manifest itself in a firm's view that it is the quality of its good which is attracting customers and not, for instance, the firm's strategy of pricing or tying the good which is forcing competing goods from the market. A rule may be a better means to control such behaviour arising from such unwarranted confidence or optimism.

In spite of their advantages, rules – particularly in antitrust – are not a panacea. There is the over- and underinclusiveness problem described above. In addition to this, areas of law governed by a rule-based regime suffer from the shortcoming that categorisation of an activity so that it falls within the scope of a given rule may be determinative of the legal treatment of that activity. Thus significant time, effort and legal costs are spent (or, perhaps, wasted) in an effort to describe certain forms of conduct in a particular way, so that they fall under that rule which gives them the most favourable treatment. A caricature of tax law is that this legal specialism exploits such behaviour. And certainly, adjudicators may also choose the wrong rule to determine the outcome of a dispute.

In antitrust, characterisation of a practice as vertically imposed or horizontally agreed can have significance. In *Sealy*, the USSC remarked:

> Because this Court has distinguished between horizontal and vertical territorial limitations for purposes of the impact of the Sherman Act, it is first necessary to determine

---

[117] See above pp 130–32.
[118] Ola Svenson, 'Are We All Less Risky and More Skilful than Our Fellow Drivers?' (1981) 47 *Acta Psychologica* 143.

whether the territorial arrangements here are to be treated as the creature of the licensor, Sealy, or as the product of a horizontal arrangement among the licensees.[119]

The arrangement there concerned a mattress company (Sealy) owned by its licensee-manufacturers. As the Court noted: 'Sealy agreed with each licensee not to license any other person to manufacture or sell in the designated area; and the licensee agreed not to manufacture or sell "Sealy products" outside the designated area.'[120] Although there were both vertical and horizontal elements to the arrangement, the Court characterised it as horizontal and agreed that the arrangement was per se illegal. This decision was condemned. However, this incorrect result was a consequence of judicial error in choosing the wrong rule, and not necessarily with the rule itself.

This sort of reasoning is often derided as 'formalism', and is used as an example of what is wrong with a rule-based approach to antitrust. This sort of reasoning, it is said, focuses too much on the form or characterisation of the practice, and ignores any rigorous analysis of its economic effects.[121] But such a comment may confuse rule-based reasoning with judicial error in applying the rules.

B. Certainty: A Case for Specified Rules

The conclusion which can be drawn from the above is that competition regulation will necessarily be imperfect. The imperfection will arise from both the form (rule or standard) and content of the principles used in this regulation. These principles may fail because they are over- or underinclusive, may be drafted (or administered) by a regulatory body which has been captured by a rent-seeking constituency, the legal process could have been manipulated by strategic litigation or opportunistic behaviour (exacerbated by information asymmetries) during litigation, judicial error in applying those rules, or for other reasons.[122] However, as imperfect as these principles may be, firms and courts require guidance to plan and adjudicate future commercial arrangements.

The fact that such regulation will necessarily be imperfect should not be taken as a fatal blow for any regulatory scheme. Rather, those designing an antitrust

---

[119] *US v Sealy Inc*, 388 US 350, 352 (1967).

[120] ibid.

[121] For one statement of this type of criticism, see Julie Clarke, 'The Opinion of AG Wahl in the Intel Rebates Case: A Triumph of Substance over Form?' (2017) 40 *World Competition* 241, 257:

Existing case-law on Article 102 has, with some justification, been described as 'economic wasteland', focusing too much on form and making presumptions about consumer harm not firmly grounded in economic principles. In particular, existing presumptions suffer from a general failure to accurately predict either competitor or market level foreclosure. Although a minority of commentators maintain that the current form-based classifications enjoy sound economic foundation, this position is difficult to sustain in light of the context-specific nature of anti-competitive effects arising from rebates.

[122] Christiansen and Kerber (n 103) 223–24.

regime should accept that though such perfection is impossible, they should design a system which appropriately controls the unwanted behaviour, given the costs and uncertainties inherent in the market and in the commercial practices prevalent in the given market. Further, there will be a cost to all regulatory regimes. These costs include not just the losses occasioned by over- and underinclusiveness of principles (ie the type I and type II errors of concerned to those focusing on error cost analysis), but also costs involved in formulating and promulgating, litigating and adjudicating under the principles, monitoring and compliance costs, and taking advice in regard to appropriate commercial strategies given what is known of the principles.[123] These may be viewed as a form of transaction costs.[124]

The aim of an antitrust regime should include the elimination of market failures associated with the monopoly problem, in a manner which is consistent with or promotes other legal values (to the extent that these are recognised by the jurisdictions legal/antitrust regime); and to do so in a manner which minimises costs to all market actors.

An extreme effects-based approach, where every arrangement is individually scrutinised in an effort to determine its legality, is costly. As Christiansen and Kerber note:

> [I]t is one of the most important economic insights that applying more general rules instead of a case-by-case investigation can economize on information and decision costs .... From that perspective it becomes clear that a fullscale analysis of all positive and negative welfare effects is desirable only in rare cases, whereas for the millions of everyday business transactions simpler rules are preferable that can be more easily monitored and complied with.[125]

Rather, with transaction costs in mind, the focus ought to be on rules that are of more general application and work for the vast majority of cases. Joskow makes this argument in the following terms:

> Just as the choice of governance arrangements for private transactions requires an evaluation of the comparative costs and benefits of alternative imperfect governance arrangements, so too does a TCE [transaction costs economics] perspective imply that the test of a good legal rule is not primarily whether it leads correct decision in a particular case, but rather whether it does a good job deterring anticompetitive behavior throughout the economy given all of the relevant costs, benefits, and uncertainties associated with diagnosis and remedies.[126]

Good rules, from an administrative perspective, have an element of generality to them. This leads to correct decisions in most cases. Good rules are also reasonably

---

[123] See ibid 231–33.

[124] Paul L Joskow, 'Transaction Cost Economics, Antitrust Rules, and Remedies' (2002) 18 *Journal of Law, Economics, and Organization* 95, 96–100.

[125] Christiansen and Kerber (n 103) 233, their reference to Frank H Easterbrook, 'Ignorance and Antitrust' in TM Jorde and DJ Teece (eds), *Antitrust, Innovation, and Competitiveness* (New York, Oxford University Press, 1992) 119 omitted.

[126] Joskow (n 124) 99–100.

simple and cheap to apply – or at least simpler and less costly – than what a 'full-blown' effects-based analysis would require. As such they have the benefit of being able to give ex ante guidance. In this way, such a regime using such rules more closely approximates the rule of law ideal than one which compels case-by-case scrutiny.

To complete the outline of this approach, there needs to be some indication of how specific such rules need to be, and if (or how) these rules can be developed (or allowed to evolve, if a more organic metaphor is needed) in the face of the changes in the economy and in society's response to these economic changes. This latter point recognises the possibility that there may be a legal requirement that competition policy take into account concerns other than a strict focus on advancing consumer welfare.

Christiansen and Kerber provide a compelling argument for the appropriate degree of specificity which antitrust rules should possess. These authors follow Kaplow's definition of complexity in rules as a function of the 'number and complexity of the distinctions incorporated in the set of rules'.[127] More precise rules contain more assessment criteria, which in turn permit a more accurate analysis of the case at hand. They note: 'The main advantage of more precise (or more differentiated) competition rules is that their complexity might allow a more effective distinction between procompetitive and anticompetitive behavior.'[128] But such complexity (or in their terms 'differentiation') and its corresponding accuracy comes at a cost: in particular, highly differentiated rules impose greater transaction costs (or, in Christiansen and Kerber's terms, 'regulation costs'). These are the costs involved in shaping and promulgating rules, the costs involved in assessing individual cases, monitoring and compliance costs, and 'costs through legal uncertainty'.[129]

Christiansen and Kerber note the obvious: in designing a set of rules, particularly in antitrust policy, there will always be a cost trade-off between the costs of a more general rule, which may be over- or underinclusive, leading to type I and type II errors and their resultant costs, and those costs involved in producing highly specific analysis (via either a highly differentiated rule or case-by-case consideration).[130] The insight is to develop optimally differentiated competition rules, ie rules designed to incur the least cost through the sum of regulation and error costs.[131] Such rules will not get the answer correct in every case (as doing so

---

[127] Christiansen and Kerber (n 103) 221, referring to Louis Kaplow, 'A Model of the Optimal Complexity of Legal Rules' (1995) 11 *Journal of Law, Economics, and Organization* 150 and Louis Kaplow, 'General Characteristics of Rules' in B Bouckaert, and G DeGeest (eds), *Encyclopedia of Law and Economics* (Cheltenham, Edward Elgar, 2000) vol V, 502.

[128] Christiansen and Kerber ibid 221.

[129] ibid 231–33.

[130] This tension is not unique to antitrust (or legal reasoning generally); it can be found in utilitarian ethical theory as well. See my '*Intel*, Consequentialist Goals and the Certainty of Rules: The Same Old Song and Dance, My Friend' (2016) 11 *Competition Law Review* 215, 218–24, which relates this issue to antitrust in the context of the GC's decision in *Intel*.

[131] Christiansen and Kerber (n 103) 223: 'The basic idea is that the optimal rule is characterized by the minimum of the sum of welfare losses through wrong decisions (error costs) and regulation costs.'

is prohibitively expensive); but over the long run they will reduce both types of costs,[132] and therefore 'a limited number of wrong decisions through the application of the optimal rule are accepted because the costs of avoiding these decision errors are higher than their costs'.[133]

The authors note that, applied generally, a particular arrangement is not prohibited or permitted because of that arrangement's effects in a given case. Rather the legal question (or purpose in setting the rule) is to determine whether or not arrangements of the type in question will maximise welfare over the long run. The optimal rule will be sufficiently differentiated (or complex) to arrive at this long-term solution, and the costs of any further differentiation (or addition of complexity in the rule's content) will not result in an offsetting (long-term) benefit. Hence, legal reform in changing from (or rejecting) a differentiated rule can never be justified on the basis that a different (or a more differentiated) rule is justified in a particular case.[134] Hence economics is used, not on a case-specific basis, but to shape and differentiate the competition rules.[135]

With two reservations, we accept this line of reasoning. The first reservation regards the strict economic focus the line of reasoning contains. This needs to be relaxed. If there are non-welfarest goals which competition policy-makers must take into account (as the account of the EU's regime suggests), these goals need to be incorporated at the rule-making stage. Hence the rule formulation process may need to take into account a number of standards (eg the welfarest goal of contemporary antitrust policy, non-welfarest goals mandated by other elements of a jurisdiction's legal order, and a standard for comparing these). However, an attribute of standards is that they are more amenable than rules for use in balancing tests. And similar balancing standards can be applied in the subsequent differentiation of rules. This regime is somewhat more complicated than that envisaged by Christiansen and Kerber; however, its complexity is caused by its recognition of the multiple norms which underlie some jurisdictions' antitrust regimes. To fail to acknowledge this and take it into account in constructing the antitrust rules (or the process by which such rules are constructed) would be a rule of law failing.

The second reservation is more of a caveat. It relates to the above concern about how rules can be made to evolve, or become specified, when necessary. Further refinement, or differentiation, requires appropriate evidence of general tendencies, not a specific advantage in a given case. Thus significant changes in antitrust rules, such as of the sort found in *Leegin*, are acceptable only when a wide variety of data is acquired on business practices throughout the economy. In *Leegin*, this should have included the pervasiveness of free-riding, the welfare benefits of the enhanced service which RPM would provide, and whether or not such benefits

---

[132] ibid 224.
[133] ibid 225.
[134] ibid 238; see the authors' analysis of whether a move from a per se approach to resale price maintenance is justified.
[135] ibid 239–40.

could be obtained through means other than RPM. Such data should also have been collected from industries beyond the luxury leather goods sector of which Leegin was a part. Under this approach the sweeping conclusion of the majority in that case was almost certainly unwarranted and without a rational foundation.

This tells us that change of legal rules should therefore be incremental. Assuming that legislators and adjudicators have sufficient knowledge to make these decisions (and this knowledge cost is implicitly among the transaction costs involved in shaping and differentiating competition rules), it is unlikely that wholesale changes of the *Leegin* sort are ever warranted. The approach this chapter suggests is that the form of precedential reasoning we should expect in antitrust will more closely follow traditional 'common law' reasoning. That is, a process of a slow and careful structuring of a legal doctrine, rather than a radical restructuring of long-standing antitrust rules. The consequence of this is that antitrust rules will be more certain, thus firms can rely on them in shaping their future plans and practices. This, needless to say, better reflects the rule of law ideal than an alternative approach where accuracy and predictability are based on the vicissitudes of case-by-case analysis; and where overgeneralisation of one isolated instance may be regarded as the catalyst for an extensive revision of competition policy.

III. Conclusion

The primary merit of the effects-based approach to competition policy is its purported ability to allow competition authorities and adjudicators to make determinations on a case-by-case basis, ensuring that only business arrangements that reduce consumer welfare are prohibited. Advocates of this policy recognise that a significant degree of rule-scepticism is needed, if the approach is to be effective. Such rule-scepticism has manifested itself (at least in the US) in a weakened version of *stare decisis*, and in both the US and EU in scepticism towards the nature of the legal rules which govern the competition regime. This chapter has argued that these two approaches to the nature of legal rules draw antitrust (or at least an antitrust regime incorporating an effects-based approach) away from the rule of law ideal.

Certainty and predictability are features of any legal system, and as has been seen, are key components of a rule of law ideal. A legal system which incorporates the rule of law ideal is one which allows for rational agents to plan their future activities. This requires that legal rules allow for certainty and predictability in such planning. Precedent (or at least the ability to rely on the past rulings of administrators and tribunals) and certainty and clarity of legal rules are key positive features which bring a legal system closer to the rule of law ideal.

Precedent is significant in this regard. When a court follows earlier precedent, it does two things. First, it ensures the continuity of previous rules, affirming that reliance on these rules was a rational choice. Second, it ensures that like cases are treated alike, another important feature of the rule of law. In the US antitrust regime, precedent has come to play a diminishing role in directing the behaviour of market participants. Further, there is disconnect between what the USSC says and what it does. In statutory matters, should a Supreme Court decision be unsatisfactory, it is the job of Congress to rectify it: except in antitrust.[136] This leads to a situation recognised by that Court that *state decisis* has less than usual effect in antitrust cases. This is hardly a satisfactory situation for anyone seeking or giving advice on commercial arrangements. Indeed, such acknowledgement of increasing uncertainty in antitrust matters is also an implicit recognition that this body of law has moved away from the rule of law ideal, with the explicit assistance of the Court.

In the EU the situation is somewhat different. The effects-based approach has been a Commission-driven initiative. The CJEU has accepted it, but without the unbridled enthusiasm of the USSC. This slower European process is reflective of a different legal understanding of the role of previous decisions. It is informed by a view of *jurisprudence constante* where a lengthy history of cases is persuasive of the disposition of the dispute at hand. There is no underlying single precedent, no *Dr Miles*, to reject on the basis of a new view of economic theory. As such the CJEU has ensured a degree of stability in the EU competition regime. The rule of law threat in Europe comes not from a judicial willingness to discard precedent, but from the Commission, by its reshaping of competition policy. The European Treaties take a multifaceted view of the Union's goals. But since the turn of the century with the adoption of the MEA, the Commission has appeared to ring-fence competition from the other values of the Treaties. This approach, in effect an administrative rewrite of the Union's law, takes Europe's competition regime a step away from the rule of law ideal.

For an effect-based competition regime to achieve its full potential, the form of the legal principles used in competition matters must also be amenable to case-by-case analysis. To this end, courts and adjudicators have been increasingly reliant on standards, at the expense of rules. As there is a continuum of legal principles, running from more general standards to highly specific rules, the standards–rules distinction is a false dichotomy. Nevertheless, this effects-based approach requires a preference that competition policy be governed by legal principles which are more toward the standards end of the continuum. This has significant rule of law implications.

It is of course true that rules can have their deficiencies. They can be over- or underinclusive, they can yield silly and inconsistent results, and the legality of the activity may be a function of judicial characterisation of the practice rather than commercial reality (*Sealy* and *Topco* come to mind). These are problems with rule formulation and selection, and not problems with rules per se. Notwithstanding this, rules do provide certainty, which in turn can be used for ex ante guidance about a given practice.

---

[136] And, of course, baseball is the exception to the exception; see above p 31, n 71.

Standards, we have seen, do not possess these needed characteristics. While, ex post, they may be useful in determining whether or not a particular practice was anticompetitive, they lack the virtues of foresight and ex ante administrability. To move a legal regime towards a system with greater reliance on standards moves that regime away from the rule of law paradigm. Yet this is not to say that some of the benefits of a standards-based, economics-focused regime cannot be captured by an improved competition regime. Basing appropriately complex legal rules on inter alia the tools of economics is one way of doing this, as we have suggested. This is one of the principal results of the present chapter.

Conclusion: Putting the Rule of Law Back into Antitrust

From both a normative and positive perspective, the rule of law is an important constituent of any legal system. If we take Rawls's account as a guide,[1] law is a system of rules addressed to rational agents. This system is backed by the coercive power of the state and is designed to regulate the agents' conduct in a way that provides a 'framework for social cooperation'.[2] Social cooperation among rational agents entails an ability to rationally plan for the future with the confidence that such plans can come to fruition. This in turn requires that legal rules promote the ability to plan rationally, ie the rules are sufficiently stable, certain and clear so that parties can rely upon them while making arrangements for the future. This is a very minimalist understanding of the rule of law, and one which we have suggested must be inherent in any theory of the rule of law. We considered such a conception of the rule of law in our first chapter.

Our minimalist understanding of the rule of law is formal, or process oriented. It contains no substantive normative content. It does not suggest that a purported law is void (or 'not a law') if it violates some substantive normative precept. For that matter it does not even suggest that a law which is unclear to a rational agent, or introduces uncertainty about the rational agent's future plans, is somehow not a 'law'.[3] Rather this idealised conception of the rule of law is a paradigm, which legislators, adjudicators and policy-makers should keep in mind and strive towards when developing a legal system and its rules. It is an idealised goal, which may never be realised. Indeed, both the United States and the European Union explicitly recognise their commitment towards the rule of law, and hence implicitly recognise a need to strive toward that paradigm.

Our paradigm of the rule of law gives prominence to formal criteria such as clarity, consistency between the law as written and as implemented, stability and prospectivity.[4] These are the very characteristics of law which not only guide, perhaps idealised, rational agents in their plans for the future, but are relied upon by actual individuals and firms when they develop commercial plans. This understanding of rule of law therefore also has positive value, in addition to being a normative aspiration. These formal criteria are also the sorts of features which

---

[1] See above pp 18–21.
[2] John Rawls, *A Theory of Justice*, rev edn (Cambridge MA, Harvard University Press, 1999) 207.
[3] In this regard, our theory of the rule of law is amoral, in the literal sense.
[4] See above pp 18–21.

are necessary conditions for commercial certainty. Unsurprisingly, we noted that societies characterised by a closer approximation to this paradigm are better developed in both an instrumental sense (ie that measured by metrics such as GDP, life expectancy at birth, public health indicators, etc) and in the normative sense identified by Sen (with the relevant metrics including democratic elections, political participation and civil liberties).[5] Countries such as the United States and the Member States of the European Union invest heavily in rule of law programmes to promote these values abroad, in the hope that these instrumental and developmental benefits of the rule of law will enhance not just the business environment, but also the quality of life, in the receiving regimes.

In light of this internationalisation strategy, rule of law considerations also have an important symbolic force. A regime that promotes the virtues and values of the rule of law abroad needs to ensure those virtues are practised and implemented domestically.

It is against this background of a formal theory of rule of law that this work considered recent developments in both US and EU competition law and policy. We have shown the influence of a particular school of economic thinking, the so-called Chicago School, on the development of antitrust law and policy on both sides of the Atlantic. The focus of antitrust analysis has under this influence shifted towards a series of case-by-case examinations of the pro- and anticompetitive consequences of a given arrangement on an ex post basis. It is now less concerned with the development of general rules which can be considered ex ante, and which give prospective guidance for appropriate commercial conduct.

This has been shown by the discussion of the US courts' shift in antitrust analysis. This shift was driven by the USSC to alter US antitrust law from an approach that was significantly reliant on numerous per se prohibitions to a legal regime in which the rule of reason is now the default mode of analysis. A similar shift occurred with the European adoption of the MEA, where case-by-case analysis (mandated by considering 'all the circumstances') is now the new norm. In both jurisdictions this case-by-case analysis is conducted through the lens of classical price theory. The result of this is that this effects-based approach to antitrust analysis has moved antitrust law away from the ideal of the rule of law.

To be fair, before the advent of the effects-based approach to antitrust analysis, there were some fundamental inconsistencies in the then approach. In the US, *Sealy* and *Topco* only need to be mentioned; in Europe, inadequate analysis in merger cases, a 'formalistic' approach to categorisation, and consideration of Article 101 and 102 matters resulted in market players being uncertain about how authorities may regard their practices. And, with the decentralised European regime brought in by Regulation 1/2003, there was a need to provide guidance to undertakings which they could use in their self-assessment of the acceptability of future business plans.

---

[5] See above pp 36–38.

The toolbox of the economist could help here. The principles of price theory could be used to identify conduct which could increase (or decrease) consumer welfare. The over- and underinclusiveness of antitrust rules could be seen through the use of these tools; but more significantly, if rules could be relaxed (or even abandoned), these tools could be used to ensure that the legal regime permits the welfare-maximising alternative in any given case. To the extent that the maximisation of consumer welfare is (or should be) the goal of competition policy on either side of the Atlantic, liberal use of this toolbox would advance the goal.

Further, by using this approach the Commission can signal to those market participants engaging in self-assessment of their business practices for compatibility with Articles 101 and 102 that only the tools of the economist are needed to complete this analysis. By restricting the scope of self-assessment to the self-assessment of only economic consequences, not only is the process simplified, but the ability of undertakings to manipulate the assessment process by manipulating Article 101(3) to introduce values that are not immediately reducible to, or incommensurate with, consumer welfare[6] is reduced – if not eliminated.

There is an elegant appeal to this approach. First, it ostensibly gets the right result in all cases. Second, the analysis required by this approach mandates the consideration of one value, consumer welfare; hence there will be no need to compare consumer welfare against any other (perhaps incommensurable) goals or norms adopted by the competition regime. The elegance of this approach's analytic method and potential accuracy of its results would provide strong persuasive justification that, ceteris paribus, this approach be adopted.

But things are not otherwise equal, as this book has argued. The final three chapters of this book have shown this. More significantly, these chapters have also demonstrated that the adoption of this approach has set antitrust law and policy on both sides of the Atlantic on a trajectory that is retreating from a rule of law paradigm.

The first point of concern is the nature of the economic 'tools' deployed in competition analysis. Obviously, not all tools are useful for every situation. An orthopaedic surgeon's bone saw is quite useful for amputations, but dangerous for eye surgery. The tools deployed by the economist in antitrust analysis have their limitations as well. The rule of law problem associated with incorrect analysis, driven by an improper or questionable methodology, is that such analysis may produce results that are incongruent with the goals of the law. Hence what the law says and what the law does will be two different – and possibly inconsistent – things.

---

[6] It could be suggested that Art 101(3)'s criteria of 'promoting technical or economic progress' and 'a fair share' could be manipulated in this way. I have previously argued that these values may not be reducible to consumer welfare (or consumer welfare in the sense envisaged by the Commission in its Guidelines on Art 101(3)). The argument is that Art 101(3) includes more than welfarest goals and that the Commission is wrong in ignoring these. See above pp 167–71; and Bruce Wardhaugh, 'Crisis Cartels: Non-Economic Values, the Public Interest, and Institutional Considerations' (2014) 10 *European Competition Journal* 311. However, it is not acceptable to 'read out' or otherwise ignore the force of a particular legal standard or objective merely because it is subject to manipulation by rent-seekers.

This work has focused on two difficulties with the economic tools in the 'orthodox' toolbox. First, the construction of the orthodox toolbox was based on traditional price theory, as elaborated by the Chicago School. It is highly theoretical, and until possibly quite recently, its adherents have used little empirical analysis to develop or verify its axiomatic assumptions and propositions. Some of these assumptions are quite strong. Indeed, this work has noted the assumptions of the self-correcting nature of markets, and its corollary, a preference for type II over type I errors, are significant to the effects-based approach. This preference exists even in the presence of evidence of the longevity of cartels. If cartels (a form of monopoly) can survive over a period of years (even in the face of enforcement activity), then markets may not be as self-correcting as the approach assumes. Hence type II errors may not be as benign as assumed.

A more fundamental problem with the economic tools of this orthodox approach is the assumption of rationality in market participants. If this assumption is relaxed, a number of different results follow. These results diverge significantly from the predictions of the orthodox approach. This is the lesson which our brief consideration of behavioural economics has taught us.

The significance of the behavioural approach to economics is that it demonstrates that people possess bounded rationality, and are not the unboundedly rational economic agents which the orthodox approach presupposes. People, rather than calculating the utility-maximising outcome in every situation, use heuristics (or short cuts) to facilitate their choice among alternatives; and their decisions are often influenced by biases which lead to suboptimal (from a utility- or welfare-maximising approach) decisions. If this is the case, and a significant amount of empirical evidence suggests that it is, then the approach to antitrust dictated by orthodox analysis will, in a non-trivial number of cases, lead to an incorrect result. Chapter 4 considered how the behavioural approach analyses tying, predatory pricing and market entry. The result of that analysis was that in each of these cases, the behavioural approach's conclusion differed significantly from that predicted by the orthodox approach.

The significance of this cannot be dismissed. If the behaviourist approach accurately captures what people in fact do, ie how they behave in a market situation, then much of the orthodox thinking regarding (at least these) antitrust issues is likely incorrect. If this is so, this poses a rule of law problem: the aims of antitrust law are thwarted by the (orthodox) analytical methodology compelled by the effects-based approach. This divergence between what the law says and what the law does moves antitrust law away from the rule of law paradigm.

The rule of law concerns associated with the use of the orthodox methodology are exacerbated by how the methodology has been deployed, and how it is used in the adjudicative process. The legal implementation of the effects-based approach was judicially driven in the United States, and Commission driven in the European Union. However, in both jurisdictions there is a legislative (or Treaty) basis for antitrust, and it is only the function of the (US) courts and European Commission to interpret this. Further, in both jurisdictions, the legislative (or Treaty) basis promotes values other than the maximisation of consumer welfare. By adopting an antitrust methodology that focuses exclusively on the maximisation of consumer welfare, the US courts and the European Commission have rewritten the antitrust law of their respective jurisdictions. This, as was argued, is a profound problem raising concerns of democratic legitimacy.

This issue of democratic legitimacy is also a rule of law concern. Typically, democratic societies (and both the US and EU are typical in this respect) separate and divide powers among their institutions. This separation of powers provides a link between governmental exercise of power and a democratic authorisation of such use of power. Waldron has expressed this connection in terms which explicitly relate the link to our formal understanding of the rule of law.[7] As such we have argued that this reorientation of competition law and policy, driven by the USSC and the European Commission, away from a multivalued legal field to one which focuses exclusively on the maximisation of consumer surplus, is a rule of law threat. In effect, administrative or judicial preferences have now usurped democratic choices in competition policy. Given that competition policy is one of the main means by which the market is regulated, and the central significance of the market as a means of distribution of resources in US and European societies, this is no small matter.

Further, even if the orthodox approach to antitrust is the appropriate methodology for antitrust analysis and its introduction into antitrust policy is democratically legitimate, then the use of this methodology in the context of litigation raises a number of other rule of law questions. The role of a judge is to decide the matter before her, giving a reasoned account why the case was decided in the manner it was. In order to do so, the judge needs to have knowledge (or at least reasoned belief) of the facts she has found. The orthodox approach to competition law requires an understanding and analysis of matters that are typically beyond a judge's competence. This is why a significant amount of evidence needs to be presented through experts. But experts, particularly in contested competition matters, may not always agree with each other. Thus a judge is called upon to make a reasoned determination between two (or possibly more) opposing interpretations of the same market conditions.

The rule of law issue here is clear. The certainty and predictability of legal rules that is required for these to serve as guides for future conduct of rational agents presupposes that those applying (or adjudicating under) those rules can do so rationally, rather than in an arbitrary unreasoned manner. As the effects-based approach makes such rational determination of the appropriate determination of litigation more difficult, it represents a retrograde step in the path towards the rule of law.

But most significantly, the effects-based approach represents an attack on the certainty of the legal principles which may be used to resolve a competition

---

[7] See above pp 162–64.

dispute. This approach eschews the certainty of rule-based decision-making for the accuracy of a case-by-case analysis using standards. In doing this, at least in the US, the judiciary is willing to cast precedent aside and give *stare decisis* a less central role in the adjudicative process. Case-by-case decision-making, and a view of precedents which makes them weak, makes it difficult to determine in advance if a proposed business arrangement is likely to pass muster. Indeed, this is the greatest rule of law threat posed by this economic, or effects-based, approach.

To its credit, the CJEU has resisted efforts to alter its view of its previous jurisprudence. This may be a reflection of that Court's unwillingness to jump wholeheartedly on the bandwagon of the more economic approach, or it could be driven by an understanding of *jurisprudence constante*, which differs from that of *stare decisis*. Under the former, there is not one driving decision which anchors and determines subsequent interpretation of the law, rather there is a body of decisions which provide persuasive guidance on how future disputes should be resolved. The threat in Europe, however, stems from a different source: the Commission's adoption of the MEA and its subsequent rewriting of competition policy to focus exclusively on a consumer welfare goal.

All of these developments have pushed competition law and policy away from the rule of law paradigm we identified in Chapter 1. As an ideal, it is doubtful that any legal system (or element of a legal system) could ever fully instantiate the rule of law; however, this should not prevent us from attempting to bring our legal system to better approximate this ideal. But the economic approach does the very opposite.

This criticism of the MEA must not be taken as a rejection of a place for economic analysis in antitrust policy. There is a place for this approach, but it should play a less prominent role than it presently does. First, and foremost, the goals of antitrust must be identified. We see this happening at the political and academic level in the US. The 'New Brandeis Movement' (or sometimes, 'hipster antitrust') is challenging the orthodox view of antitrust's exclusive focus on consumer welfare.[8] While it may be premature to assess, and hence reject, the influence of this movement, its arguments need to be listened to and be taken seriously. The history of US antitrust shows that it was more than prices which concerned the public, legislators and administrative bodies in the development of this area of law. Similarly in Europe, the Commission's blinkered focus on consumer welfare is under challenge. Perhaps reflecting an inevitable interval between a US and European approach to competition policy, this European challenge is not as advanced as the challenge in the United States. However, the challenge must be accepted. The European Treaties do not fence off the Articles dealing with competition from other Treaty provisions. The opposite is true: they are clearly linked through the Union's goals. It is perhaps time to read the Treaties in this light.

---

[8] See above pp 157–58 and eg Lina M Khan, 'The New Brandeis Movement: America's Antimonopoly Debate' (2018) 9 *European Journal of Competition Law and Practice* 131.

Once these goals are identified, the task for those charged with the development of antitrust policy is to establish a set of principles which can be used in assessing future conduct. To this point, antitrust is no different from other areas of the law. The main source of difference which distinguishes antitrust from the bulk of other areas of the law is its reliance upon the methodology and insights of economics to a greater extent than the vast majority of other areas of law. This is unsurprising as antitrust is one of the main sources of market regulation.

As has been suggested throughout this work, the source of the problem leading to the rule of law concern is the locus of economic theory within antitrust analysis. The current orthodox approach identifies the maximisation of consumer welfare (itself a concept from traditional price theory) as the goal of antitrust law and policy. With the exception of a small set of obviously hard-core cartel cases, economic analysis is used in considering the facts of any dispute, to identify whether or not a given practice is welfare enhancing. For this approach to legal analysis to operate, it is necessary that the legal principles governing antitrust are sufficiently flexible so as not to prevent a court or administrative body from holding that a welfare-enhancing result is permissible.

The previous chapter argued that the orthodox approach's use of economic analysis at the case-by-case level is a source of much of the rule of law concerns generated by effects-based, economics-focused antitrust. The cure, we suggested, is to focus the insights of economics at a different location in the analytical process: the point of this analysis is to develop rules that, over the long term, will get the vast majority of cases right, with the rules being improved through an incremental process. While such rules may produce erroneous results (in the sense of type I and II errors) in the occasional case, the cost of these sorts of errors should be less than the sum of the administrative costs required to produce a 'correct' answer in each case and the costs arising from uncertainty resulting from the absence of guidance regarding whether or not the authorities will look upon a particular future arrangement kindly. Incremental improvement of these rules is possible through a 'common law' (in the original sense) approach to precedent. This approach is the slow and incremental development of a particular area of law, as witnessed in, for example, tort and contract doctrines. In these areas of law judges develop the rules, albeit slowly and with regard to previous decisions and (in the case of contract and commercial law) with reasonable commercial expectations in mind. This is our suggested approach to putting the rule of law back into antitrust law.

Since the 1970s, US antitrust law has been moving away from the rule of law paradigm. Starting around the turn of this century, European competition law followed this US trajectory. It would be reasonable to suggest that Europe has moved slower than its US counterparts, likely as a result of the CJEU's reticence to completely abandon its previous thinking. The Commission, on the other hand, is a greater rule of law threat. The Commission has produced a number of soft law instruments to guide the conduct of undertakings. These are binding on the Commission, and their production leads to some certainty in the law. However, these documents, while possessing persuasive force, are not binding on the courts (whether European or of Member States) nor are they binding on the competition authorities of Member States. The difficulty with these soft law instruments is the Commission's use of the MEA in them. This approach, as argued, is inconsistent with a broad reading of the European Treaties – one that does not view the competition provisions as existing in isolation and fenced off from other Union values and objectives. An approach which is in greater alignment with the Treaty objectives as a whole would closer approximate the rule of law ideal.

In the United States, the current state of antitrust law shows there to be a need to reverse the trend away from the rule of law paradigm. This is not unnoticed in the academic community, and the desire for a change to antitrust's approach is also entering into political discourse. Unfortunately, the rule of reason approach with the goal of maximising consumer welfare is well entrenched in US antitrust thinking. The word 'unfortunately' is used deliberately, for two reasons. First, dislodging the orthodox approach will require action by either the Supreme Court or Congress. And in the current US political environment, neither is likely.

But second, the US move away from the rule of law paradigm is lamentable. Rule of law considerations have played a significant role in the jurisprudence of the USSC since *Marbury*[9] in 1803. The stability and certainty of its precedents has been a cornerstone of these considerations throughout its history. The Court recognises the need for stability. Given the difficulties of amending the US Constitution, it has taken a flexible approach to Constitutional precedents. It has also taken a firmer view of *stare decisis* with its precedents in matters of statutory interpretation. From a rule of law perspective this guarantees the stability and certainty which precedents play in the legal system. This recognises the division of powers mandated by the Constitution, namely that it is the legislature's – not the Court's – role to make such legislative changes.

However, while this may be the professed state of affairs, the situation in antitrust law is different. In spite of its claims to the contrary, the USSC will from time to time overturn its interpretations of non-antitrust statutes. This in itself may not be too problematic, so long as the Court provides clear criteria of when it is appropriate to reverse a statutory precedent. As we saw, the Court seems to have done this. But in antitrust matters, this respect for precedents and division of powers is absent. This is a significant rule of law problem, and one that strikes to the core of antitrust. Given the essential role which antitrust plays in the regulation of the market, this rule of law problem is of wider social significance.

Although no legal or political system is likely to fully instantiate the rule of law, it is proper that any such system do its best to realise it as completely as possible. This is not just for some sort of ideal normative satisfaction, but for its instrumental and symbolic value. The rule of law is productive of those characteristics which allow for certainty in planning for the future, leading to enhanced commercial and developmental opportunities. Similarly, while governments and international

---

[9] *Marbury v Madison*, 5 US (1 Cranch) 137 (1803).

organisations such as those of the US, and the EU and its Member States promote the idea of the rule of law and proselytise its virtues abroad, these jurisdictions should look into their own backyard to notice how this fundamental aspect of their legal regime diverges from the ideal that they promote. But significantly and from a less rarefied perspective, antitrust's move away from the rule of law paradigm has introduced a non-trivial element of uncertainty into that area of law. This uncertainty acts as a transaction cost, which – if too great – will frustrate beneficial transactions and practices.

BIBLIOGRAPHY

—— 'President Trump's Contempt for the Rule of Law' *New York Times* (20 July 2017).

—— 'Press Undermined Rule of Law in Brexit Case Coverage, Says Supreme Court Chief' *The Independent* (16 February 2017).

Acemoglu, Daron, Simon Johnson and James Robinson, 'The Colonial Origins of Comparative Development: An Empirical Investigation' (2001) 91 *American Economic Review* 1380.

Akman, Pinar, *The Concept of Abuse in EU Competition Law* (Oxford, Hart, 2012).

—— 'The Reform of the Application of Article 102 TFEU: Mission Accomplished?' (2016) 8 *Antitrust Law Journal* 145.

Antitrust Chronicle April 2018.

Aquinas, Thomas, *Summa Theologica*, literally translated by Fathers of the English Dominican Province, 2nd rev edn (London, Burns Oates and Washbourne, 1927).

Areeda, Phillip and Donald F Turner, 'Predatory Pricing and Related Practices under Section 2 of the Sherman Act' (1974) 88 *Harvard Law Review* 697.

Arkes, Hal R and Catherine Blumer, 'The Psychology of Sunk Cost' (1985) 35 *Organizational Behavior and Human Decision Processes* 124.

Atiyah, PS, 'Common Law and Statute Law' (1985) 48 *Modern Law Review* 1.

Authority for Consumers and Markets (Competition Authority of the Netherlands), 'ACM's Analysis of the Sustainability Arrangements Concerning the "Chicken of Tomorrow"' ACM/DM/2014/206028 (26 January 2015).

Ayer, AJ, *Language Truth and Logic* (London, Pelican, 1936).

Baker, Jonathan B, 'Taking the Error Out of "Error Cost" Analysis: What's Wrong with Antitrust's Right' (2015) 80 *Antitrust Law Journal* 1.

Banner, Stuart, *The Baseball Trust: A History of Baseball's Antitrust Exemption* (Oxford, Oxford University Press, 2013).

Bannon, Leah and Douglas H Ginsburg, 'Antitrust Decisions of the US Supreme Court' (2007) 3(2) *Competition Policy International* 14.

Barber, BM, T Odean and L Zheng, 'Out of Sight, Out of Mind: The Effects of Expenses on Mutual Fund Flows' (2005) 78 *Journal of Business* 2095.

Bartalevich, Dzmitry, 'The Influence of the Chicago School on the Commission's Guidelines, Notices and Block Exemption Regulations in EU Competition Policy' (2016) 54 *Journal of Common Market Studies* 267.

Bartholomew, Christine P, 'Death by *Daubert*: The Continued Attack on Private Antitrust' (2014) 35 *Cardozo Law Review* 2147.

Baye, Michael R and Joshua D Wright, 'Is Antitrust Too Complicated for Generalist Judges? The Impact of Economic Complexity and Judicial Training on Appeals' (2011) 54 *Journal of Law and Economics* 1.

Berghahn, Volker, *The Americanization of West German Industry 1945–1973* (Cambridge, Cambridge University Press, 1986).

Bork, Robert, *The Antitrust Paradox: A Policy at War with Itself*, rev edn (New York, Basic Books, 1993).

Bouckaert, Boudewijn and Gerrit De Geest (eds), *Encyclopedia of Law and Economics*, vol I: *The History and Methodology of Law and Economics* (Cheltenham, Edward Elgar, 2000).

—— *Encyclopedia of Law and Economics*, vol V: *The Economics of Crime and Litigation* (Cheltenham, Edward Elgar, 2000).

Brewer, Scott, 'Scientific Expert Testimony and Intellectual Due Process' (1998) 107 *Yale Law Journal* 1535.

Brook, Or, 'Struggling with Article 101(3) TFEU: Diverging Approaches of the Commission, EU Courts, and Five Competition Authorities' (2019) 56 *Common Market Law Review* 121.

Buehler, Roger, Dale Griffin and Michael Ross, 'Exploring the "Planning Fallacy": Why People Underestimate their Task Completion Times' (1994) 67 *Journal of Personality and Social Psychology* 366.

—— 'Inside the Planning Fallacy: The Causes and Consequences of Optimistic Time Predictions' in Thomas Gilovich, Dale Griffin, and Daniel Kahneman (eds), *Heuristics and Biases: The Psychology of Intuitive Judgment* (Cambridge, Cambridge University Press, 2002) 250.

Calabresi, Steven G, 'Text v Precedent in Constitutional Law' (2008) 31 *Harvard Journal of Law and Public Policy* 947.

Camerer, Colin and Dan Lovallo, 'Overconfidence and Excess Entry: An Experimental Approach' (1999) 89 *American Economic Review* 306.

Cardozo, Benjamin, *The Nature of the Judicial Process* (New Haven, CT, Yale University Press, 1921).

Carey, George W and James McClellan (eds), *The Federalist* (Indianapolis, IN, Liberty Fund, 2001).

Carnap, Rudolf, 'Überwindung der Metaphysik durch logische Analyse der Sprache' (1932) 2 *Erkenntnis* 219.

Carothers, Thomas, 'The Rule of Law Revival' (1998) 77 *Foreign Affairs* 95.

Carrier, Michael A, 'The Real Rule of Reason: Bridging the Disconnect' [1999] *Brigham Young University Law Review* 1265.

—— 'The Rule of Reason: An Empirical Update for the 21st Century' (2009) 16 *George Mason Law Review* 827.

Cavanagh, Edward D, 'Whatever Happened to Quick Look' (2017) 26 *University of Miami Business Law Review* 39.

Chesterman, Simon, 'An International Rule of Law?' (2008) 56 *American Journal of Comparative Law* 331.

Christiansen, Arndt and Wolfgang Kerber, 'Competition Policy with Optimally Differentiated Rules Instead of "Per Se Rule vs Rule of Reason"' (2006) 2 *Journal of Competition Law and Economics* 215.

Cicero, *The Laws.*

Congressional Record (51st Session) (18 and 20 March 1890).

Clarke, Julie, 'The Opinion of AG Wahl in the Intel Rebates Case: A Triumph of Substance over Form?' (2017) 40 *World Competition* 241.

Coase, Ronald, 'The Problem of Social Cost' (1960) 3 *Journal of Law and Economics* 1.

Craig, Paul, 'Formal and Substantive Conceptions of the Rule of Law: An Analytical Framework' [1997] *Public Law* 467.

Crane, Daniel A, 'Rules versus Standards in Antitrust Adjudication' (2007) 64 *Washington and Lee Law Review* 49.

De, Oindrila, 'Analysis of Cartel Duration: Evidence from EC Prosecuted Cartels' (2010) 17 *International Journal of the Economics of Business* 33.

Devlin, Alan and Michael Jacobs, 'Antitrust Error' (2010) 52 *William and Mary Law Review* 75.

Djelic, Marie-Laurie, 'Does Europe Mean Americanization? The Case of Competition' (2002) 6 *Competition and Change* 233.

—— 'From Local Legislation to Global Structuring Frame: The Story of Antitrust' (2005) 5 *Global Social Policy* 55.

Dolzer, Rudolf and Christoph Schreuer, *Principles of International Investment Law*, 2nd edn (Oxford, Oxford University Press, 2012).

EAGCP, Economic Advisory Group for Competition Policy (Jordi Gual, Jordi, Martin Hellwig, Anne Perrot, Michele Polo, Michele, Patrik Rey, Klaus Schmidt, Rune Stenbacka) 'An Economic Approach to Article 82', Report by the European Advisory Group on Competition Policy.

Easterbrook, Frank H, 'Predatory Strategies and Counterstrategies' (1981) 48 *University of Chicago Law Review* 263.

—— 'The Limits of Antitrust' (1984) 63 *Texas Law Review* 1.

—— 'Allocating Antitrust Decisionmaking Tasks' (1987) 76 *Georgetown Law Journal* 305.

—— 'Ignorance and Antitrust' in TM Jorde and DJ Teece (eds), *Antitrust, Innovation, and Competitiveness* (New York, Oxford University Press, 1992) 119.

Eatwell, John, Murray Milgate and Peter Newman (eds), *The New Palgrave Dictionary of Economics* (New York, Stockton Press, 1987).

Ehrlich, Isaac and Richard Posner, 'An Economic Analysis of Legal Rule Making' (1974) 3 *Journal of Legal Studies* 257.

Ely, John Hart, *Democracy and Distrust: A Theory of Judicial Review* (Cambridge, MA, Harvard University Press, 1980).

Emmett, Ross B (ed), *The Elgar Companion to the Chicago School of Economics* (Cheltenham, Edward Elgar, 2010).

Eskridge, William N, Jr, 'Overruling Statutory Precedents' (1988) 76 *Georgetown Law Journal* 1361.

European Commission, *XIIth Report on Competition Policy* (Brussels, Office for Official Publications of the European Communities, 1982).

—— 'DG Competition Discussion Paper on the Application of Article 82 of the Treaty to Exclusionary Abuses Public Consultation' (Brussels, 2005).

—— Press release, 'European Commission Acts to Preserve the Rule of Law in Poland' (26 July 2017).

European Council, 'Outcome of the Council Meeting' (19 February 2018) 6547/19.

Fallon, Richard H, '"The Rule of Law" as a Concept in Constitutional Discourse' (1997) 97 *Columbia Law Review* 1.

Federalist 47 (Madison) (1 February 1788) in George W Carey and James McClellan (eds), *The Federalist* (Indianapolis, IN, Liberty Fund, 2001).

Federalist 78 (Hamilton) (28 May 1788) in George W Carey and James McClellan (eds), *The Federalist* (Indianapolis, IN, Liberty Fund, 2001).

Feldman, Gabriel A, 'The Misuse of the Less Restrictive Alternative Inquiry in Rule of Reason Analysis' (2009) 58 *American University Law Review* 561.

Finnis, John, *Natural Law and Natural Rights* (Oxford, Clarendon Press, 1980).

Fox, Eleanor M, 'We Protect Competition, You Protect Competitors' (2003) 26 *World Competition* 149.

Friedman, Michael, *Reconsidering Logical Positivism* (Cambridge, Cambridge University Press, 1999).

Fuller, Lon, *The Morality of Law*, rev edn (New Haven, CT, Yale University Press, 1973).

Gavil, Andrew I, 'Defining Reliable Forensic Economics in the Post-*Daubert/Kumho Tire* Era: Case Studies from Antitrust' (2000) 57 *Washington and Lee Law Review* 831.

—— 'Moving Beyond Caricature and Characterization: The Modern Rule of Reason in Practice' (2012) 85 *Southern California Law Review* 733.

Gavil, Andrew I, William E Kovacic and Jonathan B Baker, *Antitrust Law in Perspective: Cases, Concepts and Problems in Competition Policy*, 3rd edn (St Paul, MN, West, 2017).

Gerber, David J, 'Constitutionalizing the Economy: German Neo-liberalism, Competition Law and the "New" Europe' (1994) 42 *American Journal of Comparative Law* 25.

—— *Law and Competition in Twentieth Century Europe: Protecting Prometheus* (Oxford, Oxford University Press 1998).

Gilovich, Thomas, Dale Griffin, and Daniel Kahneman (eds), *Heuristics and Biases: The Psychology of Intuitive Judgment* (Cambridge, Cambridge University Press, 2002).

Gilovich, Thomas, Robert Vallone and Amos Tversky, 'The Hot Hand in Basketball: On the Misperception of Random Sequences' (1985) 17 *Cognitive Psychology* 295.

Gimbel, Ronald W, Martin A Strosberg, Susan E Lehrman, Eugenijus Gefenas and Frank Taft, 'Presumed Consent and Other Predictors of Cadaveric Organ Donation in Europe' (2003) 13 *Progress in Transplantation* 17.

Ginsburg, Tom and Tamir Moustafa (eds), *Rule by Law: The Politics of Courts in Authoritarian Regimes* (Cambridge, Cambridge University Press, 2008).

Giocoli, Nicola 'Competition versus Property Rights: American Antitrust Law, the Freiburg School, and the Early Years of European Competition Policy' (2009) 5 *Journal of Competition Law and Economics* 747.

Goyder, Joanna, *EU Distribution Law*, 4th edn (Oxford, Hart, 2005).

Grimm, Pamela, 'Social Desirability Bias' in Jagdish N Sheth and Naresh K Malhotra (eds), *Wiley International Encyclopedia of Marketing* (Hoboken, NJ, John Wiley, 2011).

Haita-Falah, Corina, 'Sunk-Cost Fallacy and Cognitive Ability in Individual Decision-Making' (2017) 58 *Journal of Economic Psychology* 44.

Harding, Christopher and Julian Joshua, *Regulating Cartels in Europe*, 2nd edn (Oxford, Oxford University Press, 2010).

Harrison, John, 'Substantive Due Process and the Constitutional Text' (1997) 83 *Virginia Law Review* 493.

Hawk, Barry E, 'System Failure: Vertical Restraints and EC Competition Law' (1995) 32 *Common Market Law Review* 973.

Hayek, FA, *The Constitution of Liberty*, ed Ronald Hamowy (Chicago, University of Chicago Press, 2011).

Hemphill, C Scott, 'Less Restrictive Alternatives in Antitrust Law' (2016) 116 *Columbia Law Review* 927.

HM Treasury, *Green Book* (London, HM Treasury, 2018).

—— *Supplementary Green Book Guidance: Optimism Bias* (London, HM Treasury, 2018).

Hildebrand, Doris, *The Role of Economic Analysis in EU Competition Law: The European School*, 4th edn (Alphen aan den Rijn, Woulters Kluwer, 2016).

Hovenkamp, Herbert, 'Post-Chicago Antitrust: A Review and Critique' [2001] *Columbia Business Law Review* 257.

—— *Federal Antitrust Policy: The Law of Competition and its Practice*, 5th edn (St Paul MN, West, 2015).

—— 'The Rule of Reason' (2018) 70 *Florida Law Review* 81.

Hume, David, *A Treatise of Human Nature* (1738).

Hutcheson, Allan C and Patrick Monahan (eds), *The Rule of Law: Ideal or Ideology* (Toronto, Carswell, 1987).

Hylton, Keith N (ed), *Antitrust Law and Economics* (Cheltenham, Edward Elgar, 2010).

Ibáñez Colomo, Pablo, 'Beyond the "More Economics-Based Approach": A Legal Perspective on Article 102 TFEU Case Law' (2016) 53 *Common Market Law Review* 709.

—— 'Why Rules Do Not Always Give Legal Certainty – And Why They Are Not Necessarily Administrable' *Chillin' Competition* (2 May 2018, 11:44 am).

Jacob, Marc, *Precedents and Case-Based Reasoning in the European Court of Justice* (Cambridge, Cambridge University Press, 2014).

Johnson, Eric J and Daniel Goldstein, 'Do Defaults Save Lives?' (2003) 302 *Science* 1338.

Jones, Alison, Brenda Sufrin and Niamh Dunne, *EU Competition Law: Text, Cases and Materials*, 7th edn (Oxford, Oxford University Press, 2019).

Jorde, TM and DJ Teece (eds), *Antitrust, Innovation, and Competitiveness* (New York, Oxford University Press, 1992).

Joskow, Paul L, 'Transaction Cost Economics, Antitrust Rules, and Remedies' (2002) 18 *Journal of Law, Economics, and Organization* 95.

Kalintiri, Andriani, *Evidence Standards EU Competition Enforcement: The EU Approach* (Oxford, Hart, 2019).

Kanemann, Daniel, *Thinking Fast and Slow* (New York, Farrar, Strauss and Giroux, 2011) 344.

Kaplow, Louis, 'A Model of the Optimal Complexity of Legal Rules' (1995) 11 *Journal of Law, Economics, and Organization* 150.

—— 'General Characteristics of Rules' in Boudewijn Bouckaert and Gerrit De Geest (eds), *Encyclopedia of Law and Economics*, vol V: *The Economics of Crime and Litigation* (Cheltenham, Edward Elgar, 2000) 502.

—— 'Rules versus Standards: An Economic Analysis' (1992) 42 *Duke Law Journal* 557.

Kauper, Thomas E, 'Influence of Conservative Economic Analysis on the Development of the Law of Antitrust' in Robert Pitofsky (ed), *How the Chicago School Overshot the Mark: The Effect of Conservative Economic Analysis on US Antitrust* (Oxford, Oxford University Press, 2008) 40.

Khan, Lina M, 'Amazon's Antitrust Paradox' (2017) 126 *Yale Law Journal* 710.
—— 'The New Brandeis Movement: America's Antimonopoly Debate' (2018) 9 *European Journal of Competition Law and Practice* 131.
Kieran, Francis, 'A Separation of Powers Approach to Non-efficiency Goals in EU Competition Law' (2103) 119 *European Public Law* 189.
Kobayashi, Bruce H, 'The Law and Economics of Predatory Pricing' in Keith N Hylton (ed), *Antitrust Law and Economics* (Cheltenham, Edward Elgar, 2010) 116.
Korobkin, Russell B, 'Behavioral Analysis and Legal Form: Rules vs Standards Revised' (2000) 79 *Oregon Law Review* 23.
Kovacic, William, 'The Quality of Appointments and the Capability of the Federal Trade Commission' (1997) 49 *Administrative Law Review* 915.
Krattenmaker, Thomas G, 'Per Se Violations in Antitrust Law: Confusing Offences with Defences' (1988) 77 *Georgetown Law Review* 165.
Lande, Robert H, 'Wealth Transfers as the Original and Primary Concern of Antitrust: The Efficiency Interpretation Challenged' (1982) 34 *Hastings Law Journal* 65.
Lao, Marina, 'Free Riding: An Overstated, and Unconvincing, Explanation for Resale Price Maintenance' in Robert Pitofsky (ed), *How the Chicago School Overshot the Mark: The Effect of Conservative Economic Analysis on US Antitrust* (Oxford, Oxford University Press, 2008) 196.
—— 'Ideology Matters in the Antitrust Debate' (2014) 79 *Antitrust Law Journal* 649.
Lenaerts, Koen and José A Gutiérrez-Fons, 'To Say What the Law of the EU Is: Methods of Interpretation and the European Court of Justice' (2013) 20 *Columbia Journal of European Law* 3.
Leslie, Christopher R, 'Rationality Analysis in Antitrust' (2010) 158 *University of Pennsylvania Law Review* 261.
Letwin, William L, 'Congress and The Sherman Antitrust Law: 1887–1890' (1956) 23 *University of Chicago Law Review* 221.
Levenstein, Margaret C and Valerie Y Suslow, 'What Determines Cartel Success?' (2006) 44 *Journal of Economic Literature* 43.
Locke, John, *Second Treatise on Government* (1689).
Louis, Frédéric and Cormac O'Daly, 'Unfulfilled Promise: Is the Commission's Guidance Going the Way of the Dodo?' *Global Competition Law Review* 15 August 2017, 1.
Lovedahl Gormsen, Liza, 'Why the European Commission's Enforcement Priorities on Article 82 Should Be Withdrawn' (2010) 31 *European Competition Law Review* 45.
Lovett, AW, 'The United States and the Schuman Plan: A Study in French Diplomacy 1950–1952' (1996) 39 *Historical Journal* 425.
Mackaay, Ejan, 'History of Law and Economics' in Boudewijn Bouckaert and Gerrit De Geest (eds), *Encyclopedia of Law and Economics*, vol I: *The History and Methodology of Law and Economics* (Cheltenham, Edward Elgar, 2000).
Madrian, Brigitte and Dennis Shea, 'The Power of Suggestion: Inertia in 401(k) Participation and Savings Behavior' (2001) 116 *Quarterly Journal of Economics* 1149.
Maziarz, Aleksander, 'Do Non-Economic Goals Count in Interpreting Article 101(3) TFEU?' (2014) 10 *European Competition Journal* 341.
Marvel, Howard P, '*Leegin* and the Economics of Resale Price Maintenance' (2017) 50 *Review of Industrial Organization* 221.
McGraw, A Peter, Barbra A Mellers and Ilana Ritov, 'The Affective Costs of Overconfidence' (2004) 17 *Journal of Behavioral Decision Making* 281.
McGregor, Douglas, 'The Major Determinants of the Prediction of Social Events' (1938) 33 *Journal of Abnormal and Social Psychology* 179.
Medvedovsky, Konstantin, 'Hipster Antitrust – A Brief Fling or Something More?' *CPI Antitrust Chronicle*, April 2018.
Meese, Alan J, 'In Praise of All or Nothing Dichotomous Categories: Why Antitrust Law Should Reject the Quick Look' (2016) 104 *Georgetown Law Journal* 835.
Miller, H Laurence, Jr, 'Chicago School of Economics' (1962) 70 *Journal of Political Economy* 64.

Montesquieu, Baron de (Charles Louis de Secondat), *The Complete Works of M de Montesquieu*, 4 vols (London, T Evans, 1777).

Monti, Giorgio, 'Article 82 EC: What Future for the Effects-Based Approach?' (2010) 1 *Journal of European Competition Law and Practice* 2.

Moore, GE, *Principia Ethica* (Cambridge, Cambridge University Press, 1903).

Nadakavukaren Schefer, Krista, *International Investment Law: Text, Cases and Materials* (Cheltenham, Edward Elgar, 2013).

Nagy, Csongor István, 'The Distinction Between Anti-competitive Object and Effect after Allianz: The End of Coherence in Competition Analysis?' (2013) 36 *World Competition* 541.

Neumann, Franz L, 'The Change in the Function of Law in Modern Society' in William E Scheuerman (ed), *The Rule of Law Under Siege* (Berkeley, University of California Press, 1996).

North, Douglass, *Institutions, Institutional Change and Economic Performance* (Cambridge, Cambridge University Press, 1992).

Olsen, Robert, 'Desirability Bias Among Professional Investment Managers: Some Evidence From Experts' (1997) 10 *Journal of Behavioral Decision Making* 65.

Orbach, Barak, 'How Antitrust Lost Its Goal' (2013) 81 *Fordham Law Review* 2253.

Padilla, Jorge, 'Whither Article 102 TFEU: Comments on Akman and Crane' (2016) 8 *Antitrust Law Journal* 223.

Peeperkorn, Luc, 'Defining "By Object" Restrictions' [2015] no 3 *Concurrences* 40.

Peritz, Rudolph J, *Competition Policy in America: History, Rhetoric, Law*, 2nd edn (Oxford, Oxford University Press, 1996).

Peterman, John L, 'The International Salt Case' (1979) 22 *Journal of Law and Economics* 351.

Pitofsky, Robert, 'The Political Content of Antitrust' (1979) 127 *University of Pennsylvania Law Review* 1051.

—— (ed), *How the Chicago School Overshot the Mark: The Effect of Conservative Economic Analysis on US Antitrust* (Oxford, Oxford University Press, 2008).

Plous, Scott, *The Psychology of Judgment and Decision Making* (New York, McGraw-Hill, 1993).

Popofsky, Mark S, 'Defining Exclusionary Conduct: Section 2, the Rule of Reason, and the Unifying Principle Underlying Antitrust Rules' (2006) 73 *Antitrust Law Journal* 435.

Posner, Richard A, 'The Rule of Reason and the Economic Approach: Reflections on the *Sylvania* Decision' (1977) 45 *University of Chicago Law Review* 1.

—— 'The Law and Economics of the Economic Expert Witness' (1999) 13 *Journal of Economic Perspectives* 91.

—— *Economic Analysis of Law*, 9th edn (New York, Wouters Kluwer, 2014).

Pound, Roscoe, 'Common Law and Legislation' (1908) 21 *Harvard Law Review* 383.

Priest, George L, '"The Limits of Antitrust" and the Chicago School Tradition' (2009) 6 *Journal of Competition Law and Economics* 1.

Quigley, Muireann, 'Nudging for Health: On Public Policy and Designing Choice Architecture' (2013) 21 *Medical Law Review* 588.

Radcliffe, Nathan and William Klein, 'Dispositional, Unrealistic, and Comparative Optimism: Differential Relations with the Knowledge and Processing of Risk Information and Beliefs about Personal Risk' (2002) 28 *Personality and Social Psychology Bulletin* 836.

Rawls, John, *A Theory of Justice*, rev edn (Cambridge, MA, Harvard University Press, 1999).

Raz, Joseph, *The Authority of Law: Essays in Law and Morality*, 2nd edn (Oxford, Clarendon Press, 2009).

Reeves, Amanda P and Maurice E Stucke, 'Behavioral Antitrust' (2011) 86 *Indiana Law Journal* 1527.

Reiss, Julian, *Philosophy of Economics: A Contemporary Introduction* (London, Routledge, 2013).

Reksulaka, Michael,William F Shughart II and Robert D Tollison, 'Innovation and the Opportunity Cost of Monopoly' (2008) 29 *Managerial and Decision Economics* 619.

Ritter, Lennart and W David Braun, *European Competition Law: A Practitioner's Guide*, 3rd edn (Alphen aan den Rijn, Kluwer, 2005).

Roderick, Dani, Arvind Subramanian and Francesco Trebbi, 'Institutions Rule: The Primacy of Institutions over Geography and Integration in Economic Development' (2004) 9 *Journal of Economic Growth* 13.

Royal Society, *Forensic DNA Analysis: A Primer for the Courts* (London, Royal Society, 2017).

Rutherford, Malcolm, 'Chicago Economics and Institutionalism' in Ross B Emmett (ed), *The Elgar Companion to the Chicago School of Economics* (Cheltenham, Edward Elgar, 2010) 25.

Sagers, Chris, 'Rarely Tried, and … Rarely Successful: Theoretically Impossible Price Predation among the Airlines' (2009) 74 *Journal of Air Law and Commerce* 919.

Samuelson, William and Richard Zeckhauser, 'Status Quo Bias in Decision Making' (1988) 1 *Journal of Risk and Uncertainty* 7.

Sandbrook, Dominic, 'How Will History Treat David Cameron?' *New Statesman* (29 August 2016).

Scherer, FM, 'Conservative Economics and Antitrust: A Variety of Influences' in Robert Pitofsky (ed), *How the Chicago School Overshot the Mark: The Effect of Conservative Economic Analysis on US Antitrust* (Oxford, Oxford University Press, 2008) 30.

Scheuerman, William E (ed), *The Rule of Law Under Siege* (Berkeley, University of California Press, 1996).

Schinkel, Maarten Pieter, 'Forensic Economics in Competition Law Enforcement' (2007) 4 *Journal of Competition Law and Economics* 1.

Schlag, Pierre, 'Rules and Standards' (1985) 33 *University of California at Los Angeles Law Review* 379.

Schmalensee, Richard, 'Thoughts on the Chicago Legacy in US Antitrust' in Robert Pitofsky (ed), *How the Chicago School Overshot the Mark: The Effect of Conservative Economic Analysis on US Antitrust* (Oxford, Oxford University Press, 2008) 11.

Selk, Avi, 'Trump Says He's a Genius. A Study Found These Other Presidents Actually Were' *Washington Post* (7 January 2018).

Sen, Amartya, *Development as Freedom* (Oxford, Oxford University Press, 1999).

Sharot, Tali, 'The Optimism Bias' (2011) 21 *Current Biology* R941.

Sheth, Jagdish N and Naresh K Malhotra (eds), *Wiley International Encyclopedia of Marketing* (Hoboken, NJ, John Wiley, 2011).

Shklar, Judith N, 'Political Theory and the Rule of Law' in Allan C Hutcheson and Patrick Monahan (eds), *The Rule of Law: Ideal or Ideology* (Toronto, Carswell, 1987) 1.

Simon, Herbert A, 'A Behavioral Model of Rational Choice' (1955) 66 *Quarterly Journal of Economics* 99.

—— 'Behavioral Economics' in John Eatwell, Murray Milgate and Peter Newman (eds), *The New Palgrave Dictionary of Economics* (New York, Stockton Press, 1987).

Sirri, ER and P Tufano, 'Costly Search and Mutual Fund Flows' (1998) 53 *Journal of Finance* 1589.

Stöckl, Thomas, Jürgen Huber, Michael Kirchler and Florian Lindner, 'Hot Hand and Gambler's Fallacy in Teams: Evidence from Investment Experiments' (2015) 117 *Journal of Economic Behavior and Organization* 327.

Stucke, Maurice E, 'Does the Rule of Reason Violate the Rule of Law?' (2009) 42 *UC Davis Law Review* 1375.

Summers, Robert S, 'A Formal Theory of the Rule of Law' (1993) 6 *Ratio Juris* 127, 139.

Sussman, Shaoul, 'Prime Predator: Amazon and the Rationale of Below Average Variable Cost Pricing Strategies Among Negative-Cash Flow Firms' (2019) 7 *Journal of Antitrust Enforcement* 203.

Svenson, Ola, 'Are We All Less Risky and More Skilful than Our Fellow Drivers?' (1981) 47 *Acta Psychologica* 143.

Tamanaha, Brian Z, *On the Rule of Law: History, Politics, Theory* (Cambridge, Cambridge University Press, 2004).

Tashima, A Wallace, 'The War on Terror and the Rule of Law' (2008) 15 *Asian American Law Journal* 245.

Thaler, Richard H and Cass R Sunstein, *Nudge: Improving Decisions about Health, Wealth, and Happiness* (New Haven, CT, Yale University Press, 2008).

Thorelli, Hans, 'Antitrust Policy in Europe: National Policies after 1945' (1958) 26 *University of Chicago Law Review* 222.

Tor, Avishalom, 'The Fable of Entry: Bounded Rationality, Market Discipline, and Legal Policy' (2002) 101 *Michigan Law Review* 482.

—— 'Illustrating a Behaviorally Informed Approach to Antitrust Law: The Case of Predatory Pricing' (2003) 18 *Antitrust* 52.

—— 'Understanding Behavioral Antitrust' (2014) 92 *Texas Law Review* 573.

Townley, Christopher, *Article 81 EC and Public Policy* (Oxford, Hart, 2009).

Trebilcock, MJ and Ronald J Daniels, *Rule of Law Reform and Development: Charting the Fragile Path of Progress* (Cheltenham, Edward Elgar, 2008).

Tversky, Amos and Daniel Kahneman, 'Judgment under Uncertainty: Heuristics and Biases' (1974) 185 (NS) *Science* 1124.

Van Alstine, Michael, 'The Costs of Legal Change' (2002) 49 *UCLA Law Review* 789.

van de Gronden, Johan W, 'The Internal Market, The State and Private Initiative' (2006) 33 *Legal Issues of Economic Integration* 105.

Vanberg, Viktor J, 'The Freiburg School: Walter Euken and Ordoliberalism' (2011) Freiburger Diskussionpapiere zur Ordnungsökonomik/Freiburg Discussion Papers on Constitutional Economics No 04/11, 6.

Waldron, Jeremy, 'Separation of Powers in Thought and Practice?' (2013) 54 *Boston College Law Review* 433.

Wardhaugh, Bruce, *Cartels, Markets and Crime: A Normative Justification for the Criminalisation of Economic Collusion* (Cambridge, Cambridge University Press, 2014).

—— 'Crisis Cartels: Non-Economic Values, the Public Interest, and Institutional Considerations' (2014) 10 *European Competition Journal* 311.

—— '*Intel*, Consequentialist Goals and the Certainty of Rules: The Same Old Song and Dance, My Friend' (2016) 11 *Competition Law Review* 215.

Weatherhead, Patrick J, 'Do Savannah Sparrows Commit the Concorde Fallacy?' (1979) 5 *Behavioral Ecology and Sociobiology* 373.

Werden, Gregory J, Luke M Froeb and Mikhael Shor, 'Behavioral Antitrust and Merger Control' (2011) 167 *Journal of Institutional and Theoretical Economics* 126.

Wessling, Rein, *The Modernisation of EC Antitrust Law* (Oxford, Hart, 2000).

Whish, Richard, *Competition Law*, 6th edn (Oxford, Oxford University Press, 2009).

Wilkinson, Nick and Matthias Klaes, *An Introduction to Behavioral Economics*, 3rd edn (London, Palgrave, 2018).

Wilks, Stephen and Lee McGowan, 'Disarming the Commission: The Debate Over a European Cartel Office' (1995) 32 *Journal of Common Market Studies* 259.

Witt, Anne C, 'Public Policy Goals under EU Competition Law – Now Is the Time to Set the House in Order' (2012) 8 *European Competition Journal* 443.

—— *The Economic Approach to EU Antitrust Law* (Oxford, Hart, 2016).

—— 'The European Court of Justice and the More Economic Approach – Is the Tide Turning' University of Leicester Law School Research Paper No 18-10.

World Bank, Worldwide Governance Indicators.

Wright, Joshua D and Angela M Diveley, 'Do Expert Agencies Outperform Generalist Judges? Some Preliminary Evidence From the Federal Trade Commission' (2013) 1 *Journal of Antitrust Enforcement* 82.

Wright, Joshua D, Elyse Dorsey, Jan Rybnicek and Jonathan Klick, 'Requiem for a Paradox: The Dubious Rise and Inevitable Fall of Hipster Antitrust' (2019) 51 *Arizona State Law Journal*, forthcoming.

Zamir, Eyal and Doron Teichman, *Behavioral Law and Economics* (Oxford, Oxford University Press, 2018).

Zeng, Xiaohua, Srabana Dasgupta and Charles B Weinberg, 'The Competitive Implications of a "No-Haggle" Pricing Strategy When Others Negotiate: Findings From a Natural Experiment' (2016) 33 *International Journal of Research in Marketing* 907.

INDEX